Between Crown and Swastika

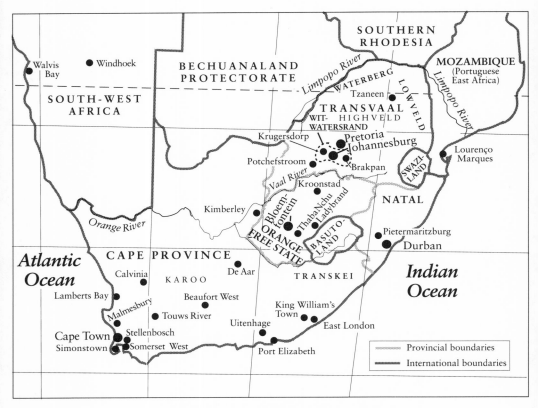

SOUTHERN AFRICA IN 1939

The following labels appear on the map:

Walvis Bay · Windhoek

SOUTH-WEST AFRICA

BECHUANALAND PROTECTORATE

SOUTHERN RHODESIA

Limpopo River · WATERBERG · LOWVELD

MOZAMBIQUE (Portuguese East Africa)

Limpopo River

Tzaneen

TRANSVAAL · WIT-WATERSRAND · HIGHVELD

Krugersdorp · Pretoria · Johannesburg

Potchefstroom · Brakpan

SWAZI-LAND · Lourenço Marques

Vaal River · Kroonstad

NATAL

Orange River · Kimberley · Bloem-fontein · ThabaNchu · Ladybrand

ORANGE FREE STATE · BASUTO-LAND

Pietermaritzburg · Durban

Atlantic Ocean

CAPE PROVINCE

De Aar · TRANSKEI · Indian Ocean

Calvinia · KAROO

Lamberts Bay · Beaufort West · King William's Town

Malmesbury · Touws River · Uitenhage · East London

Cape Town · Stellenbosch · Simonstown · Somerset West · Port Elizabeth

Provincial boundaries
International boundaries

Between Crown and Swastika

The Impact of the Radical Right
on the Afrikaner Nationalist Movement
in the Fascist Era

Patrick J. Furlong

Wesleyan University Press
Published by University Press of New England
Hanover and London

Wesleyan University Press
Published by University Press of New England, Hanover, NH 03755

Parts of chapters 8 and 9 first appeared in different form in *Ufahamu* (UCLA), volume 16, number 1, © 1987 by the Regents of the University of California. The author is grateful for permission to reprint.

The author and publishers have made every effort to trace the copyright holders of illustrations, but if they have inadvertently overlooked any, they would be pleased to make the necessary arrangements at the first opportunity.

Printed in the United States of America   5   4   3   2   1
CIP data appear at the end of the book

For my parents and grandparents

Contents

Illustrations

Preface

All South Africans who lived through the Second World War have their stories to tell of experiences "up north" in Ethiopia or the Libyan desert, or of how those tumultuous years were spent on the home front. Through many cold Cape evenings, I was regaled by my mother's father, an ambulance driver with the South African forces in North Africa, with tales of the great adventure remembered vividly by so many men of his generation. He particularly loved to tell me of the maneuvers of his ambulance as he sought to evade General Rommel's airplanes.

For those like my father or like my other grandparents who remained at home there were vivid memories of the nightly blackouts, though air raids never came, of submerged sea-spikes, designed to ward off German U-boats, which, in consequence, stayed a respectable distance offshore, and of the experiences of neighbors who spent the war years in internment because of widespread disaffection from the Allied cause among many white South Africans.

Many of those who spent the war behind barbed wire for varying degrees of support for the Axis cause were not, in the postwar period, reviled as "collaborators," as often happened to persons of similar views in Europe. Indeed, when the victorious wartime prime minister, General Jan Smuts, leader of the pro-Allied United Party, was unceremoniously dumped in the first postwar election, those who had been convicted of war crimes were promptly freed by the pro-neutral National Party, the wartime "official opposition," which swept to power by a narrow majority. The National Party has ruled South Africa ever since. Many who had supported the cause of the Axis, or at least of the pro-fascist extreme Right, much more explicitly than had the more cautious among the Nationalists were brought into the heart of the government in the next few years. They included a future prime minister (John Vorster), two state presidents (Vor-

ster and Nico Diederichs), the leader of the National Party in
Namibia (Johannes Strauss von Moltke), a head of the Bureau
of State Security (Hendrik van den Bergh), the longtime chief of
the state broadcasting system (Piet Meyer), in addition to individual cabinet members, senators, and members of Parliament.
Under Nationalist rule, South Africa moved from old-style "segregation" to a more comprehensive and systematic form of white
supremacy, *apartheid* (Afrikaans for "apartness").

Very little of the literature on South Africa and the age of the
dictators is based on serious archival, or even newspaper, research. One category of literature on the period is liberal and
anti-Nationalist, which saw the National Party as "Nazis." Two
of its best-known works are William Henry Vatcher's *White
Laager* (1965), which includes a chapter on "The Impact of Nazism,"[1] and Brian Bunting's classic leftist exposé, *The Rise of the
South African Reich* (1969), complete with introductory chapter
epigraphs from Hitler's *Mein Kampf*.[2] Bunting's book, long
banned in South Africa, is perhaps the archetypical work of its
genre, with a thesis that is a virtual identification of modern
Afrikaner nationalism with Nazism, but lacking the scholarly
apparatus that would give the work greater credibility.

A closely related approach is represented by the works of Hans
Strydom, Ivor Wilkins, and J. H. P. Serfontein on the secret Afrikaner Broederbond, an exclusive all-male society long linked
by liberals in South Africa to responsibility for orchestrating the
rise of the National Party and the consolidation of its rule after
1948,[3] a conspiracy theory of history that is suspect in scholarly
circles.[4]

A second major school of thought about the relationship of
Afrikaner nationalism to European fascism is Afrikaner nationalist scholarship that rejects as simplistic the linking of nationalist history to the rise of European fascist regimes. D. W.
Krüger, for instance, argues that the wartime leader of the National Party, Daniel F. Malan, and his conservative followers
"swore by parliamentary democracy after they had temporarily
and gently toyed with the new ideas."[5] So also, B. J. Liebenberg
stresses Malan's conflict with the "foreign ideology" of National
Socialism, and subordinates the pro-Nazi sympathies of many of
Malan's followers.[6]

Similarly, J. C. Moll summarizes the attitude of many younger Afrikaner academics in his argument that the South African state and government, for all their democratic shortcomings, do not display the minimum characteristics of fascism.[7] Moll's study, while valuable, does not pretend to be anything more than a survey of the secondary literature, along with some newspaper analysis.

A more formidable contribution in the Afrikaner nationalist tradition is that of historian Frederik van Heerden, whose doctoral dissertation on National Socialism as a factor in South African politics is the only study in the field to be based on extensive research in South African archives.[8] This work concludes that Nazi or even broader fascist influence on mainstream white politics in South Africa was, on balance, insignificant. Much more so than Moll, Van Heerden defends the Nationalist government. He makes little use of documentation other than the records of Afrikaner nationalism. There are, for instance, striking omissions in the area of Jewish records on anti-Semitism in South Africa, Nazi documents, or government intelligence reports and other reports on pro-Nazi activity presented to General Smuts's wartime cabinet. Van Heerden concludes that the Nationalists stood squarely behind the values of Western democracy throughout the period 1933 to 1948, except for a brief flirtation with Nazi political theories. He describes such flirtation as "superficial experiments with National Socialism" that never reached a "thoroughgoing application."[9] He does not address whether such a flirtation may have had any long-term significance for Afrikaner politics.

Such studies tend to indulge in either polemic or apologetic. None has attempted seriously to grapple with the archival evidence of connections between the rise of fascism in Europe and the formative period of the modern National Party prior to its accession to power in 1948.

Certain more recent works, such as those of George Visser and Heribert Adam, have attempted a less ideologically oriented analysis, but they either do not take seriously the possibility of *any* fascist-Nationalist connection or otherwise work from a limited data base that restricts the significance of their findings. For instance, Visser in his *OB: Traitors or Patriots?* denies that Balthasar Johannes ("John") Vorster, prime minister from 1966 to 1978, who was interned during the Second World War, was pro-Nazi. Vorster was detained for several years because of his participation in the pro-German Ossewabrandwag (Ox-Wagon Guard or OB), a paramilitary and quasi-fascist Afrikaner movement whose symbol was the ox-wagon of their pioneer ancestors.[10] Visser distinguishes sharply between the South African government since 1948 and the OB and organizations like the anti-Jewish Greyshirts, although his conclusion is not supported by persuasive documentation.[11]

Even Heribert Adam, one of the best-known liberal scholars of South African politics, made light of the role of fascism in Afrikaner political history. He wrote in *The Rise and Crisis of Afrikaner Power* that "contemporary South Africa hardly resembles fascist Germany . . . the differences outweigh the similarities, and . . . the fascist analogy obscures a proper understanding of the South African system."[12] The arguments by which Adam reaches this conclusion suggest that he would apply a similar judgment to the National Party of the thirties and forties.

Many earlier Marxist writers have taken the fascist model more seriously. Nevertheless, Dan O'Meara, the historian who has written perhaps the most substantial Marxist work on Afrikaner nationalism of this period, has distanced himself from an analogy between nationalism and fascism. Working out of a decidedly structuralist Marxian tradition, O'Meara argues that "comparative insights gained through the use of the concept of fascism do not compensate for the lack of historical specificity" and do not enhance a "theoretical understanding" of Afrikaner nationalism.[13] O'Meara relies almost totally on published source material, a limitation, ironically, on the scope of his own "historical specificity."

Also working from the left, but with a less specifically Marxian agenda, are Sipho Mzimela, with his *Apartheid: South African Nazism,* and Alexandre Kum'a N'dumbe of Lyons University, author of a number of studies in French, German, and English.[14] Kum'a N'dumbe's principal contribution is his systematic searching of relevant German records. His work focuses, however, on German foreign policy in Africa, not on Afrikaner nationalism itself, and, moreover, as is true also of Mzimela, his scholarship is heavily polemical. Both his and Mzimela's work contain factual slips. Kum'a N'dumbe repeatedly asserts that the first two South African prime ministers, Louis Botha (1910–1919) and Jan Smuts (1919–1924 and 1939–1948), were "English immigrants." Botha and Smuts were in fact Afrikaner generals who had fought in the Boer armies during the South African War of 1899 to 1902, a struggle which had pitted Afrikaner against Briton.[15] Mzimela, for his part, incorrectly describes J. G. Strijdom, prime minister of South Africa from 1954 to 1958, as having studied in Germany.

One author whose work is a serious theoretical effort within the neo-Marxian tradition and which is reliable from a scholarly point of view and also, to some extent, successful in avoiding both polemic or apologetic is Howard Simson of Sweden's Uppsala University.[16] Yet his work fails to use letters or diaries as sources. He relies on newspapers and published government documents of the period.

Influenced by the work of Nicos Poulantzas, Simson defines fascism as a form of capitalist state in which a mass movement, based primarily on the petite bourgeoisie, uses both legal and violent tactics to seize power. In this model, a fascist regime is rooted in a strongly anti-working-class ideology and a massive expansion of monopoly capital in the name of a strong national economy.[17]

Simson concludes from his identification of such elements in the post-1948 Nationalist government that the socioeconomic base and function of the Afrikaner nationalist movement is sufficiently similar to the "classical" fascism of Mussolini and Hitler that, when seen in the light of the limited, virtually all-white electoral politics in South Africa, "Afrikaner Fascism" and classical fascism are more similar than different.[18] Simson is mistaken; Afrikaner nationalism did not draw its support only from the wealthy but from all classes. Also, the parliamentary system is much more central to white South Africans, including Afrikaners, than he maintains.[19]

Simson, like O'Meara and those liberal and Marxist scholars who have considered this question, not only has depended on inadequate source material, but has attempted to treat Afrikaner nationalism as though it were a monolith. Apologists for the

National Party have readily demonstrated the obvious limitations of such a generic approach, pointing out that most South African groups who were clearly identified with fascism and who were proponents of a South African variety of National Socialism faded into political oblivion soon after the war, and some, even before the war was over. The National Party, which remained, represented a much more moderate, even a conservative, variety of Afrikaner nationalism.

The Van Heerden and Moll approaches identify the National Party as radically different from and even hostile to the representatives of the Radical Right in South Africa during the thirties and forties. This study attempts to pick up the debate at precisely that point, the essential distinction between the National Party and its rivals on the Radical Right. The really important question concerns the relationship between these two poles of Afrikaner nationalism, a central issue that none of the literature has addressed. Have these two groups always been hostile to each other? What issues have divided them? Did these groups in South Africa, as sometimes in Germany, form an alliance of convenience against the center and the left? Why did so many radicals later rise to eminence in the Nationalist government, if the Radical Right and the Nationalists were earlier mutually opposed? Were certain groups inside the National Party favorably disposed to the Far Right? Scholars have not asked these questions. Nor have they asked *why* there was such ambivalence toward Germany inside the National Party, nor why it took so long for the Nationalist establishment to recognize the threat of Nazism to its own cause.

This study investigates these issues by examining the possibility that mainstream Afrikaner nationalists had come under the spell of the fascists, but by far more veiled and subtle means than was true of their more extreme compatriots. To consider the dynamics of the relationship between Afrikaner nationalism and fascism seriously, we must examine not only the direct impact of European fascism, especially German National Socialism, on the National Party, but also the indirect, perhaps much more significant, influence of the indigenous Radical Right on "mainstream" Afrikaner nationalism.

As many of the archives begin at last to surrender their wartime secrets, scholars need to dig deeply and carefully; we can no longer be content with broad structuralist analyses or journalistic reminiscences. Historians must move beyond the defense of or attacks on old and cherished political positions.

Considering the central role of the "South African question" in the contemporary world, the topic of this study is more than a matter of antiquarian interest. When antiapartheid activists describe the Nationalists of today as "modern Nazis," is this an ugly lie or a profoundly disturbing truth, or something in between? Historians should not shy away from the question on the grounds that it is tasteless or needlessly provocative. Historians know that documents always have something to reveal, and they believe that evidence must be allowed to speak for itself, regardless of the outcome, in this as in other important matters.

This study addresses these questions. It does not come from an outsider. As a white South African with at least some Afrikaner ancestry, I try to speak from within the situation. The issues have fascinated me ever since I first was tantalized by my elders' wartime tales, and they are issues with which I have long felt a need to come to terms.

All white South Africans who travel abroad, and not only committed Afrikaner nationalists, experience something like that of German travelers: the assumption that we are modern-day "Nazis." As a historian, I have felt that the question underlying this charge needs an answer, one based not on a defensive need to apologize, but on an unembarrassed desire to seek the truth, however old-fashioned that may sound to some contemporary scholars. We cannot escape our past; we must address it and try to understand it, regardless of where that may lead us.

Any book of this scope owes a very considerable debt to the many institutions and individuals who helped to make it possible. I would like to express my gratitude to them for helping me realize this project and for assisting in smoothing out the many obstacles in the way. Those pioneers in open archives in South Africa, the Archives and Manuscripts departments of the libraries at the Universities of the Witwatersrand and Cape Town, deserve special mention. In addition, Sharon Friedman of the Kaplan Center for Jewish Studies at the University of Cape Town and the South African Jewish Board of Deputies made it possible to examine the many important collections of the Cape Jewish community now housed at that school. The State Archives in Cape Town and Pretoria not only kindly made available their open collections, but also gave special permission for consultation of the General Hertzog and Albert Geyer Papers.

No study of Afrikaner nationalist politics would be complete without the services of the Instituut vir Eietydse Geskiedenis (Institute for Contemporary History) at the University of the Orange Free State. The staff went out of their way to make all too brief a stay as fruitful as possible. Their hospitality was matched by the kindness of the Boyce family, who made it much easier to bear those long days in the archives during my stay in the Transvaal.

Academics at various South African and American universities were most generous in sharing their time and scholarship. I would like to mention J. P. Brits, Richard Elphick, Hermann Giliomee, Richard Mendelssohn, J. C. Moll, Newell Stultz, and Charles Villa-Vicencio. Leslie Rubin deserves my special gratitude for sharing many hours of his time, and also the fruit of his years of research on Nazism and South Africa. Jeffrey Butler read the entire manuscript and offered some helpful suggestions for improvements. Like all others mentioned here, none of these scholars is responsible for any of the views expressed in this study nor for its shortcomings.

In the United States, the library and archives of the Hoover Institution at Stanford University and the libraries of the University of California at Los Angeles and Santa Barbara were also invaluable resources. The staff of the interlibrary loan department at Santa Barbara made it possible for many of the more hard-to-find materials to find their way into this study.

The members of my dissertation committee at UC Santa Barbara, Professors Robert Collins, Edward Alpers, Albert Lindemann, and Joachim Remak, supervised the original version of this work, and were always there with encouragement and advice. The constant moral support and helpful criticism of Robert Shell at Princeton and, at Presbyterian College, of Booker T. Ingram and Charles Mckelvey, also went a long way toward helping me realize this project, especially in the latter stages. Connie

Colwell kindly assisted me in translating some of the more obscure passages in Nazi sources. Generous funding by the University of California at Santa Barbara, including a Regents' Special Fellowship, a Graduate Research Travel Grant, and a University General Affiliates Dissertation Fellowship, and by Presbyterian College and the Irwin Belk Fund, made all of this feasible in the first place. Jeannette Hopkins's insightful and experienced editing and the friendly staff of Wesleyan University Press helped to make the transition from dissertation to print a smooth one.

Finally, my parents were always there, whenever difficulties arose, to step into the multiple roles of agent, banker, and even secretary. I would particularly like to thank them and Karel Schoeman of the South African Library for their assistance with many of the illustrations for this book, which are from the *Cape Times* Collection of the library. In addition I would like to thank Anna Cunningham and the South African Institute of Race Relations for permission to reproduce items from collections in the Cullen Library at the University of the Witswatersrand, Leonie Twentyman-Jones for allowing reproduction of parts of a document held jointly by the Jagger Library and Kaplan Center at the University of Cape Town, and the Argus Group for permission to reproduce photographs from the *Cape Argus* and the *Pretoria News*. My father and grandparents inspired the choice of this topic in the first place. Those many stories of the home front in South Africa had some surprising consequences.

Abbreviations

AB	Afrikaner Broederbond (Union of Brothers)
AHI	Afrikaner Handelsinstituut (Afrikaner Institute for Commerce)
ANS	Afrikaner Nasionale Studentebond (Student Union)
AO	Auslandsorganisation (External Organization of the German Nazi Party)
AP	Afrikaner Party
BOSS	Bureau of State Security
FAK	Federasie van Afrikaner Kultuurverenigings (Federation of Afrikaner Cultural Organizations)
HNP	Herstigte Nasionale Party (Reconstituted National Party)
NGK	Nederduitse Gereformeerde Kerk (Dutch Reformed Church, the largest white Afrikaans Reformed body)
NIOO	Nasionale Instituut vir Onderwys en Opvoeding (National Institute for Education and Training)
NJ	Nasionale Jeugbond (National Youth Union)
NP	National Party
OB	Ossewabrandwag (Ox-Wagon Guard)
RDB	Reddingsdaadbond (Union for the Act of Salvation, economic body)
RSU	Republican Student Union
SABRA	South African Bureau of Racial Affairs
SAIRR	South African Institute of Race Relations
SAP	South African Party
UP	United Party
USNAMS	United States National Archives Microfilm Series
UUTS	Union Unity Truth Service

Between Crown and Swastika

Introduction: Between Crown and Swastika

It is no secret that certain individuals prominent in the Afrikaner nationalist regime that came to power in South Africa in 1948 were, at the very least, sympathetic to the Nazi cause and in many cases were strongly attracted to the various fascist movements and philosophies of the thirties and forties.[1] There has been an understandable attempt on the part of the ruling National Party to distance itself from such associations. Charges of "Nazism" or "fascism" tend to elicit angry denials from those in power.[2] Indeed, any who bring such charges find little support today in the world of scholarship. Yet during the two decades after 1948 many opponents of the South African government, white liberals and Marxists alike, were convinced that successors of the Nazis were now ensconced in Pretoria, that 1948 had marked not only the triumph of the most militantly nationalist Afrikaners, the descendants of the early Dutch, German, and French settlers, but also the decisive juncture in the long march of South African history toward totalitarianism and a racial Armageddon.[3] This fear was the genesis of the later charges of activists such as Archbishop Desmond Tutu of Cape Town, yet by the 1970s and 1980s such charges were met with some embarrassment among contemporary scholars, even on the left. For by the seventies a new generation of radical scholars was arguing that 1948 had not been all that important in any case since the structures of racial repression in South Africa had long predated apartheid, and that the alliance of capital and the white state, which they saw as the root of the South African sociopolitical system, had been firmly in place at least a generation before the Nationalists came to power.[4] More conservative individuals in the white opposition, for their part, began to wonder whether the Nationalists were as malevolent as they had once been depicted; they noted with satisfaction the growing pragmatism of Nationalist rule, and, despite unhappiness over individual acts of official callousness, expressed gratitude that the government had at least prevented a "communist" takeover.

Even among white liberals, discussions of the connection between prewar and wartime fascism, on one hand, and the present system of government, on the other, now often seemed at best softheaded and at worst tasteless.[5] The subject itself seemed dead in scholarship, although continual reminders in the newspapers showed that some journalists were not about to let a good story go.[6] One relatively safe way of handling the issue was to acknowledge the very real differences between the wartime National Party, which still claimed to support an indigenous variety of democracy, and the more explicitly pro-Nazi organizations like the fiercely anti-Semitic Greyshirts and especially the huge Ossewabrandwag (OB), the uniformed "Ox-Wagon Guard," whose membership at its height was said to be close to two hundred thousand and which was inspired by their pioneer ancestors and the bulky ox-drawn vehicles that had helped to open up the South African interior to white settlement in the preceding two centuries.[7] Ossewabrandwag subversive activities and Nazi attempts to use the OB for their own ends were detailed in books such as the popular history of the Ossewabrandwag by George Visser, based on his own police investigation of this group, and Hans Strydom's best-selling *For Volk and Führer*, about a Nazi-organized plot to overthrow the pro-Allied government and set up a puppet state.[8]

Focus on the more colorful Afrikaner Radical Right allowed commentators to see the now governing National Party itself as intrinsically different and as a more respectable movement.[9] My own research rejects the view that such an all-embracing distinction can be made between the Radical Right and the party. The National Party's relationship with the Afrikaner Radical Right and with fascism more broadly must be examined if historians are to make sense of what the age of the dictators really meant for South Africa. To seek a greater understanding of this period of Afrikaner nationalist history is not "Boer-baiting," but an honest attempt to throw some light on an inescapable historical problem. Historians believe that the truth cannot but help free people from the shackles of past obfuscation.

The present study does reject simplistic sweeping analogies between "fascism" and "Afrikaner nationalism." The substantial variety of such ideologies and movements are acknowledged by an empirical and phenomenological approach. Individual points of comparison need to be noted where these are borne out by the evidence, and specific areas of fascist influence suggested where these are indicated by the sources, but such connections should never obscure the important nuances that differentiate patent and serious pro-fascist trends from less obvious and more passing interest in Far Right ideologies.

The difficulties presented by the striking differences between the "original" Fascism, that of Mussolini, and its most radical and totalitarian variant, Nazism,[10] are obviated in this study by the blurring of these two types in the minds of most Afrikaner nationalists. The Mussolini model formed the basis of most serious theoretical attempts at a South African variety of fascism, for example, Oswald Pirow's New Order, but it was the Nazi regime that provided the core inspiration for most fascist-style groups in South Africa.

Nazi symbols like the swastika, Nazi characteristics like anti-Semitism, which was not intrinsic to Italian Fascism, and Nazi labels like "national socialism," which was commonly used to describe the ideology of the Afrikaner Radical Right, completely eclipsed references to Mussolini or fascism in South Africa. There was a small "South African Fascist Movement," led by the ex-Greyshirt Johannes Strauss von Moltke, later leader of the National Party in South-West Africa (now Namibia), but both the Greyshirts and the much larger Ossewabrandwag preferred to adhere to "national socialism." Mussolini's reputation was understandably overshadowed by that of Hitler, especially after the massive expansion of the Nazi state in the late thirties. In addition, the ethnic and linguistic affinities between the Germans and the Afrikaners were far greater than those between the Afrikaners and the Italians, whose Catholicism did not help to make their system especially attractive to the fiercely Calvinist Afrikaners. I use "national socialism" in a broader sense than the philosophy of the Nazi state itself because in the minds of most Afrikaners, this term was interchangeable with "fascism." The word "fascism" has a variety of possible connotations; it can be used narrowly to describe the Mussolini and Hitler regimes, plus movements directly derivative of these, such as the Dutch Nazi Party or, in the South African case, Louis Weichardt's Greyshirts.[11] A broader definition, however, will also include both the Ossewabrandwag in South Africa and the Catholic clerico-fascist regimes of Dollfuss in Austria, Franco in Spain, and Salazar in Portugal.[12] Groups belonging to either category of "fascism" are, in recognition of the difficulties associated with the term, usually described here as belonging to the newer "Radical Right," in contrast with the more conservative Old Right of traditional, more moderate nationalism. Those more consciously aligned with "classical fascism" are described here as fascists or national socialists, depending on which term they preferred and which term more accurately describes their allegiances. Those subscribing only to a high proportion of characteristics typically ascribed to Mussolini's Italy or Hitler's Germany are described in my study, for want of a better term, as "semifascist." These distinctions are, of course, not narrowly drawn. There was a considerable overlap even between conservative nationalism and the New Right, an area of debate of the most relevance to students of mainstream Afrikaner nationalism.

It is certainly debatable whether the Radical Right movements in South Africa were better described as "Nazi" or "fascist," but the principal concern here is not this question but rather to establish how clearly identifiable fascist regimes, movements, and thought, especially of the Nazi variety, *influenced* the direction of white South African politics, either directly or obviously in the sense of specific prewar or wartime experiments with the language or outward symbols of fascism, or more subtly.

For example, if there was indeed the profound gap of method and principle between the National Party and the extremists of the Radical Right that seems to be the basis of current Afrikaner orthodoxy on the subject, why the later warm embrace offered by the ostensibly more "constitutionalist" Nationalists to Radical Right zealots? It is also a matter of public knowledge that anti-Semitism was rife in the National Party in the thirties and early forties. In other areas as well, Nazi or more broadly "fascist" intellectual influences may have had a substantial and lasting influence on Nationalist ideology and policy. This study examines the evidence.

All those who experienced the changeover from the old paternalistic segregation of Generals J. B. M. Hertzog and Jan Smuts to the apartheid system of government after 1948 can attest that the degree of authoritarianism increased after that date and also that the National Party had a vision of a future South Africa far more inclusive and total than the slipshod racist measures of its predecessor, the United Party government of prime ministers Hertzog and Smuts. This study argues that this underlying shift in outlook was a consequence in considerable part of the war years and the period of fascist dominance in Europe. Nor did the Nationalists have to be Nazis to be impressed with the achievements of authoritarian nationalism. Even the ill-fated Edward VIII of England, driven into exile as the Duke of Windsor, expressed admiration for the Nazi "miracle" in the mid-thirties.

As noted, I do acknowledge the very real differences between the National Party and the overtly pro-Nazi organizations. But the focus here is the triangular nexus between the growth of European fascism, and especially the rise of Nazi Germany, the concomitant rise of influential Radical Right factions in South Africa, and their cumulative impact on the principal prewar Afrikaner nationalist opposition group, Daniel Malan's National Party. Particular emphasis is therefore placed on the shaping of the National Party in its organization, its ideology, and its policy.

One area of investigation is the scope of pro-Nazi or pro-fascist activity engaged in by individuals connected either at the time with the National Party or later with the ruling Nationalist establishment. Such activity is clearly borne out by the evidence. Apologetic arguments that try to downplay, or even ignore, such an important part of the historical record must be countered if later generations are to understand the ideological milieu in which the nationalism of Malan's party came to dominate not only Afrikaner politics, but South Africa as a whole.

While such a task is not the sole purpose of this study, which otherwise could descend to the level of "Boer-bashing," intellectual fairness requires that unpleasant parts of the past not be overlooked. A more complete and more sober picture than that widely held of the National Party (and Afrikaner nationalism in general) of the thirties and forties must be recreated. And, since the analytical dimension of history is at least as important as reconstructing the past, it is crucial to understand how Nationalist leadership sought to maneuver its way through political mine fields, to what degree this meant directing policy toward the widespread Radical Right sentiment of the time, and to what extent National Party involvement with the radicals of the right influenced the course of mainstream Afrikaner nationalism.

The subject is too vast to cover in every aspect of the relationship between fascism, or even Nazism, and Afrikaner nationalism. Hence, this study does not deal with English-speaking white South Africans, who, in any case, figured only peripherally, usually as members of the South African government charged with uncovering and suppressing pro-Nazi subversion. Also, this study does not include the responses of African, mixed-race "colored," and Indian South Africans, although their attitudes to fascism would make a fascinating book. Their presence reverberates in the records of Nationalist and pro-Smuts figures concerned with the Nazi phenomenon; nevertheless, white politicians saw them primarily as an eternal "problem," almost never as a political force with which to reckon. The African National Congress, today the most popular political party among the majority of Africans, "coloreds," and Indians, wholeheartedly supported the struggle against fascism,[13] yet it is not mentioned once in any of the voluminous Afrikaner nationalist or Nazi sources consulted in researching this work.

This study is also not a social history of Afrikaner nationalism, a history of individual Radical Right organizations, either before or after 1948, nor another attempt to explain why the National Party came to power in that momentous year. The fundamental question under examination is whether the National Party that won power in 1948 was intrinsically different from the old pre-1934 National Party in any sense that is a consequence of the rise of fascism. If it is, then the rise of fascism would seem to have had a fundamental and lasting impact on mainstream Afrikaner nationalism. I believe the answer is that it has.

The concerns of ordinary Nationalists are not ignored in this study, but the primary emphasis is on the leadership cadres, to some extent because serious scholarship on the National Party or the Radical Right as sociopolitical phenomena is comparatively meager, which suggests an important subject for future research. Also, researchers find access to appropriate data difficult to obtain.[14] In addition, an emphasis on elites is justified by the tradition of strong leadership in the party, a tradition that has tended to mold the rank and file to the wishes of party bosses. The Nationalist leaders central to this study in many respects epitomize the fundamental philosophies of the various regional and ideological factions in the National Party, factions that still survive.[15] In that sense, the study of the party elite provides one of the easiest ways to understand the broad trends in that organization.

It is possible, through the study of party leadership, to examine in considerable detail even in a limited study the changing dynamics of Nationalist politics, both internally and in relation to the Radical Right at home and abroad. Most available archival sources, primarily the personal papers of leading politicians, are of leadership activity. More detailed social histories can supplement such an approach, even alter some of its findings, but the limitations of a "traditional" political-historical analysis are less than the advantages. As the Russian composer Sergei Prokofiev has so aptly observed, there is still much to say in the simplest and most straightforward key, C Major.

The byzantine complexities of South African politics are not easy to follow. It is well known, of course, that whites, who constitute about one-sixth of the population, have historically sought to control exclusive access to power in South Africa. At times the dominant theme of struggle between white and black has overlapped with or been superseded by that of conflict among whites, between the numerically dominant Afrikaners (about three-fifths of the white population), who were the earliest white settlers and who speak Afrikaans, a variant of Dutch, and the English-speakers (about two-fifths of the white population), largely descendants of nineteenth- and early twentieth-century immigrants from Britain, who as latecomers have found it difficult to become accepted by the Afrikaners as "real" South Africans. After one hundred and fifty years of inefficient, and often corrupt, control of the Cape of Good Hope by the Dutch East India Company, the century of rather more vigilant British rule (from 1795 to 1910) over a rapidly expanding empire in South Africa left a tradition of Afrikaner resentment of Britain, distrust of English-speakers' loyalties, and often violent disagreements over how eventually to incorporate the black majority into a "white" South Africa.

These tensions were only partly resolved by unification in 1910 of the two coastal British colonies, the Cape and Natal, with the two interior Afrikaner-dominated republics, the Orange Free State and the Transvaal. These individual political units became the four provinces of the new state, which enjoyed nearly complete internal autonomy with a British-style system of government, but real independence in matters of foreign relations took another twenty-four years to achieve. By then, this new "Union of South Africa" had gained a status as a British "dominion" similar to that of Canada, Australia, and New Zealand.

The British monarch, the symbolic head of state, was represented in South Africa by a royal appointee, the governor-general, initially invariably a white male British aristocrat. He had few substantial powers; he was bound to sign laws passed by the Union Parliament, and could intervene in the political process only if the South African Parliament failed to provide clear majority support for the prime minister and his government. In such a case, the governor-general enjoyed some discretion in appointing a prime minister capable of commanding such a majority. As in Britain, sovereignty was vested in Parliament; there were two chambers, the House of Assembly, elected for a maximum of five years by constituent districts, and a Senate, elected indirectly by the Assembly and the provincial legislatures. The electorate consisted almost exclusively of adult white males; white women did not receive the vote until 1930, and the few Africans, "coloreds," or Indians permitted to vote (only in the Cape Province and Natal—in the latter case Indians had lost the right to vote in 1896) were gradually disenfranchised.

The Senate, with no absolute veto over bills passed in the lower house, could only delay or amend legislation. As in Britain, the party or parties enjoying the support of a majority in the lower house formed the government. The majority party leader became prime minister, with the right to appoint a cabinet of ministers. Again as in Britain, only the Assembly could vote on budgetary matters.

A curious special feature of Union elections was that, in deference to the difficulties of campaigning in and caring for the interests of vast and thinly populated rural electoral districts, in the rural districts a significantly smaller population than in urban constituencies provided equivalent voting power. According to this provision, referred to as "loading" or "unloading" a district, urban areas with up to 15 percent more and rural areas up to 15 percent less than the national average of voters per district had the same weight. The effect was profound: since rural constituents were, except in Natal, overwhelmingly Afrikaans-speaking, Afrikaner parties were substantially overrepresented in Parliament. One person, one vote never existed in South Africa, not even for whites.

A significant source of tension in the post-1910 Union was the retention by the new Cape Province of the old practice in the Cape Colony of granting the franchise to African and mixed-race "colored" men who possessed the required property and educational qualifications to vote, although they could not sit in Parliament (in the Cape they could be elected to the provincial legislature and in some cases to municipal councils). Natal permitted a similar practice, but with restrictions that in practice gave the vote to only a handful of African and "colored" males. The northern provinces so disliked this tradition, despite its affecting at most 15 percent of the Cape electorate, that in 1936 African voters were placed on a separate roll and permitted to send a small delegation of three white representatives to the House of Assembly. Africans nationwide would henceforth also elect four white senators, but this token representation was abolished in 1959 in favor of Prime Minister Hendrik Verwoerd's "homelands" scheme. "Colored" male voters in the Cape remained on the common roll until the Nationalist government succeeded in removing them in 1956; thereafter, they had representation similar to that enjoyed by Africans, from 1936 to 1959, until the "colored" voters lost this concession in 1968. The Cape "colored" community, like the Indians who were concentrated in Natal and who previously had no voting rights at all, is now represented in a separate chamber of Parliament under the 1983 "tricameral" constitution. Limited power-sharing was extended under that constitution to both "coloreds" and Indians.

Because enfranchised Africans and "coloreds" played a crucial role in some Cape constituencies, early on they found themselves wooed by diverse white political parties; the struggle over the Cape franchise was part of the much larger conflict between Afrikaner and English-speaker for dominance in South Africa. Exclusively English parties had no real political future: the pro-empire Unionist Party, the first Union "official opposition" (the largest party in the Assembly which did not support the government of the day), had by 1920 merged into the ruling South African Party, led by moderate Afrikaners, such as Jan Smuts, who sought conciliation with the English.

Exclusively Afrikaner parties, on the other hand, could gain power on their own, or with the support of a splinter party. Thus, the National Party, founded in 1914 by J. B. M. Hertzog to promote Afrikaner interests, was able to gain control in 1924 in alliance with the small Labour Party, led by English-speakers, and appealing to white workers of both language groups. When, in 1934, Smuts's South African Party merged with an older and more mellow Hertzog to form the United Party, some Afrikaners again preferred to remain in an ethnically exclusive party, and formed the Purified National Party under D. F. Malan. While their opposite numbers among Smuts's followers formed the small and staunchly pro-British and anti-Hertzog Dominion Party, which never achieved much success, the Purified Nationalists went from strength to strength and were rejoined by most of Hertzog's followers in 1940 as a result of a split in United Party ranks over participation in the war. Smuts was able to govern with a smaller and now predominantly English-speaking United Party, in part because in wartime he had support from the small Labour and Dominion parties. However, the Reunited Nationalists, as the followers of Hertzog and Malan were now called, had the demographic advantage in the long term; they rebuilt their forces and, a few years after Hertzog's exit from politics at the end of 1940, were able to gain victory under Malan in 1948 in alliance with another splinter group, the small Afrikaner Party. The latter merged with the Reunited Nationalists in 1951 to form the National Party, reassuming the name of Hertzog's old pre-1934 organization. In this study, the term "National Party" is used to refer to the successive groups describing themselves as "Nationalist," whether "Purified" or "Reunited." The United Party itself never recovered from the defeat of 1948 and went into a long and slow decline, eventually disbanding in 1977.

Ironically, in power the National Party, like Smuts's South African Party and Hertzog's United Party, eventually appealed increasingly to English-speakers as well as to Afrikaners; it modified its racial policies somewhat to placate its foreign and internal critics, and came to occupy the center of the white South African political spectrum. Like its predecessors, it also came to be opposed from the right by claimants to the mantle of exclusive Afrikaner nationalism who saw the National Party as a reincarnation of the old "centrist" United Party. Extremism in this, as in other matters, had given way to a degree of moderation and pragmatism.

A significant shift in attitudes can also be detected in the influence on Afrikaner nationalism of fascism and the Radical Right in the broadest sense. This influence was not uniform, but went through several phases. In the thirties, when the Afrikaner was confronted by the threats of drought, depression, and rapidly increasing black economic competition, various uniformed "shirt" movements had emerged, devoted primarily to attacking that oldest of scapegoats, the Jew, and showing a marked preference for adopting the language and symbolism of Nazism, in particular. But although fascism exerted some influence on mainstream Afrikaner nationalism in this period, it remained on the fringe of white South African society.

With the outbreak of the Second World War and the remarkable German military successes in Europe in the first three years of that struggle, fascism began to affect Afrikaner politics on a much wider front and with much more visible success, peaking in 1940 to 1941, when for a time it seemed that the National Party might work toward a full-fledged alliance with South African Radical Right groups like the Ossewabrandwag, and conceivably even with the Nazis themselves. By the end of 1941, and more so during the next two years, however, this relationship began to sour.

A different outcome might have been possible had the Axis powers remained victorious, but the growing resistance of the Allies led to a pragmatic response on the part of the National Party leadership, which, especially from 1943, began to distance itself ever more clearly from Far Right groups. By that time the chances of German victory were more dim. This new attitude among mainstream Afrikaner nationalists led to fragmentation on the right of white South African politics and to increasing attempts by the National Party to reintegrate the many Afrikaner factions under its own banner in preparation for taking power by the ballot box rather than by revolutionary means. In preparing for assuming leadership of a postwar South Africa, the Nationalists did not merely co-opt the estranged Radical Right, but were also influenced by them. When the Nationalists' attempt to build a new and more effective Afrikaner political alliance led to a surprising electoral victory in 1948, the wartime political triumph over the Radical Right that had been crucial in achieving electoral success could now be seen, in a certain sense, as a Pyrrhic victory. The Nationalists had entered into a compromise with the Radical Right the effects of which would be felt for decades, particularly on the political philosophy and style underlying much of Nationalist policy in the fifties and sixties. This influence on the National Party after 1948 is discussed only briefly in this book; its full extent remains to be examined thoroughly in the literature, and will require much more research than is presently possible.

In recent years, the Nationalist compromise with Far Right thinking proved increasingly unworkable. Government by centralized, obsessively segregationist blueprint and by the iron fist was succeeded by rule by a mixture of more sophisticated repressive and ad hoc reformist measures. The wartime generation has largely died or gone from politics, and, under pressure both internal and external, the Nationalist government was gradually compelled to be more vocal in its disavowals of modern-day supporters of fascism than in the past.

In this respect, political circumstances have changed so dramatically that the Nationalists, while far from liberal in European or American terms, find themselves confronted not only by opponents on the left but also by a growing array of powerful enemies on the right. Afrikaners, faced by the impending collapse of the sociopolitical system under which they have always lived, once again are finding attractive the seductively simple slogans of the Radical Right, whether in the milder guise of the Conservative Party, which seeks to find a more workable form of the classical apartheid of the sixties, or in the shape of the many extremist and more or less quasi-fascist groups like the Afrikaner Resistance Movement, with its Nazi-style paraphernalia and its talk of a "Boer State," or the mysterious White Wolves, reminiscent of the murderous death squads of Latin America.

In the eighties the Afrikaner once again, as in the thirties and forties, lived in a time of profound crisis. With Afrikaners feeling threatened, the Radical Right is again on the march. This time the Nationalists are as much the enemy as Smuts and the United Party once were. However curiously ironic this may seem, it is entirely in keeping with past political patterns. Any talk of conciliation, of compromise with other groups, has always provided fertile soil for the extremists. Purely English white parties are a distant memory today; parties of moderation and cooperation with blacks, however limited they may seem in the international or even the broader South African context, are more viable than before, yet they find themselves challenged from the right. It is too early to tell whether the New Right of today will, like its wartime predecessors, have a long-term impact, but the past suggests that it could be much more than a passing phase.

Chapter One

The Coming of the Shirt Movements

The Emergence of the Nazi Movement in Southern Africa

Adolf Hitler came to power in January 1933. By then, the German National Socialist German Workers' Party (generally known as the Nazi Party) had already established organizational structures both in the Union of South Africa and in neighboring South-West Africa (now Namibia), the vast former German colony administered by the Union, under a League of Nations mandate, since the close of the First World War. Because in southern Africa the Nazi Party was exclusively an organization for South African residents of recent German extraction, and therefore had comparatively little direct impact on the Afrikaner population, this study does not focus specifically on the history of the Nazi movement in South Africa. A brief outline of the principal features of this movement is nonetheless important in understanding the background for the emergence of groups with a more direct influence on the shaping of modern Afrikaner nationalism. These groups were the so-called "shirt" movements of the 1930s, modeled on the Italian Blackshirts, German Brownshirts, and similar uniformed fascist organizations of interwar Europe, and were the first indigenous South African imitations of European-based fascism. (See chapter 3 for a more detailed discussion of the impact of Nazi activities on the German-speaking community and indirectly on the Afrikaner nationalist movement.)

During 1936 and 1937 investigations of Nazi activities, the South African administration in South-West Africa discovered that as early as 1928 a Nazi Party member, Hans Schwabe, a resident of the small South-West African port town of Lüderitz, had approached party headquarters in Berlin about enrolling members locally; by the following year another party member, Karl Schröder of Windhoek, the territorial capital, was writing to Berlin to obtain membership forms. The potential for Nazi recruitment was certainly present in South-West Africa, since so many of the local white minority were German-speakers; they had settled before the First World War in that arid and sparsely populated country. The overtures of Schwabe and Schröder met with a favorable response; Schwabe was initially placed in charge of enrolling members, but, after his departure from the territory for Germany in April 1930, Schröder took on this role.[1]

In South Africa, with a proportionately much smaller German-speaking population, the Nazis took only slightly longer than in South-West Africa to begin the task of recruiting supporters from among German citizens (*Reich* Germans) resident in the Union and from naturalized South Africans of recent German origin (*Volk* Germans). According to an unpublished 1945 Union government report detailing Nazi activities in South Africa, the Nazi Party was founded in the Union in early 1932 by Hermann Bohle, an engineering professor at the University of Cape Town and a founder of a local German-speaking community organization, the Deutsche Verein (German Union). After Bohle received complaints from the latter group, which included many Jews, about a projected lecture series on Nazism he was planning to give, he decided to set up a Nazi Party branch in Cape Town. The South African government took no action and initial press hostility soon died down. The party rapidly extended its operations to all the major population centers: Johannesburg, Pretoria, Durban, East London, Port Elizabeth, and Bloemfontein, as well as to a number of smaller towns, such as Tzaneen in the northeastern Transvaal. In addition, the party began to expand more rapidly in South-West Africa.[2]

Baron Otto von Strahl, the German consul in Durban, who defected to the Allied side after dismissal in 1938 because of his refusal to join the Nazi Party, and apparently the biggest single source of intelligence on prewar Nazi activity in South Africa, reported that Bohle, as the first Nazi *Landesgruppenleiter* (country group leader) of South Africa, headed a complex and growing network of *Ortsgruppen* (local groups) and *Stützpunkte* (support points), each with male and female members.[3] This organization was, ironically, under the direct control of Bohle's own son, Ernst, who headed from Berlin the huge Auslandsorganisation (foreign organization or AO) of the Nazi Party, the umbrella agency that supervised party activities in every country with a sizable German-speaking minority. Ernst Bohle, born in England in 1903, had grown up in South Africa; in 1920, when he was sixteen, he first went to Germany.[4]

The main purpose of establishing a local Nazi organization was, as stated publicly in South Africa as also elsewhere, to disseminate Nazi ideology within the German-speaking community.[5] Both Hermann Bohle and his successor after his return to Germany, Bruno Stiller, the German consul in Cape Town and later the legation counsellor in Pretoria, kept a tight rein on their compatriots; Stiller, for instance, threatened to withhold government stipends from uncooperative German clergymen who worked in the Union.[6]

Many of the organizations most commonly associated with the Nazi movement in Germany were also active in South Africa in the years leading up to the outbreak of the Second World War. Nazi documents seized by the Union government after the outbreak of war showed that a small number of Germans who had emigrated to South Africa during the preceding ten to fifteen years had joined the Nazi Brownshirt organization, the Stürmabteilung (stormtroopers or SA); however, Von Strahl believed that the actual numbers involved were much higher.

Von Strahl stated in one of his many wartime reports to Interior Minister Harry Lawrence that, in addition to the SA, the Nazi Schützstaffel or SS itself (the elite black-shirted paramilitary Nazi units under command of Heinrich Himmler) had also operated in South Africa. SS members, he said, were employed not only in the German legation in Pretoria, but also in commerce, in the mines, and at mission stations, where as agents of the German government they supplied secret reports to the Gestapo in Berlin, which kept a very accurate card index on almost every German citizen living abroad. Three Gestapo agents were employed by the legation in Pretoria to watch local Germans' activities and also to establish and fund a spy network in the Union.[7]

This latter aspect of Gestapo activity indicated that the Nazis were not interested simply in coercing and controlling German-speakers; South African government intelligence later established that in the prewar years Berlin had provided a special telegraph code ("A.O.," a reference to the Auslandsorganisation) for the use of the local party organization and also secret addresses for communicating with Germany. This suggested the existence of an extensive espionage network; this, in turn, would have fitted in well with evidence in the possession of government intelligence of a separate German naval espionage organization operating in South Africa just before the outbreak of war.[8]

The importance the Nazis attached to obtaining detailed information on events in South Africa is underlined by a December 1937 directive from the press office of the Auslandsorganisation in Berlin to Wilhelm Stark, editor of the Nazi newspaper in South Africa, *Der Deutsch-Afrikaner*. In addition to his usual role of promoting Nazi propaganda among German-speakers through the pages of his newspaper (copies of which I have not been able to locate), Stark was, according to the official South African White Book on Nazi Activities in South Africa, instructed to collect complete volumes of all South African newspapers and periodicals, and to send them to Berlin. The same report indicates that in January 1939 the press bureau of the Foreign Section of the German Labor Front (the Nazi organization that replaced trade unions and employers' associations) in Berlin instructed the leader of the Labor Front in Johannesburg, W. Krause, to submit a report giving the names, designation, nature, circulation, and manner of publication of all English, Afrikaans, and German newspapers and periodicals published in South Africa. He was to send a copy of each of these publications to Berlin and to supply a detailed report of comments, stories, and songs antagonistic to Nazis and to Nazi Germany.[9] Such concern was complemented by regular reports from the Pretoria legation to the German Foreign Office on developments in South African politics, with particular interest shown in events inside the white political parties.[10]

From the time of the establishment of the Third Reich, this sometimes exhaustive interest was reciprocated in a remarkably concrete way by South African admirers of the new Germany who were not necessarily of German ethnic background themselves, and so from an early date Nazi concern with South African events began to take on a much more than purely academic character. South Africa soon represented not only one district of the international German-speaking community, but a window of opportunity for fascist influence that was without equal among the British dominions.

The Advent of the Anti-Semitic Shirt Movements: The Nazi Connection

Within months of Hitler's accession to power, a variety of uniformed ultrarightist "shirt" movements had arisen in South Africa, centering their programs not on antiblack feeling, with which white South Africans had long been associated, but on a distinctively imported European variety of anti-Semitism. Starting in the Western Cape, movements like the Greyshirts, the Blackshirts, and the South African Fascists spread rapidly across the entire country. In the Cape they attracted thousands to their meetings. The Nazi press in Germany carefully chronicled their activities.

By far the most important of these organizations was the Greyshirts, led by a former hairdresser of German extraction, Louis Weichardt, who founded the South African Gentile National-Socialist Movement after his debut as an orator on 26 October 1933 at the Afrikaner Koffiehuis in Cape Town.[11] The Koffiehuis was a familiar meeting place for nationalists of all kinds, not merely those of the fascist persuasion. Leaders of the National Party itself had long haunted this basement restaurant.[12]

Although the Nazis' anti-Jewish campaign in Germany had almost immediately elicited indignant reaction in South Africa, pro-Jewish protest meetings in Cape Town in 1933 were disrupted by anti-Semitic agitators, encouraged by people of German extraction or sympathies. Soon anti-Semitic pamphlets began to appear. By the last few months of 1933 the agitators had organized into groups such as Weichardt's, replete with swastikas, Nazi-style salutes, uniforms, and parades. The Eastern Cape, like the West, soon became a center of Greyshirt activity, while to the north in the Orange Free State Jewish shops in Bloemfontein were plastered with swastikas, and in the Transvaal the Afrikaner Manie Wessels founded the parallel anti-Semitic Blackshirt movement.[13]

Details on shirt movements other than the Greyshirts are fragmentary, not least because since their records have not been collected in a single location, information is limited largely to scattered references in documents on anti-Semitic activity. One of the most notable features of these groups was their tendency to continue to splinter and regroup. Their ephemeral nature also helps to explain why documentation on their membership and programs is difficult to find.

A pamphlet issued in July 1936 by the principal Jewish organization in the Union, the South African Jewish Board of Deputies, outlined the principal anti-Semitic groups active at the time, noting that Weichardt had been the major initiator of these movements, and that several of these groups were splinters that had broken away from the Greyshirts.[14] There were five groups in addition to his movement, reorganized in May 1934 as the "South African National Party" (not to be confused with the more familiar and much larger mainstream "National Party," led by J. B. M. Hertzog and later by Daniel Malan). The uniformed Greyshirts were the "vanguard" of the new party (presumably analogous to the role of the Brownshirts in the Nazi Party in Germany).[15]

One of the splinter shirt movements, the South African Fascists, was led by Johannes Strauss von Moltke, like Weichardt a South African of recent German extraction, and at first a close associate of Weichardt as Greyshirt leader in Port Elizabeth. Von Moltke's Greyshirt breakaway group was active primarily in the Orange Free State and in the Eastern Cape, where he had his headquarters in the small interior town of Aberdeen. Another Greyshirt splinter group was the Gentile Protection League, led by J. H. H. de Waal, Jr., son of a prominent National Party politician of the same name. De Waal, previously a lawyer in the Western Cape town of Hopefield, was later based in the remote village of Vredendal, on the edge of the arid Namaqualand desert region in the northwestern Cape Province. In January 1935 his group broke away from the Greyshirts, in which De Waal had been organizing secretary, on the grounds that the Greyshirts had become too "political" and that Weichardt was aiming at the establishment of a dictatorship. De Waal proposed to focus exclusively on the "Jewish menace." It may have been difficult to sell such a more limited program without the quasi-Nazi mystique of the Greyshirts; apparently at the time the Jewish Board produced its pamphlet not much had been heard for some while from De Waal's group.[16]

In Cape Town was based yet another anti-Jewish group, the People's Movement, led by H. S. Terblanche, which had initially issued a journal, *Terre Blanche*; the movement had been reduced to issuing a variety of leaflets promoting anti-Semitic sentiment. More important was Manie Wessels's South African National Democratic Party or "Blackshirts," based in Johannesburg and operating in the Transvaal and the Orange Free State. Wessels's group, active since December 1933, published a newspaper, *Ons Reg,* based in the small southeastern Transvaal town of Ermelo. Like the Greyshirts, the Blackshirts suffered from splintering: Chris Havemann, a former associate of Wessels, broke away with his own Blackshirt organization, Die Volksbeweging (the people's movement), to operate in the Johannesburg area; its Afrikaans name suggests a more narrowly ethnic appeal.[17]

All of these groups shared with the Greyshirts a virulent dislike of the Jews, but unlike the Greyshirts, the others remained on the perimeter of political life and had little impact on mainstream Afrikaner politics. The available evidence suggests that only the Greyshirts were still a viable albeit minor political force by the beginning of the war, when new groups such as the Ossewabrandwag and, to a lesser extent, former Defense Minister Oswald Pirow's New Order, rapidly eclipsed even the Greyshirts as proponents of a South African variety of fascism. Individually, therefore, the lesser shirt movements are of secondary importance to this study, but as a group the Greyshirts and their imitators were significant for the atmosphere of fear and violence that they created in South Africa in tandem with the emergence of the Third Reich in Germany.

The question of whether these shirt movements were funded or directed by Berlin has still to be answered. The general assumption that there is no evidence of a direct link between them may rest on a lack of substantial evidence in the surviving Nazi records, or it may depend simply on the repeated denials of

Weichardt of any such connection. In 1935 and again in 1939 Weichardt offered to open his party records to government purview in order to establish his innocence of a direct link to Nazi Germany, and on one occasion he offered to resign as Greyshirt leader if such a connection with the Nazis could be shown.[18]

Still, the matter is by no means resolved. For one thing, Weichardt ordered all his party documents removed from headquarters just eight days before Germany invaded Poland on 1 September 1939 at the start of the Second World War; he did so ostensibly to protect members from government persecution.[19] But were his operation as free of links to the Nazis as he claimed, he should have had nothing to fear from an investigation, which he elsewhere openly invited for publicity reasons. Suspicion must therefore remain that he destroyed any incriminating material while or after the papers were moved.

In 1935 Weichardt stated that the Greyshirts had no connection *whatsoever* with any organization overseas, specifically with the German Nazi organization, or any group in South Africa.[20] But there are some suggestions of rather closer cooperation than this. His party had a contract to send copies of its organ *Die Waarheid* (The Truth) to the Berlin Deutsche Kolonialgesellschaft, a front organization for Nazi interests in former German colonies like South-West Africa,[21] and also to exchange *Die Waarheid* with *Der Deutsch-Afrikaner,* the principal Nazi organ in southern Africa.[22] Although evidence of this kind does not establish the fact of substantial Nazi support, it certainly undermines Weichardt's denials of *any* kind of connection with the Nazis. If he could cloud the true state of affairs at such a trivial level, he may also have concealed matters of a more significant order.

Some fragments of evidence suggest he did just this. After the war it became clear that the Nazis in Germany had encouraged their nationals to join organizations like the Greyshirts and that lesser-known anti-Semitic groups like the "Blackshirt" National Democratic Movement were also infiltrated by the Nazis or their sympathizers.[23] Otto von Strahl listed Weichardt as one of those Germans considered a "reliable Nazi," one to whom it could be presumed attempts were continuously being made to smuggle information.[24]

By October 1939 the South African government was aware through its own intelligence sources that Bruno Stiller, the Nazi Party leader in South Africa and the counsellor at the German legation in Pretoria, had for some time been carefully cultivating the Greyshirts, the Blackshirts, and also the later ultrarightist organization the Ossewabrandwag (Ox-wagon Guard), and that Stiller had some system for contacting them.[25] This information became available after the confiscation of materials from the evacuated German consulate in the South-West African capital of Windhoek.

The influence of Nazi activity among the German-speaking people of South-West Africa had compelled Pretoria to ban the Nazi Party in the territory in 1934. It set up a commission of inquiry into Nazi activities there, and that commission reported that it had uncovered important evidence about a Nazi relationship with the Greyshirts.

The use by Weichardt's movement of Nazi symbols and political ideas like the *Führerprinzip* (leadership principle)[26] not surprisingly enhanced Nazi interest in the Greyshirt cause. According to evidence presented to the South-West Africa Commission, the Nazis considered Weichardt "an honest fanatical Nazi"; they referred to his organization as "the South African Sister Movement," and Nazi officials met with him to ask his opinion of South-West African affairs.[27]

According to other captured evidence before the commission, Weigel, leader of the Nazis in South-West Africa, had written Hermann Bohle on 29 April 1934 that it might "be possible for us to establish with the Greyshirts a united front based on similar world-views." Weigel asked Bohle to interview Weichardt about this possibility and to arrange for Greyshirt propaganda material to be sent to South-West Africa, where local Nazis already were distributing issues of *Die Waarheid* among South African nationals.[28] On 27 May Weigel wrote to the Auslandsorganisation in Hamburg:

Perhaps it would be possible to make provision for a nominal amount, say several hundred pounds, out of some political fund, which one could then place in some suitable form at the disposal of the Greyshirt Movement along devious ways. It is obvious that I must avoid any open fraternization with the South African sister movement. The support of the movement can only take place through intermediaries without any direct contact with us.[29]

The best explanation for the eagerness of the Nazi leadership in South-West Africa to let the growing Greyshirt movement in the Union expand into their own strongest base is, it seems to me, that they hoped to undermine the strength of the moderate governing United Party of Generals Hertzog and Smuts among Afrikaners there. One E. Muller, a Nazi *Gruppenleiter* (group leader) in the territory, underlined Weigel's sentiments on how best to achieve this in a letter to his superior on 11 June, 1934:

Naturally [Nazi] Party members must only support the movement anonymously. It is also in the interests of the Greyshirt movement that it should not be made known that it is being supported financially from the German side. I will get in touch with Comrade Bohle in Cape Town and in this manner endeavour to influence Weichardt to support his party here in South West Africa.[30]

Muller's letter suggests why Weichardt denied receiving any financing by the Nazis. He may, indeed, have been kept in the dark about a financial Nazi connection. There is no reason to believe that the Greyshirts were actually *initiated* by Berlin, yet all the evidence points to Weichardt's knowledge of close Greyshirt contact with the Nazis in southern Africa. A letter of 25 May 1934 from one of his followers, L. Kunze, notes disapprovingly that he met at least once with Karl Schröder, then leader of the Nazi Party in South-West Africa. Weichardt's reply to this letter, dated 29 May, indicates that he was familiar with local Nazi internal squabbling, with which he refused to interfere, since he felt that this infighting only hurt the cause of the campaign against world Jewry.[31] He was aware of the Nazis' ideological, if not financial, support for his movement's activities. More generally, the Greyshirts and their smaller rivals took naturally to national socialism's style and philosophy and imitated its standards enthusiastically.

J. H. H. de Waal, Jr., who was Weichardt's right-hand man before breaking away to form his own Gentile Protection League, epitomized this connection of common goals and practices. The "Programme of Principles" of his league was uniformly anti-Semitic in orientation, and advocated policies such as the denial of Union citizenship to Jews who received citizenship after 1918 and such as a ban on Jewish employment in government offices. The preamble to this document set forth clearly the central aim of De Waal's group: "The League desires to remove the ever increasing control obtained by the Jewish nation over the life and destiny of the South African Nation."[32]

According to the South African Jewish Board of Deputies' 1936 pamphlet on the anti-Jewish movements in South Africa, De Waal's anti-Semitic tract *My Ontwaking* (My Awakening) had copied an illustration from the notorious "blood libel" issue of Julius Streicher's *Die Stürmer,* which claimed "to show an actual incident of Jews drawing the blood of Christian children for ritual murder." The pamphlet commented:

One of the most wicked libels ever perpetrated against the Jewish people . . . is that the Jewish religion enjoins the use of the blood of Christian children for ritual purposes. When the *Stürmer,* the notorious Nazi newspaper edited by the fanatical Jew-hater, Julius Streicher, revived this accusation two years ago, a storm of protest arose throughout the civilised world, so that even the Hitler Government had to withdraw that issue from public circulation. Our South African anti-Semites, however, have not shrunk from reviving even this charge.[33]

In the same spirit, the Greyshirts published ditties like "The Song of the Gentile," replete with guitar chords, which included the following verse:

These aliens came with mad delight;
In blood our land to soak.
We'll work for right; we'll stand and fight,
And break the Jewish yoke.[34]

Anti-Semitism had characterized South African society earlier, but this was a quite different kind, one that owed its tone and substance, after 1933, to the advent of the Nazi regime. By example and through direct contact, the Nazis encouraged a climate of virulent anti-Semitism. White South Africans, and especially German-speakers, were bombarded with anti-Semitic propaganda from Germany. The activities of the shirt movements were consistent with it. So much of this literature was sent to South Africa from Germany that local Nazi officials could not distribute it all and had to store vast piles of pamphlets at German consulates.[35]

The Historical Context of the Emergence of the Shirt Movements

The political environment which these developments helped to create encouraged mainstream politicians of the Afrikaner right like Daniel Malan's Purified Nationalists to embrace the anti-Semitic message central to both Nazi and shirt movement ideology. Weichardt early on recognized the value of an anti-Semitic political program for politicians seeking to reach less privileged whites. He declared prophetically to his cohorts at their first congress in December 1934:

We know that party politicians are only out to catch votes and however strong [sic] they condemn us today, I predict that before long even Dr. Malan and others will be able to pronounce the word JEW, and the next you will hear that they are also against the Jews, we must compromise or we must leave the work to them.[36]

Weichardt's words showed a perceptive grasp of the opportunities available to any politician who chose to include anti-Semitism in his party platform. The circumstances in South Africa were ripe. The shirt movements, that most visible manifestation of growing fascist influence in South Africa, could not have existed without the example and encouragement of the Nazi regime. They could not, however, have spread as rapidly as they did if local conditions had not been favorable. The confusion surrounding a drastic realignment of white political parties left many on the right in the political wilderness. Political loyalties were temporarily fluid. In that atmosphere extremists moved swiftly to try to fill the vacuum.

To understand the rise of the new South African right in the thirties, one must understand the historical context of the preceding years. The roots of the pro-Nazi, anti-Jewish movement are there. The Nazis exploited what they found.

When in 1914 General Hertzog founded the original National Party, he provided a political home for those who felt that the Afrikaners, the descendants of the original white settlers, had become overshadowed in their own land by the much more affluent English. The National Party became the voice of the populist right in white South African politics. It was critical of the ruling political establishment, a coalition of English-speakers and of Afrikaners who supported some accommodation with the former, but was utterly opposed to any opening to further rights for the black majority. Hertzog won power in 1924 in alliance with the white Labour Party. The interests of Afrikaner culture and of the white worker seemed at last secure against both the old economic establishment of English-dominated capital and the competition from rapidly urbanizing African workers who were beginning to stream to the cities.

By 1930 the radical fervor had gone out of Hertzog's nationalist revolution. He had provided jobs for many poor whites (at the expense of the black workers), partly by greatly expanding state involvement in the economy; he had strengthened the symbolism of a separate white South African nationalism through a new Union flag (the old Dutch of the seventeenth century, with superimposed small Union Jack and the flags of the two nineteenth-century Boer republics, the Orange Free State and the Transvaal) and a new anthem, "The Voice of South Africa." Both were to enjoy equal status with the Union Jack and "God Save the King." He had replaced Dutch with the creole patois, Afrikaans, as an official language, and he had enforced a policy of civil service bilingualism, greatly undermining English dominance over the bureaucracy.

The Hertzog government was looking like some of the nationalist regimes of southern and east-central Europe, which had grown fat on several years in power. Italy under Mussolini, Spain under Primo de Rivera, Portugal after the collapse of its First Republic, Poland under Pilsudski, and the quasi-democracies of Bulgaria, Rumania, and Yugoslavia all come to mind here, gradually losing their initial radical fervor after an early flurry of reforms. Hertzogism, once uncompromising in its "Afrikaner" "nationalism" and closely identified with promoting the interests of Afrikaner workers and farmers, had moderated on its ethnic platform and become, in effect, a semi-authoritarian oligarchy, offering extensive political rights and a limited share in power to English-speakers but not to the African majority.

To many poorer Afrikaners it could well seem that their leader was losing interest in their cause now that he had achieved most of his major aims and, with a landslide victory in 1929, a com-

J. B. M. Hertzog, founder of
the National Party, who served
as prime minister from 1924 to
1939. After his angry departure from the Reunited National Party in late 1940, he
became an advocate of national
socialism.

From the Cape Times *Collection
in the South African Library*

Cabinet, with the Prime Minister J. B. M. Hertzog, and the Governor-General, the
Earl of Clarendon, c. 1931. Front (left to right): Daniel Malan, Earl of Claren-
don, Hertzog; back: C. W. Malan, Colonel F. H. P. Creswell, P. G. W. (Piet)
Grobler, E. G. Jansen, General J. C. G. (Jan) Kemp, A. P. J. Fourie, N. C.
("Klasie") Havenga, Oswald Pirow.

Daniel Malan held a powerful position as Cape Nationalist leader until Fusion
led to his founding of the Purified National Party in 1934. Kemp was a wartime
co-leader of the "Reunited" Nationalists in the Transvaal. Pirow visited with
Hitler, Mussolini, and Franco in the thirties.

From the Cape Times *Collection in the South African Library*

fortable parliamentary majority. For none of his reforms had substantially changed one painful truth: the less affluent remained far behind the English-speakers. A substantial minority were still poor unskilled laborers; only a minuscule proportion of Afrikaners had entered the prosperous urban merchant class.[37] For the others, mainstream Afrikaner nationalism had achieved only limited gains. They were therefore extremely vulnerable to simplistic solutions offered by the emergent Far Right.

The opportunity for the growth of a sizable New Right came with the Great Depression, which, as in Europe, changed all the axioms of political life and led to a drastic realignment among the ruling classes. As in much of east-central and southern Europe, where peasant societies were similarly dominated by privileged oligarchies in a more or less "democratic" framework, "democracy" here became ever more restrictive. In all these countries the system of government was strengthened around the most reliable traditional pillars of power—the major political parties or established ruling cliques, or the monarchy or presidency. The result was "national" governments of broad coalitions, as in the established western European democracies of Great Britain or France, or governments ruled by "strongmen" like Marshal Pilsudski in Poland and General Metaxas in Greece, King Alexander in Yugoslavia and King Carol in Rumania. Such regimes were often characterized by at least some of the elements associated with fascism: the curbing of civil liberties, extreme nationalism and militarism, and reliance on mass propaganda that appealed romantically to the supposed glories of the past. They were, however, at most "semi-fascist," often retaining at least the vestiges of their previous governments.[38]

Pre-1948 South Africa, with its curious combination of the western European liberal democratic tradition (for whites) and southern and eastern European paternalist authoritarian tradition (in respect of blacks), had not abandoned constitutionalism. But Hertzog could not meet the growing crisis on his own. Common sense dictated joining Britain in abandoning the gold standard, but Hertzog reaffirmed his neglected "nationalism," sticking to the gold standard as a sign of economic independence. The results were disastrous, especially for the many poor Afrikaner farmers.[39] The Carnegie Commission of Enquiry into the

Poor White Question found in 1932 that 17.53 percent of white families with children at school were "very poor," largely supported by charity, especially in the big cities, or living in dire conditions on farms. A further 30.97 percent of white families were too poor to clothe and feed their children adequately. Nine out of ten such families were Afrikaans-speaking.[40] In these circumstances, a dramatically new approach to party politics was considered: a grand coalition, on the lines of the western European "national" governments, but headed, as in so many central European countries, by conservative generals: Hertzog, the Afrikaner nationalist, and Jan Smuts, the longtime symbol of Anglo-Afrikaner reconciliation. Despite a considerable improvement in the economy following Hertzog's belated agreement to abandon the gold standard, there was a growing demand in both parties for a new vision.[41] A coalition agreement was reached in 1933 between the Nationalists and Smuts's pro-British South African Party. An equal number of ministers from each party was to be included in the coalition cabinet with Hertzog, representing the National Party, as prime minister and Smuts, representing the South African Party, as his deputy.[42]

Just as in Europe, rightist elements in South Africa would have nothing to do with such coalition arrangements, no matter how fundamentally conservative or even authoritarian. So the Rumanian Iron Guard and Christian National Party and the Hungarian Arrow Cross opposed the authoritarian Carolist and Horthy regimes in those countries, just as the Austrian Nazi Party opposed the stern Christian Social regime of Dollfuss. Such Radical Rightist movements flourished especially where there was no base for communist support among the poorer classes, either because of a legal ban or, as in the South African case, because communism had become increasingly associated in white eyes with black advancement.[43]

In South Africa Daniel Malan's "Purified" Nationalists, the most radical elements in the National Party, centered principally in the small towns and rural areas of the Cape, participated only reluctantly in the coalition. They were enticed by the prospect of otherwise losing their seats when Hertzog and Smuts went to the country for a popular mandate for a coalition.[44] Their core region of support, the southwestern Cape (apart from Cape

Town itself), was the one part of the country with an established and fully developed Afrikaner bourgeoisie that could lead an ethnic-based populist movement to mobilize whites on the socio-economic fringe. Here was a region with its own major Afrikaans newspaper, *Die Burger,* the respected Afrikaans university and Dutch Reformed seminary at Stellenbosch, and wealthy farmers and financiers in wheat, wine, wool, and insurance. English-dominated capital had never penetrated as deeply into the rural economic fabric here as in the north. Moreover, the wheat and wine farmers were far less oriented toward export, particularly to Britain, than the agriculturists of the northern provinces. There were no obvious material reasons to support rapprochement with the "imperial" interest in this home of the first Afrikaner nationalists of the late nineteenth century. Malan's supporters were well positioned to opt out of any more permanent type of realignment with Smuts.[45]

The Malanites balked at the next step: the fusion of Hertzog's and Smuts's followers into a new party to form a great white front and to turn the Union into a virtual one-party state. For many committed Afrikaner nationalists, with the prospect of "Fusion," as the merger of the United Party and the Nationalists came to be known, the world seemed to be coming apart. Hertzog, their hero, had appointed Smuts as his deputy prime minister, a man viewed widely as a traitor for his support of British capital and culture. He had crushed striking white miners in 1913, 1914, and again in 1922 with brutal force; when Afrikaners rebelled rather than fight for the British in 1914, he ordered the execution of a rebel leader, Jopie Fourie. How could Hertzog work with such a man? What had happened to the old Nationalist dream of reviving the Afrikaner republicanism of the nineteenth century? Nobody could be trusted anymore.

Late in 1933 and early in 1934, when it still seemed that Malan and other less radical elements on the right of Hertzog's National Party might be persuaded to support Fusion, hard-line Afrikaner nationalism was in chaos. A. J. Werth, the former administrator of South-West Africa from 1926 to 1933, later a leading figure in the Purified National Party in the Orange Free State,[46] and a known anti-Semite, was one who despaired of what militant Nationalists should do under such circumstances. He

bitterly pronounced Malan a leader with feet of clay.[47] The political vacuum could be exploited by ultrarightists like the Greyshirts' Weichardt, himself a former Nationalist. Even after Malan
had decided in the middle of 1934 to break with Hertzog and
secede with fellow republicans, Werth continued to believe that
no leader had captured the imagination of the *volk* (Afrikaner
people) and claimed that the volk did not trust Malan's new
party.[48]

During the year preceding Malan's secession, the situation was
so fluid that J. H. H. de Waal, Sr., a former speaker of Parliament, longtime key ally of Malan in the Cape National Party and
later a prominent Purified Nationalist, held discussions with
Weichardt about an "Afrikaner Union" to promote an uncompromising Afrikaner nationalism.[49] These talks broke down,
partly because Weichardt's movement was aimed also at English-
speakers,[50] and probably also partly because of his uncompromising adherence to a philosophy even the crusty old De Waal
could not stomach. De Waal, after all, was an ultraconservative,
not a Radical Rightist. Whatever the case, there was clearly an
opportunity to recruit dissatisfied right-wingers of all persuasions into a new movement, provided it was done carefully and
with tact, neither of which Weichardt possessed in abundance.
The opportunity did not escape his notice, as he later explained
to his supporters at a Greyshirt conference in 1938:

The Nationalists were about to fuse and the formation of a new party
in view of this was necessary. It was considered an ideal moment for
the then National-Socialist Movement to become a party [the SANP].
. . . We honestly believed that the reaction would be greatly in our
favour. After we had formed the Party, however, the Nationalist papers
came out and said that they were not after all going to fuse. Otherwise
I am convinced that whole Branches would have joined us.[51]

The bombastic Weichardt was fond of hyperbole but he was
probably telling the truth here. The Greyshirts long retained a
sympathetic ear among many Purified Nationalists, when they
confined themselves to anti-Semitism and refrained from standing against Nationalist candidates. In 1937 several Greyshirt
leaders in Malmesbury begged Weichardt not to put up a candidate for the upcoming elections in this Cape Malanite stronghold, because it would only hurt their cause. Most local Grey-

shirt financing, it was argued, came from generous Purified Nationalist supporters![52]

Grass-roots Nationalist sympathy with the Greyshirt cause may well have had its roots in the confused period before the foundation of the Purified National Party. Many ordinary Purified Nationalists, without necessarily accepting the full-blown national socialist program of the Nazis, recognized similarities between the aims of the two organizations. Like the National Party, the Greyshirts found a key constituency among poor whites and working-class people. The Greyshirts had one special advantage, for their bilingualism provided a home for some sections of the shrinking pool of English-speaking workers. Anti-Semitic propaganda was aimed in these closing years of the Depression at the disadvantaged of all groups: poor whites, white railway workers, and even black South Africans.[53]

Manie Wessels's Blackshirts, on the other hand, were popular only among poor Afrikaners in the Transvaal. As a May 1934 Blackshirt flyer put it, their appeal focused on the "economical and financial oppression of the Christian Afrikaans volk."[54] One onlooker at several Greyshirt meetings at the Koffiehuis in mid-1934 commented that it was impossible to reason with the sort of people who attended such gatherings, "crowded mostly with tramdrivers, railway workers, unskilled laborers, shopwalkers, etc."[55] The same observer found substantial support for the Greyshirts among rural Afrikaners in small Cape towns like Tulbagh. General Manie Maritz, the hero of the 1914 Afrikaner Rebellion, who had crossed over to the Germans in South-West Africa at that time, was now sharing Weichardt's platform in these rural areas. *Die Waarheid* was freely distributed there, and the notorious anti-Semitic forgery, *The Protocols of the Elders of Zion*, was making a powerful impression on these ordinary country people.[56]

In addition to the urban poor and Afrikaners in rural areas, a third constituency for the shirt movements was the youth. When J. H. H. de Waal wrote to his son about the Greyshirts' use of uniforms, De Waal, Jr., replied, "It is the world-order of the day to wear a uniform to distinguish the identity of political parties. All the young Afrikaners (English as well as Dutch) are ready to wear uniforms."[57]

The Purified Nationalists were not slow to recognize this point. F. C. Erasmus, secretary of the Cape National Party and one of the most prominent younger party leaders, organized the uniformed "Junior Nationalists" during 1934. Extremely detailed guidelines were issued for the uniforms of these "Orangeshirts," including the size of their belts and the material to be used for their neck scarves.[58] Very little else is known about this organization, which receives mysteriously little mention in the available records, but its mere existence is significant. The Nationalists were, however, affected by the new political climate. Their radical populism was more significantly influenced by the shirt movements in anti-Semitism than in any other respect. The Nazis made their first visible impact on Afrikaner nationalism in the anti-Jewish campaign.

Nationalists, Anti-Semitism, and the Greyshirts

It is perhaps not surprising, given the activity of the shirt movements among the Nationalists' key constituencies—workers, farmers, the poor, and the youth—that the Malanites were soon forced to adopt a strongly anti-Semitic message. The traditional appeals to anti-British and antiblack sentiment were no longer enough: Smuts's supporters in the "Fusion" "United" Party had accepted Hertzog's hard-line policy on the removal of Africans from their last foothold in mainstream electoral politics, the presence of a few thousand Cape African men on the common voters' roll. In return, Hertzog had agreed to drop an openly republican platform, claiming that Afrikaner and English-speaker had achieved parity in status, thereby making a separate Afrikaner nationalism superfluous.[59] Most whites were not going to quibble, given the beginnings of a massive economic boom that had followed within a year of the return to the gold standard.[60] Soon only those least affected by the improved economic situation were still vulnerable to the appeal of the irreconcilable right.

In public, at least, the Purified Nationalists were initially loath to attack the Jews directly. In the months leading up to the Malanite secession from Hertzog's "Fusion" Nationalists, Malan's newspaper, *Die Burger,* dismissed the Greyshirts as a political movement that was foreign in nature and claimed that the 1930 Quota Act, which had excluded most immigrants from eastern and southern Europe, dealt with the "Jewish question" quite adequately.[61] But three issues forced the Purified Nationalists to change their stance once they had become a distinct opposition party: the growing influence of the Greyshirts among their own people, the resurgence of the Jewish immigration question, and a latent anti-Semitism within the Purified National Party itself.

A careful examination of Nationalist documents shows that even in the early years of the Malan party anti-Semitism was sometimes just beneath the surface. The position of W. Bruckner de Villiers is a case in point. One of the most senior members of the party, close to Malan, he headed the board of Nasionale Pers (National Press), owner of the two principal Nationalist newspapers of the mid-thirties, *Die Burger* and the Bloemfontein-based *Die Volksblad*. Yet despite De Villiers's credentials as a comparative moderate, in his notes for an undated speech from the early thirties, in which he discusses the errors of Fusion, he refers to "our archenemies" as forming an unholy alliance between "Imperialists," "Capitalists" and "Communist Jews." He obviously thought better of this reference, because he later crossed it out.[62]

On 15 November 1934 yet another leading moderate in the Purified Party, A. L. Geyer, editor of *Die Burger,* launched an outspoken attack on "Hoggenheimer," a mythical ludicrously fat and cigar-smoking stereotype of Jewish capitalism long popular among Afrikaner nationalists. The notes for this editorial were among a handful kept by Geyer in his personal archive, which suggests that it dealt with a subject particularly close to his heart. Under the title "The Chief Enemy in the National Struggle," Geyer contrasted "Hoggenheimer" to the Imperialist, who was obsessed with love of another country, Britain: "But Hoggenheimer has no patriotism and no National feeling at all. Not the interests of the volk nor even of humanity, but self-seeking and own interests pure and simple control his actions. The Dark Money-Power is a tumor in the body of the capitalist system."[63] Geyer was unambiguous here. He did not actually "name the Jew," but he did not have to do so, since his public clearly understood the reference.

By late 1934 the shirt movements had created an atmosphere of hysteria against Jews that could not be ignored by the Nationalists, and which perhaps explains Geyer's attack. In Johannesburg the streets were filled with anti-Semitic posters in Afrikaans bearing the swastika. Jewish refugees from Germany were horrified to find the streets of Cape Town similarly littered with Greyshirt newspaper posters adorned with the headline "Kaffirs [the South African equivalent of 'niggers'] and Jews indecently assault white girls."[64]

Already J. Conradie, a United Party loyalist, was warning the liberal South African Institute of Race Relations not to expect any assistance from *Die Burger* or associated newspapers in combating anti-Semitism: "It is an open secret that although the new nationalist party (with its orangeshirts) and the Greyshirts are opposed to each other, there are very strong nationalist influences at work in the Greyshirts, and in the event of a General Election tomorrow an election pact will be formed."[65]

As it happened, there was no Greyshirt–National Party alliance in 1934, and nothing more was heard about this for some time. But the rapid increase in Jewish immigration over the next three years provided grist for the mill of anti-Semites in the National Party. By 1937 opposition to Jewish immigration was not enough for the Transvaal National Party; it now banned Jews from party membership. Yet Malan, a cautious and experienced politician, still tried to sidestep the issue.

In the north such obfuscation and evasion did not satisfy ordinary Transvalers, who were ripe for Greyshirt recruitment. In October 1937 one M. Kotze, a Pretoria Greyshirt, wrote to his friend Willie Laubscher, the Greyshirt secretary in Cape Town, that Weichardt wanted him to keep up a friendly stance toward the Nationalists:

The Nationalists are courting us seriously here in the Transvaal, but it is just because of the attitude which we are taking up towards the National Party. . . . We now have gained old Nationalists as members of our party and they inform me that they are tired of the standpoint of the federal council regarding the Jew as a member of the Nat. Party.[66]

An electoral agreement between the National Party and two smaller groups, the Blackshirts and Von Moltke's South African Fascists, had already been achieved by October 1937, according to J. L. Basson in his biography of J. G. Strijdom, the Transvaal National Party leader. Although Basson does not discuss the contents of these arrangements, they apparently involved not opposing Nationalist candidates in the upcoming 1938 general election, and in at least one case a Blackshirt leader, D. A. J. de Flamingh, stood as a Nationalist candidate in the blue-collar Johannesburg constituency of Vrededorp. Despite the appeal the Blackshirts had always made to working-class Afrikaner interests, De Flamingh lost the seat to a United Party candidate by 507 votes. Vrededorp was one of only two seats held by the National Party in the Transvaal, and had previously been won in a 1937 by-election by a Nationalist majority of 475 votes.[67] De Flamingh's defeat suggests that in practice candidates with his radical political affiliations proved less useful to Nationalist purposes than might have seemed likely.

The Greyshirts were a more problematic group, because they insisted on putting up their own candidates in the 1938 election. A prior electoral agreement therefore seemed particularly urgent if three-cornered contests with the United Party were to be avoided. With widespread sympathy for the Greyshirts at the grass-roots level, such an arrangement seemed a real possibility in late 1937. Individual Nationalists were sometimes generous donors to the Greyshirts, but did not want to see them undermine their own candidates' chances against the hated United Party at election time.[68] The management of the *Transvaler,* the main Nationalist newspaper in the Transvaal, established in 1937, was soon on friendly enough terms with the Greyshirts to exchange its issues with *Die Waarheid,* the Greyshirt organ.[69]

In this environment both sides could explore the possibility of negotiations, which led to an extended correspondence between Erasmus of the Cape National Party and Laubscher of the Greyshirts, the chief secretaries of each group.[70] The management committee (*Dagbestuur*) of the Cape National Party appointed a committee to act on behalf of the Cape Executive in furthering these negotiations.[71] In other words, all correspondence bore the

clear stamp of approval of Malan himself; it was not the initiative
of a few isolated extremists. There are indications that Malan
actually met with Weichardt, the Greyshirt leader, at least three
times during this process, following approaches, according to
Greyshirts records, by "leading Nationalists in the Cape" to
work toward some kind of compromise.[72]

Negotiations began in a cordial spirit. The Nationalists argued
that a victory by their common enemies, "Fusionist-Liberalism"
and "Labor-Communism," would be disastrous, and urged a
coalition of "national, anti-liberal and anti-communist" groups
to defeat this "anti-national" front. Although the Greyshirts had
not raised the Jewish issue, the Nationalists brought it up in this
same letter, with a view to a more detailed joint declaration of
intent.[73]

As it happens, negotiations failed miserably, partly because
Weichardt insisted on a purely tactical pact, with no compromise
on policy content, and partly because the Malanites became fearful of too close an identification with a party so similar to the
German Nazis. The Greyshirts' rejection of a multiparty system perhaps suggested that Weichardt hoped to repeat Hitler's
"arrangement" with Alfred Hugenberg's German Nationalists,
which had led to the annihilation of that organization.[74] Local
jealousies were probably also important. Individual Nationalists,
such as P. J. van Nierop, a member of Parliament, sabotaged
mutual goodwill with claims in September 1937 that the Greyshirts were funded by, of all things, Jewish money![75]

The fundamental issue, however, was that the Malanites were
above all *Afrikaner* nationalists, and notwithstanding their recognition of German friendliness, they could not be seen to be
working too closely with an apparent German puppet organization.[76] Erasmus perhaps inferred this with his mysterious comment in canceling further negotiations that, apart from the
Fusionist-Liberal and Labor-Communist dangers, "there are also
others."[77]

The Greyshirts remained keen to put up candidates in the
wake of this disastrous exchange, but just before election day
Weichardt decided to let his supporters fall in behind the Nationalists, except in three constituencies. In all other districts,

including Piketberg in the Cape, where Weichardt himself with-
drew at the last moment in favor of Malan, the Greyshirts in
effect supported the Nationalists.[78]

It would not be fair to conclude that the Purified Nationalists
in any real sense "supported" the Greyshirts. The Greyshirts,
like the other shirt movements, were simply too extremist to have
substantial value as allies. On the other hand, ordinary Nationalists, patently sympathetic to the Greyshirt cause, especially to
its anti-Semitism, gave donations to the movement.[79] The Greyshirts would never have made such headway in the rural areas
had they not enjoyed so much popular support among ordinary
Nationalists, especially in the heavily Malanite Cape.

At a higher institutional level, the Nationalist leadership openly
used the anti-Semitic bandwagon created by Weichardt and his
lieutenants for their own political advantage; they were willing
to enter into a serious and lengthy exchange with a group already
exposed as closely allied with Berlin, a point recognized by the
Nationalists themselves. As Erasmus put it in writing to Laubscher on 28 September 1937, Weichardt's group was "a Party
which apparently is so closely in solidarity with and inspired by
the political activities of another country, however friendly we
may be with that land."[80] Malan himself did not conceal his
pleasure at the opportunities presented from 1936 on by the
"Jewish question." He wrote gleefully to a leading Nationalist
anti-Semite, Eric Louw:

We are advancing particularly well with our volk cause. What has
helped us a great deal are Hertzog with his bitterness, Hofmeyr with
his liberalism, the Jews with their storming of our land and the King
with his antics [a reference to Edward VIII's entanglement with Wallis
Simpson, which cost him his throne].[81]

When the Nationalists closed their correspondence, Erasmus
was at pains to thank the Greyshirts for their anti-Semitic activity:

My party wants very much to express its real appreciation for the
valuable work which has been done in one respect by the Greyshirts,
namely that they have very pertinently drawn the attention of the volk
to the Jewish question, which has indeed taken on very threatening
proportions.[82]

But while Nationalists felt politically indebted to the Greyshirts, Malan's party could not, in my view, because of its special

claim to represent the Afrikaner volk, permit the identification of the anti-Jewish forces in South Africa with a Nazi or Fascist movement. In Erasmus's view, such a move could only weaken the Greyshirts' anti-Semitic "service" to the nation:

Towards Nazism in Germany and Fascism in Italy they [National Party supporters] are not of an unfriendly disposition, because each volk must ultimately choose for itself its own form of government. But they disapprove of the transfer of those movements to South African soil.[83]

When the Nationalists carefully considered the consequences of an "official" alliance with the Greyshirts, it was obvious that the temporary tactical advantages were greatly overshadowed by its implications for the central role of the National Party in Afrikaner politics. Hitler's harsh treatment of Hugenberg's Nationalists in Germany provided an additional warning to those on the Old Right who were considering dabbling in formal political arrangements with the fascists.

The Von Moltke Case

If it is difficult to demonstrate a definitive link between the Greyshirts and the Nationalists in the thirties, the picture is even more complex in the case of Johannes Strauss von Moltke, the leader of the Greyshirt breakaway group, the South African Fascists. A former Greyshirt leader in Port Elizabeth, Von Moltke had been expelled by Weichardt, who alleged that he had failed to account fully for funds he had collected in the Eastern Cape, that he had conspired against the Greyshirt movement, and that he had spent an afternoon with a Jewish woman in a hotel room during 1934.[84] Like the Greyshirts, Von Moltke's group drew many Nationalist supporters.[85]

Von Moltke's more significant link to the Nationalists was related to his own anti-Semitic activities. In 1934 a Rev. Abraham Levy of the Western Road Synagogue in Port Elizabeth brought a libel suit against Von Moltke and two lower-level Greyshirt leaders, Harry Inch and David Olivier, for publishing in the 13 April issue of Olivier's newspaper, *Die Rapport*, circulated privately in the Aberdeen district of the Eastern Cape, a South African variant of the notorious *Protocols of the Elders of Zion*. The Greyshirts alleged that this document had been removed from Levy's synagogue, and that it bore a signature purporting to be that of the "rabbi" of that congregation.[86]

Von Moltke himself had read the document to a crowd of some two thousand at a mass meeting in Port Elizabeth on 4 April. The document, according to Von Moltke, had been issued by "the Select High Circle of the Anti-Nazi Propaganda Vigilance Committee" in Port Elizabeth and was entitled "Our Plan of Attack." According to its stated purpose, this group aimed at world domination by the Jews, stood for "World Communism," and advocated violence, including murder, as the means of destroying the Greyshirts. The inflammatory anti-Christian language of "Our Plan of Attack" included these words: "Christ, in the Jewish sense was a false prophet born of the womb of a foul bitch whose husband was in our eyes never married to Joseph [*sic*]. In our Talmud, Torah and other holy books, it does say that the gentiles will be made to drink the Piss and eat the dung of the Jews."[87]

On 24 August 1934 the court, with Sir Thomas Graham, Eastern Cape Judge-President, presiding, reached a judgment awarding 1,755 pounds to Levy to be paid by the three Greyshirts said to have been involved, including 750 pounds in damages assessed against Von Moltke. *Die Burger*'s lengthy report on the judgment noted the court's findings that the document had never been in the Western Road Synagogue, that it had been compiled instead by one or more Greyshirts, and that it "could easily have been composed by Inch or Von Moltke or one of the two."[88]

Harry Inch, who had told the court that he had found the document when he had broken into the synagogue, was subsequently tried for making false statements in affidavits and for perjury in the case.[89] He was sentenced to six years and three months' imprisonment with hard labor, but the governor-general, the Earl of Clarendon, after receiving a petition of several thousand signatures from Weichardt, reduced the sentence to three years and three months with hard labor.[90]

Levy's suit was important to the Jewish community. General anti-Semitism under South African law could not be prosecuted, but in this case an individual Jew had been able to seek redress under libel law. Thus, the South African Jewish Board of Deputies had assisted Levy in preparation of evidence to expose the document.[91] During the libel trial, one of the defendants had read out to the court a letter that had been in the offices of the Cape Committee of the Board of Deputies in Cape Town and that had, so it was reported, disappeared in a burglary in June 1934, along with other records, including letters and minutes.[92] One can only speculate on how access to such a document had been achieved; the question of the missing Board of Deputies records was to resurface in another trial just two years later.

In June 1936, by which time Von Moltke was no longer a Greyshirt, he was criminally prosecuted for contravening the Insolvency Act, and according to a brief drawn up in the following year by two attorneys for the Board of Deputies, P. Millin and I. Isaacs, in this trial Von Moltke raised questions about the contents of some of these missing letters and minutes, and claimed that while he did not possess the originals, he did have access to them. Later he indicated to a Mr. Schauder, a member of the Eastern Cape Committee of the Board of Deputies, whom he had subpoenaed to appear in the case, that these originals were in the hands of the National Party, and that some had been sent to Germany![93]

According to the brief of Millin and Isaacs, by 1937 Von Moltke was editing a pro-fascist journal, *Patria,* in which several references to material in the missing records appeared, and some of these references had acknowledged their source. (I have been unable to locate this journal.) Von Moltke announced in this paper that he would soon publish a book, *The Jews of South Africa*; Millin and Isaacs said in their brief that they feared he might use some of the missing documents in that book.[94]

In October 1937, amid abortive Nationalist-Greyshirt negotiations, then under way, the Greyshirt secretary, Willie Laubscher, discovered to his annoyance that Von Moltke, by now heartily detested in Greyshirt circles, was making the most of his Nationalist connection—Nationalists were collecting money to assist him in publishing his book, and were planning to present the text before Parliament and to demand a government commission of inquiry into the role of Jews in South Africa. Laubscher commented in a letter to Weichardt: "In this manner they hope to show the Volk that they are anti-Jewish."[95]

On 22 February of the following year, the Board of Deputies succeeded in obtaining an injunction from the Cape Supreme Court against the use or publication of any missing documents, or of "the contents of such letters, minutes, documents, extracts or copies of any information derived therefrom." The court also ordered Von Moltke to hand over to Isaac Goodman, the applicant by virtue of his position as board secretary, all copies of these documents and any plates, type-matrixes, and typesetting of this material.[96]

In a sworn affidavit that he had presented to the court in attempting to forestall this injunction, Von Moltke spelled out the nature of the documentation in his possession. In his affidavit, he gave several pages of examples of the Deputies' influence over South African newspapers and politicians, particularly in combating anti-Jewish activities, but nowhere in this document did he demonstrate that he had material indicating that the Board of Deputies had engaged in any illegal or unethical acts. In the political climate of the time, however, it is understandable that the board feared that a distorted presentation of its efforts to protect the good name of the Jewish community was likely to abet the propaganda of its enemies. Von Moltke claimed, in his affidavit to the court, that the Board of Deputies was "a secret Jewish parliament" and "that the Jewish members of the Senate, Parliament and the Provincial Councils of South Africa, only nominally represent their constituencies, while in reality they are the secret representatives of the Board on the said State bodies, and that, as such, they will oppose any legislation which, although in the interests of the State and its subjects, might be in conflict with the policy of the Board."[97] He concluded that "organised Jewry in South Africa uses all kinds of underhand and dishonest methods in furtherance of its interests and welfare."[98]

Despite the board's victory in gaining an injunction, on 27 June 1938 the United Party organ *Die Suiderstem* reported that Von Moltke was now in charge of collecting certain funds for the National Party and added, "Two books about the Jewish question in South Africa will also shortly make their appearance, and although it cannot be said that the publication of these books has any connection with the fund, their writers have thrown in their lot with the 'Purified' Party and they were, during the elections, assisting the 'Purified Party' in their Campaign."[99] My sources do not indicate whether these books were, in fact, ever published.

Von Moltke's South African Fascists, the group which he had formed after his breaking with the Greyshirts, reached an understanding with the Nationalists in the 1938 election. As Afrikaner historian J. L. Basson notes, Von Moltke's group "created no problem in giving their support to the NP." Basson points out that Von Moltke addressed gatherings in the Transvaal to bring to the attention of voters the agreement with the Nationalists and that he made personal contact with National Party office-bearers in various constituencies.[100] Nor did Von Moltke's involvement with the Nationalists end there, for he joined the party later and ended his days as the postwar leader of the National Party in South-West Africa, where sections of the wartime German community had been known for pro-Nazi sentiment.[101]

As with the Greyshirts, because of the sparseness of available evidence, the exact nature of the relationship between Von Moltke and the Nationalists remains not wholly clear. What the evidence does suggest is that the Nationalists, on some occasions at least, did enter into a de facto alliance with self-identified fascists.

Chapter Two

Jewish Immigration and the Tide of Nationalist Anti-Semitism

Anti-Semitism as a political phenomenon in South Africa was both older and wider in scope than the very visible activities of the shirt movements. There had been many outbreaks of anti-Semitism before 1933, especially following sudden increases in Jewish immigration,[1] but the tide of anti-Jewish activity that swept the country from 1933 was of a decidedly different order, more intense, more sustained, and more threatening to the rights of Jews, even those who had long lived in South Africa.

Coinciding almost exactly with the coming to power of Hitler in Germany, the new anti-Semitism was most dangerous precisely because it reached rapidly beyond the ranks of the shirt movements to become an essential element of the program of the official opposition, Malan's Purified National Party. For although the informal alliance between Purified Nationalism and the shirt movements was in itself a significant indicator of the forces unleashed by the advent of the Nazi regime, anti-Semitism gradually became more than a tool to lure voters from the Radical Right.

When examined in juxtaposition with the flirtations with the shirt movements, the manner in which the Purified National Party slowly integrated anti-Semitism into the core of its platform tells a great deal about what was happening to mainstream Afrikaner nationalism in these years.

Early Anti-Semitism in South Africa: From Ambivalence to Quotas: To 1930

In the nineteenth century, when most Jewish immigrants were either British or anglicized Germans, there was little marked anti-

Semitism in South Africa, as General Jan Smuts noted years later, surprised when he visited Europe to discover that the Jews were often hated there.[2] The rural Boers saw wandering Jewish traders, called *smouse* (hawkers), as a "Chosen People," a designation increasingly ascribed by the Boers to themselves toward the end of the century. Only from the 1890s did English-speakers and Afrikaners begin to express ambivalent feelings about the Jewish community.[3]

Anti-Semitism became a serious problem in the aftermath of the turn-of-the-century Anglo-Boer War, when the number of Jewish immigrants into the Cape Colony and the Transvaal increased notably. These were now, generally, impoverished Jews from the "Lithuanian" regions of western Russia and northeast Poland, and thus easily identifiable in terms of culture and the Yiddish language. The new climate of hostility was as much one of xenophobic antialienism as of anti-Semitism; not only Jews but, for instance, Indians and Chinese laborers imported into the Transvaal after the war were targets of resentment.[4]

The aggressively industrious Lithuanian, or *Litvak*, Jews were regarded as a threat to the economic well-being of the poorer white classes in particular. They seemed especially "foreign" to the Britons and the anglicized Dutch-Afrikaners of the larger towns, where most Jews settled. It was in these years in the early twentieth century that the notorious "Hoggenheimer" cartoon character first appeared in South Africa, in the anti-Semitic Cape Town journal *The Owl*.[5] The obese Hoggenheimer, with his greedy eyes, massive hook nose, protruding lips, ill-fitting suits, and large cigars, was the caricature of what seemed to these Britons and anglicized Dutch-Afrikaners to be the epitome of the new class of large-scale capitalists that was emerging in the wake of the mineral revolution. Hoggenheimer was later popularized in the National Party newspaper, *Die Burger,* associated particularly with Daniel Malan, its first editor.

The South African Jewish Board of Deputies, which later fought strenuously to combat the activities of the shirt movements, was organized in 1903 to defend Jewish rights in the face of this first major anti-Semitic campaign.[6] After the establishment of the Union of South Africa in 1910, the board was vigilant against attempts to control Jewish immigration by administrative rather than statutory means, for example by using vague wording in the 1913 Immigration Act aimed at preventing further Indian immigration that, while not naming the Jews as the target, could nevertheless be used against them. In terms of this law, the minister of the interior could bar anybody from entering South Africa on the grounds of economic or social unsuitability.[7]

Despite Malan's exploitation of Hoggenheimer, anti-Semitism was not yet particularly associated with Afrikaner nationalism. In the turbulent early 1920s it was not a leading Nationalist, but Interior Minister Patrick Duncan, a member of Smuts's South African Party government, who on the grounds of economic unsuitability employed the Immigration Act against Jewish immigrants. At this time Jews were also accused by supporters of Smuts's government of collusion with Russian "Bolshevism" and of having helped to instigate the bloody Rand Revolt of 1922,[8] an unsuccessful attempt by white miners to stave off their replacement in semiskilled positions by cheaper black labor.

Ironically, in the late twenties the National Party, in power from 1924, actively sought the Jewish vote, hoping to capitalize on Jewish anger at such South African Party bigotry. The Nationalists, who had also taken up the cudgel on behalf of white workers, were in no position to attack the Jews for involvement in a workers' protest that they themselves had supported in spirit, if not in fact. Surprisingly, despite the contrary views of some South African Party members, Smuts himself had always shown strong support for Zionism, was a longtime friend of Chaim Weizmann, Zionist leader and future president of Israel, and had been backed by the overwhelming majority of Jewish voters, who considered him a valuable ally.[9]

However, the Nationalists failed to attract significant numbers of Jewish voters in either the 1924 or 1929 general elections, not least because South African Jews had little sympathy for secession from the British Empire, which had generally provided a safe haven for their communities. In addition, despite Duncan's exclusions of prospective Jewish immigrants, Smuts was considered the most reliable major South African politician, in contrast to General Hertzog and his Nationalists, whom South African Jews still regarded as a relatively unknown quantity in 1929, even after five years of rule.[10]

On the other hand, also in the late twenties, several Jews, among them Louis Karovsky and Bernard Alexander, brother of the leader of the Cape Board of Deputies, Morris Alexander, participated in Nationalist politics, some even standing as candidates.[11] In these years Malan expressed himself in thoroughgoing philo-Semitic terms, cruelly ironic in light of his radical volte-face in the next few years. Upon assuming office as interior minister under Hertzog in 1924, Malan assured Morris Alexander that he would not use anti-Asian legislation against the Jews, as had his predecessor Duncan. He promised that "no discrimination will be made against any particular European race or nationality."[12]

In 1929 Malan addressed a largely Jewish audience in the Hof Street Zionist Hall in Cape Town, in support of Morris Alexander, who was standing as an independent against the South African Party. According to *Die Burger,* Malan was forthright in his praise:

Of all the members who directly represented the Jewish race, he [Alexander] was the only one who throughout had advocated the cause of that race. The speaker could not understand how a member of the Jewish race could allow their champion to be thrown out of Parliament. "Although he often has differed from us," the speaker declared, "we have much in common as regards great principles. We know that his ideal is: South Africa for the South African people. We Nationalists have for years emphasized the principle of South Africa first."[13]

Yet only a year later Malan introduced legislation that was to provide a foretaste of things to come: his key Immigration Quota Bill, which was intended to limit the growing number of Jewish immigrants from eastern Europe to a mere trickle.[14] Jews were not mentioned in this legislation, but its purpose was clear: all countries not mentioned in a special schedule (all of them western European and North American countries, along with Australia and New Zealand) were to be limited to no more than fifty immigrants per year. Since Asian immigration was already controlled by 1913 legislation, the Quota Bill clearly was aimed at immigrants from southern and eastern Europe, almost all of whom were Jewish, a point conceded in an editorial by the relatively liberal *Cape Times,* which was surprisingly one of the more outspoken supporters of this bill.[15]

Such bipartisan support shows that too much should not be made of the Nationalists' introduction of this legislation. Smuts, who recognized that the Jews were in practice the principal target of the bill, returned from overseas in time to speak vociferously but in vain against it at its third reading in the House of Assembly.[16]

Malan argued that he did not aim to exclude Jews per se, but immigrants of all types from southern and eastern Europe. The crux, he claimed, was not race, but the country of origin, since the Jews of western Europe were not excluded.[17] He was keen to underline the allegedly nonsectarian nature of his legislation:

I think that the inhabitants of South Africa, in general, belonging to all parties and all sections, are desirous of conceding to the Jews in our country complete equality in every regard, to give them all the opportunities which the other sections of the community enjoy: to let them participate to the fullest in the national life and I am happy to say that we are in the position today to appreciate, and to appreciate in the highest degree, what the Jews have done for the country.[18]

The Quota Bill was in the tradition of the antialienism of past anti-Semitic activity in South Africa, in the sense of not being specifically targeted at Jews long resident in the country, and in its support by sections of white opinion who did not regard themselves as particularly anti-Jewish. The Jewish community was nevertheless deeply concerned about the potential for further, still more restrictive, legislation and protested strongly against it.[19] A mass meeting of Jews on 6 February 1930 in the Johannesburg city hall voted to send a telegram to the prime minister, the minister of the interior, and all members of Parliament, stating that the assembled community "emphatically protests against the proposed Immigration Quota Bill on the ground that it is based on unjust and illiberal principles and would in its incidence discriminate against Jews." Such protests were to no avail, as the bill soon passed into law.

The National Party and Anti-Semitism: 1930–1934

South African Jews had interpreted their situation far more correctly than those who accepted Malan's reassurances at face value. In June 1930 Malan wrote to Eric Louw, then outside the country in the diplomatic corps but soon to become the leading spokesman of anti-Semitism among Malan's Purified National-ists. Malan was rapidly coming to the conclusion that Jews were a threat to the Afrikaner volk. He showed that he was well aware of the nature of the step he had taken, declaring that the new measure was popular and overdue. He noted that he knew it would meet with Louw's approval:

Party advantage it will not bring us and for the rest of my days I will be for the Children of Israel like the Canaanite and the Philistine, but at least something was done for the volk on which its life depends, and that is altogether enough for me. It is only a pity that already so much has been permitted for our country to make commercial demoralization and exploitation a terrible and permanent reality.[20]

With the passing of the Quota Act, the days of the immigra-tion of *Litvak* Jews were over. The Jewish population of the Union was now a little more than 4 percent of the whites. The Jews of South Africa soon had reason to fear for their future. Their principal advocate inside the National Party, its Transvaal leader, Tielman Roos,[21] faded rapidly from the political scene during the tumultuous days of Coalition and Fusion in 1933–1934. The Jews' most powerful ally, Smuts, was forced to take a backseat to Hertzog; he was now less able to speak out against their enemies, since he was required to follow the Westminster tradition of cabinet unity now that he was no longer in oppo-sition.

With Fusion, the most right-wing elements of the Nationalists, who had rejected joining the new United Party, were clustered in Malan's Purified National Party, unfettered by the moderates among Hertzog's supporters, who opted to go into Fusion. Nei-ther Nationalist faction was likely to assist the Jews in a crisis situation, since their attempts in the twenties to obtain Jewish votes had been largely ineffective.

The Jewish community was therefore particularly vulnerable from 1934, with a "Purified" Nationalism rid of the ambivalence of an older Nationalist tradition. The "dual loyalty" charge be-came one angle of attack against Jews. South African Jews, because of their predominantly Orthodox *Litvak* origins, had always been enthusiastic Zionists, unhindered in their desire for a separate Jewish state by the assimilationist western European Reformed Judaism or the anti-Zionist Polish-Jewish Hasidism.[22]

Before 1934, Zionism had not evoked in South Africans the common charge of a dual loyalty, as in so many other countries. Afrikaner nationalists had accepted the communal separateness of the Jews, as well as their desire for a national homeland.[23] In 1929 the Nationalists had specifically reassured Jewish voters on this score:

The National Party like the Jewish people feel that they are a minority who must do all in their power to keep alive their language and racial characteristics. We have nothing but admiration for that race who have for two thousand years struggled to keep alive their national culture and prevent themselves being swamped by the nations among whom they dwell. We, like most Jews, are Zionists. Our Homeland is South Africa; to us it is sacred soil.[24]

But this was the voice of a broader Afrikaner nationalism, one that governed with the support of the English-led Labour Party, one that courted both mixed-race Cape "colored" and Jewish voters on purely pragmatic grounds, and that, even under Hertzog's leadership, happily extended the term "Afrikaner" to English-speakers who regarded South Africa as their home. Hertzog's party still retained vestiges of the inclusive and pragmatic Afrikaner nationalist tradition that had won out over more doctrinaire, exclusivist tendencies in the nineteenth-century Cape Colony. There had been elements of such an inclusive tradition even in the speeches of Paul Kruger, president of the old Transvaal Republic, who as the symbol of defiance of the British Empire would become the hero of the Purified Nationalists.[25]

Now that the Jewish vote, still loyal to Smuts, had failed to move over to the Nationalist cause, and with Malan's Purified Nationalism focusing on a far narrower, defensively "ethnic" definition of "Afrikaner,"[26] the very distinctiveness of Jews as a community exposed them to a real threat. It could not have helped matters that a community identified as inimical to local interests looked to the distant land of Palestine as the focus of its energies and enthusiasm.

Despite widespread rejoicing over the formation of the new United Party, there was much bitterness among Afrikaners over this rapprochement with the British-sponsored "organized" *geld-mag* (money power). Amid the terrible living conditions of poor Afrikaners and Malan's bitterness over the new divisions in Afrikaner nationalist ranks, a scapegoat had to be found. Malan had identified one at the very founding of his new movement: Hoggenheimer.

It has been said that the coalition must be formed to put an end to racial hatred. Experience has taught, however, that as soon as there is talk of so-called racial hatred, something else lies behind this. When that mask is removed, one always sees there the steely, calculating, greedy visage of Hoggenheimer.[27]

No Jew could feel safe, given the understandable identification of the Hoggenheimer stereotype in the popular South African imagination with Jewish businessmen. The Hoggenheimer cartoon character appeared with increasing frequency in *Die Burger*.[28] The "Purified" leadership, in keeping with its radical populist nature, was not going to spare the sensibilities of those who might consider this to be blatant anti-Semitism.

In any case, Nationalist radical populism by its very nature was likely to target the Jews as "capitalists." Despite the widespread belief of many Marxian historians that the apartheid state is essentially a creature of capitalism,[29] its creators, the Malanite Nationalists, had nothing but scorn for large-scale capitalism. An anticapitalist message was at the heart of the Malanite program, on a par with the protection of Afrikaner identity, not least because capitalism was seen as synonymous with British and Jewish oligarchy. The minutes of the crucial 1934 Cape National Party congress, which voted to secede from Hertzog's "Fusionists," redound with anticapitalist slogans. In his address to the congress, Malan denounced the failure of the coalition government of Hertzog and Smuts to address the root causes of the economic problems of South Africa: "The Government ought to recognize that the major cause of the problem lies in over-capitalized farms as a result of tumbling prices. Today improved prices cannot save the farmer, but only bring relief."[30] Malan condemned the coalition because it had, in his view, been formed "not . . . to the advantage of the farmer and the poor man, but to the advantage of [*tot voordeel van*] the money power [*geld-mag*] and the imperialist, his ally, who behind the scenes was exceptionally active in obtaining this policy."[31] The Malanites on the Federal Council of the old National Party had stated to the press on 19 June 1934:

We feel that the basis as it stands of the new Party [the United Party] is going to make a stronghold for imperialism and capitalism, and that it is impossible for the farmer, the worker and the poor man in the long run to find safety in it and must necessarily find a new home.[32]

Nationalist anti-capitalism, however, faded almost imperceptibly into anti-Semitism, particularly in the new ideological climate. To grow, the Purified Nationalists had to focus their appeal, in the generally healthy economy, on the remaining outsiders of white society, the very elements most susceptible to the scapegoating of the Jews.

Despite the earlier indications during the passing of the 1930 Quota Act that Malan was moving toward the adoption of anti-Semitism, in 1934 Malan himself was still guarded about his attitude to the Jews, in contrast with his grass-roots supporters, who provided fertile soil for recruitment into the shirt movements.[33] This underlines a broad trend in Nationalist thinking in the thirties: ordinary Nationalists were often far more amenable to extremism than was the party leadership itself, especially the leadership in the Cape.

Malan's attitude was encapsuled in a speech at Potchefstroom on 23 February 1934, before an audience of more than a thousand people. He criticized "parasites" who did not work but who nonetheless manipulated financial markets and exploited the common people. In the popular imagination, of course, "parasites" meant "Hoggenheimer," and Hoggenheimer meant Jew. But Malan stated that there were Jews who were parasites, and Jews who were not parasites, and that other groups were similarly divided. The parasites had to be "removed," he announced to applause. When a questioner asked him what action would be taken against those Jews who were "parasites," he replied enigmatically that he was unwilling to say directly what ought to be done; the resolution of this problem should be left to "the various departments."[34]

The Purified Nationalists and Jewish Immigration

In December 1933 the Greyshirt leader, Louis Weichardt, had turned up at a Malanite "circle conference" at Somerset West near Cape Town, seeking to persuade the conference to pass a resolution asking for stricter enforcement of the 1930 Quota Act. His resolution was adopted in a modified form.[35] Whether or not Weichardt's relative success indicates a reservoir of anti-Jewish Nationalist feeling at the local level, within a year the Nationalist press was giving extensive publicity to the activities of the shirt movements, to the chagrin of the Jewish community.[36] The rise of these major competitors of the National Party was noted with considerable interest in Germany by the Nazis, with particular attention given to their incitement of anti-Jewish feeling.[37]

Apart from the threat from the shirt movements, the single most important reason for the Nationalists' volte-face on the Jewish issue was the rapid increase in Jewish immigration from Germany during 1934–1936. The statistics are very instructive in this regard. In March 1935, 73 Jewish immigrants arrived in the Union. Twenty-five of these came from the traditional source countries, Lithuania and Poland (probably the Wilno district, which is part of modern Lithuania), despite the limitations of the Quota Act. By far the largest single group, 23, came from Germany. In August, 73 immigrants arrived, 29 from Lithuania and Poland, 38 from Germany. In November, out of 152 Jewish immigrants, 25 were from Lithuania and Poland, 12 from Latvia, and 99 from Germany.[38]

In 1932 five German Jewish immigrants came to South Africa; in 1933, 1934, and 1935, in response to Hitler's persecution, 204, 452, and 421. In 1936, 2,577 Jews fled to South Africa.[39]

Ironically, during the first three years of the Nazi regime fewer than half of German immigrants to South Africa were Jewish, 1,044 out of 2,664 arrivals. Despite the big increase in *German* immigration, there were fewer Jewish immigrants overall than in the pre–Quota Act days. The anti-Jewish hysteria that struck South Africa in 1936 was stimulated, in part, by the sudden boost in migration; 3,344 immigrants came, compared to 1,078 in 1935.[40] Yet the proportion of Jews to the total white population of the Union had increased only a fraction, from 4.28 percent in 1926 to just under 4.75 percent in 1936, or 95,000 out of more than two million people.[41]

The Transvaal Nationalists, in particular, were incited to extraordinary anti-Semitic fervor. At the provincial party congress of 1936, draft resolutions (*Beskrywingspunte*) from local branches sought further restrictions on immigration. Some used the veiled language of the thirties, such as a motion "that only whites who will be of benefit to the country be allowed as immigrants."[42] Seven branches asked that trade licenses be granted to none but naturalized Union citizens who had been legal residents for at least five years,[43] a commercial version of President Paul Kruger's residence-period franchise requirements for the *Uitlanders* (foreigners) of the nineteenth-century "South African Republic" in the Transvaal. A resolution from the working-class Pretoria suburb of Hercules provided a much more direct example of the fears incited among blue-collar Afrikaners, with its plea in a draft resolution that "no Jew, Colored or Asiatic may become a member of the Party."[44] The intensity of grass-roots Afrikaner fears of "swamping" were directed at many groups. There were even proposals that Africans be forbidden to drive white-owned automobiles, that motorcar licenses no longer be issued to Africans, and that "coloreds" not be permitted to handle petrol pumps at gas stations![45]

Anti-Jewish sentiment was addressed at three points in the manifesto that was published with the minutes of the 1936 party congress. "Hoggenheimer grows ever richer while the rest of the population sinks deeper every day into the morass of ever increasing poverty," it claimed. According to the manifesto, the Hertzog government was unwilling to stop a boycott of German goods (a boycott backed widely in the Jewish community) and the government seemed "powerless to take effective measures to stop the present stream of Jews from Germany to South Africa."[46]

The Transvaal leader of the party and future prime minister, J. G. Strijdom, made a spirited attack on Jewish immigrants, and in veiled terms criticized resident Jews as well:

We have the right to say that we do not want to become a Jewish or Italian nation or whatever, but want to remain an Afrikaner nation.

S.A. GREY SHIRTS · S.A. GRYSHEMDE

S.A.N.P.

SUID-AFRIKAANSE NASIONALE PARTY | **SOUTH AFRICAN NATIONAL PARTY**

PHONE 2-4864   FOON 2-4864

HOOFKANTOOR: 166 LANGMARKSTRAAT, KAAPSTAD.   HEAD OFFICE: 166 LONGMARKET STREET, CAPETOWN.
P.O. BOX 2432.   POSBUS 2432.

14th August, 1934.

S.A. Institute of Race Relations,
Box 1176,
JOHANNESBURG, Tvl.

Dear Comrade,

The mainstay of our Party and the S.A. Greyshirts is our
Official Organ "The Truth", and as you can well realise we need
every financial assistance to make same a success. With the
little finance so far at our disposal we have done wonders in
establishing a fortnightly issue of four pages (occasionally
six pages).

The Municipalities with its Jewish Mayors'and Jewish Coun-
cillors will not allow us to hold "street-collections". Like-
wise no Halls are at our disposal for bazaars and functions.
In addition the powerful Jew-press fights and ridicules us,
making our struggle very hard. Nevertheless we are determined
to fight and must expand "The Truth" and in order to do so need
every financial assistance.

For that purpose we are calling on you and others to assist in collecting funds for us. We enclose herewith a proper
Official collection-list and a book of stamps to the value of
£4-8-0 made up as follows:-

```
        4 @ 10/-  £2  0  0
        4 @  5/-   1  0  0
        8 @  2/6   1  0  0
        8 @  1/-      8  0

                  £4  8  0
```

These stamps act as receipts and at the same time constitute an Official record.

We appeal to you to do your bit and trust that you will
endeavour to dispose of all your stamps before the end of this
month. Please note that all lists, with amount collected and
unsold stamps must reach our Office on or before 30th instant.

Depending upon your support. Hail South Africa!

Yours faithfully,

Organising Secretary.

Letter of 14 August 1934 from the South African National Party (not the same as
the National Party), one of many Greyshirt aliases. The liberal South African Institute of Race Relations collected archival material on ethnic strife from all sources,
but the Greyshirts' letter implied that a request for information from the institute
was an effort to collect funds for their movement.
From the SAIRR Records, Cullen Library

(This pamphlet was distributed at Capetown and other towns at the coast. — Ed. D. A. P.)

CIVIL WAR?

According to adv. Morris Alexander K. C., M. P., uncrowned king of the Jews, there will be "Civil War and Bloodshed" in South Africa if the Government fails to introduce legislation to stop the Anti-Semitic movement, as he calls it.

(See "Die Burger", Wednesday, 24 January, 1934.)

According to adv. Alexander:—

(1) "This movement is nothing but sheer racial hatred and barbarism."

(2) "I as well as other Jews have time and again been threatened in anonymous letters with our lives."

(3) "False statements are being spread everywhere among the people and is done with great determent to the Jewish Community."

(4) "If this continues and these things take root among the unenlightened section of the nation, it must result in Civil war and bloodshed."

(5) "Jews having large business and factories are bing harmed."

(6) "There are proportionally more poor among the Jews in South Africa than any other section of the nation, excluding the poor whites."

(7) "In Cape Town the Jewish community spend up to £2000 per month on poor Jews."

(8) "Legislation must be introduced to prevent the spreading of the racial poison in the country."

Our Reply:—

(1) "It is sheer racial hatred and barbarism if we plead all South Africans to be pro-Gentile?"

(2) "Who would waste a bullet on any Jew?"

(3) "It is false to state that racially everything is in Jewish hands; and besides to plead for narrower Gentile co-operation?"

(4) "Whom does he refer to as unenlightened? The farmers? The University Students? The Attorneys? The whole South African nation? Or are all Gentiles unenlightened? We craves bloodshed? The Jews or the unenlightened?"

(5) "[With whose money did they built up these businesses? With that of the "truely" unenlightened or did they bring it from Palestine?"

(6) "True, if the poor whites are excluded only the Jews remain and we quite believe that there are still poor Jews because there are thousands pouring into our country continuously without a penny in their pockets!"

(7) "Out of whose pockets does the £2000 per month come which is distributed among the poor Jews? Out of ten Gentile's pocket! How much is spent on the poor white Christian? Nothing! Everything goes to the Jews, Jews, Jews!"

(8) "Who must introduce that legislation? Must the Gentile members of Parliament prevent the Gentiles to be pro-Gentile?"

J. H. H. De WAAL.

Printed by Moorreesburg Press, Main Street, Moorreesburg, and published by Mr. J. H. H. de Waal, P.O. Box 11, Hopefield.

Circular attributed to J. H. H. de Waal, Jr., Greyshirt leader, scoffing at a prediction of "Civil War and Bloodshed" in South Africa in the wake of anti-Semitism ("Who would waste a bullet on any Jew?").
From the SAIRR Records, Cullen Library

The National Party has the task of keeping the white race white. . . . Another task for the National Party is the economic salvation of the volk. It sets for itself the goal of ensuring for the farmer a civilized existence and to prevent parasites from sucking dry the consumer.[47]

Strijdom was well known for the directness of his language; it was now left for the more moderate Nationalists in the Cape like Malan to adopt a similar line. Malan had to contend with pressure from Cape anti-Semites like Louw, still in the diplomatic corps, but readying himself to enter parliamentary politics, who led a pressure group to convince Hertzog to pass stringent anti-Jewish immigration legislation.[48] The Louw group included South African diplomats abroad who were either Malanite or Hertzogite Nationalists in political inclination: H. D. van Broekhuuzen, A. Heymans, C. T. te Water, and S. F. N. Gie.[49]

By mid-1936 even the Hertzog government was contemplating some kind of restrictions on Jewish immigration, giving rise to deep divisions between the liberal interior minister, J. H. Hof-

secretary. S. A. N. D. M.

Box 4998,

Johannesburg.

YOU! BLADY BASTARD !

            I defy you to read this letter at your meeting publicly — I don't suppose that you have enough guts to do it — Am specially writing this in large letters and distinctly as an igno rant idiot like you may not be able to read it otherwise and I do want you to read this letter.

            I don't know yet — what you are — a bastard fool — Lunatic — Mampara or what — I shall write and tell you after your meeting and when I saw and Heard you I may(?) be able to judge but one thing I am certain and that is that Y O U A R E A B L A D Y IGNORANT GOD DAMNED F O O L and that is putting it mildly.

                    Your statistics for instance

             A R E   A L L   B A L L S !!!

             If the Jewish population is $7\frac{1}{2}\%$ therefore out of

750 Jews there are 740 Jewish Butcher and 10 Christians Think it

over.

           Now I shall give you a statistic

Goal birds	90%	Christians	10%	Jewish
Murderers	100%	"	0%	"
Laufer	100%	"	0%	"
Lazzy Bastards (Like you)	100%	"	0%	"
Brainless Idiots like you	95%	"	5%	"
Idiots like you	95%	"	5%	"
Rapers	100%	"	0%	"
Drunkards	100%	"	0%	"
Beggars	100%	"	0%	"

              W   H   Y   ?

If you just look at this figures — you will see why the Jews are more progressive they are industrious — they look to the future — they use their brains and don't sit on it like you they are clever and most of all while you think of racial Differences, hatrets, they think of progress. Now you Fool if you would use your brains and learn from the Jew how to be a man and preach what you have learned, you may do a better service to yourself your country and your fello man ———————————————what would you and South Africa have been without the Jews.

     K A F F I R S

Further let me give you a word of warning you fool — You and your followers (Idiots) are going to get on Wednesday such a damn good bludy Hiding that your own mother won't know you from a monkey

        Ta — ta You shuthuse

        Till   Wednesday !!!!!!???

"You! Blady Bastard!" leaflet purporting to be a letter from a Jew to the secretary of the (fascist) South African National Democratic Movement.
From the SAIRR Records, Cullen Library

Cover and page of pamphlet issued by the South African Jewish Board of Deputies. The board was attempting to alert the South African community to such anti-Semitic propaganda. The cartoon "Ritual Murder" purports to reflect Jewish slaying of Christian infants; it is said to have been reproduced in *My Ontwaking* by J. H. H. de Waal, Jr., former organizing secretary of the Greyshirts, from *Der Stürmer*, an anti-Semitic journal of the Nazi Party in Nuremberg, Germany.

From the A. M. Jackson Miscellany, Kaplan Center for Jewish Studies

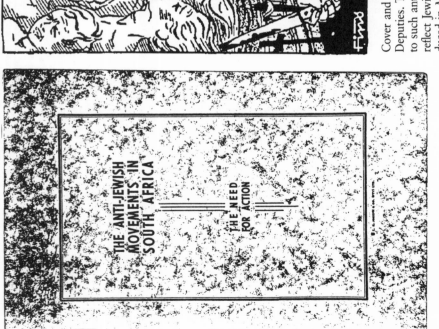

THE ANTI-JEWISH
MOVEMENTS IN
SOUTH AFRICA

THE NEED
FOR ACTION

meyr, a devoted Smuts adherent, and Hertzogite civil servants like S. F. N. Gie, best known as the prewar South African minister in Berlin, and A. Broeksma at the Department of Foreign Affairs.[50] The matter was exposing many of the weaknesses in the fragile coalition of the ruling United Party.

The Transvaal Nationalists, in keeping with their tendency to take the most militant positions in the Purified National Party, at their October congress adopted a program of principles that included a ban on "unassimilable" immigrants and on those who would by their presence "lower the material living-standard or the moral level of the white population."[51] "Unassimilable" immigrants meant *Jewish* immigrants. The congress rejected "unlimited and undesirable" Jewish immigration.[52]

One anti-Semitic motion made clear that on this score the Transvaal National Party was only marginally different from the Greyshirts—the motion to the usually more moderate Federal Council of the party on Jewish membership: "That this Congress, in view of the adopted motion concerning Jewish immigrants, urgently requests the Federal Council in its Program of Principles to ban the admission of Jews as members of the National Party anywhere in the Union."[53]

Malan was not yet ready for such drastic measures, but he did give considerable attention to the "Jewish question" in his speech to the congress. According to the congress minutes, he used an argument of which he became increasingly fond in arguing for restrictions on further Jewish immigration: "Prominent Jews acknowledge that no country can assimilate more than a certain number of Jewish immigrants. That limit was long ago exceeded in South Africa. South Africa appears to be third on the percentage list of the world. Palestine has eleven percent and Poland ten. Third, the speaker thought, is South Africa. This has already made anti-Semitism grow in the Union."[54] Just a month later in Bloemfontein, Malan told the provincial party congress that he would introduce in Parliament a private bill to halt "unassimilable" immigration, to cease recognizing Yiddish as a European language in respect to immigration law, and to prohibit the granting of Union citizenship to any person who belonged to "a class which cannot be assimilated."[55]

The wave of anti-Jewish hysteria was capped by the arrival in

October 1936 of a ship, the *Stuttgart,* from Germany with more than five hundred Jewish refugees aboard, trying to get into South Africa before further restrictions were enacted. The Greyshirts led a mob to the Cape Town docks, in the hope that they could prevent their landing, but in vain. The *Stuttgart* became a cause célèbre in the Jewish community.[56]

With the Greyshirts at the dockside were also five Nationalist professors from the Afrikaner Harvard, Stellenbosch University, among them H. F. Verwoerd, a future prime minister, who within a year was to be appointed the first editor of *Die Transvaler,* the key Nationalist organ in the north. The first issue of *Die Transvaler* hailed the professors with the headline "They Took the Leadership Role upon Themselves" and praised them for contributing to awakening "volk consciousness" and preventing impulsive, violent behavior.[57] The Nationalists increasingly followed this tack during 1937; adopting a "respectable" anti-Semitism, they would show that they were concerned about the alleged threat of Jewish immigration to the economic needs of the volk, but they would distance themselves from actual physical abuse of Jews. In this way, their platform would not be confused with that of the shirt movements.

The Hertzog government responded with its own variety of "respectable" anti-Semitism. Despite the wooing of the Jewish vote in the twenties, Hertzog had never been very sympathetic to the Jews, although he was opposed to the violence of the shirt movements.[58] He was far more concerned with not upsetting trade with Germany through anti-Nazi publicity in the English-language press than with responding to the fears of South African Jews. For instance, although Hertzog's papers show only the curtest responses to Jewish appeals for action against the shirt movements, his secretary, H. D. Bodenstein, sent a letter on his behalf in August 1934 to the Jewish Board of Deputies, drawing the board's attention to the need not to offend certain unnamed foreign countries with "unsympathetic" press treatment.[59] Hertzog's attitude toward the Jews on at least one occasion bordered on open hostility. When the Board of Deputies in July 1936 requested the prime minister's assistance against the anti-Semitic movements, he replied through his secretary that their fears of "any serious interference" with Jewish rights were unfounded. The Jewish community itself, he said, was in part responsible "in no small measure" for anti-Jewish feeling, especially in relation to promoting the anti-German boycott, which hurt the broader South African community:

There is a fast-growing conviction that members of the Jewish community in the Union, in order to promote the interests of the Jewish race, whether in South Africa or elsewhere, do not hesitate to avail themselves of measures and means in direct conflict with the interests of the rest of the population and of the state. This source of grievance with the non-Jewish section of the population has on more than one occasion been pointed out to the leaders of the Jewish people by the Prime Minister. . . . With respect to [the boycott of German goods], you will readily realize that it is difficult for the rest of the community to understand why they should be called upon by South African Jewry to make sacrifices for people in foreign lands who are not their fellow subjects, but complete strangers both to them and to South Africa.[60]

Hertzog complained in the same letter about "the indiscriminate immigration" of Jews, and closed with a stern warning:

When, therefore, the Jewish Community, in spite of provocative conduct by fellow Jews of the kind referred to, appeals to the Government for assistance against possible acts of molestation, your Committee will appreciate that the Government is bound to give its attention to all the aspects of the situation and to consider in how far, and what, measures ought to be taken, in order to safeguard the interests not only of South African Jewry, or any other section of the community, but also those of the people of the Union as a whole.[61]

In the light of this official attitude, it was scarcely surprising in January 1939 that Hertzog's amenable new interior minister, Richard Stuttaford, introduced an Aliens Bill that, without "naming the Jew," would screen all would-be immigrants not born British subjects. Aliens would be forbidden to change their occupations for three years; any changing of last names was to be stringently curbed. Malan made great play in the ensuing debate on Stuttaford's failure to pinpoint the Jews as the target of this legislation, while Smuts displayed evident discomfort over the interior minister's vacillating tone.[62] Stuttaford stated that the bill could be used to stop Nazis from coming to South Africa. Hertzog, however, while disclaiming anti-Semitism, used Malan's own favorite argument: the bill's aim was to curb Jewish immigration from Germany in order to reduce the threat of anti-Semitism in South Africa.[63]

Malan was now ready to go much farther. The Cape National Party, unlike the Transvaal Nationalists, had not banned Jews from membership, and therefore the Federal Council of the party, lacking the authority to override the provincial party congresses, could not act on the Transvalers' request to extend their own ban. On this one issue Malan would not shift, but he succeeded in hedging it enough to keep his leadership cadres quiet.

As late as June 1939 the Executive Council of Malan's Cape party responded to a request for clarification on this issue that party policy had been made abundantly clear in the bills introduced by Nationalist members of Parliament.[64] This could only mean Malan's draft 1937 bill, nipped in the bud by Stuttaford's Aliens Act, and Louw's still more virulent Aliens Act Amendment Bill, introduced in early 1939. The message from Malan's Cape Executive was simple: the party showed a negative attitude toward Jews; if Jews wanted to join the Nationalists nonetheless, they would not stop them.[65]

Anti-Semitism as Mainstream Nationalist Politics: 1937–1939

Despite the remaining scruples of the Old Guard in the Cape party, the years 1937–1939 saw the rapid assimilation of open anti-Semitism into mainstream Nationalist politics. There was close cooperation at various levels between the National Party and the shirt movements.

With the approaching 1938 elections, Malan began to look ever more urgently to anti-Semitism, particularly with the looming threat to his own radical populist appeal from the Greyshirts. He continued as far as possible to play a careful game of straddling both sides of the fence, yet it was becoming increasingly evident where he was more likely to fall.

This was perhaps most apparent in his speech at Stellenbosch on 12 April 1937. It incited outrage from Jews and liberals alike. The *Cape Argus*, relatively liberal by South African standards, declared that "too much musing on the Jews has made Dr. Malan a little mad" and that the Nationalists had "gone over lock, stock and barrel to anti-Semitism."[66] It is difficult to disagree with such sentiments, given comments like the following linking Jews to communism, interracial sex, and "anti-nationalism":

Coalition and Fusion were to a great extent the result of Jewish organization. The Jews did everything in their power to keep the Afrikaners from uniting, as they feared that South Africans would rise from their lowly and insignificant position to save South Africa for the South Africans. . . . Throughout the world the Jews availed themselves of democratic institutions for their own profit and that was why they joined the Labourites. There is yet another aspect of Jewish Communism in South Africa. The Jews oppose discrimination because they fear discrimination against them. In South Africa this means miscegenation.[67]

This was no longer the language of a man who hoped to halt anti-Semitism.

In striking contrast with such vitriolic language, however, Malan remained personally cordial toward individual Jews. In February 1938, just before the elections and after the failure of the Greyshirt negotiations, he welcomed a request from the Jewish Board of Deputies for an interview, stating that his party did not view the Jewish question "from the point of view of a particular race," but "with a view to the interest of South Africa as a whole."[68] In a similar spirit, he received Morris Alexander, Cape Jewish Board of Deputies leader and United Party member of Parliament for Cape Town–Castle, courteously for tea in his office. Alexander noticed also that he had recently received unusually friendly greetings in the Assembly lobby from Nationalist members of Parliament and that anti-Semitic attacks from that quarter had for the moment ceased.[69]

Such apparent friendliness may have been for purely tactical reasons, but it is hard to explain, considering Malan's vituperative attack only months before and the specific anti-Jewish proposals in the 1938 Nationalist Election Manifesto, adopted at last by the entire party and not just by the hard-liners in the north. Yet the actual wording of the manifesto suggests that the Nationalists were still acting in keeping with Malan's adherence to Hertzog's old "South Africa First" principle, a form of anti-Semitism with which the Malan of earlier years apparently could still live, but which would serve to placate extremists among rank-and-file Nationalists.

> While the Party in general welcomes the immigration of suitable assimilable white elements, it will, with a view to South Africa's specific problems, take measures to end further immigration of Jews, to act against the use of name-changing, to exercise stronger control over naturalization, and to create an occupational permit-system for unnaturalized aliens, like those which exist in England, France and other countries. Furthermore it will take all possible steps to train South Africa's own indigenous [oorspronklike] Afrikaans- and English-speaking volk elements for a livelihood in all fields and to protect them against unfair competition.[70]

In one sense this was merely a strongly nationalist position, another expression of the antialienism to which South Africa had resorted in times of economic hardship. In another sense, however, this proposal threatened not only prospective immigrants, but the Jewish community of South Africa as a whole. The thousands of non-Jewish German immigrants, for instance, were not even mentioned. Here was not the language of a Weichardt, perhaps, but to the well-informed Jew it heralded the first steps against local Jewry, just as in Germany the anti-Semitic campaign had begun on a limited scale. At a fundamental level, anti-Semitism had become an acceptable part of mainstream white South African politics. The shirt movements had been the first to "name the Jew"; now the Nationalists, even in the Cape, were no longer embarrassed to do so.

Some in the Purified Party were willing to go much farther than Malan. In *Die Transvaler,* the newspaper of the radical Nationalists of the north, Hendrik Verwoerd, its zealously brilliant young editor, derided the 1938 United Party triumph at the polls as "a Jewish victory."[71] In the preceding months Verwoerd's provincial leader, J. G. Strijdom, had attacked the Jewish community for refusing to advertise in his paper.[72] After sections of the Jewish community had expressed the view that *Die Transvaler* should be boycotted, the management of the paper expressed Strijdom's outrage in a threatening letter to the Jewish Board of Deputies: "If this is meant as a challenge to Afrikanerdom backed by responsible Jewish opinion, we shall be compelled to accept it, and with all the forces and influence at our command, make it an economic fight to the finish."[73] Although the author, A. J. Van Zyl, tried to present the Nationalist view as entirely reasonable, seeking an "amicable solution" of "an urgent problem," the Jewish question, he closed with an ultimatum that left the board in no doubt as to the central issue:

Responsible National leaders wish to calm feelings which may lead to excesses, but will not be able to restrain their followers much longer unless a disclaimer as to a boycott of *Die Transvaler* is provided very soon by the leaders of Jewry in South Africa, and actual proof to the contrary is given by the reappearance of advertisements from Jewish firms. . . . Action on your part on the lines suggested will calm matters down for the time being, and if the advertising columns of *Die Transvaler* show within the next weeks that there is in reality no boycott, we have little doubt that the anticipated economic clash between Afrikaner and Jew throughout the country will not eventuate.[74]

The Jewish Board of Deputies responded that it opposed any boycott, but noted that the other Nationalist newspapers had not experienced a similar level of Jewish antipathy.[75] These other journals were controlled by Malan's more moderate Nasionale Pers (National Press). Van Zyl expressed great pleasure at such apparent compliance, but closed his exchange with the board on a sour note, stating that its reassurances "eased the situation *for the time being*" (my emphasis).[76]

Just over a year later it became clear how little the board's accommodation had eased circumstances. Malan had apparently abandoned the courteous niceties of his attitude of early 1938. At the beginning of 1939 his party threw its weight behind a new Aliens Amendment Bill, introduced in the Assembly by Eric Louw.

Louw's bill shocked the more liberal sections of the pro-government press, such as the *Cape Argus* and the *Rand Daily Mail*.[77] It specifically declared Jews to be "unassimilable" as immigrants, including even British-born subjects of the Jewish faith, a group Malan had excluded in his own 1937 proposals before Parliament. The bill excluded all refugees by denying entrance to immigrants whose passports did not permit reentry into the country of issue. Any person who supported in any way any "communistic organization" was also to be excluded. Furthermore, all entrants since 1930 would be subjected to the provisions of the bill, a proposal that went far beyond the past language of the Nationalists.[78] Louw's test for Jewish parentage was redolent of Hitler's Nuremberg Laws: one "whose father and mother are or were either wholly or *partly* Jews [my emphasis], whether or not they profess the Jewish religion."[79] This was bald racial anti-Semitism, departing wholly from the veiled arguments of the past. Although the Nationalists could not muster anything like a Parliamentary majority, and the bill had no hope of passing, pressures on Malan from party extremists were mounting constantly.

By the beginning of the war Malan threw the last vestiges of caution to the winds, when even the Cape party threw its support behind anti-Jewish resolutions. On 6 November 1939 he told a rural audience at Koringberg: "We have, moreover, the Jewish problem which hangs like a dark cloud over South Africa. Behind organised South African Jewry stands the organised Jewry of the world. They have so robbed the population of its heritage that the Afrikander resides in the land of his fathers, but no longer possesses it."[80]

By that time, too, the Malanites had become firmly attached to a policy of "neutrality" toward Germany that bore signs of considerable sympathy for the Nazi cause. *Die Transvaler* had attacked what it said was the anti-German bias of its anti-Nationalist rivals. Numerous articles praising conditions in Germany had been featured in the Nationalist press, including a series by A. J. R. van Rhyn, editor of the Orange Free State Nationalist organ, *Die Volksblad,* and Eric Louw had tried to create the impression that news from the United States was colored by the Reuters press agency to give it an anti-Nazi appearance.[81]

By late 1938 and early 1939 the shirt movement leaders had found their way into the Nationalists' ranks. Von Moltke was one of the first, followed, later in 1938, by Willie Laubscher, the Greyshirt secretary. Then just before the introduction of Eric Louw's bill in January 1939, Weichardt himself joined the party and called on his followers to do the same, since Louw was now attacking the Jewish issue "as a whole." *Die Burger* hailed Weichardt's action, on the grounds that there was no place for small parties in South Africa. The real struggle was to be between nationalism and the evil alliance of imperialism, money-power, and liberalism.[82]

Those who had most ardently promoted the National Socialist cause, the leaders of the shirt movements, had found at least a temporary home in what had once seemed a most unlikely place: the Purified National Party. Now that full-blown anti-Semitism had become acceptable to mainstream Nationalists, just as Weichardt had prophesied it would, there seemed no reason for those on the extreme right to insist on a separate political existence. If opportunism had originally been behind the adoption of anti-Semitism by Malan's party, by 1939 this was certainly no longer evident to the shirt movement leaders; the Purified Nationalists had ultimately been affected by their own adoption of this cause at a much deeper level, something that eventually caused avowed supporters of fascism to feel reasonably comfortable in their ranks.

As early as 1938, when a Nationalist delegation went to Germany to study "the achievements of anti-Semitism," a German Foreign Office official cryptically expressed his gratitude to them for "showing such explicit faith in our methods." He expressed disappointment in the lack of recent support from South Africans in general, but said that: "We have not been unconscious of the faith of the Malan party in Germany. Germany had every reason to believe that the Nationalists look to Germany for inspiration and leadership."[83]

With the invasion of Poland and the outbreak of the Second World War, Berlin would have an opportunity to see whether the Nationalists' alleged "faith" in Nazi methods extended beyond the realm of anti-Semitism. There were indications in the thirties that fascism had indeed made significant inroads in South Africa into other areas of Nationalist political life and thought.

Chapter Three

The Berlin Connection

The Historical Background to Nazi Activity

From the start of the Hitler regime, Germany considered South Africa an eminently suitable target for Nazi propaganda. Here was the weakest link in the chain of self-governing British dominions, with the possible exception of Ireland, which from 1937 on was, in any case, an independent republic with no remaining constitutional ties to the British Crown.[1] The long-standing ties of culture and common ancestry between Germany and the Afrikaners were considered particularly important in influential German circles.[2]

Apart from some French Huguenot background and a small but significant Afro-Asian admixture,[3] the seventeenth- and eighteenth-century settlers who were ancestors of the Afrikaners were as often German as Dutch; by 1700 one-sixth of Cape whites were of German origin. The Dutch East India Company regime encouraged this trend when it stipulated at the end of the seventeenth century that only Dutch or German married men, of good character, could receive land. Lutherans were the only denomination, other than the Dutch Reformed Church, that the Company tolerated (from 1784).[4]

Although, because of company policy to preserve an official Dutch cultural monopoly, the Dutch language and the Dutch Reformed Church emerged dominant in the cultural and religious spheres, the German component in the embryonic Afrikaner society remained a significant part of its heritage. One has only to consider the many prominent Afrikaner families of German origin to establish the importance of that strand simply from a genealogical perspective: alongside the many recognizably Dutch names, such as Van der Merwe or Van Deventer, and the

French ones, like Du Plessis, Malan, and De Villiers, there were such notable names as Botha, Kruger, Muller, Hertzog, Vorster, Leibbrandt, and Meyer.

After the second British occupation of the Cape in 1806, German influences continued. A nearly three-thousand-strong contingent of German former soldiers, including some of their families, arrived in 1857. There was also a steady stream of German missionaries, first Protestant but later also Catholic, whose well-organized mission stations came to resemble German towns in their size and comprehensiveness. Some of the better known examples are Hermannsburg and Marrianhill in Natal. Both these missions and concentrated later German settlements such as New Germany, also in Natal, were to provide focal points for the later activities of the external wing of the German Nazi Party, the Auslandsorganisation (AO).[5]

In addition to the high proportion of German ancestry among Afrikaners and the impact of newer German immigrants, the history of Germany's relationship with the nineteenth-century Boer republics, and with Britain, the traditional Afrikaner foe, reinforced the potential for Nazi influence in South Africa. Thomas François Burgers, president of the Transvaal "South African Republic" from 1872 to 1877, and Jan Hendrik Brand, president of the Orange Free State Republic from 1864 to 1889, had both hoped to interest Germany in establishing a foothold at Delagoa Bay (now Maputo, capital of Mozambique), an old trading post held by Portugal, which had long ago ceased to show much concern about developing a more formidable presence in the area. Britain was genuinely concerned that the Germans might become involved in Southern Africa as Boer allies.[6] The German press showed considerable concern at Britain's annexation of the Transvaal in 1877, and after the restoration of independence in 1881, Transvaal president Paul Kruger led a deputation to Europe that met Bismarck and Kaiser Wilhelm II.[7]

By the mid-1890s Germany was becoming increasingly interested in South Africa,[8] spurred on not only by the great wealth of the new Witwatersrand gold mines, but also by the substantial German strategic and economic interest in the region created by the annexation of South-West Africa in 1884. When in January 1896 Leander Starr Jameson failed in his mission to seize the

Transvaal for Britain, Kaiser Wilhelm sent his notoriously un-
diplomatic telegram congratulating Kruger on repulsing the raid-
ers "without summoning the aid of friendly powers," a gesture
that confirmed the worst British fears about German intentions
in the region.[9] The kaiser's reference in the telegram to preserv-
ing Transvaal "independence" furthermore implied rejection of
British claims to suzerainty under the 1884 Anglo-Boer London
Convention.[10] The Boers took note of the kaiser's sympathy, and
a massive arms trade ensued, including 73,000 modern Mauser
rifles as well as German heavy artillery to protect the Transvaal
against a possible British invasion.[11]

Germany's annexation of South-West Africa and its growing
interest in the subcontinent as a whole, particularly St. Lucia Bay
in Zululand on the east coast, was a major factor in promoting
the British policy from the 1880s of encircling the landlocked
Boer republics.[12] This policy could only cement long-term German-
Afrikaner sympathies against a common enemy. Britain was not
about to permit the turbulent republics to establish a physical
link with German territory; the incipient Afrikaner nation in
turn was not going to forget quickly this attempt to strangle its
only chance of a non-British outlet to the wider world.

When war came in 1899 between Britain and the Boers, however, despite overwhelmingly anti-British sentiment in the European press as a whole, the kaiser's hands were tied for the
moment by an alliance system that threatened a far greater conflict than Germany was as yet ready to fight,[13] and the republics
were forced to stand alone against the British Empire. Short of
actually going to war against Britain, Germany had been quite
willing to take concrete steps to demonstrate its support of the
Boers, as with the sending of a cruiser to Delagoa Bay in 1894
to emphasize to the British its interests, as the official German
explanation put it, "both on the coast and in the Transvaal."[14]

A full-fledged war was something else, but there was now an
historical basis for supporting Germany in the future when it in
turn came to blows with Britain. This helps to explain the refusal
of so many Afrikaners to support the South African war effort
in 1914 and the widespread Afrikaner sympathy in the thirties
and forties for Germany when the latter, humiliated at Versailles
just as the Boers had been at the close of the Anglo-Boer War,

sought to turn the tables on the victors of 1918. The Nazi leaders in Berlin recognized the possibility of such a sympathetic hearing among their distant African cousins, and also the potential for developing this sentiment with a view to undermining British interests in the region.

Within months of Hitler's accession to power, a strong anti-Semitic movement had taken hold in South Africa. Its Nazi source of inspiration was evident from the start. Swastikas began to adorn its uniforms, banners, and the title page of the Grey-shirts' official organ, *Die Waarheid*. The provenance of the literature with which the country was now swamped was equally unmistakable. Leslie Rubin, a longtime student of Nazi influence on Afrikaner nationalism, recalls reading one anti-Semitic pamphlet during the 1930s in Durban which, although in Afrikaans, had been printed in Erfurt, Germany.[15]

German interest in South Africa had a very personal point of focus, since the first leader of the South African Nazis, Hermann Bohle, had taught at the University of Cape Town before returning to Germany to take up an important consulting position for the Nazi Party. His South African-educated son, Ernst, had returned to Germany and rose to become head of the sprawling Auslandsorganisation in Berlin, which coordinated and led all party activities overseas.[16] Ernst Bohle's organization controlled the diplomatic representatives of Germany abroad, since the Foreign Office professionals themselves were considered by the Nazi Party bosses to be too independent-minded.[17] One consequence was that the official and the real hierarchies of power in the German diplomatic corps were by no means identical. For instance, the apparently lowly Lierau, the consul-general in the South-West African capital of Windhoek, was actually responsible for all Nazi interests in southern Africa.[18]

The Nazis' activities in the subcontinent had two dimensions. One was the creation of a power base among German nationals and naturalized Union citizens of German descent, many of whom, like the family of Hertzog's defense minister in the United Party government, Oswald Pirow, were now assimilated into the Afrikaner population. The second dimension of Nazi activity was the promotion of the Nazi cause among non-Germans, particularly Nationalists. In the first regard the Nazi campaign was most thoroughgoing, but their propaganda activities in promotion among non-Germans were by no means ineffective either. The growth of interest in the anti-Semitic issue was just the most visible example of the effectiveness of this effort.

The Nazis and the German-Speaking Community

The central focus of Nazi activity in South Africa was the German-speaking community. Hermann Bohle's South African wing of the Nazi Party was just the peak of a subterranean network of considerable dimensions, which went beyond the organizations typically associated with the Nazi movement, such as the Brownshirts and the SS. In Pretoria the Nazis rapidly gained control of the *Deutsch-Afrikaner,* the most important German-language newspaper in the country. Its editor, Wilhelm Stark, assisted the German legation as an agent of the Auslandsorganisation and reported to Berlin cases such as those of German pastors who refused to accept national socialist doctrines. According to Otto von Strahl, who had served as a German diplomat in South Africa in the late thirties, families in Germany were punished for their relatives' views.[19] The *Deutsch-Afrikaner* and several lesser German-language newspapers functioned both as key propaganda organs within the German-speaking community and as sorting houses for the flood of propaganda from Germany.[20]

Von Strahl's lengthy wartime report on Nazi press activities in South Africa, written for Interior Minister Harry Lawrence, describes in considerable detail the role and nature of the *Deutsch-Afrikaner* as a Nazi organ geared to the German-speaking immigrant community. This newspaper made regular use of semiofficial essays on Nazi foreign policy from the German Politico-Diplomatic Correspondence Service, an agency attached to the German Foreign Office which attempted to put Hitler's expansionist moves in the best light while attacking Britain and the Soviet Union.[21]

In addition to printed leaflets praising the accomplishments of the Third Reich in matters such as social welfare and technology, which the Auslandsorganisation sent from its National Socialist Service for Foreign Papers, the *Deutsch-Afrikaner* received numerous photographs of German personalities and events, as for example the 1936 Berlin Olympic Games, Hitler's involvement in the German "Winter Relief" fund, and functions held by the Nazi recreation organization, "Strength Through Joy." The *Deutsch-Afrikaner* was expected not only to publish these photographs, but also to distribute them among the South African press and among individuals sympathetic to Nazism or with potential for such sympathy.[22]

Besides publishing a wide variety of material from Berlin, Stark's newspaper gave extensive coverage to Nazi functions in South Africa: Nazi Party branch activities, Winter Relief Fund events, Nazi youth movement gatherings, Nazi fund-raising bazaars, and celebrations whenever German ships arrived in Union harbors. The financing of this key Nazi publicity organ was at least partly local: Von Strahl noted that companies owned by German-speakers were intimidated by local Nazi Party representatives into advertising in and subscribing to the paper.[23]

Another key role of the *Deutsch-Afrikaner* was to promote a militantly anti-British and anti-Smuts political attitude among German-speakers and Afrikaner nationalists who, if they could read German, would have found exhortations to look to Germany for friendship, to adopt anti-Semitism, and to support a pro-German policy in South-West Africa. On all these counts the newspaper questioned the policies of the Hertzog-Smuts government and the attitudes it seemed to represent among a majority of white South Africans. Thus an article in the 8 November 1934 issue, entitled "We Utter a Warning," contained the following passage (the translation is by Von Strahl):

Isolation means becoming Anglicized to the Afrikaans nation. It would become stunted and demoralized and only that nation of Helots would remain of which General Sir Ian Hamilton spoke recently. If the Africander nation wants to preserve its originality against British culture, it cannot forego friendly relations with other nations, and who else would primarily deserve consideration in this respect as an unselfish friend, if not Germany? Sensible Africanders have therefore always set value on maintaining friendly relations with the German nation.[24]

On 22 November 1934 another article set forth similar ideas more bluntly:

A country which through the mouths of its responsible statesmen pampers Jews and orientals [the latter reference, probably to Indians, is puzzling in light of the lack of any government attempts to improve their position] and eulogizes them as being the most valuable citizens, and at the same time ill-treats its German blood relations in South West Africa [a reference to the banning of the Nazi Party in that territory], is suffering from racial softening of its bones. . . . The teutonic culture whose champion in Africa the Afrikaans nation proudly professes to be, can only be developed with Teutons. The task is so tremendous that it needs the collaboration of all the racially related teutonic nations whose colonial tradition is rooted in Africa.[25]

The German South African community was indoctrinated at every level: through not only newspapers but also the German-language schools, German pastors and priests, and front organizations such as "reading circles," through which Nazi literature was disseminated. Several teachers in the German schools, and at least two principals, belonged to the South African branch of the National Socialist Teachers' Organization (Nationalsozialistische Lehrerbund or NSLB), a Nazi professional organization.[26]

The Lehrerbund, which aimed at educating German-speaking youth according to the principles of national socialism, held regular conferences in the various regions of the Union, and its leaders and members who were school principals were expected to provide detailed reports to a central "Ausland Section" office of the Lehrerbund in Berlin on matters such as the influence of German-language schools in the local German-speaking community, the percentage of German-speaking children attending these schools, and activities of alumni. In January 1939 the Ausland Section began its own magazine, *Der Deutsche Erzieher im Auslande* (The German Educator Abroad), to which all members were required to subscribe, and were encouraged to send contributions on themes like racial doctrines, world philosophy, character building, and national politics.[27]

Although, according to a Lehrerbund circular dated 8 March 1939 detailing a new membership fee structure, there were only fifteen active members in the Union, these members came from at least eight schools in diverse centers like Durban, Cape Town, Johannesburg, Hermannsburg, and East London. It is possible that, like the party, the Lehrerbund was intended to function as an elite body through which a few committed Nazis could exercise influence over other German-speakers in the workplace and in the local community.[28]

Professional groups such as the Lehrerbund fell under an umbrella organization, the Verband Deutsche Berufsgruppen (Association of German Vocational Groups), an arm of the German Labor Front (Deutsch Arbeitsfront or DAF).[29] The Labor Front was the largest of the Nazi front organizations operating in southern Africa. Such associations were crucial to Nazi activity, because German-speakers who were ineligible for or uninterested in party membership could be pressured into joining less overtly Nazi groups. According to Otto von Strahl, a tremendous effort was made to persuade all German-speakers in employment of any kind to join the DAF, which was ostensibly intended to provide a means of overcoming friction between the various classes of Germans, for instance in labor disputes in German-owned companies, through arbitration and discussion. Members paid a subscription fee in return for which they received benefits in the event of unemployment, illness, or death.

But, as the evidence collected by Von Strahl shows, the Labor Front had a much more important underlying function: it permitted the Nazis to enjoy some degree of influence over a much larger proportion of German-speakers in South Africa and South-West Africa than would have been possible through regular party structures. In each country where the Labor Front operated a reliable Nazi Party member was delegated to exercise disciplinary control over those belonging to the DAF,[30] and worked directly under the senior political official of the Nazi Auslandsorganisation in that territory.[31] At the local level, each individual Labor Front branch was headed by the leader of the Nazi Party branch in that area or by a deputy nominated by him. To complete the picture of efficient party control, Labor Front members were required to attend monthly meetings and other occasional gatherings, to cooperate with the front leadership, and to act "in a manner becoming of a German," in the words of a 1935 party directive.[32] Thus the Nazi policy of *Gleichschaltung* (roughly equivalent to "bringing into line") of German-speakers was effected at the southern tip of Africa just as in Germany itself.

Afrikaner Leaders and German Exchanges

A stream of visitors flowed back and forth between Germany and South Africa. The Deutsche Akademie of Munich, a key cultural organization for the promotion of the interchange of ideas between Germany and other countries, had twenty-three members on its South African committee in Germany, compared with twenty-one for the entire United States. Related organizations were the Goethe Institute, which held classes at Pretoria and Kingwilliamstown in the Eastern Cape, and the Kultuurraad (Cultural Council) in the Orange Free State capital, Bloemfontein.[33]

Trade between Germany and the Union was also a priority. Helmut Schacht, the powerful president of the Reichsbank in Germany and Hitler's top economist, stressed the "ties of blood" between the two countries in a 1936 speech at the launching of the new vessel of the Woermann shipping line, significantly named the *Pretoria*. He noted that Germany was South Africa's second-best customer, outranked only by Great Britain. Excluding gold exports, no less than 14 percent of Union exports went to Germany, 42 percent to Britain.[34] In order to encourage this practical relationship, a German economic delegation that toured South Africa in late 1937 and early 1938 provided five bursaries for young South Africans to pursue studies in Germany.[35]

Educational exchanges of this sort contributed to the intellectual formation of a generation of leading Nationalists. They helped to create a climate receptive to German propaganda in South Africa, and encouraged a new kind of Afrikaner youth culture, shaped by student leaders and teachers who had been exposed to fascist ideas abroad.

An important source of cultural cooperation and scholarly exchanges was the German-Afrikaans Cultural Union, under the presidency of J. F. J. ("Hans") van Rensburg,[36] an Afrikaner who served as secretary of justice under Minister Jan Smuts in the Fusion government and then administrator of the Orange Free State until the outbreak of war. Like Pirow, a powerful minister in the United Party government, Van Rensburg was both a devoted adherent of Prime Minister Hertzog and an admirer of the Hitler regime. His admiration for Hitler's new Germany is evident from the Nazi response when he visited Germany in 1936. A certain Herr Dieckhoff at the German Foreign Office wrote to General Smuts that his government had been glad to receive so important a guest: "All the more as in his case we have made the acquaintance of a personality of great value whose fundamental knowledge of the German character and lively interest in conditions in Germany we especially know how to appreciate."[37]

Van Rensburg was a Hertzogite of unusually Radical Rightist inclination. He was also the president of the Afrikaanse Nasionale Studentebond (Afrikaner National Student Union or ANS), founded by Piet Meyer in 1933 at Bloemfontein in order to provide an Afrikaner nationalist alternative to the "liberal" National Union of South African Students, which was dominated by English-speakers.[38] The Nazis watched Afrikaner student activities with interest, noting, for instance, their support for neutrality in the event of a war between Britain and Germany.[39] Bruno Stiller, the leader of the Nazi Party in South Africa, commented appreciatively on an address given in Stellenbosch in April 1937 by Van Rensburg to the Studentebond in which he discussed his impressions of Hitler's Reich:

The Administrator particularly emphasized that national socialism meant a synthesis of nationalism and socialism and that through this synthesis Germany was being saved from the great danger of communism. The fact that Van Rensburg has frankly and freely upheld national socialism as an example to the Afrikaners, not only to the German-Afrikaans Cultural Union, but also before the student body of Stellenbosch, from which the future leader of Afrikanerdom will be drawn, shows how lasting are the impressions which he gained on his visit to Germany.[40]

Berlin retained an interest in several potential allies among Afrikaner nationalists, including Malan's party, but those connected with the ANS seemed to be among their most promising possibilities. Apart from Van Rensburg, the most important of these individuals were Piet Meyer and Nico Diederichs.

Meyer would become chairman of the influential secret and militantly pro-Afrikaner nationalist Afrikaner Broederbond (Afrikaner Union of Brothers, or AB) in 1960 and he headed the state-controlled South African Broadcasting Corporation (SABC) for most of the 1960s and 1970s. In the early 1930s he was offered a Rhodes scholarship to study at Oxford, but his uncompromising nationalism kept him from accepting it, electing to do a doctorate in philosophy and education at the Free University in Amsterdam instead, and to attend occasional courses in Germany as well.[41]

The other founding father of the ANS, Diederichs, studied at the graduate level in Germany in Munich, Cologne, and Berlin, apart from his main doctoral program in philosophy at Leiden in the Netherlands.[42] Diederichs, like Meyer, would later head the Broederbond, but he reached equally elevated heights in office as longtime finance minister under B. J. Vorster after 1966 and he crowned his career as state president of South Africa from 1975 to 1978.

Hendrik Verwoerd, prime minister from 1958 to 1966 and one of the most powerful figures in the Transvaal National Party from the late thirties, also studied in Germany, in Hamburg, Leipzig, and Berlin, preceding Meyer and Diederichs.[43]

There can be little doubt that these decades were of particular importance to the intellectual formation of these men. Professor Walter Markov, Emeritus, of Leipzig University, informed Leslie Rubin that the Nazi Party was beginning to gain a powerful hold over many students at this university as early as the mid-twenties.[44] Both Meyer and Diederichs were profoundly influenced by the antiliberal German Romantic mood, modeled after ideas of the early nineteenth-century philosopher Johann Fichte, the fashion at German universities at the time. It upheld the nation and Volk as the highest ideal of human existence. South African scholars have generally described the variant of this philosophy adopted by Afrikaner intellectuals such as Diederichs or Meyer as "neo-Fichteanism," a practice I follow in this study.[45]

At a much more practical level, the ANS leadership (Verwoerd did not belong, but many of his views were similar) was encouraged by Nazi cultural organizations to learn about national socialism at first hand. Meyer was invited in 1934 to lead the first Studentebond tour group to Europe, and he later recalled how excited he and his colleagues were to learn skiing in the Alps with none other than Rudolf Hess, Hitler's chief of staff, and to see Hitler himself close up.[46]

There was a more serious purpose to this tour, since the Studentebond took the opportunity to forge links between these South Africans and a number of German organizations, including the National Socialist Students' Association, the Colonial Society (which worked for the return of South-West Africa to Germany), Hitler Youth, and the German Academic Exchange Service.[47]

A series of Studentebond-sponsored tours of Germany followed. For young Afrikaners, with their parents' bitter memories of the devastation of the Anglo-Boer War, it must have been impressive to see how a nation in misery had succeeded in reclaiming its former eminence. In 1937–1938 no fewer than eighteen Studentebond members participated in the Berlin University celebrations honoring the fifth anniversary of Hitler's accession to power. Everywhere such groups were received warmly and feted by representatives of the various Reich departments.[48]

Senior ANS representatives received even more lavish treatment. Van Rensburg, of course, not only had the opportunity to meet top Nazis like Goering and Goebbels, but was also granted an interview with Hitler.[49] Diederichs, although strictly a private citizen, unlike Van Rensburg, gave a lecture in Goering's palatial "Aviation House" in Berlin. It was attended by many top Nazis, as reported in the *Deutsch-Afrikaner*. Diederichs's lecture must have been a rather dull affair, dealing as it did with the constitutional options open to the Union, but it was received with hearty applause. He did not use the opportunity to launch an attack on Britain or to advance his own political ideas.[50]

Diederichs was privately more forthright in expressing his views to Nazi officials. According to a transcript from captured Foreign Office records, in a two-hour discussion in May 1939 with Herr Kirschner, a Foreign Office official in Berlin, Diederichs confided his doubts about Malan's ability to transform the Purified National Party into an instrument for fundamental change. He was convinced that the old leader was burdened by traditional liberal-democratic institutions. A new party name was needed, as was a clear program resting on a broader policy than anti-Semitism. Diederichs felt that the problem with the National Party lay not only with Malan: "Very many of its currently leading members are still too extensively caught up in democratic ideas. Consequently, a far-reaching change of leadership becomes a prerequisite for a full-scale Nationalist takeover. Hope lies with the youth and all in the Nationalist camp are unanimous that every newborn Boer will one day become a Nationalist. Therefore nobody doubts the final victory."[51]

In addition to the promise of the youth, there was also the potential inherent in the Broederbond:

... the main concern should be the education of experts who would then be in a position to take over the government by virtue not only of their convictions but also of their professional training. The Broederbond will in the future devote itself to this task, starting with the smallest matters. With the request that I keep this strictly confidential, Prof. Diederichs then told me that he had recently taken over the leadership of the Broederbond. According to him, the Broederbond was a secret organization to which it was possible to be admitted only after a thorough investigation. He maintained that the goal of the organization was to infiltrate the whole country, especially the leadership, and in this way to take over the whole state apparatus from within.[52]

Diederichs's own sympathies were made clear in the following passage from Kirschner's transcript of the interview: ". . . he did not believe that the inner strength of the National Party would suffice to form a government according to the model of the authoritarian states. But in the long run only such a government could ensure the position of South Africa south of the equator."[53]

Diederichs's doubts about the ability of the National Party to promote radical nationalism in South Africa were reflected still more broadly in the former South African Nazi leader Hermann Bohle's opinion of South Africans. Since his return to Germany in the mid-thirties, he had become the influential senior expert in Berlin on South African affairs. According to a German Foreign Office memorandum by Bohle, he noted that none other than Eric Louw, a South African diplomat in Paris and later a prominent Nationalist cabinet minister, "the so-called Streicher of South Africa," as Bohle put it in praise of his anti-Semitic stance, had returned to the Union to stand for Parliament in 1938 as a Malanite. Yet behind the scenes, Louw had written to Malan's archenemy, Hertzog, asking whether he could have his post back as "minister in Paris" in case he lost the election! Bohle wrote scathingly: "This lack of character is typically South African, hence in Germany one should have little faith in all South Africans and only allow oneself to be guided by absolute facts."[54]

The Nazis' Propaganda Network in South Africa

Distrust of this kind did not prevent the Nazis from pouring a fortune in propaganda material into South Africa. Two agencies were particularly important in this regard: the Hamburg Fichtebund (Fichte Union) and the Weltdienst (World Service), an agency that published a weekly bulletin in eight languages. The Fichtebund, founded in 1935 to disprove German "war guilt" in the First World War, sent more than five million leaflets abroad in its first year. Much of the material sent to South Africa was written in excellent Afrikaans, which suggests how important this audience was thought to be. The shipments were often sent into the country wrapped in other merchandise, or posted directly to individuals. Dutch Reformed clergymen received many of these pamphlets on the "Jew-Bolshevist" threat and the achievements of the Nazi regime.[55]

The Weltdienst specialized in what it regarded as Jewish machinations; it charged among other things that Jews killed Christian babies for ritual purposes. The bulletin had a still more useful purpose, the promotion of anti-Semitic organizations around the world. Advertisements from shirt movements everywhere were featured regularly; their activities in South Africa received extensive coverage. Roosevelt and Smuts were referred to as Jews; the parliamentary system of government itself was also described as "Jewish."[56]

Such an avalanche of propaganda could well have had an influence, particularly on those with a limited educational background, those isolated in remote areas, the youth, and the poor. This may help to explain why there was so much pressure for action against the Jews from rank-and-file Nationalists. A grave crisis of faith in liberal-democratic institutions and values ensued. German propaganda fed on the discontent of whites least affected by the post-Depression recovery and on the anger of militant Afrikaner youth. The Nazis used Nationalist bogeys like Smuts and "Communism" for maximum effect.

Yet Hermann Bohle, three months before the war began, expressed an underlying unease about the Nationalists, although it was the largest right-wing political organization in South Africa: "In general no unity reigns in the camp of Malan. Malan is moreover a genuine democrat, who for egotistical reasons has adopted anti-Semitism. He is by vocation a Calvinist pastor."[57]

Since Malan himself seemed so unpromising a client leader, if the Nazis were to have any real impact on the Afrikaner nationalist movement, it seems to me, their only practical option was to subvert the sections of the grass-roots Nationalist following most sympathetic to Radical Right ideas, and thus force the apparently softheaded elders of the party, like Malan, to make the necessary changes.

It is true that the Nazis did also have potential support among some of the Hertzogite ex-Nationalists in the United Party, but the coalition nature of that party, including so many English-speakers, limited its potential value for developing a "Berlin-Pretoria axis" on the lines of the relations Germany enjoyed with Mussolini's Italy, Imperial Japan, or right-wing regimes in Europe such as those in Hungary and Bulgaria. Nevertheless, there were a few striking cases of individual pro-German sentiment in the Hertzogite faction.

In addition to Hans van Rensburg's contact with Nazi officials during his 1936 trip to Germany, Oswald Pirow, Hertzog's minister of defense, who not only was the son of German immigrants but also had attended Kiel University in northern Germany,[58] made several visits to the fascist countries during the thirties. Pirow held discussions with Mussolini, Franco, and the Portuguese strongman, Salazar, and even met with Hitler at the Führer's private retreat at Berchtesgaden,[59] inciting unfavorable reaction about the purpose of such meetings.

For instance, in November 1938 the South African writer Sarah Gertrude Millin, a woman who enjoyed a wide range of contacts in political life, and a champion of her own Jewish community, noted in a letter to Smuts that the British politician Ramsay MacDonald had expressed his concern at Pirow's visit to Germany earlier that year; she added that in light of this visit England did not trust Pirow.[60] Jan Hendrik Hofmeyr, an unusually outspoken liberal United Party member of Parliament (for Johannesburg North) and until September 1938 a minister holding a variety of portfolios in Hertzog's cabinet, concurred with these sentiments in a letter written to her the next month: "I don't think Pirow has done himself much good in South Africa by his peregrinations through Europe. He is undoubtedly more distrusted than ever before."[61]

Hertzog himself, despite his own moderate attitude toward the British, refused to believe the stories of Nazi atrocities. Hofmeyr noted in a letter to Sarah Millin that Hertzog, who never had much patience with his strong opinions about racial prejudice, "steadfastly refuses to believe that the Germans, in whom he still has a pathetic confidence, really are ill-treating the Jews!"[62] Hofmeyr, whose anti-Nazi reputation was such that Berlin instructed the German consul in Johannesburg not to attend a banquet at which Hofmeyr was to speak,[63] was so convinced that Hertzog would pay no attention to any protest of his about Nazi Germany that he decided, against his own better judgment, not to speak to Hertzog about stopping Pirow's 1938 trip.[64] As he informed Sarah Millin in June 1938, when he was still a cabinet member, although he wanted desperately to express his outrage at Nazi treatment of the Jews, the response of the Hertzog government would be a foregone conclusion: "Sometimes I wonder whether I should not be gloriously indiscreet and say exactly what I think about Hitler's policy in this respect. Then no doubt the P.M. would send an apology to Germany and I would have to resign."[65]

But, despite Hertzog's sympathetic attitude to Germany, his advanced years must have limited his usefulness to the Nazis. If Hitler were to need an ally among the leading white political parties in South Africa, it seems that, even if Malan was an unlikely potential local führer, Malan's party, unfettered by the avowedly pro-British Smuts wing of Hertzog's United Party, and both openly anti-Semitic and anti-British in its rhetoric, must have been a far more promising candidate for a possible connection in the event of a war in Europe.

For such reasons, no doubt, Nationalist politics was carefully monitored from Berlin. Attempts at cooperation between the Greyshirts and the Malanites were considered natural. In October 1937 in a lengthy anonymous report from Cape Town to Berlin detailing the preparations for the 1938 general election, a local German agent did concede that "the fundamentals of both parties are radically different [grundverschiedene]."[66] But the report noted that, when considered in the light of a prospective electoral alliance between the equally dissimilar United Party and the small, left-wing Labor Party, "the natural assumption of a rapprochement between the Malan Party and the Greyshirts is quite obvious. Both stand in honest and open opposition to the government, both retain the Jewish Question and Bolshevism as an essentially crucial element in their programs, and both want to secure the independence of the South African money market from international Jewry by establishing a purely South African National Bank."[67] The report showed that to the Nazi official mind the prospect of an arrangement between the Malanites and the Greyshirts was most reminiscent of the earlier similarly largely tactical alliance between Hitler and the more traditionally conservative nationalist, Alfred Hugenberg, in Germany: "While the National Party corresponds in essence with the earlier German National Party, the South African National Party (Greyshirts) is thoroughly fascist in orientation."[68] Indeed the Nazi records on South Africa were littered with references to the Malanites as the "National Opposition," a term used in Germany to denote the Old Right of the Weimar Republic.[69]

The analogy could only evoke memories of how nationalists in Germany had assisted in bringing Hitler to power in a right-wing coalition, believing him to be easily manageable, only to find that they had been quietly removed from the political scene within the year.[70] That was a scenario of which the Afrikaner Nationalists of Malan were only too well aware, as their correspondence with the Greyshirts showed. As F. C. Erasmus noted in writing to Greyshirt secretary Willie Laubscher, Weichardt's aim of a "united volk state" (*eenheidsvolkstaat*) would mean the destruction of all parties, including its allies, because such a state could only come about "when all other parties either have willingly disbanded or have been forcibly compelled to do so. That it would happen voluntarily is unthinkable under the democratic system. Therefore only the second alternative remains." Nor did Erasmus accept the Greyshirts' position that they were not really a political party and that they also intended eventually to disappear as a separate political group: "That it in practice means the forced liquidation [*uitskakeling*] of all political parties besides your own is confirmed by your acknowledgment that in the five years of the existing German 'united volk state,' the National

Socialists have always continued to exist."[71] Such a recurring nightmare dictated Malan's attitude to national socialism throughout the next few years, particularly in his often stormy wartime relationship with the Ossewabrandwag. It seems that the only practical response to such a threat was for the Nationalists to use the New Right without, in turn, becoming used.

The Nazis misjudged the true nature of the Purified Nationalists if they saw their relationship to the Greyshirts as mirroring that of Hugenberg's Nationalists to themselves. The ultranationalism, anti-Semitism, and anticommunism of the Hugenberg bloc was certainly shared by the Malanites, but while Hugenberg's support was drawn from the German upper classes,[72] Malan had no such constituency. The Purified Nationalist following itself more nearly coincided with that of the Nazis: young Afrikaners, some workers, small farmers and businessmen, schoolteachers, and other petit bourgeois elements. Only in the Cape did Malan have support of more affluent Afrikaans-speaking farmers.[73] If anything, South African Nationalists were more concerned than the Nazis themselves to reach out to the poor and oppressed of their own people, as "the champion of the worker and the farmer."[74]

Although the history of the Purified Nationalists shows an ability to build an ever-expanding support base that rapidly eclipsed the constituency of the pro-Nazi shirt movements in South Africa, the Hertzog-Smuts alliance drew a far larger proportion of support from wealthy capitalists, comparable in this regard to Hugenberg's Nationalists, than did the Malanites. The Hugenberg analogy is therefore quite inadequate, although useful for indicating what the Nazis *thought* the Nationalists in South Africa represented. As the future was to show, this was not the only instance in which Berlin misjudged Malan and his party.

The Intellectual Impact of Fascism on Afrikaner Nationalism

If the relationship of Afrikaner nationalism to the New Right was far more complicated than a simple analogy to that between traditional and radical nationalists in Germany, the influence of Radical Right thought on individual leading Afrikaner nationalists was nevertheless far more clearly identifiable. Those who had gone abroad for graduate studies, most notably Meyer and Diederichs, drank deeply of the intellectual waters available there.

But other important younger Afrikaner thinkers had had similar experiences, among these, Geoffrey Cronjé, professor of sociology at Pretoria University College and one of the architects of the apartheid ideology; J. Keyter, professor of sociology at Bloemfontein University College; and Albert Hertzog, son of the prime minister and a prominent Broederbond leader and right-wing labor organizer.[75] Hertzog, who mobilized Afrikaner workers for the Nationalist cause in the thirties and early forties, in the sixties was to become identified with the extreme nationalist wing in John Vorster's government.

The German Romantic philosophy espoused by these academics upheld an authoritarian and idealist type of nationalism, rooted in the thought of Johann Fichte (1762–1814), J. D. Herder (1744–1803), and Friedrich Schleiermacher (1768–1834). The key document in this tradition is Fichte's *Addresses to the German Nation* (1807–1808), an emotional series of appeals to the fragmented German people to unite in order to liberate themselves from Napoleon's rule. Fichte obviously struck a chord in the German-speaking world, because in 1809 the Prussian authorities appointed him a professor at the University of Berlin.[76] At the heart of his philosophy were the Volk (people—in the ethnic sense) and the nation. Hitler was far less concerned with statism and Volk-worship itself than with a cult that equated Volk and nation with himself;[77] thus Nazism, in this sense, was much more radical than any previous German philosophy, however ardently nationalist, and more radical than Afrikaner radical nationalism, in the main.

Yet Alfred Rosenberg (1893–1946), an important early influence on Hitler's thinking and the official Nazi Party "philosopher,"[78] made the Volk and its glorification a central concept in his ideological scheme. Rosenberg, whose *völkisch* nationalism was closely tied to his hatred of Jews as racial outsiders, was profoundly affected by the German Romantic tradition, with what historian Robert Pois calls its "glorification of the mysterious and the abstruse and its elevation of intuition, emotion and nationalism."[79] Fichte combined such emphases with the exaltation of German supremacy over other peoples and a marked dislike of the nobility and the Jews.[80]

Such ideas were appealing to many in the new generation of Afrikaner intellectuals. Excluded from access to the corridors of power by Hertzog's merger with the English-speaking elite, led by Smuts, they were suspicious of the established classes. And many shared a dislike of the Jews, perhaps because of the heavy representation of the latter in the professions and in business. Diederichs is a case in point, despite the sociologist Dunbar Moodie's denial that he was anti-Semitic.[81] In the interview with German Foreign Office representative Herr Kirschner discussed earlier, Diederichs responded to a question regarding government successes in recent by-elections by stating, in the words of this report, that "the United Party essentially had solely to thank the votes of the Jews for these seats."[82]

The ideas of Diederichs and of Piet Meyer are worthy of some elaboration, partly because of the positions of power both men ultimately held in the Afrikaner establishment, and partly because of the considerable influence they were already able to wield in the thirties through the ANS, the Broederbond, and other extraparliamentary groups.

Diederichs's doctoral dissertation, written in German at Leiden University, entitled *Vom Leiden und Dulden* (On Suffering and Patience), stressed the Romantic themes of pain, the irrational, and ways of overcoming suffering. In it he explicitly rejected liberal rationalism, which he hated passionately, focusing instead on the historical attitude toward suffering not only in Judaism and Christianity, as well as in ancient Greece, but rather more exotically in Brahmanism and Buddhism. He also treated these themes as they appeared in Schopenhauer and Nietzsche, philosophers whose work was diligently mined by Nazi academics.[83]

Such a palette of ideas inspired Diederichs's most famous work, published in 1936, *Nasionalisme as Lewensbeskouing en Sy Verhouding tot Internasionalisme* (Nationalism as a Worldview and Its Relationship to Internationalism). This work explicitly addressed the problem of a politically divided Afrikanerdom by an appeal to "a more lasting and noble terrain in which

Louis Weichardt, c. 1937, leader of the anti-Semitic Greyshirt movement, modeled on the German Nazi Party. Weichardt later became a Nationalist senator.

From the Cape Times *Collection in the South African Library*

Nico Diederichs, 1940. With Piet Meyer, Diederichs founded the extremist Afrikaner Nasionale Studentebond; he served as Broederbond chairman from 1938 to 1942 and 1951 to 1952), headed the Reddingsdaadbond, the Bond economic front organization, and became a Nationalist member of Parliament in 1948. Later he served under Verwoerd and Vorster, ending his career as state president (1975–1978).

From the Cape Times *Collection in the South African Library*

Piet Meyer with one of his many awards. Meyer and Nico Diederichs founded the Afrikaner Nasionale Studentebond; Meyer was secretary of numerous Broederbond front organizations and Bond assistant secretary from 1936 to 1943. During the war he was, briefly, information director of the Ossewabrandwag, from 1952 a member of the Bond Executive, and Bond chairman from 1960 to 1972. Later Meyer was rector of the Rand Afrikaans University in Johannesburg and chairman of the South African Broadcasting Corporation (1959–1981).

Courtesy The Argus

Die Waarheid
The Truth

Official Organ of the S. A. Gentile Nat.-Socialist Movement.

SOUTH AFRICAN NATIONAL PARTY

Offisiële Orgaan van die S. A. Christ. Nas.-Sos. Beweging.

P.O. BOX 2432

P. K. BUS 2432

CAPE TOWN

KAAPSTAD

Earnest Appeal !

An earnest appeal is hereby made to all true and devoted S o u t h A f r i c a n s for financial assistance to enable us to expand and propogate our Official Organ "THE TRUTH" with a view to rid our beautiful country from parasites and undesirable alien exploitation.

Hail
South Africa !

LOUIS T. WEICHARDT.
Born at Paarl, 21st May, 1893.

SONG OF THE GREYSHIRTS.

Watch in the world the Swastika,
The sign of awakening nations!
The Greyshirts march in South Africa
To free us from Jewish explcitations!
Cast off now your fear, let's unite
    now at once
Down with foreign domination and
    down with our bonds!
    Hail, Greyshirts, Hail!
    Hail, Greyshirts, Hail!

Watch in our country the rising tide
Of Greyshirts determined and faithful
The Greyshirts march bravely to free
    and unite
The country they love and they
    treasure!
If British, if Dutch — Be South
    African now
But the Jews in our nation we do not
    allow
    Hail, Greyshirts, Hail!
    Hail, Greyshirts, Hail!

Now then, South Africans, come
    along,
And join in the world's great endeavour!
"Sunny South Africa" must belong
To white men and Gentiles for ever!
Come forward, fght bravely, your
    dear ones to guard!
Ours is the victory! Ours the reward!
    Hail, Greyshirts, Hail!
    Hail, Greyshirts, Hail!

Ernstige Beroep !

Hiermee word n ernstige beroep op alle ware en egte A f r i - k a n e r s gedoen om finansiele steun teneinde ons amptlike orgaan

DIE WAARHEID'

tot groter uitbreiding te bewerkstellig teneinde langs hierdie weg ons land en volk van parasietiese en ongewenste vreemde uitbuiting te suiwer.

Heil
Suid-Afrika !

P.E.D./1890/34.

Front page of an early issue of *Die Waarheid/The Truth,* Greyshirt newspaper. It is identified by one of the organization's first aliases, S.A. Gentile National Socialist Movement; South African National Party, another alternative name, is stamped over the bannerhead.

From the SAIRR Records, Cullen Library

all of us, despite political division, can still be one."[84] This appeal to rise above the merely natural world of fratricidal intra-Afrikaner political strife attacked Bolshevist and liberal cosmopolitanism in favor of a nationalism that went much further than liberal-national aspirations to a common political heritage and institutions: "Only in the nation as the most total, most inclusive human community can man realize himself fully. The nation is the fulfilment of the individual life." And further on: "To work for the realization of the national calling is to work for the realization of God's plan. Service to the nation is therefore part of my service to God."[85]

This is not the language of traditional Afrikaner Calvinist nationalism. Afrikaner heroes such as Paul Kruger would have found such views dangerously close to idolizing the state. H. G. ("Bram") Stoker, a leading Afrikaner philosopher at the University of Potchefstroom, expressed such a concern in reviewing Diederichs's book in *Die Volksblad* in April 1935, writing: "By placing my nation above me and God above the nation, [Diederichs] attributes to the nation at least in part that which belongs to God alone, and in so doing he deifies the nation."[86] Nor is it the language of the twentieth-century variety of neo-Calvinism, so influential among modern Afrikaner academics and first promoted by the conservative turn-of-the-century Dutch theologian and politician Abraham Kuyper, with its respect for traditional institutions and a clear sense of the boundaries among the various spheres of life, family, church, and state.[87] Here Diederichs was breaking away from the Calvinist intellectual heritage of the Afrikaner universities; his views were a distinct part of the worldview of the new Germany.

Such ideas of the Studentebond leadership were extremely controversial on Afrikaner campuses, and never accepted in unadulterated form by the broader Afrikaner public.[88] Yet the Studentebond leadership became increasingly powerful in the Afrikaner Broederbond, which did happily accommodate at least a modified form of Romantic neo-Fichteanism, blending its secular nationalism with a respect for Calvinist sensibilities.[89]

It is not surprising that the Broederbond did so. Its stronghold lay in the Transvaal, its original base in the twenties, where Afrikaner nationalism was most deeply fractured. After most Afrikaners, especially farmers, had gone over to the Hertzogite Fusionists in 1933 and 1934,[90] the Broederbond rapidly filled the political vacuum left there by the weak position of the Purified Nationalists. After the loss of the Vrededorp seat in 1938, there was only one Malanite member of Parliament in this province, J. G. Strijdom.[91] The Transvaal Purified Nationalist finances were in a desperate state until the late thirties, and the party there was riven by internal personality and policy differences.[92] Under these circumstances, the message of Diederichs, Meyer, and others proved a real boon to those who sought to fill the space left by the Purified Party and sought ultimately to bring Afrikaners together under the name, preferably, of the Purified Party itself. Staunch Potchefstroom neo-Calvinists who dominated the Broederbond Executive during the thirties, men like Professors L. J. du Plessis, J. C. van Rooy, and Bram Stoker,[93] therefore accommodated to a modified form of the Studentebond doctrines of Meyer and Diederichs.

Diederichs's message was addressed to specific concerns not unlike those facing the pre-Hitler German "National Opposition." Both countries confronted the fragmentation of the volk into hostile factions and classes, the poorest of which were increasingly vulnerable to the slogans of the internationalist left, which derided nationalism as a capitalist trick to divide the workers of the world. Diederichs attacked communism on the grounds of its antinationalism:

Its striving is not to protect and strengthen the natural unity of a volk, but to break it down and destroy it; not to advance harmonious co-operation between groups and classes in the volk, but to drive these groups and classes against each other in a spirit of hate and enmity. . . . The highest task which according to Communism rests on the worker of every state, is to tear himself from his natural bond to other parts of his volk and to unite himself in a mythical world-proletariat in the struggle against his own fatherland and compatriots.[94]

Diederichs's message was promulgated not only to academics but also to Afrikaners; several chapters of his treatise against communism appeared in the popular journal *Die Huisgenoot*.[95]

Nor were the Nationalists entirely unconnected with the propaganda activities of the ANS leadership. Both of Diederichs's principal works were published by Nasionale Pers, the Malan-controlled company that produced the Cape Party's *Die Burger.* In collaboration with Van Rensburg and others, Diederichs brought out a short polemical account of current political movements, published by the other major Nationalist publishing house, Voortrekkerpers, which was responsible for *Die Transvaler.*[96]

Piet Meyer, who spent much of his time as secretary of various Afrikaner nationalist organizations (see next chapter), produced even more complex theoretical systems. When Meyer first returned from his studies abroad at the beginning of 1936, he still displayed the concerns of a neo-Fichtean nationalist such as Diederichs, for instance working to mobilize Afrikaners against the dual threats of class conflict, which he, like most Afrikaner nationalists, saw as inspired by communism, and of the United Party philosophy of conciliation between Afrikaner and English-speaker. To achieve this end, he strove to unite, in a new Afrikaner Nasionale Kultuurraad (National Cultural Council) not only middle-class Afrikaners involved in cultural, educational, and church organizations, but also Afrikaner workers. Through such organizations Afrikaner workers would, he hoped, be detached from leftist labor groups and be organized into "Christian National" labor unions, financial backing for which would come from a National Council of Trustees (Nasionale Raad van Trustees), which he, Diederichs, and Albert Hertzog were instrumental in founding in October 1936 in Johannesburg.[97] Thus, as in Fascist-ruled Italy and Nazi-ruled Germany, where employer and employee belonged to a single umbrella body in the interest of national unity, the worker would be co-opted into the national movement and the class divide would be bridged by organizations stressing a common nationhood or ethnicity rather than class conflict.

Although Meyer's concerns were therefore more practical than those of the more academically oriented Diederichs, he did produce some theoretical work, primarily during the Second World War, when he moved closer to national socialism by stressing the roots of Afrikaner unity in the "organic" concepts of race and family.[98] Like Diederichs, he believed that the Afrikaner had a divine calling, which he attempted to explain in a highly convoluted argument stressing the organic, vital nature of the volk in his book *Die Afrikaner* (1941):

The People as a faith-unit [*geloofseenheid*] fulfils its own calling on the one hand by realizing the value-whole [*waardegeheel*] and on the other the life-order [*lewensordening*] ordained by its faith. . . . The people is at the same time a social [*lewens*] and a cultural community. In the realization of its unique life-form the People creates its culture and in the creation of its culture it realizes its own life-form. These are the two sides of its unique calling as given in its faith.[99]

Ultimately Meyer attempted to combine national socialism and Kuyperian neo-Calvinism more explicitly than other Studentebond and Broederbond figures had done. The result was a curious transformation of Kuyper's theory of "sovereignty in own sphere" into one of "totalitarianism in each sphere":

The totalitarianism of the *volksbeweging* [people's movement], which is subordinate to the Word of God, means on the one hand the struggle toward an organic community on the part of the estates of the People (*volksstande*) which are integrated into the *volksbeweging*, and on the other hand it means the independent existence alongside the People of other organizing human entities like the individual, the family and the church.[100]

Beneath this strange potpourri of ideas was a far more serious theme: the wedding of the new ideas of a fascist Europe to the old emphasis on church, family, and volk (used without any German Romantic connotations of ethnic superiority and purity) of traditional rural and small-town Afrikaner society. It was to bear fruit in the emerging political philosophy that increasingly underpinned the Nationalists on their road to power: "Christian Nationalism," a curious mixture of Nazi ideas, Kuyper's neo-Calvinism, and ideas inherited from the old Boer republics.

Diederichs had made it plain in his discussion with Kirschner in May 1939 that he desired some type of authoritarian state to replace the liberal-democratic parliamentary system, although he did not elaborate on what he meant by this.[101] Meyer was more forthright: his admiration for the new regimes abroad almost equaled the passionate expressions of Van Rensburg, his co-leader of the Studentebond. On 3 October 1937 Meyer told a great crowd at the ANS annual congress on the subject of Italian-style Fascism: "Dictatorship is actually the real form of democracy. . . . The freedoms of the individual are not negative, as in liberal democracy, but positive. The volk rules itself through bringing to the fore its own leader and is not ruled by a little minority group."[102]

After expressing pleasure in Mussolini's belated acceptance of the role of religion, Meyer went on to discuss the importance of adapting Fascism, "the new thing in Western culture," to South African conditions. He suggested Kruger's Transvaal Republic as a model for such a hybrid state. He was particularly enthusiastic about the volk as "the real employer, and not the capitalist" in a fascist state, and advised his audience to pay serious attention to the practical work of effecting change in South Africa so that it would fit in with the volk life-style.[103]

With Afrikaner students exposed to such beliefs from their own leaders, it is perhaps comprehensible why the Greyshirts found such an easy appeal in the second point of their program (the first point supported "religious freedom," an important item in a Calvinist society): "We stand for the welfare of each member of the State where the National Interests of South Africa are placed before Self or Party Interests. The interests of the State must always precede the individual. We consider the present political democracy corrupt and exploded."[104] The worship of volk and state had, however, been adopted not only by the shirt movements, but increasingly by respected Afrikaner nationalist thinkers and the leaders of the youth.

The examples of Germany and Italy, along with the overt and clandestine propaganda work of the Nazis, had found a ready South African audience, from intellectuals like Diederichs to streetside orators like Weichardt. The great question was whether such views would be taken up, as anti-Semitism had been, by the largest and nationally the most organized voice of the Afrikaner right, the Purified National Party itself. Only in this way could the Nazis' propaganda network make a real difference to white South African politics. National socialist and broader fascist influences would otherwise be limited, as in so much of Europe and Latin America, to a small extremist fringe.

Chapter Four

The Initial Transformation of the National Party

With the emergence of Malan's Purified Nationalists as the heirs of the old radical Hertzogite tradition, their policies became reinvigorated and altered by the new wave of political thought from abroad. Malan's party drew closer to those Afrikaner intellectuals who had been most influenced by European authoritarian nationalism.

The influence of fascist doctrines on the Malanites needs to be considered first, through the direct evidence of party records and Nationalist politicians' correspondence; and second, perhaps more important, from the evidence of the increasingly complex relationship between the party and Afrikaner organizations that had come more obviously under the influence of the Radical Right.

The Malan Party and the Beginnings of Authoritarian Nationalism

Direct evidence of fascist influence on the Purified Nationalists is hard to find, at least in the thirties. The southern wing of the party in particular provided something of a restraining influence on the radicals of the north, as in the matter of anti-Semitism. Too many wealthy men in the Cape party, often large-scale sheep farmers, had too much to lose to be willing to become seriously estranged from their British trade partners and therefore tempered their anti-imperialist rhetoric with a certain degree of economic realism. It is true, however, that Cape wine and wheat farmers, another key Cape Nationalist constituency, were far less dependent on the export trade than many farmers in the heavily pro-Fusion northern provinces, where farming centered on maize production.[1] But conservative veterans of the old Hertzog Party continued to be important in the southern Purified Nationalist organization, men like Malan, R. L. Geyer, and Bruckner de Villiers. They were naturally suspicious of anything that threatened a system, whatever its shortcomings, from which they had long profited. The radical populism of the Cape Nationalists was therefore framed in the language of reform, not of revolution. As in the case of anti-Semitism, matters were rarely quite as simple as a clear north-south divide. Even Geyer and De Villiers occasionally used the openly anti-Semitic language of their northern cousins.[2]

The Transvaal leader, J. G. Strijdom, on the other hand, despite his bluntness, essentially an old-fashioned Afrikaner in the mold of President Kruger and the Boer leaders of the nineteenth century, was an unlikely fascist. He spoke with a traditional directness that is associated even today with the Afrikaners of the rural northern Transvaal. When his co-leader, Mrs. Mabel Jansen, was attacked from certain party quarters, he dismissed these accusations, claiming that they were based on hearsay gathered from "certain Coolies and a Colored."[3] Still, his forays into radical rhetoric were tempered by a distrust of *volksvreemde* ("alien-to-the-Afrikaner volk") ideologies, as fascist teachings came to be known among more traditionally minded Afrikaner nationalists such as Malan, Strijdom, and even Verwoerd.

Strijdom's impatience with quasi-mystical authoritarian doctrines was reflected in the manner in which he rejected the suggestion of one of his lieutenants, J. J. Erasmus, that the defeat of a candidate in the election of party Executive members was "the work of the Lord" and therefore should not be questioned. Strijdom saw this as an extremely dangerous line of thought, and replied caustically: "Remember that what happens is often the work of Satan and not always of the Lord. No matter what, our Party is a democratic Party and if the majority decides, the minority concedes. It nevertheless remains true that the majority often does incorrect and unfair things."[4]

Strijdom cannot simply be put together with Diederichs, Meyer, and others of the ANS school of thought. He was too much of a practical politician to indulge in pseudofascist flights of fancy.[5] His views in this respect were entirely in keeping with the principles of the Cape moderates of the "mother" Purified National Party, espousing an unapologetically nationalist and pro-republican policy,[6] yet suspicious of taking any drastic steps away from traditional parliamentary systems.

Nevertheless, as early as 1934 some elements in Cape National Party policy indicated a less than total commitment to the principles of parliamentary liberal democracy. There was, for example, a provision to limit immigration to "assimilable" elements, and the recognition by the party, in traditional white South African fashion, of the "basic rule of the domination in South Africa of the European race."[7] This was admittedly not a departure from the language of traditional Afrikaner nationalism, and was not radically different from the United Party's insistence on "the Christian trusteeship of the European race," or its encouragement of "desirable European immigration."[8] The United Party was merely marginally more circumspect in its language, as was to be expected of a large coalition.

Nevertheless, from the very beginning the Cape Malanites had insisted that Purified Nationalism be represented by "a real volk party,"[9] a concept which, if narrowly interpreted, was open to much abuse in the hands of extremists. The ban on Jewish membership in the Transvaal party demonstrates this point all too well. Furthermore, volk democracy encouraged extraparliamentary mass "direct action" such as the monster segregationist "color petition," signed by 231,000 white adults, presented to the House of Assembly by Malan in May 1939. This petition was intended to force Parliament to act "without hesitation" to pass race legislation in accordance with the resolutions of Nationalist congresses.[10]

Racial purity had, of course, been a subject of Nationalist concern for many years. As far back as 1925, the Cape National Party had overwhelmingly adopted a resolution in favor of legislation to ban marriages between whites and those of other groups.[11] But during the 1930s the obsession with racial purity reached hysterical proportions, just as it did in Hitler's Germany. In South Africa this wave peaked during the 1938 general election campaign, which, like that of 1929, was fought largely on the theme of the *swart gevaar* (black danger), and this time anti-

Semitism was an important additional ingredient. But on this occasion what had worked previously in the Nationalists' favor did not produce the desired results, perhaps in part because of the generally good economic conditions that had followed Hertzog's agreeing to go off the gold standard in 1932.

On the contrary, when in the 1938 election campaign the Nationalists produced a notorious poster portraying a white woman, a black man, and their children, with the attached slogan "Mixed Marriages," and which, given the context of a fiercely fought campaign, by implication suggested that the United Party championed such unions, the UP responded that this was an attack on white women, who it claimed had never been so insulted. The United Party demanded that these posters be removed from the streets.[12] The Nationalist tactic subsequently failed at the polls to make any dent in United Party support. Only in the Orange Free State and especially the Cape did the Nationalists demonstrate any significant strength.[13] White voters apparently felt sufficiently secure to continue supporting Hertzog and Smuts.

The Nationalists showed in reacting to the United Party response to their poster that they had misread the white electorate. In the Orange Free State the Nationalists simply refused to remove the posters,[14] while in the Cape a meeting of Nationalist women in the arid interior town of De Aar resolved to express "the strongest protest" that the "Jewish-imperialist press," by attacking the poster, was trying to draw the attention of the volk away from "the real danger of miscegenation." In the view of the meeting, Afrikaner women were being "misled" by the "Jewish press."[15]

The use of such language indicates that the Nationalists felt driven to use extremist rhetoric to obtain votes. Apparently they did not have sufficient confidence in their republican program to believe that standing strictly on this platform would improve their position in Parliament. Yet the adoption of extremist tactics did not attract voters in sufficient numbers to give them more than 27 seats, 20 of them in Malan's old Cape stronghold, against 111 for the United Party and 11 for the small Labor and Dominion parties.[16]

The linking of *swart gevaar* politics to anti-Semitism provides

an important clue to the nature of the atmosphere in right-wing
South African politics at that time. Jews, communists, liberals,
and the "black danger" were regarded as a single web of inter-
linked conspirators against the volk, a theory strikingly reminiscent of the theories then prevalent in European fascist circles.
Just as the women of De Aar believed that the Jews were promoting miscegenation, so at the 1937 Cape party congress, Malan charged the "liberal and Communist-inclined" with threatening the existence of South Africa as "a white man's country."
He tied these scare tactics to his party's populist program of
uplifting poor Afrikaners, newly arrived in the cities: "The white
man who lives in the slums, goes about in a condition of fear
and anxiety when he thinks of the future of his children. And
the state refuses to provide him with protection where he is
crowded together with the non-white. . . . Along this road South
Africa is becoming ever more a black man's country."[17] Malan
followed this statement with an ominous warning about communism in South Africa, noting that most South African delegates to the Comintern were Afrikaans-speakers.[18] The same
congress duly adopted a resolution proposed by no fewer than
twenty-seven branches, advocating racial segregation in every
area of life.[19]

The Nationalists were thus moving from old-fashioned segregation, with its many loopholes and exceptions, to full-scale
apartheid, although that word was not yet in use. The segregation advocated by Hertzog did not, for instance, embrace mixed
race "coloreds," except in social matters such as residential
areas, and even there, Hertzog did not move to actual legislation,
relying for the moment on traditional white practice. The National Party explicitly included "coloreds" in its segregation
plans, proposing, for instance, to remove them from the common
voters' roll in the Cape. The skimpy wording of earlier Nationalist race policy was already being rapidly fleshed out. This can
be seen in the numerous references to segregation in the National
Party's 1938 Federal Program of Action.[20]

In the Transvaal, the impact of overseas extreme right thought,
with its penchant for radical and all-encompassing solutions, was
much more clearly felt than in the Cape. One form of expression
lay in the multifarious racial draft resolutions presented at party

congresses. One even proposed bans against blacks driving automobiles. Resolutions advocated Afrikaans as the first language of the Union, removing Indians from positions in state service, and, most significantly, returning South-West Africa to Germany, "the rightful owner."[21]

Without restraining influence like that of older Cape Nationalists such as Bruckner de Villiers or Malan himself, the struggling Transvaal party was far more likely to be influenced by extremist ideas. The role of the Broederbond, with its strong Studentebond presence, is also relevant here. Strijdom occupied the middle ground, an adherent of volk democracy, but far less constrained than the southerners in his expression of nationalism. Transvaler Purified Nationalism became a striking hybrid variant, combining a militant radical populism with signs of a creeping authoritarianism, nowhere near the dimensions of full-blown European fascism, but it was a tendency that would reach its culmination in the still headier days of the Second World War.

The significant urban element in the Transvaal National Party (rural Transvalers still were mainly UP supporters) made its populism essential. In 1937 the Transvaal Executive adopted a remarkably progressive plan intended to satisfy two of its most important potential recruiting pools: women and blue-collar workers. Henceforth the Executive would have the right to choose six members to represent miners, railway workers, and factory workers, who were concentrated in the less affluent areas of Pretoria and the Johannesburg-Witwatersrand industrial complex. In addition, every rural "electoral circle" was to elect a woman to the Executive, while the urban areas, the Witwatersrand and Pretoria, were to send two female delegates each.[22] A few days later the party congress underlined this radical plank with a resolution to nationalize the mines.[23]

The representation of workers according to trade, rather than of party members as a whole by geographic area, is similar to the form of popular representation in Italian Fascist-style corporatism.[24] It is noteworthy, too, that these representatives were to be appointed, not elected. The proposed nationalization of the mines was not inconsistent with such an interpretation: state involvement in the economy was a widespread feature of fascist policy platforms, even if less often of fascism in power.

This view is confirmed when account is taken of certain other more obviously authoritarian steps adopted by the Transvaal National Party at its October 1937 congress. It agreed that the Executive would have the right to expel any member without giving reasons, subject to consultation with the member's branch and divisional leadership, and that the Executive would have the right to dissolve any level of party management and then reconstitute it. In all such cases the decision of the Executive was to be final.[25]

Just five months before, in May 1937, the Executive had taken the principle of centralization of authority even further, giving the small Management Committee, in charge of day-to-day matters, the power to appoint or dismiss members of either body or of the powerful Organizing Committee, and to fix, raise, or lower party officers' salaries. The Management Committee decided at the same time that all decisions of the Organizing Committee were to be subject to its own approval.[26]

The concentration of power in the hands of the Nationalist leadership in the province was entirely in keeping with the neo-Fichtean inclinations of its sponsors in the secret Broederbond. Such concentration of power also made it easier to coordinate Bond and party policy in the very province where the Broeders were most long established and most influential. In the Cape, where the Nationalists had by far the greatest voting strength, the Broederbond did not establish a branch until 1931, thirteen years after its foundation in the Transvaal, and the Bond did not hold an annual meeting in the Cape until 1947. Annual meetings were not held outside the Transvaal until the 1938 gathering in Bloemfontein.[27] The corporatist elements in the new party proposals had all the flavor of an imported system, but at the same time they were likely to please the sections of Afrikanerdom most obviously excluded from the male-only Broederbond elite: women and workers.[28]

The sympathies of the Transvaal Nationalists were made most clear with a resolution adopted unanimously by the 1937 congress on the so-called colonial question:

That the Congress requests the Government without delay to bring to the attention of the League of Nations the question of territorial possession by European powers on the African continent with the aim of having a discussion with Germany and Italy, in order to resolve the issue peacefully by way of agreement.[29]

While they sympathized with the colonial aspirations of the fascist powers and opposed a violent confrontation with these countries on that issue, they did not necessarily identify themselves with the methods Germany and Italy were using to achieve these ends. The Nationalists, even in the Transvaal, were not yet willing to abandon their traditional policies. Only those elements of New Right thinking that were tailored to specific Nationalist needs were attractive enough to be adopted. On the other hand, in a variety of subtle ways, Nationalist thinking had in a much more fundamental sense taken a sharp turn to the right. By 1939 the old policies of segregation and of Afrikaner solidarity between all classes became greatly intensified, while new elements were added to the ideological menu, including full-blown anti-Semitism and some dabbling in authoritarianism, applied now even to their own people.

The considerable gap between main-line Purified Nationalists, even in the north, and the Studentebond leaders and other radical intellectuals who had become far more clearly influenced by imported Radical Right thinking becomes far more elusive when the actual structure of Afrikaner nationalist organizations is examined, particularly the membership of their elite cadres. There was not a terribly significant difference, for example, between the positions of Diederichs and men like the *Transvaler* editor Verwoerd, who stood to gain most from a resolution of the 1937 Transvaal congress, one which could easily have come from his own pen, underlining the fast-changing character of Afrikaner nationalism in the late thirties: "It is generally decided that Afrikaners will be exhorted to support National-oriented businesses, and that only businesses which advertise in *Die Transvaler* will be supported."[30]

The National Party was not just another democratic political party. It claimed to be *the* volk party. As the political expression of the Afrikaner nationalist *Volksbeweging* (people's movement), it seemed only natural that it should receive the support of Afrikaners. The identity of volk and party in so narrow a sense was something new in South Africa, but it would have been considered perfectly normal in Italy or Germany, or in the clerico-fascist countries like Salazar's Portugal or Dollfuss's Austria. In Germany, Jews and other "un-national" elements were exposed to official boycott. In South Africa it was not the government but the official opposition that promoted such policies.

Purified Nationalism and the Rise of the Broederbond Front Network

It is surprising that the Purified Nationalists were not even *more* influenced by neo-Fichtean authoritarian nationalism since the ANS clique in the Broederbond, along with their Transvaal neo-Calvinist allies from the theologically ultraconservative Potchefstroom University College, such as professors L. J. du Plessis and J. C. van Rooy, dominated the great majority of Afrikaner nationalist organizations, particularly those based in the Transvaal. The only important, albeit partial, exception, was the group of older business enterprises linked to the Cape Nationalist leadership, most notably the powerful Cape Town–based Afrikaner insurance houses, Santam and Sanlam, founded in 1918 by Malan's old friend W. A. Hofmeyr, and the Cape National Party's publishing house, Nasionale Pers, founded in 1914.[31] The influence of the Studentebond-Potchefstroom alliance would have been less significant if it had not been interconnected with the National Party leadership itself.

The Broederbond was founded in 1918 by a group of young Afrikaners who felt humiliated after a Nationalist meeting addressed by Malan had been disrupted by rowdy English-speakers.[32] Sixteen years later, when Malan was undecided on whether to join Hertzog in Fusion, the Broederbond sent a deputation to ensure that he was not a party to this insult to unadulterated nationalism. The deputation was successful; although for some time the Bond still included Hertzogites as ordinary members, the leadership was solidly behind the Malan secession.[33]

Strijdom, later the Transvaal nationalist leader, was convinced to take the secession route in 1934 after a whole night of persuasive wrangling with his father-in-law, W. J. de Klerk, a founder of the Broederbond. A series of top Nationalists joined the Bond soon afterwards: not only Strijdom, but also Malan, Verwoerd (still a Stellenbosch University professor), and N. J.

van der Merwe and C. R. Swart, the two most powerful men among the Orange Free State Purified Nationalists.[34] At least two influential younger Nationalist politicians who had been active Broeders for some years[35] had been elected to the Executive Council of the Broederbond by October 1940: Verwoerd and Eben Dönges, who had stood for the party in the 1938 election.[36] A third Nationalist joined the ranks of the Executive Council in 1940: J. H. Conradie, a member of Parliament.[37] With Dönges and Conradie on the Executive, there was at least a substantial voice in the Broederbond leadership for Cape Afrikaners.

In the late thirties there was personal cooperation between individual members of the Broederbond Executive Council, such as Albert Hertzog, and important Nationalists. For instance, Hertzog, Jr., wrote to Otto du Plessis, editor of *Die Oosterlig*, the National Party organ in the Eastern Cape, to thank him for his encouragement of the northerners' efforts in the field of Afrikaner labor relations. Hertzog encouraged Du Plessis to use as an informer a former Communist, one J. G. Ferreira who, according to Hertzog, claimed to have been encouraged by the Jewish Board of Deputies to accept the position of secretary in a Communist front organization, the "League for the Maintenance of Democracy." Hertzog commented with satisfaction: "Such indications of cooperation between our enemy groups can often later come in very handy for us. Although we do not always obtain big facts, the little facts are also sometimes very valuable."[38]

Hertzog was very close to the Studentebond-Potchefstroom alliance in the Broederbond leadership, referring to this clique as "our little group." He considered himself relatively independent of the National Party, although in sympathy with its broad aims.[39]

Albert Hertzog and his allies dominated Afrikaner nationalist political and cultural organizations to an extraordinary degree. The Executive of the huge Federasie van Afrikaner Kultuurverenigings (Federation of Afrikaner Cultural Organizations or FAK) was the most important of these, with branches in every town and village, embracing every activity connected to Afrikaner cultural life. Although publicly strictly a cultural organization, at least for most of its history, the FAK had been the creature of the Broederbond from its foundation in 1929, and initially had been bold enough to include the name of the Broederbond on its letterheads.[40] In 1937 the FAK Executive included among its members Professor T. J. Hugo, a longtime deputy chairman of the Broederbond, as its own vice chairman, and I. M. Lombard, the powerful full-time secretary of the Bond, until then also secretary of the FAK. In that same year, the ANS founder, Piet Meyer, succeeded Lombard as FAK secretary.[41]

Other Broeders sat on the FAK Executive in a more ambiguous capacity. N. J. van der Merwe, the National Party leader in the Orange Free State, was chairman of the FAK from its inception. Eben Dönges, who would become a key Nationalist cabinet minister under Malan, Strijdom, and Verwoerd from 1948, was another Executive Council member who wore two hats as both a cultural and a political leader. The presence of these party men underlines the complexity of the relationship between the official Nationalist political organization and extremists in the Broederbond and Studentebond.

The Broederbond operated in circuitous but effective ways. With top FAK and ANS figures among its leadership, both organizations enjoyed the Broederbond secret stamp of approval. Afrikaners were treated to a public spectacle of "close cooperation" between both front groups. Thus at a 1937 FAK congress a formal ceremony was held to hand over the new FAK *Volksangbundel* (volk song anthology) to N. J. van der Merwe and I. M. Lombard in their FAK capacities, and also to Diederichs as the chairman of the newly founded ANS.[42] In this way the Broederbond ensured that ordinary Afrikaners attending the meeting of the highly respected FAK would give the smaller, younger, and perhaps therefore more questionable ANS similar legitimacy.

Delegates at the 1937 FAK congress demonstrated their support for comprehensive segregation in a way that, in effect, demonstrated the pro-Nationalist bias which was contrary to the public image of the FAK as a purely cultural body. The congress expressed itself in favor of "the maintenance of the color line" and supported legislation to outlaw employment of whites by other groups. It expressed opposition to the holding of conferences or discussions in South Africa with "equal sitting rights" for both black and white.[43]

Considering the frequency with which the Malanites used every opportunity to embarrass the Hertzog government about its failure to introduce thoroughgoing segregation,[44] it is difficult to see how any impartial observer could have described FAK behavior on this occasion as nonpartisan. The truth was that the FAK could not be nonpartisan, given the web of connections between the National Party, on the one hand, and the Broederbond front network, on the other, a relationship that was also necessarily reciprocal, with all that this implied for the impact of fascist-influenced Broederbond extremists on mainstream Nationalist politics.

Besides the FAK, other Afrikaner organizations, which proliferated from the mid-thirties, demonstrated their Broederbond "front" character through the composition of their leadership. The "Christian National Education Institute"'s secretary was the ubiquitous Piet Meyer, who was also secretary of the powerful Economic Institute, headed by Meyer's Potchefstroom ally in the Broederbond, L. J. du Plessis. The Management Committee of the Education Institute comprised Studentebond chief Diederichs, I. M. Lombard, and Albert Hertzog, as well as Eben Dönges and two others.[45]

Similarly, the organization intended to realize the aims of the Economic Institute, the newly founded Reddingsdaadbond (Union for the Act of Salvation), was headed by none other than Diederichs, the champion of Romantic German-style authoritarian nationalism in South Africa.[46] Some observers maintained, perhaps unfairly, that he was appointed to this post in 1939 on the basis of his interest in the similarly run Nazi Winterhilfe (Winterhelp) organization in Germany.[47] Diederichs also sat on the Council of the Institute for Volk Welfare, founded after a great Volkskongres on the poor-white question in 1934. The chairman of this institute was Professor J. C. van Rooy, another of Diederichs's Potchefstroom University College allies on the Broederbond Executive Council. The secretary was, once again, Piet Meyer.[48]

Meyer was also secretary of the labor front of the Broederbond, the National Council of Trustees, founded to promote Afrikaner nationalism among railway workers, and including Diederichs, Lombard, Albert Hertzog, and Van Rooy.[49] According to the liberal Afrikaner journalist J. H. P. Serfontein, author of one of the few major investigative reports on Broederbond activities, *Brotherhood of Power* (1979), Meyer enjoyed comparing his many roles to those of Stalin, who had successfully used his own multiple secretarial roles in the Soviet system to outwit the more visible Trotsky and thus emerge as the strongman successor to Lenin.[50]

Indeed, the case of Meyer shows very well how in such a system one man could effectively propagate his own rather extravagant beliefs across a wide spectrum of society. Extraordinarily ambitious, he went far beyond the usual role of a mere minutes-keeper to ensure the realization of his vision of an organized Afrikanerdom. He bullied organizations into participating in the ceaseless series of volk congresses, a key weapon in mobilizing Afrikaners for the Broederbond cause. His circulars to FAK member bodies veered between studied politeness and implied threats. In an invitation to a 1939 congress on Christian volk education, Meyer made this pronouncement: "It is the duty of all organizations and bodies for Afrikaners to let be heard unequivocally their support in this great matter. . . . Every body which does not involve itself in this, forfeits the right later to object to the formulated policy in the educational field."[51]

On other occasions, Meyer appealed to Afrikaner ethnic solidarity and especially to religion in order to elicit support for his authoritarian vision. His circulars often redound with a passionate conviction in keeping with the authoritarian nationalist style that he had absorbed in Europe, but which reads strangely in ordinary bureaucratic correspondence. Meyer closed a circular on the 1939 Volkskongres on economics in terms that superbly elucidated his comprehensively totalitarian political vision, citing the special vocation of the Afrikaner volk in southern Africa:

This calling stretches out and embraces all the different spheres of life, including the economic sphere. Vocational fulfilment means that the Afrikaner attitude to life, with all the capabilities which it contains, must come to full deployment in our special life-circumstances. In this way in every area of life must be created an [sic] own cultural form on the basis of our own life- and world-view. We are not free only to choose certain spheres of life and leave out others.[52]

Meyer's final sentence in this circular makes the deterministic dimension of his appeal most explicit: in a reference to Dr. Kestell, an elderly Afrikaans Reformed minister and much-loved father-figure in the Nationalist movement years before, Meyer noted that Kestell had said that the economic salvation of the Afrikaner should be a "divine deed." Meyer's ideas, with their curious combination of Romantic nationalism and Kuyperian neo-Calvinism, along with the latter's emphasis on the autonomy of the various spheres of society, had one foot in Germany, but the other solidly in the soil of Afrikaner Calvinism. This was precisely what made the views of the Broederbond leadership so appealing and, in such an indigenized form, allowed authoritarian nationalism eventually to put down deep roots in the broad Afrikaner population.

The Broederbond had penetrated into every sphere of Afrikaner life. The *völkisch* philosophy of its leaders spread into education, labor relations, finance, culture, and politics. Malanite Nationalists, and to a lesser extent the Hertzogites in the United Party, breathed the all-encompassing air of this *völkisch* neo-Fichtean ideology. It was pervasive in Diederichs's presidential address to the Broederbond in October 1940: "The legend of a strict division between culture, economics and politics has fallen away. We will no longer be blinded by it. The *volk* is an organic whole. Its different parts are closely connected with each other and cannot be separated."[53]

In keeping with the attempt to co-opt the Afrikaner worker, no fewer than 21,000 of the 40,000 Afrikaans-speaking railway workers had been persuaded to join the Spoorbond (Railway Union), an FAK member, by mid-1937.[54] And in the same spirit, Van der Merwe, a party man, spoke to the 1937 FAK congress in the *völkisch* rhetoric of Diederichs:

The FAK has taken the hand of the impoverished and it will never let go of it again. The blood of the poor is noble and if they also grab hold of the hand of the FAK, their struggle for self-preservation will be made easier. On them depends the future of our volk. Therefore the FAK will strive and battle against the anti-national attempt to divide our volk into classes.[55]

The Ossewatrek and the Volksbeweging

The emotionalism aroused by the growing *Volksbeweging* (Afrikaner volk movement) was harnessed above all in the elaborate 1938 Ossewatrek (Ox-wagon Trek), a centennial reenactment of the Afrikaner pioneers' (*Voortrekkers*) epic "Great Trek" into the South African interior, in which ox-wagons followed the old routes of the Voortrekkers right across the Union. Women rushed out to baptize their children in the shadows of the passing wagons, and special wedding ceremonies were held in the costumes of the Voortrekkers. Across the nation, Afrikaner men grew beards and women wore bonnets, known as *kappies,* to commemorate the deeds of their forefathers. An unprecedented wave of Afrikaner nationalist feeling swept the land.

Amid this outpouring of ethnic sentiment was born the Ossewabrandwag (Ox-wagon Guard), a paramilitary organization intended to continue the spirit of the centenary, but soon to become the most eloquent instrument of fascist sentiment in South Africa.[56] (See chapter 6.) The organization of the Ossewatrek had not been left to chance. The composition of the organizing bodies strongly suggests that the Broederbond had ensured that its personnel were in key positions on the Central Volk Monuments Committee, which was in overall charge of the celebrations. The management committee of this body included Broederbond secretary I. M. Lombard as treasurer and senior Bond member T. J. Hugo. Other members of the monuments committee included N. J. van der Merwe and Willem Nicol, Broederbond chairman from 1924 to 1925 and one of the most powerful figures in the Afrikaans Reformed churches. Mrs. M. Jansen, Strijdom's former co-leader of the party in the Transvaal, was also on the management committee.[57] (The absence of Diederichs and Meyer can be explained by their relative youth, since the committee had been elected in 1931, when they were still completing their studies.)[58]

The development of Afrikaner nationalism as a broad movement into a tightly organized, all-embracing *Volksbeweging* suggests influences that were not merely indigenous. The control of this movement lay primarily in the hands of men like Diederichs or Meyer, directly influenced by fascist thought, or strongly sym-

The 1938 Ossewatrek (Ox-wagon Trek), commemorating the nineteenth century Afrikaner pioneers' migration into the interior, a powerful means of mobilizing Afrikaner sentiment for the Nationalist cause. At top, members of the Voortrekker Youth Movement at an Ossewatrek celebration in Cape Town (note the speaker's Trekker-style beard and quasi-military uniform). At bottom, members of the Voortrekker Movement participate in a torchlight parade in Cape Town.

From the Cape Times *Collection in the South African Library*

Afrikaner families wearing traditional dress, including the distinctive wom-
en's *kappies* (bonnets), at an Ossewatrek celebration at the Rosebank
Showgrounds in Cape Town, 1938.
From the Cape Times *Collection in the South African Library*

pathetic to a home-grown variant. In such an environment the
Purified National Party had no choice but to make some kind of
arrangement with those in control of the *Volksbeweging,* or to
abandon the cause altogether, adhering to a truly liberal nationalism, but this was impossible for a party trying to secure the
political ground to the immediate right of a conservative such
as General Hertzog.

Hertzog, whose own liberal credentials were questionable, and
who was enamored with the successes of the new Germany, had
long leaned toward a dictatorial style of management. A. L.
Geyer, Malan's trusted confidant and formerly a Hertzog supporter in the pre-Fusion days, stated in private notes in 1933
that once Malan's supporters had chosen to break with Hertzog,
the general would never permit a return to the former unity of
the National Party, because "Hertzog is by nature vindictive."[59]

Hertzog became increasingly intolerant of the more liberal members of the United Party who, like Hofmeyr, sometimes voted independently on racial matters. When, early in 1939, Hofmeyr and Leslie Blackwell, a member of Parliament of similarly liberal disposition on the rights of the Indian community, voted against a bill to restrict Indians' right to buy land, Hertzog arranged for them to be censured by the United Party parliamentary caucus, and in consequence they were forced to resign from that body.[60] Hertzog did not take kindly to being crossed, particularly by his own followers. His dalliance in 1939 with the idea of a bill to curb the press was along the same lines, prompting L. R. Macleod of the Johannesburg *Rand Daily Mail* to observe sardonically: "I am sure that Hitler could devise nothing better suited to serve his needs."[61]

Apart from outspoken admirers of the Hitler regime, such as Pirow and Van Rensburg, others in the ranks of the Hertzogites showed authoritarian tendencies. One was Piet Grobler, one of Hertzog's senior cabinet ministers. In 1936 he had proposed abolition of the parliamentary system.[62] In that same year, Jan Pienaar, another senior Hertzogite, tried unsuccessfully to win passage of a private bill to outlaw interracial marriage.[63]

If those outside the inner orbit of organized Afrikanerdom expressed such sentiments, it was hardly surprising that many Malanites, free from the Broederbond ostracism of Hertzog's supporters, at least dabbled in the new ideological fashions. Malan himself was not above capitalizing on the current mood. In August 1939, on the eve of war, A. J. Bosman, a South African trade representative in Germany, presented to the Berlin Foreign Office a letter signed by Malan and other Nationalists asking for an increase in the number of German automobiles sold in South Africa. As Bosman put it, Afrikaners had a strong preference for German cars.[64]

Younger men in the party were still more likely than their more cautious seniors, like Malan, to express an openly Radical Right sentiment, and this eased cooperation with the shirt movements and other extremist groups. For instance, Eric Louw, one of the best-known hard-liners in the Cape party, enjoyed sufficient popularity with the radical Studentebond to be invited in July 1939 to address it at Stellenbosch University. His lecture, "Ireland Shows the Way: Constitutional Development Since 1921," may well have disappointed his expectant listeners with so apparently tame a theme, but the Irish secession from the Commonwealth to become an independent republic was by no means uncontroversial. English-speakers could only find the discussion of such a step highly offensive, especially in the explosive international climate. In any case, Malan's Nasionale Pers thought Louw's talk important enough to publish,[65] possibly reflecting Malan's own preference for reaching a republic by constitutional rather than revolutionary means.

Moderates among the Hertzogites were expressing concern about the role of youthful National Party extremists who had founded the Ossewabrandwag without consulting Malan.[66] On the eve of war, *Die Vaderland* complained bitterly and prophetically:

It was from the first moment clear that this semi-military movement is no ordinary cultural movement. Whatever the admirers of the overseas dictatorships have in mind . . . , there can anyway be no doubt that such an organization can easily be used by people with more ambition than a sense of responsibility. Dr. Malan and his democratically-minded supporters in the Purified Party ought to realize that such a possible attack on our democratic form of government can be aimed as much against themselves as against any other supporter of democracy. And still they do not dare to denounce the movement definitively.[67]

A pattern was being set that Malan would follow repeatedly in the coming months; extremists moved so fast that he could only go along with them or abandon the Nationalist cause entirely. In the long run, this was not a road to be taken halfheartedly, picking and choosing only what was most suitable to party needs. By mid-1939 even inside the party, old-style Nationalists were concerned about the course their colleagues were taking. Naas Coertze of Pretoria University warned *Oosterlig* editor Otto du Plessis:

The German philosophy of today is a danger to us. Their point of departure [*uitgangspunt*] is foreign and if a person loses his worldview [*lewensbeskouing*], then he sells away his birth-right for a dish of lentil soup [*vir 'n skottel lensiesop*]. You are a newspaperman. Just don't walk away with the whole German thing because there are a few good things in the German system—like some of your fellow party members are doing.[68]

The real problem was that some of the Nationalists had long been dabbling in undemocratic notions, even in the context of a largely whites-only political system such as that of South Africa. They had always been ambivalent toward Germany, and even after Hitler had marched into Czechoslovakia, these Nationalists were talking about returning South-West Africa to the Germans.[69] Nor were Nationalist designs on the right of enfranchised Cape "coloreds" to vote on a common roll or the exclusion of Jews from the Transvaal party consonant with a commitment to democratic values. Neither of these developments had ever been part of mainstream white South African politics, including under Hertzog's pre-1933 Nationalist government.

Of course, it might be argued that minority rule based on race, always central to South African political life, was not and never could be democratic, but the Purified Nationalists aimed at narrowing political participation in still more fundamental ways, going beyond even Hertzog's long-standing (and—in 1936—eventually successful) attempts to remove Cape Africans from the common voters' roll. The Nationalists had gone yet one step further when they accommodated themselves to the role of the secret, extraparliamentary, elitist Broederbond in Afrikaner life, unlike Hertzog, who had shown the courage to denounce it vigorously as early as 1935.[70]

The Purified Nationalists were therefore moving decisively away from the basic arrangements of 1910: a Westminster-style parliamentary system restricted primarily to whites, whether Afrikaners or English (including Jews), but including a limited franchise in the case of the Cape for other communities. Although Hertzog had never been happy about the presence of African voters on the common roll, and in this regard opened the door to the Purified Nationalists' more extremist proposals, he had never proposed tampering with the political rights of the Cape "coloreds," and it is well known that in the past he had left open the possibility of extending these rights to "colored" women and to "colored" men in the northern provinces. The Malan party was moving in the opposite direction, toward a system in which only those fully committed to the aims of an exclusive Afrikaner nationalism would enjoy real political power.

Such aims did not yet prove attractive to a majority of Afrikaans-speakers, and understandably alienated the English. The results of the 1938 election show this clearly. Despite the attempts of the Broederbond to seize control of Afrikaner cultural organizations, many Afrikaners, especially in the Transvaal, where the National Party was still suffering from inadequate organization and funding, remained loyal to Hertzog and Smuts. Thus only Strijdom retained a National Party seat in that province. Perhaps because of the Nationalists' failure to make much headway with the electorate there, intellectuals behind the scenes hoped that shrill and radical rhetoric would win votes among the most marginalized and disaffected whites. Nationalist failure to make a breakthrough in the key urban working-class districts of the southern Transvaal suggests that this was an error of judgment, but it was still too early to tell whether the emergent *Volksbeweging* would ultimately deliver Nationalist votes.

As Alan Paton notes in his acclaimed biography of Hofmeyr, even if in 1938 perhaps one-third of Afrikaners were for Hertzog, one-third for Smuts, and one-third for Malan:

The Afrikaner universities were turning out, not Smuts men and women, or Hertzog men and women, but Malan men and women. The Afrikaner scout movements and the cultural movements were not excited about the Commonwealth of Nations or [Hertzog's] bi-racial policy [for English and Afrikaners], but about being Afrikaners, about the day when Afrikaners would govern, about the time when all the wickedness and the loose sentimentality of the last hundred years would come to an end, and all the people of South Africa would be ruled firmly and resolutely by the Afrikaner people, whom God had sent into Africa.[71]

Nor were the 1938 election results a total rout for the Nationalists. Malan gained seven seats overall, principally in the Cape, but including two in the Orange Free State, where Hertzog, who had been unopposed in 1933, defeated his Malanite opponent by only 526 votes. Malan obtained only 24 percent of the United Party's number of seats, but 58 percent of the United Party's total votes.[72] Given the South African winner-take-all political system, the Nationalists' failure to gain many seats obscured a slow but steady increase in voting support, one that would bear fruit in the next election, and victory in that of 1948. The Afrikaner nationalist movement in 1938 was better organized than at the time of the secession of the Purified Nationalists in 1934 and had time on its side for further gains. It had also shifted considerably to the right in the intervening years.

So many in the Malanite and even the Hertzogite wings of Afrikanerdom had ingested the ideas of European authoritarian nationalism that it had begun to transform the nature of Afrikaner politics. The men in Berlin could see still more potential here by 1939 than they had seen in 1934. Radical ideological experimentation in a land deeply rooted in racism was an explosive idea in peacetime. In wartime, with the ancient enemy Britain pitted against Germany, self-proclaimed friend of the Afrikaner, the Nationalists' adherence even to a semblance of parliamentary democracy would face its severest test yet.

Chapter Five

A Pro-War Majority in a Climate of Subversion

The Hertzog government hoped that somehow the Union might be spared involvement in the world crisis, after war was declared in Europe in September 1939, despite all the pent-up forces of Afrikaner nationalism, anti-British sentiment, anti-Semitism, residual white economic distress, and disenchantment with parliamentary democracy. But with a parliamentary pro-war, pro-Allied majority, South Africa was confronted with the possibility of direct German retaliation through armed intervention. It had to muster a credible war effort in the face of a deeply divided white population, much of which was embittered by South Africa's involvement in yet another of Britain's wars.

In these circumstances, there was an increasing danger of a "fifth column," with Berlin beginning to capitalize on radical Afrikaner nationalist sentiment for its own purposes. With the growing impact of metropolitan authoritarian nationalism in the Afrikaner nationalist movement, this threat soon began to assume alarming proportions.

Neutrality or War?

Hertzog, supported by his ex-Nationalist followers in the United Party cabinet, was convinced that the 1934 Status Act would protect the Union from involvement unless South African interests were threatened. In the view of his faction in the government, South Africa had no "vital concern" in a war that was the result of a strictly European conflict.[1] This perspective was in keeping with the stand taken by the entire cabinet during the Munich crisis. Smuts and his followers had accepted a resolution drafted by Hertzog and adopted on 28 September 1938 that suggested that neutrality was the official Union position "in the event of war in Europe with England as one of the belligerents." The resolution stated: "The existing relations between the Union of South Africa and the various belligerent parties shall, so far as the Union is concerned, remain unchanged and continue as if no war were being waged." There was one important specific proviso, that existing contractual relationships, such as the agreement with Britain permitting the Royal Navy to use the base at Simonstown (near Cape Town), would "remain unaltered." There was also a vague final statement, perhaps out of deference to Smuts's English-speaking supporters, that no change would occur in "the relationships etc., [which] must be regarded *impliciter* [*sic*] as flowing from the free association of the Union with the other members of the Commonwealth."[2]

Such convoluted language, attempting to hold to a position of neutrality without damaging relationships with the rest of the British Empire, was still possible when war was a threat but not an immediate reality, and to some extent was essential if the old Anglo-Afrikaner divisions were to remain reconciled inside the United Party. But, as Sir Keith Hancock points out in his biography of Smuts, while Hertzog made no public declarations about the heightening tensions in Europe during the following year, hoping that such a written resolution would keep Smuts to neutrality even in the event of war, he misunderstood his deputy prime minister. Smuts, Hancock notes, could foresee that if the military situation changed it might be necessary for South Africa to take her stand with Britain and the Commonwealth.[3] But even if Smuts did break with Hertzog on the war issue in September 1939, with both Hertzog's supporters in the United Party and the Purified Nationalists favoring neutrality,[4] it seemed likely that Hertzog as prime minister would prevail in this policy; Smuts's changing personal opinions, therefore, may have seemed of purely hypothetical importance.

Smuts, increasingly convinced that neutrality would not be an option, decided that nothing in the relationship with Britain had fundamentally changed since the First World War, and that South Africa would have to stand with Britain against Hitler. As in 1914, when the Botha government had considered the Union automatically engaged in any war involving Britain, so in 1939 Smuts relied on this same rationale. The pro-war group in the 1939 cabinet held that South Africa had certain obligations that flowed from its membership in the British Commonwealth. Despite the sovereignty of the Union, it could not abandon cooperation with its "friends and associates."[5] It was Smuts's view, according to a letter from British High Commissioner L. H. Clark to Sir Patrick Duncan, now the governor-general, that, contrary to Hertzog's assessment, South African freedom and independence *were* at stake, and that therefore it *was* in the direct interest of the Union to oppose the German use of force.[6] Hertzog remained proudly attached to the notion of national independence. Smuts was deeply committed to loyalty to the friends of the Union in their hour of need, especially in a war against an aggressor.

The situation was made more complex by the past role of the neutrality issue as a divisive factor in South African politics. There loomed large the fear of a repetition of the 1914 Rebellion, when many Afrikaners, still bitter over their recent defeat in the Anglo-Boer War, had resorted to an armed uprising rather than be conscripted to fight against Germany. With this memory still very much alive, and arguing that the right to neutrality was intrinsic to any claim of South African independence from Britain, the Malanites had tried to make political capital from the neutrality issue in the 1938 general election.[7]

Both the pro-neutralist and the pro-war faction knew that South Africa had to take certain precautions, no matter which policy was followed. The common border with South-West Africa, to which Germany still laid claim, and the presence of Portugal, with its clerico-fascist Salazar regime, in nearby Angola and Mozambique, suggested that it might be difficult to ride out the war peacefully.

The stakes were high. Neutrality, especially a pro-German neutrality such as was likely if backed by Hertzog's pro-Hitler lieutenants and the radicals among the Malanites, could seriously hurt Allied interests, particularly if the Germans could manage to be reinstalled in South-West Africa, where they would have a superb submarine base at Walvis Bay, accessible to South Atlantic Allied convoys.

Hertzog insisted, as in 1938, that the Union agreement with Britain guaranteeing the Royal Navy facilities at the still more strategically important Simonstown base should continue to be honored, even if a neutral stance were adopted.[8] Since English-speakers would be unlikely to support a neutralist government, however, such a regime under Hertzog would depend heavily on the political support of those very radical Afrikaner nationalist elements least likely to favor the continuance of the Simonstown agreement. If anything, they might be amenable to the Germans using Simonstown themselves. There was a real possibility that this key base would fall into Nazi hands.

Even if Simonstown were not handed over to the Germans, without a substantial Allied military presence in the Union an invasion would, in theory, be possible. In September 1939 South Africa lacked the equipment to put even one regiment into the field and its air force had bombs for only one day's action.[9] Harry Lawrence, one of Smuts's right-hand men, later argued that Hertzog and his defense minister, Pirow, favored neutrality not out of any anti-British feeling, but from fear of Hitler's might.[10]

Yet it is doubtful that Hertzog's war policy was motivated altogether by fear since his ambivalence toward Germany was no secret. His sympathies were now brought to the surface. By chance, Parliament had been summoned at the beginning of September to prolong the Senate session, which was due to expire, and the international crisis exploded in what was planned to be the briefest of sessions.

Hertzog used the opportunity to try to obtain parliamentary support for neutrality. Actually there was no other choice, since the cabinet was divided down the middle on the war issue. Two opposing motions were placed before the House of Assembly, one by the prime minister, one by his deputy. It was a unique moment in the history both of the war and of the British Empire. This was the only dominion in which the government itself was deeply divided over whether to go to war against Germany. The two motions were predictable, Hertzog's for neutrality, Smuts's for war.[11]

Hertzog entered the House of Assembly on 4 September convinced that he had a guaranteed majority, because in addition to the old Hertzogites in the United Party, whose support he could assume natural, the previous day Malan had given the prime minister written assurance of Purified Nationalist support for neutrality in case of a vote on entering the war.[12] Perhaps because Hertzog was so confident of victory, he dispensed with the usual parliamentary niceties that had always been necessary to preserve the United Party coalition and provided a rare glimpse into his true state of mind on international affairs. One of his arguments was the strictly nationalist claim that this was merely England's war, that England had gone to war because it "has certain obligations towards Poland." "We have no such obligations," he pointed out.[13] On this point, Hertzog was most explicit: "It must not be forgotten that we are concerned here with a war in which the Union has not the slightest interest. We are not interested in the war between Poland and Germany."[14] Another argument was more surprising, at least to those who had come to respect Hertzog as a moderate nationalist who had buried the enmities of the past. Hertzog's deepest feelings on the German question came out into the open: "Now it is argued that we should take part in the war because the German Chancellor has demonstrated that he is out to obtain world domination. Let me say this. I have carefully followed his actions step by step, and I have asked myself where is the proof that this man is out for world domination? . . . Let us be honest. Where can we find proof?"[15]

Hertzog's own deeply held views on the sufferings of his people in the Anglo-Boer War came explicitly to the fore in this debate. His address must be considered one of the most revealing speeches by a South African prime minister. He explained that he had told the British authorities in 1935 that they would have to deal with the "monster of the Treaty of Versailles" and that he had put it to them at that time that he "realised what his [Hitler's] feelings were, and what the feelings of the German nation were" because "I have been through the same mill." Now Hertzog repeated the message in addressing the Assembly:

I know what it is to be humiliated and trodden . . . so that you feel that a state has been reached when you can no longer bear that humiliation. . . . Now I ask you if my interpretation is correct, what then? And is anybody going to say that it is not correct? . . . With what justification can one ask me and South Africa to take part in a war because Hitler and the German nation will no longer suffer . . . humiliation? No, you have to excuse me when I say that you have no right to expect such an action from me.[16]

At one fell swoop, Hertzog had destroyed the fragile grand coalition of the United Party, and Smuts now rose to declare that he could no longer give way to the prime minister, as he had so often done in the past:

We, as the Prime Minister has explained, have come to a point where those relations [between Hertzog's and Smuts's followers] are disturbed, where a difference of opinion, which is going to have very far-reaching repercussions, has taken place. I wish to emphasise that this difference concerns a matter which to me is of the very gravest national importance. I have never in all these years of our political collaboration made a serious point of our differences on small issues. I have always been prepared to give way, to hold the peace, and to see that the young life of this nation is given a chance, and for the people to have an opportunity to grow together. To-day we have come to a point where I have to call a halt and I have to adopt a different attitude, and I do so because I am in my soul convinced that we are up against most vital issues for the present and for the future of this country. . . . It would be wrong and it would be fatal for this country to continue to treat Germany after what has happened, as the Prime Minister proposes, as a friend, and to continue on the existing footing as if nothing had happened in the world.[17]

Smuts made it clear that his position was not entirely altruistic, but was based on a considered judgment of the Union's international position:

We have had due notice that the next demand after Danzig has been wiped off the slate is going to be the return of the German colonies, and so far as South Africa is concerned and its special interests, apart from the wider world issues raised, the question we have to face in this country is what our position is going to be within some months or some years when we are treated as Austria has been treated, as Czecho-Slovakia has been treated, and as Poland is now being treated, when we are faced with superior force and we have to surrender what we consider to be vital in the interests of the Union, at the point of the bayonet.[18]

Malan and Hertzog were on the same side now, as they had been before Fusion. While Malan, following several shorter speeches, was careful to avoid inflammatory language, he said he agreed with Hertzog's opinion of the claim that Hitler sought world domination:

The Minister of Justice [Smuts] falls back on the argument . . . that Germany is out for world domination, to achieve a position of world domination. Germany, it is said, is out not only to destroy the liberty and independence of all the surrounding nations, but after doing that she will go further and will try to dominate the whole world. I entirely agree with what the Prime Minister said in his statement, namely, that that is a propaganda argument which we got accustomed to in the world war.[19]

Germany wanted to regain its lost territory and unite all those of the German race, no more. Malan had found an argument that could compel any stout-hearted Afrikaner nationalist, but one that did not commit him to support Nazi tactics in achieving these goals:

Is that . . . such an objectionable idea that we want to bring together those belonging to the same race and speaking the same language? We may condemn it for this or that reason, but I say that such a desire is only natural and justified, and if there are no adequate reasons to remain divided, that which belongs together should not be kept apart. . . . It is a justified ideal and aim, and if that applies to the Afrikaans-speaking people . . . and English-speaking people the world over, why should it be such an unjustified, such an objectionable ideal on the part of the Germans?[20]

Malan's speech suggested more than merely neutral feelings on the war issue. He conceded that Hitler's attack on Czechoslovakia in March of that year could not be interpreted as uniting those of the same ethnic group, but he claimed that it was obvious from the map that Czechoslovakia was in a position to threaten German security.[21]

The disproportion between the might of Germany and the weakness of Czechoslovakia, stripped of its Sudeten fortifications by Hitler after the Munich crisis of the previous year, had apparently not moved Malan. Whether inspired by dislike of Britain or affection for the Germans, he now pleaded that Germany's behavior was understandable, since the League of Nations had become "the bulwark of the status quo," protecting the injustices of Versailles:

Where that is the case we can well understand that a state with self-respect, a nation with a love of liberty as the German nation, would not permanently lie down under such injustices, and where they looked in vain for relief and where the League of Nations, which should have opened the door, closed that door in their face, Germany sought refuge in another direction, took to other means to retrieve its position.[22]

Under these circumstances, to spill one drop of South African blood for a British war implied that the Union was "a country of serfs."[23] The implication of Malan's speech was that he believed that the Wehrmacht's aggression was justified, notwithstanding issues involving violation of self-determination that might have been expected to disturb so ardent an Afrikaner nationalist. Malan may well have had his own private reservations about Nazi behavior, but it was not evident in his public statement here. Not the Nazi pogroms of 1938 (including the *Kristallnacht*), nor the bullying of the Czechs at Munich and the extirpation of their Czechoslovak state a few months later, nor the concentration camps for political prisoners and other undesirables, nor the campaign against the German churches seemed to trouble him. The speeches of both Hertzog and Malan demonstrated that the sympathies of leading Afrikaner nationalists were clearly weighted on the German rather than the British side. Neutrality, if adopted as policy, would not be impartial.

But, when at the close of the debate the votes were counted, it became clear that Hertzog's and Malan's pleas had been to no avail. The decision of Parliament went Smuts's way by a vote of 80 to 67.[24] Hertzog had severely miscalculated his parliamentary strength; four of his pre-1934 National Party supporters, who had gone with him into Fusion, had voted for Smuts. In the 1938 election several formerly Nationalist United Party constituencies had returned pro-Smuts candidates because during the nominating procedure Afrikaners were split between Malan and Hertzog, and Hertzog's supporters were no longer able to win nomination.[25] The strength of the Hertzog forces inside the United Party was considerably weakened compared to the time of Fusion. Political scientist Newell Stultz argues that Hertzog committed a crucial error in going beyond the general issue of neutrality in his speech on the war crisis to what amounted to a defense of Hitler, which Stultz claims caused several wavering supporters to side with Smuts at the last moment.[26] Thus it was possible to produce a pro-war parliamentary majority in a country where it was far less certain that a majority of the electorate would have supported Smuts at the time on this particular issue. The Union was officially at war with Germany, but the leaders of both wings of nationalist Afrikanerdom were bitter, still convinced of the justice of the German cause.

Hertzog tried to force an election, which he was convinced he could win, but the governor-general, Sir Patrick Duncan, Smuts's interior minister in his 1919–1924 government, took a step unique in South African history of going beyond his usual purely ceremonial function to exercise his considerable constitutional powers. The political situation was extremely tense: Duncan had reported to Hertzog a widespread belief that calling a general election would produce great bitterness and, possibly, even violence.[27] He therefore refused to accede to the prime minister's request to dissolve Parliament, in the absence of a pro-Hertzog majority in the Assembly, and called on Smuts to form a new government, backed by those members of Parliament who had voted for war.[28] The experiment of Fusion had ended with Hertzog and Smuts parting company on this issue. The United Party, based hitherto on an alliance of Hertzogite Afrikaner nationalists and Smuts supporters of Empire (predominantly English), was henceforth to be an updated version of Smuts's old pre-Fusion South African Party, supported principally by English-speakers, in coalition with the small Labour and Dominion parties, both overwhelmingly English-speaking. The United Party Hertzogites of the pre-1934 National Party went into the political wilderness to join their longtime foes in the Purified National Party.

Ethnic polarization was prevalent. English-speakers and, increasingly, most black South Africans supported the war as one against the greatest enemies of democracy. There was a widespread belief that the overwhelming majority of Afrikaners, on the other hand, opposed involvement on the Allied side.[29]

Smuts was initially confident that Hertzog and Malan would be unable to reconcile their differences and form a united antiwar front. It seemed likely that the right could be contained because of internecine squabbling. Only direct German military intervention in southern Africa could alter Smuts's prognosis.

Nonetheless, enormous domestic forces were pushing for the reunification of nationalist Afrikanerdom. As early as January 1939 a group of professors at Stellenbosch University under A. C. Cilliers, an enthusiastic supporter of Hertzog, had promoted a scheme to bring the warring factions together, but the experiment had failed, as had a similar attempt by Albert Hertzog, the general's son, to effect reconciliation.[30] Now the Smuts-Hertzog rift greatly facilitated Afrikaner unity, since Hertzog's hands were cleansed of involvement with the archenemy of Afrikaner nationalism, General Smuts. After several months of painful wrangling,[31] a compromise acceptable to both factions was achieved when, on 27 January 1940, a joint declaration was announced by Malan and Hertzog to form a new political organization, the Herenigde Nasionale of Volksparty, the Reunited National or Volk Party, more commonly known simply as the National Party.[32]

The key compromise in this agreement involved admitting as members of the new party those who did not specifically support establishment of an independent republic, the ultimate goal of most Afrikaner nationalists. It was further agreed that such a republic would only be brought about by a decision of "the broad will of the people," including English-speakers.[33]

Despite these important concessions to Hertzog's sensibilities about English-speaking South Africans, a fundamental change in Afrikaner politics was achieved through this agreement. The great majority of Afrikaners were brought together in a party that espoused republicanism both as an ideal and as the only way to ensure neutrality. The words of the unification agreement between Hertzog and Malan expressed this dual goal:

The Party is therefore convinced that the republican state-form, separated from the British Crown, fits best with the traditions, circumstances and aspirations of the South African volk and in addition is the only effective guarantee that South Africa will not be dragged again into Great Britain's wars.[34]

The coming of war had convinced Afrikaners of the crucial importance of their republican heritage, the heritage of Kruger and the Anglo-Boer War. However, the struggle against Britain was clearly not over, as the Hertzogites had thought earlier, at the time of Fusion. English-speakers were not, and perhaps never would be, ready to sacrifice their own sectional loyalties on behalf of a broader "Afrikaner" nationalism, to use Hertzog's looser sense of the word.

Only the creation of a separate, independent republic would force the English population to merge truly into a white South African nation, Hertzog's great goal. Such a nation would necessarily be Afrikaner-dominated in the narrow, ethnic sense of Purified Nationalism. Sheer demographic weight, with Afrikaners a majority among white South Africans, dictated that a white republic would be more along the lines of Malan's exclusive ethnic vision than Hertzog's more inclusive approach. The acceptance of the need for such a republic meant also that the narrowly ethnic and elitist vision of the Afrikaner Broederbond and the Afrikaanse Nasionale Studentebond was no longer marginal. Malan's years in the wilderness were justified, for his party had preserved the flame of an unsullied and uncompromising nationalism, to which all committed Afrikaners could now subscribe in good conscience.

A Network of Subversion

Berlin watched every step of this political process with interest. After the declaration of war by the Union, diplomats at the German legation had been compelled to leave via Mozambique. One of them, Luitpold Werz, remained at the consulate there in Lourenço Marques (the modern Maputo), from which base a steady flow of telegrams proceeded to Berlin, fed by a network of Nazi spies in the Union.[35]

Werz showed particular interest in the denials of German aggression by both Hertzog and Malan, and in Nationalist dismissals of Smuts's claims as mere pro-British propaganda.[36] South Africa was ripe for Nazi trouble-making, and continual rumors of potential revolt were rife. The seriousness of the problem was made most evident by Smuts's resorting to the recruitment into the military forces of volunteers only, despite his legal power to conscript men under the Union Defence Act, in order to prevent a repetition of the 1914 Rebellion.[37] His failure to go to the country for an election in September 1939 had deeply angered neutralist Afrikaners, already disillusioned about parliamentary democracy. Now many became still more disgusted with the constitutional methods of the pro-war faction, which had been satisfied with a parliamentary vote when most Afrikaners were convinced that a majority of whites favored neutrality.[38] The antidemocratic current was considerably strengthened.

Hertzog became ever more convinced that the war would drag down South Africa along with all of Germany's defeated foes. He repeatedly tried to persuade Smuts to seek a separate peace during the next year, but was turned aside by the new prime minister, who saw the war as a crusade against tyranny.[39]

Hertzog's pleas for a separate peace may have been based on very mixed motives. Margaret Ballinger, an outspoken supporter of the war policy and a prominent liberal member of Parliament, was convinced from private discussions in the Assembly lobby that many Nationalists did fear a Nazi victory but were trying to embarrass the British.[40] The war brought out complicated feelings among Afrikaners. In many cases it is clear that pro-German sentiment alone does not provide an adequate explanation for the events that followed.

South Africa now entered one of the most tumultuous periods in its history, as militant Afrikaner nationalists fought to save their country from what they perceived as the folly of the imperialistic "jingoes" and of their leader, Smuts. Under these circumstances, the boundaries between patriotism and treason necessarily became dangerously blurred. One person's traitor became another person's hero.

The threat of subversion in South Africa was significant not only to the Union government but also to the entire Allied cause. As one Ally after another fell to Hitler's juggernaut, the importance of South Africa in the overall strategic picture increased greatly. For one thing, by 1941 the security of Suez as a route to India had become highly questionable. Indeed, the safety of India itself, the "Jewel in the Crown," was threatened from the end of that year by the Japanese onslaught in the Far East. Also, Rommel's Afrika Korps threatened the British in Egypt, while the Axis strengthened its stranglehold on large parts of the Mediterranean, advancing through the Balkans and besieging the key British base on Malta.

Until Russia and the United States entered the war on the Allied side in 1941, the mineral wealth of South Africa was crucial to the survival of Britain through its long siege. And even after the German invasion of Russia in June 1941, the Allies' only manageable supply route for Soviet minerals (the best alternative to South African) was far from assured, since it involved the perilous passage from Murmansk on the Arctic Ocean. If South Africa fell to pro-Nazi forces the Allies would be in a grievous position.

In this situation, wartime security and the attendant fear of Axis subversion were crucial, although in official circles Smuts tended to play down the threat to his government. For example, in late 1940, when the paramilitary, pro-fascist Ossewabrandwag was beginning to attract great numbers of members, Smuts telegraphed to his high commissioner in London, Sidney Waterson, arguing that the political situation in South Africa "in the opinion of competent observers is progressively improving."[41] As late as February 1942, when Japan was knocking at the gates of British India, Smuts was warned in a secret telegram from the South African legation in Washington that, according to an unnamed source in Europe, who had passed the information to the U.S. State Department, Hitler had ordered a coup in South Africa:

Hitler is at present at Berchtesgaden getting ready complete, tremendous and simultaneous spring fronts including North America, Latin America and South Africa. Hitler has issued orders that everything be prepared for a coup in South Africa and in spite of a temporary Nazi setback there he hopes that this spring South Africa will fall to Germany. All activities there are being directed from Lourenço Marques and Angola. Military and Civil Servants of Portugal have been bought and from this point explosives are smuggled to South Africa. Secret short wave senders are reported in Johannesburg, Cape Town and in German South West Africa [sic], on a farm probably. If Rommel should succeed, Nazi supporters in South Africa are preparing to declare independence and establish connections with Japan.

The general dismissed this report, claiming in his reply: "At present there is no reason for alarm as [the] internal situation [is] very well in hand." Smuts's telegram added, "No danger to Union at present anticipated from movements in Angola or Mozambique."[42]

But privately the aging prime minister was not quite so sanguine, as it became clear that the Nationalists saw a Nazi victory as their key to control of South Africa. In July 1940 Smuts wrote to M. C. Gillett in Britain, one of his oldest personal friends, a more revealing communique:

The German victories are putting great heart into my Opposition. They are holding meetings all over the country in favour of a separate peace. The Allies are finished, they say, and Smuts will be finished in a couple of months, and thereafter they will seize power and proclaim secession and a republic. There will be a new constitution, modelled on that of Italy or Portugal and an alliance with Nazi Germany.[43]

The Reunited Nationalists were certainly extremely noisy in their denunciation of the Smuts government. The officials of the party scathingly dismissed the war policy as "idiotic" (*dwaas*) and claimed "gigantic" audiences at their protest meetings.[44] Five thousand people crowded into the Johannesburg City Hall in February 1940 at one such meeting. The Transvaal National Party leader, Strijdom, used the occasion to denounce Smuts's declaration of war as an attempt to satisfy "English Jews."[45] He proceeded to denigrate the war policy as a foolhardy scheme that would cause the deaths of many innocent young Afrikaners in a foreign struggle; the policy was Smuts's "war games" (*Studeerkamer-Oorlog*), an armchair statement of solidarity with Britain that ignored reality.[46]

Cape National Party member of Parliament Eric Louw gave credence to Smuts's fears of a Nationalist seizure of power, telling a meeting in his Beaufort West constituency that, through the development of the war situation, the position of the government had been placed in question and his party could soon be called upon to take control.[47] As the Allies in Europe fell like dominoes during the first two years of the war, Louw's views continually seemed on the verge of realization.

Already in April 1939 the Hertzog government had received information that the Germans were planning a *putsch* in South-West Africa. Since I have not found evidence in captured German Foreign Office records that such a coup was indeed planned, and since relevant South African government records remain closed, it is difficult to know who was actually involved. Smuts as minister of justice was sufficiently alarmed to send in police reinforcements.[48] In August Smuts wrote to a friend in the English-speaking press, John Martin, indicating that later investigation bore out his government's earlier fears: "The Commissioner of Police who has just paid S.W. Africa a visit comes back with a very disquieting report about conditions there. It is clear that my sending the police there in April just forestalled a coup which had been planned. They say next time there will be no leakage and no forestalling."[49]

There was more potential for Berlin's carefully developed schemes than in any hasty attempt at a violent takeover, for instance in the German schools and especially the German mission stations in the Union. Charges of missionary subversion were hotly contested even by supporters of Smuts.[50] Yet there was considerable evidence of missionary involvement. According to a letter dated 25 November 1939 from Piet van der Byl, Smuts's minister without portfolio, to J. D. Rheinallt-Jones, a senator and the head of the liberal-oriented South African Institute of Race Relations, the government received detailed reports from black Christians at German mission stations indicating that their pastors were inciting converts to hatred of the English and that they were predicting that one result of a German victory would be the expulsion of all whites from the country. In this letter, Van der Byl claimed to have information that, shortly after the outbreak of war, a German pastor of the Berlin Missionary Society had told his congregation "that he was a warrior of the German Reich" who had seen active duty during the First World War. Van der Byl stressed to Rheinallt-Jones that this information was to be kept strictly between themselves, and that he could substantiate all such claims with documentary evidence. He said the missionary referred to had produced a military decoration and (somewhat puzzlingly) a swastika armband to substantiate his claim of war service, and that he had instituted a prayer to be offered by his congregation for the victory of Germany since "if the English are victorious the Berlin Missionary Society will be abolished."

Van der Byl also cited a letter he had recently received from an "educated" African, as he put it:

Us natives always read the newspapers and I saw your speech about the Nazis trying to stir up war. This is quite true, our children are being taught in the mission schools to hate the English and told that when this country is in Germany's hands all the white people will be driven out and the black people will have the white man's property and live in the white man's home, and our children have listened and now they are cheeky to we old people and the white man.[51]

Senator Edgar Brookes, like Rheinallt-Jones a liberal "native representative" with excellent contacts among his Zulu constituents, told Smuts of evidence that German mission stations in Natal were preparing for a Nazi victory. According to Brookes's sources, the missionaries were accumulating great quantities of barbed wire and cement and, expecting disruption of transport, were hoarding bicycle supplies. Vast amounts of petrol were said to be hidden under altars. Such stories may strike later observers as somewhat farfetched, but Brookes, a mild-mannered and rational man, was not given to spreading wild rumors; he himself seemed convinced that his sources were well informed. Smuts apparently took this news very seriously, since this was one of the few personal letters he received that he marked "File."[52]

Another important tool for Nazi subversion was the Zeesen Radio Service, which broadcast propaganda in Afrikaans from Europe. The person in charge of the Afrikaans service was Eric Holm, a South African expatriate who was, coincidentally, a member of the Broederbond.[53] The Nationalists considered Zeesen far more reliable than either the South African or the British Broadcasting Corporations, particularly since Zeesen gained added credibility by skillfully quoting neutral opinion.[54]

Given Zeesen's constant anti-Semitic references that sought to tie Smuts to the Jewish community, it is perhaps not surprising that reports of "extreme anti-Jewish violence" came from the area of Beaufort West,[55] which also happened to be the constituency of Eric Louw. Louw's anti-Jewish views were well known.

Zeesen exploited its credibility among Afrikaners to the fullest, praising Hertzog's courage in opposing "this destructive English war" and suggesting that Afrikaners might have to pay with their blood and liberty for refusing British demands in the name of honor.[56] Holm played on the passions of Afrikaners regarding British atrocities in the Anglo-Boer War; he referred to the Bloemfontein monument in the Orange Free State to the women and children of the notorious British camps:

In the past years the Afrikaner people have been continually asked to forget the past. But Afrikaners, we can and may only forget if we break down the monument at Bloemfontein. Women and mothers, do you still remember what thoughts you had and how many tears flowed at the unveiling of that brutal reality in 1913? Who is responsible that that monument had to be erected[;] who caused all that misery to the poor Boer nation? . . . No, we cannot and will not and may not forget.[57]

Zeesen described terrible Polish atrocities against the Germans (new graves were said to be discovered every day) and claimed that it had received thousands of letters from Afrikaner listeners. Eric Holm noted with satisfaction that Afrikaner youth had responded with anger to Smuts's policies;[58] for instance, on 10 October 1939, the birthday of Paul Kruger, children had refused to go to school and British flags had been burned.[59] Zeesen capitalized on this seething resentment to incite its listeners to still greater acts of disobedience. According to Hans Strydom's account of the later Nazi coup plotted by Robey Leibbrandt (see chapter 6), it provided weekly lessons in how to commit sabotage.[60] One Zeesen broadcast argued: "Everyone who allows a crime, is guilty of that crime and therefore it is the duty of every Afrikaner to oppose with all in his power the person and that power which drag our people into the abyss while he still has the least bit of energy to do so."[61]

Holm was careful in his station's broadcasts to keep to a minimum references to the glorification of Nazi Germany. His intended audience were ordinary Afrikaner nationalists who were not necessarily national socialists.

The National Party in the Climate of Subversion

Nor did committed Afrikaner nationalists have to be extremists to be encouraged by Holm's message. Even more cautious Cape National Party leaders, relative moderates like Karl Bremer, one of Malan's most trusted friends, could sense that a Nationalist victory would come with a victory of Germany overseas, as is evident in a speech in which Bremer declared to applause at a party meeting in Cape Town: "We must prepare our volk. It means an intensive education of the whole population. The future lies in our hands and it will demand the greatest sacrifice.

The Afrikaner volk will be prepared to make that sacrifice and it has the brains to do it."[62]

The spirit of hope, indeed of incitement, was encouraged even by the usually cautious Malan, who, in late 1940 at a giant gathering at Darling in the Western Cape to celebrate the 1838 Boer victory over the Zulu at Blood River, devoted most of his speech to the heroism of the Cape Afrikaner rebels of the Anglo-Boer War. Using much stronger language than usual, he declared that the names of Cecil Rhodes, Joseph Chamberlain, and Alfred Milner, all noted proponents of British imperialism in South Africa at the turn of the century, would always be "a swear word" (*vloekwoord*) for the volk, since these three had, he alleged, been responsible for executing thirty-three brave rebels.[63]

The Transvaal Nationalists typically went much further. At their 1940 congress they decided that once the party had come to power those members of Parliament who had voted for war on 4 September would be declared by legislation to be unfit to take their seats.[64] General Kemp, the ex-Hertzogite co-leader of the Reunited National Party in the Transvaal, underlined this increasingly revolutionary tendency with a statement to the congress that he wanted to have nothing more to do with "our present democracy." He stated that this system would have to be improved, with only the "settled section" of the white population (presumably excluding Jewish and recent British immigrants) ruling the nation. His system would follow Boer hero Paul Kruger's oligarchic nineteenth-century Transvaal republic (he did not elaborate on this point). The followers of Smuts, he said, would be forced to pay for the war.[65]

Kemp consistently showed how little distance existed between extremists among Hertzog's and Malan's followers, now reunited in one party as before the Fusion of 1934. Only months before, for example, at a meeting of Malanites and Hertzogites just prior to their formal reunion in 1940, Kemp had advocated six months' forced labor for all black Africans aged fifteen to sixty. Forced labor was, of course, nothing new in the colonies to the north, such as the Belgian Congo, French Equatorial Africa, and Angola and Mozambique, but for black South Africans who had long labored under multiple legal indignities and restrictions, such a proposal was explosive. For all that, the meeting approved this proposal.[66]

The war had brought to the surface currents of Afrikaner nationalist politics that had been seething over the previous decade but had remained submerged by the need to make Fusion work and by the division of militant Afrikaners into the Hertzog and Malan camps. The coming of war had destroyed Fusion, reunited the divided Afrikaner nationalist forces of Hertzog and Malan, and provided militants on the Far Right with a golden opportunity to further their own separate political program.

As one Ally after another fell in Europe, only Britain stood between the nationalists and their most cherished dream, a truly Afrikaner republic wholly independent of their old enemy. Berlin, clearly recognizing the predicament of the Smuts government, made the most of the situation by encouraging a climate of subversion among Afrikaner nationalists and blacks (less successfully in the latter case, given the lack of substantial black pro-Nazi activity). This problem would become much more serious with the dramatic growth of the largest pro-fascist Afrikaner group in South African history, the Ossewabrandwag.

Chapter Six

The Rise of the Ossewabrandwag and the Specter of Revolution

The Threat of the Ossewabrandwag

During the early war years there was a general sense among many Afrikaner nationalists that history was at long last about to favor them with a new republican golden age. Some moderate Nationalists were satisfied to wait until a German victory brought about the downfall of the Smuts government. Many more militant Afrikaners worked actively to hasten this process.

Certain developments pointed clearly to direct connections between the Nazis and the more radical Afrikaner nationalists. Bruno Stiller, the German counsellor at the Pretoria legation before the war, carefully developed close ties with the anti-Semitic Blackshirts and Greyshirts, and also with the much larger and more promising paramilitary Ossewabrandwag (Oxwagon Guard or OB), the child of the Great Trek centenary.[1] Wartime conditions, in which so many Afrikaners felt deeply alienated from the pro-war government and also saw Nazi success as an opportunity for furthering nationalist goals, provided an environment in which the untranationalist Ossewabrandwag could flourish and grow to become the single most visible threat to Smuts and the pro-war cause. As a Nazi victory began to appear not only possible but even probable, the atmosphere of antigovernment violence and revolutionary sentiment became increasingly widespread among Afrikaner nationalists, including many outside the Ossewabrandwag. The National Party was faced with a particularly difficult challenge. The enthusiasm and disciplined organization of the OB could help to realize the Nationalist political program but, at the same time, its rise began to pose a new threat to mainstream Afrikaner nationalism, now from the right.

First under Colonel J. C. Laas and then from 1941 under the dynamic former Afrikaanse Nasionale Studentebond president, J. F. J. ("Hans") van Rensburg, the Ossewabrandwag grew into a strong organization, with its paramilitary wing and later also groups devoted to promoting volk service in diverse areas such as religion, race relations, and "volk health."[2]

One of its great strengths was the backing of the Broederbond, even during times of tension and hostility between the Ossewabrandwag and the National Party. In March 1941, for instance, Van Rensburg was even invited to attend meetings of the Broederbond Executive Council in an advisory capacity.[3] Until conflicts over leadership and policy details led to a rift between the party and the Ossewabrandwag, Malan also provided valuable support, maintaining that all OB members were also members of the National Party, since both were needed by the Afrikaner volk, supplementing each other in the cultural and political spheres respectively.[4] Van Rensburg was so highly regarded by sections of the National Party that ten days after his retirement as administrator of the Orange Free State, he was asked, on 10 January 1941, to stand as the Nationalist candidate in Fauresmith.[5] He politely declined. He had other, bigger plans.

The Ossewabrandwag soon became much more than the merely "cultural" organization that had been its original mandate, especially under its second commandant-general, Van Rensburg, who billed himself as the "Leader of Disciplined Afrikanerdom." Van Rensburg supported an authoritarian state, explaining in an address to the Afrikaanse Nasionale Studentebond in Stellenbosch on 24 February, 1941:

It is not we who are the fifth columnists of a foreign power, not of Germany and certainly equally not of England. . . . No, if that is democracy, then we say we are sick and tired of democracy. But they say '*de mortuis nihil nisi bonum*.' Of the dead one should only speak well. And if democracy is not yet dead, it is in any case well on the way [*vinnig op die pad*].

And the irony of that is that it is precisely its pretended champions who are strangling it today. . . . And if they think that we are going to later try to revive it again whenever the wheel turns, then they think incorrectly. On the contrary, we are just going to bury it, and that without wailing and singing. And with it will be buried capitalist imperialism and its disasters. . . . They do not need to accuse us of being opposed to capitalistic democracy [*kapitalistiese demokrasie*]. It is not an accusation but rather an honor.[6]

In his inaugural oath, which illustrated his unique blend of Afrikaner nationalism and European quasi-fascism, he declared before a crowd of five thousand at Kroonstad in the Orange Free State:

I swear loyalty to the national morals and traditions of our Diets-Afrikaans [*sic*] volk connection and to South Africa as my only home and fatherland. I will always with my whole soul and all my powers alone, as well as in cooperation with my fellow-Afrikaner, struggle faithfully and to the full for the maintenance and expansion of an own, independent Diets-Afrikaans volk existence, of the Afrikaans language and the religion and church of our fathers.[7]

The oath was rooted in the best traditions of old-fashioned Malanite Afrikaner nationalism, ethnically based and enshrouded in religious language. But Van Rensburg's allusions to a Diets-Afrikaanse volk belonged to a much more distant past, a reference not only to his own people but to *all* the Dutch, Flemings, and Afrikaners in the broadest sense, an anachronistic usage from medieval times.[8]

The outspokenly fascist Flemish organization in Belgium, the Verdinaso (an acronym for "League of Netherlands National Solidarists"), had used the same unusual term in the late thirties in advocating a Dietsch Volk state to reunite Flanders and the Netherlands,[9] and like the Verdinaso, Van Rensburg and the Ossewabrandwag looked to Romantic nationalism. That same German-influenced nationalism had inspired the neo-Fichteans in the Studentebond.[10]

The Ossewabrandwag was in the mainstream tradition of fascist movements overseas, glorifying and romanticizing achievements of the remote past with a view to building a radically new future. Yet Van Rensburg himself was at first careful in public to hedge the issue of his support for National Socialism. Questioned in October 1941 on the subject at an OB meeting, he pointed out that no less an authority than Potchefstroom professor L. J. du Plessis, the intellectual godfather of radical Afrikaner nationalism, had said that even the National Party was becoming "National Socialist," indicating how loose the term had become. Van Rensburg had no desire to turn Afrikaners into Germans, he said; when specifically asked if he had ever publicly declared himself to be a National Socialist, he replied, according to the minutes of this meeting, that "on no occasion of which he was aware had he ever publicly [*nog nooit in die openbaar*] made such a declaration, especially at any Ossewabrandwag event." He indicated only that he supported a "Christian National Republic."[11]

Van Rensburg was nonetheless a committed supporter of the German National Socialist state. According to a 1946 South African police report, based on an affidavit by the wartime chief Nazi agent in South Africa, Luitpold Werz, German agents worked under Van Rensburg's protection with the active assistance of Ossewabrandwag members.[12] A report of November 1940 from a Nazi agent named Trompke to Foreign Office headquarters in Berlin indicates that he offered Nazi Germany his approximately 170,000 members to stage a coup, provided they supplied German weapons. Van Rensburg wanted to go to Mozambique, or preferably to Germany, to make arrangements. In return for providing Germany with naval and air bases, South Africa under this plan would get Southern Rhodesia (later Zimbabwe) and the three British protectorates (modern Botswana, Lesotho, and Swaziland).[13] According to German intelligence, Van Rensburg saw "himself as a bridge between his own people and the German people."[14] Werz elaborated on Van Rensburg's 1940 coup plan in his 1946 affidavit. The scheme was on a grandiose scale. Van Rensburg offered to place at Hitler's disposal, in addition to the ordinary members of the Ossewabrandwag, some 15,000 soldiers who had not taken the "Africa Oath" required of volunteers for service against the Axis outside South Africa. Van Rensburg suggested that weapons either be landed by boat off South-West Africa ("West Plan") or on an airstrip in Southern Rhodesia ("North Plan"). The more developed North Plan seems to have been his preference. According to a message from the Ossewabrandwag to Werz in Lourenço Marques, cited in Werz's affidavit, Van Rensburg proposed sabotage against transportation and communication systems.

At an hour to be determined by the German High Command, Afrikaners would then blow up all road and rail bridges connecting the Transvaal with Natal. The railway personnel, the Police and 26 000 mine workers and employees have been penetrated as the rest of the State services with Ossewabrandwag members and would go on strike. The latter, viz. mineworkers and employees, are already today urging for a strike. English newspapers are going to be blown up. Smuts and his followers are going to be asked to kill themselves. Further dispositions are left to the German General Staff.[15]

The plan, which according to Werz had first been presented to Berlin in a telegram from his Lourenço Marques office on 6 August 1940, did not materialize, probably because of difficulties in getting sufficient arms to the Ossewabrandwag.[16] As Werz notes in his affidavit, the group had very limited quantities of guns, because members had been forced to surrender to the government some eight thousand rifles, and at the time that this plan was proposed to Werz had only enough ammunition for a week's fighting.[17] In consequence, and perhaps because of the reluctance of much of the grass-roots membership to take up arms, especially as Malan grew estranged from the organization over strategy and over the leadership of the Afrikaner nationalist movement during late 1940 and early 1941 (discussed in chapter 7), real civil war did not occur. Still, a war of nerves and individual acts of sabotage were instigated by an extremist group within the Ossewabrandwag, the Stormjaers (storm troopers), whose leader was none other than Van Rensburg himself.[18]

In the southern Transvaal town of Vereeniging, for instance, the high-tension lines from the town's power station to the mines in the Witwatersrand region were blown up on the night of 29 January 1942. In the next few months attempts were made by the Stormjaers to blow up a power station at Delmas, south of Pretoria; telephone wires were cut at numerous points in the Transvaal, the Orange Free State, and the northwestern Cape, and telephone poles were often destroyed as well. The main electric cable system in the Transvaal town of Krugersdorp was damaged by an explosion, and electric power pylons were blown up in several towns, among them, Delmas and Potchefstroom. On 1 February 1942 a bomb damaged the Johannesburg offices of the black-oriented newspaper *Bantu World,* and at about the same time another bomb wrecked a corner café in Brixton, a Johannesburg inner suburb.[19]

George Visser, who as a police officer investigated many of these incidents, has stated in his book *OB: Traitors or Patriots?* that these acts were supplemented and in part funded by a series of bank robberies, the proceeds of which also helped to assist families of interned Ossewabrandwag members suspected of subversion: "A Stormjaer source stated in 1946 that it was estimated that during the war they had 'collected' about 200 000 Pounds in holdups and burglaries."[20] But, despite the wide range of Stormjaer subversive activities, it is notable that, as Visser points out, in only one case, a bomb explosion at the Benoni post office near Johannesburg that killed a passerby, did such an act involve the spilling of innocent blood.[21]

Van Rensburg was so confident of a German victory as late as mid-1942 that he openly boasted to Leo Marquard, who was to become a Liberal Party activist in the fifties, of the vast scope of OB membership and of his involvement in assisting German U-boats in sinking passing Allied ships. Marquard does not indicate in his notes recording this conversation how he responded, or even whether he did so, though he comments that Van Rensburg was obviously unaware that he worked for military intelligence![22] Extraordinarily, despite his indiscretion, Van Rensburg remained a free man.

An Upsurge of Violence

The Ossewabrandwag was a South African symptom of a universal tendency in the thirties and forties to distrust professional politicians and parliaments, as was expressed in the varieties of fascism and semifascism in Europe and Latin America. The program Van Rensburg offered included uniforms, rallies, a policy of strident nationalism, and a strong, incorruptible leader to stand above the fray of party politics.[23]

The militarism and violence associated with elements of the Ossewabrandwag was part of a much more broadly based willingness among many Afrikaner nationalists to use force against "un-national" individuals or movements. Jews had been the first targets; as the war progressed, other targets were found. The home of J. H. Hofmeyr, the one outspoken liberal in the Smuts cabinet, was attacked, in May 1942, with a homemade incendiary bomb. The bomb was placed by an unknown assailant on the verandah outside a first-floor bedroom, but the fuse went out just before it reached the flammable material.[24]

Two brothers who were Nationalist members of Parliament, Jan and Jakob Wilkens, violently disrupted a United Party *braaivleis* (barbecue) evening in Klerksdorp in the Western Transvaal on 10 January 1941. They led a crowd of some twelve hundred Nationalist supporters in an invasion of this strictly private meeting, and when Harry Lawrence, the minister of the interior, the person in charge of internal security, refused to let them take over the meeting, he was severely beaten.[25]

By 1942 the climate of political violence in the Union had in some respects begun to resemble besieged societies like the later Weimar Republic or Italy before Mussolini's 1922 March on Rome. Paramilitary movements, like the Ossewabrandwag and the Stormjaers, and secret saboteurs operated across the country.[26] Using wartime emergency regulations, Smuts was forced to intern at centers such as Koffiefontein in the northern Cape several hundred people suspected of subversion. Among the South Africans interned were two Ossewabrandwag generals, Hendrik van den Bergh, the future head of the feared Bureau of State Security (BOSS), and Balthasar Johannes ("John") Vorster, who rose to become prime minister from 1966 to 1978 and then state president.[27] Most male German nationals had been interned at the beginning of the war in separate camps, but special categories such as missionaries were usually left undisturbed.

Smuts had long been burdened with the legacy of his past tough stand against Afrikaner dissidents, as in the 1914 Rebellion or the 1922 miners' revolt. It is difficult to understand the motive for his changed methods, but this perhaps explains why he took a much more patient approach this time, unwilling to create the number of new martyrs necessary to crush his militant opponents. He may also have felt that, despite widespread Afrikaner disaffection, he still had a majority of ordinary citizens' support, since so many Afrikaners (some perhaps attracted by the need of a job) had volunteered for service against the Axis forces, fighting alongside their English-speaking compatriots. Despite Smuts's apparent hesitancy to take decisive action against groups like the Ossewabrandwag, many Nationalists viewed the steady trickle of internments, the censorship of mail, and other emergency measures as outright tyranny. For them, the wartime government appeared to have realized the worst aspects of a Jew- and jingo-dominated "un-national" regime. This sense of oppression, combined with the widespread belief that a Hitler victory was imminent, led many Nationalists to use language that was more than extraordinarily daring; in most countries in time of war these speeches would have been considered treasonable.

The Nationalist member of Parliament for Harrismith, E. R. Strauss, gave the Assembly this picture of the fate awaiting Smuts and his agents of repression: "It is a scandal. No, scandal is too good a word, but there is an end to everything, the people are waiting their time, and when organized Afrikanerdom take action, it will take definite action. . . . The Afrikaner people will take vengeance, and there will be a grudge in their hearts when they do so."[28] When a government member of Parliament asked sarcastically whether the Nationalists intended to hang their opponents, Strauss responded with grim solemnity: "I feel convinced that it will possibly be necessary to put up against the wall those who are responsible for the persecution and oppression of today, when the time comes, in order to put an end forever to that oppression."[29]

The threat of violence had become an acceptable way to express right-wing opposition to the embattled Smuts government, even in the most dignified forum in the land. Nationalists did not have to be Nazis to see Hitler as an uninvited but welcome savior who had created the circumstances by which to avenge the Anglo-Boer War and a century of British tyranny. Victory seemed in the air, and some, at least, could not contain themselves at the prospect of turning the tables on Smuts and his cohorts.

Robey Leibbrandt and Operation Weissdorn

Berlin, recognizing this potential, decided to attempt a win-or-lose venture to topple Smuts and produce a pro-Nazi state in southern Africa. The plot came extraordinarily close to success. Known as "Operation Weissdorn," it centered on a South African former Olympic boxer and sometime German paratrooper and secret agent, Robey Leibbrandt.[30] Leibbrandt was landed near a remote spot off the Atlantic coast by a German yacht in June 1941, assigned to assassinate Smuts and stage a coup with the help of the most militant Stormjaers, whom Leibbrandt called the "National Socialist Rebels."[31] Leibbrandt's followers in the Stormjaers were extremists opposed even to the Ossewabrandwag leadership which they considered unreliable. Malan's ostensibly constitutionalist Nationalists, who for their part, were rapidly becoming estranged from the Ossewabrandwag during 1941 over the issue of maintaining a multiparty framework for South Africa, were, of course, completely outside the pale, in the view of such ultrarightists.[32]

The Ossewabrandwag leadership, increasingly suspect among militant ordinary members because its chief, Van Rensburg, had not been interned, decided that Leibbrandt's impulsive fanaticism and lack of adequate planning could only hurt its cause, especially if his scheme ended in disaster. As it happens, Leibbrandt planned to execute not only Smuts's associates but also Malan, Van Rensburg, and any other possible rivals.[33] Like Hitler, Leibbrandt could not abide even right-wing competition.

It is not clear whether Van Rensburg was aware of these plans, but, according to Hans Strydom, the author of the only substantial study of the Leibbrandt affair, Van Rensburg feared that Leibbrandt would be caught, forcing Smuts's hand against the commandant-general before his waiting game in expectation of a Nazi victory could pay off. There were also rumors that the Nazis favored Leibbrandt over Van Rensburg or Malan as South Africa's future Führer.[34] Van Rensburg disclosed Leibbrandt's presence, although not his location, to the Smuts government, sending his Transvaal leader, Pat Jerling, to pass on the information verbally to Interior Minister Harry Lawrence. Since, as Strydom notes, Jerling was considered less than totally reliable by other Ossewabrandwag members, nobody would be too surprised if his role in this affair was discovered, and Van Rensburg's position as leader would not be seriously harmed.[35]

Smuts acted quickly by using one of the few policemen he felt he could trust, Jan Taillard, who in the opening stages of the war had been instructed to make a show of resigning his commission in the South African Police on the grounds of his supposed opposition to participation in the war. Taillard, it was hoped, would then be suitable for covert counterinsurgency operations at whatever point the Smuts government judged appropriate. Taillard willingly took on the dangerous role of gaining Leibbrandt's confidence and, as he explained in a memorandum to Lawrence, persuaded Leibbrandt to ride with him in his car along the main Johannesburg-Pretoria road on Christmas Eve 1941. Taillard used the pretext that Leibbrandt needed to take a short break that evening from his strenuous activities in planning his coup attempt. The police and army had been alerted earlier that Taillard would propose this route, and Leibbrandt rode unsuspectingly into the well-laid trap.[36]

Following a public trial before three judges of the Pretoria Supreme Court, throughout which Leibbrandt refused to give any evidence, he was convicted of treason and sentenced to death, but Smuts commuted the sentence to life imprisonment, on sentimental grounds, arguing that he could not execute the son of a man who had fought alongside him in the Boer War: "How can I hang the son of such a brave Boer warrior?"[37] In the end, in fact, Leibbrandt spent only a few years in prison. A month after the Nationalists' surprise victory in the 1948 general election, Leibbrandt and the Zeesen announcer Holm, who was also serving a life sentence, were freed. Indeed, the new government was apparently so determined to release them that it did not follow the legal procedure of obtaining the prior assent of the governor-general, Brand van Zyl, who privately expressed great displeasure at such an action.[38] Such haste would seem to reflect something of the Nationalists' basic sympathies during the war.

Grass-Roots Support for Subversion

One of the principal reasons for Smuts's caution in tracking down Leibbrandt was the Ossewabrandwag's deep penetration of the security forces. Already in May 1939 G. W. Wessels, a Smuts loyalist in the rural Orange Free State town of Boshof,

J. C. (Jan) Smuts, 1936. King George VI made Smuts a field marshal for his service to the Empire. Smuts had been a cabinet minister from 1910 to 1919; he served as South African Party prime minister from 1919 to 1924, and as deputy prime minister under Hertzog (1933–1939). He headed a United Party-led coalition from 1939 to 1948 and was a key figure in the founding of the United Nations.

From the Cape Times *Collection in the South African Library*

Cabinet with the Prime Minister, General J. C. Smuts, and the Governor-General, Sir Patrick Duncan, c. 1939. Front (left to right): J. H. (Jan) Hofmeyr, Smuts, Duncan, Denys Reitz, Richard Stuttaford, W. R. Collins; back: C. F. (Colin) Steyn, H. G. (Harry) Lawrence, Senator A. M. Conroy, P. G. V. (Piet) van der Byl, F. C. Sturrock, Senator C. F. Clarkson, C. F. (Charles) Stallard, W. B. Madeley.

As Hertzog's interior minister, Stuttaford introduced legislation to curb Jewish immigration from Germany. Duncan, as Smuts's interior minister in the early twenties, also tried to limit Jewish immigration; as governor-general (1937–1943) he prevented a new election, leading to Smuts's forming a pro-war and pro-Allied government. As wartime interior minister, Lawrence was in charge of internal security. Hofmeyr, Smuts's top lieutenant and the one outspoken liberal in the cabinet, was a champion of Jewish civil rights and a target of rightwing violence; he was widely blamed for the 1948 Nationalist victory.

From the Cape Times *Collection in the South African Library*

had written to Smuts about the threat of subversion in the defense force, which he said existed up to the highest echelons.[39]

Such reports began to multiply after the outbreak of war, at
a time when the reliability of the security forces had become
doubly important. In March 1940 Smuts was warned that perhaps 80 percent of the officers at army headquarters were antiwar
Nationalists, posing the threat of a repeat of the 1914 Rebellion.[40] Much of the police force was said to be of a similar
disposition. The Ossewabrandwag seems to have had so many
members in the police and also on the railways that it was decided to organize these members as separate units from the regular Ossewabrandwag structure.[41] Apart from the many who
joined in the Witwatersrand regions of the Transvaal alone, at
least 320 officers and constables belonged to the Stormjaers, leading to the spectacle of mass arrests of policemen during special
police parades in towns in the district on 20 January 1942.[42]
The threat such involvement posed to internal security cannot
be underestimated, especially considering the commitment of the
Stormjaers to violence in order to achieve their political objectives.

Nor was this all. In the early months of the war, in February
1940, according to one of Smuts's intelligence officers, Colonel
B. C. Judd, in a memorandum to Louis Esselen, reliable agents in
the Orange Free State had reported that a plan was afoot to
subvert the military still more thoroughly. Malan's supporters
were supposed to be going to join the part-time Active Citizen
Force and the District Rifle Associations. The aim of this scheme
was to be equipped with arms and organized to stage a coup
should conscription be introduced in the war against Hitler.[43]

Such reports were not the products of an intelligence officer's
wild imagination. In the northern Transvaal town of Potgieters-
rust, by mid-1940 only a quarter of the men of the Botha Regiment had taken the voluntary Africa Oath, swearing to serve
against the Axis anywhere on the continent.[44] Detailed intelligence reports showed that antigovernment and pro-Nazi sentiment was rife in the ranks of the military. Half of the Orange
Free State's Thaba Nchu Commando, for instance, were considered disloyal; the unreliability of the majority of the officers of
the Dordrecht Commando in the northeastern Cape led to a

recommendation by military intelligence that it be disbanded.[45] A secret contemporary report on individuals in the defense force includes comments such as "Admirer of Hitler," "Pro-Nazi," and "Alleges that he with others in the Air Force are in league to take action against the Government at a sign from a leader." According to this report, a major in the air force and a major of the Command Training Depot were, for example, described as having expressed "political sentiments hostile to Government," and a lieutenant of the Special Services Battalion in Pretoria, who was described as "able to influence young officers," was alleged to have said in the mess that he believed Zeesen radio "before Daventry [BBC] any day." Another lieutenant was described as having presided at meetings of an Ossewabrandwag cell in the air force, and a corporal of the command staff in Durban was said to have "Nazi leanings" and to have visited German boats in Durban before the outbreak of war. A major, commandant of a commando unit in the eastern Cape, was considered "violently anti-British," while a captain of the District Rifle Association South East Command in Pretoria was alleged "to have offered for sale ammunition he had in his possession, and also to have stated that in no circumstances would he lift a rifle in support of the Government. He stated that if conscription were enforced, there would be a revolution in South Africa." There were many more descriptions of individual officers and noncommissioned officers along similar lines.[46]

Not only the security establishment but the schools had been seriously influenced by pro-Axis opinion. The reports of the government censor in the early war years showed widespread penetration of Afrikaner schools by pro-Nazi sentiment among both teachers and students.[47] The long-term effects of this on the Afrikaner youth cannot be underestimated. At the Brakpan Commando School, for instance, lessons were opened with the Nazi salute rendered by teachers and pupils. The assistant headmaster of a school near Nylstroom arranged for the school radio to be tuned continuously into Zeesen Radio; he told the children that the only truth about the war came from that source. He also made a point of giving the Nazi salute when entering a Jewish store in a neighboring town.[48]

Despite continual charges of pro-Nazi activity in schools, especially in the Transvaal, the executive committee of the Transvaal dismissed all such allegations as baseless.[49] This may seem surprising, considering that the Provincial Council itself was dominated by the United Party, and that the Provincial executive was made up of members of the majority party in the council. But there is a simple explanation, apart from the obvious one of reluctance to admit to negligence in the supervision of schools: the provincial education department had to use school inspectors to investigate all charges, and these inspectors, uniformly senior teachers, were, many of them, as anti-British as their subordinates.[50] Schoolteachers formed one of the principal occupational groups in the Broederbond, which had its deepest roots in the Transvaal.[51]

The power of Nazi propaganda in influencing Afrikaans-speaking teachers was best illustrated by the response of the pupils. Pupils were candid; in their naiveté they spoke with a directness and honesty of expression it would have been rare to find among their more cautious elders. One pupil wrote in an article in his school magazine:

We few Afrikaners in South Africa . . . could well do with a man like Hitler for six months; then there would be a change. Hitler is a man of iron like Paul Kruger who can build a nation in the right way. If you listen to his speeches, even though you cannot understand them, then you can immediately hear and appreciate that he is a statesman in a thousand. . . . England is strong! True! But Germany. Hitler may not be a pillar of religion, but for building up a nation he is a man in a thousand. Heil Hitler![52]

There may have been more of this sort of thing in the same school magazine, since, according to Johannesburg's *Rand Daily Mail,* once the outcry over pro-Nazi activity in the schools had hit the headlines, three pages from that issue mysteriously disappeared from every copy to which the public had access.[53]

There is abundant evidence that many teachers were straying rather far from the official syllabi. When interested outsiders questioned students at some schools in the Witwatersrand area, they received unusual replies about questions such as which people in history had stood up for liberty. The answers were Paul Kruger, George Washington, Malan—and Adolf Hitler. Francis Drake was identified as a "British pirate," and when the question was put as to whether South African or German history was taught in school, one student replied proudly: "German history has an influence on South African history as all our culture is Aryan, and we and the Germans are the only Aryans."[54]

Such ideas not only reaffirmed the German-inspired Romantic nationalist philosophy of Afrikaanse Nasionale Studentebond leaders like Meyer and Diederichs, but went far beyond the teachings of the neo-Fichteans. Diederichs's hopes for Afrikaner youth were being fully realized, and on a scale and with an explicitly pro-Nazi coloring that would have seemed improbable just a few years before.

Even in the traditionally more moderate Cape, grass-roots support for the German cause was so all-embracing in some areas that by the end of 1940 most of the whites in towns like Touws River, in the arid Karoo, and Lamberts Bay, on the west coast, had gone over to the Ossewabrandwag. The local police were considered so unreliable that the few government loyalists in these centers dared not report incidents to them.[55] It is not without significance that small towns of the Cape such as these were the oldest and most loyal base of Malanite nationalism.

Ordinary Afrikaners with no intellectual pretensions had been exposed for so many years to so much anti-British Romantic nationalist sentiment, not to mention constant reports, after 1933, of the wonders achieved by the new Germany, that it was entirely understandable how wartime conditions allowed the eruption and channeling of all these forces. Simple folk in the rural areas and urban intellectuals like Diederichs and Meyer were both influenced by these developments.

A striking example of the pervasiveness of this influence is an extraordinary letter written only a few months before the war by a private citizen of Ladybrand in the eastern Orange Free State to no less a person than Adolf Hitler himself. A copy of this letter found its way into captured German Foreign Office records. The letter writer told the Führer most Afrikaners opposed British foreign policy, and she assured him of her people's solidarity with the German cause:

If war broke out again, our men and boys have decided rather to go sit in prison. Even the Government men and boys would refuse to fight against Germany. You must not forget that at least 80% of our volk

An Ossewabrandwag rally during the Second World War. Behind the band is the OB banner with an ox-wagon wheel, symbol of the Afrikaner pioneers, surmounted by an eagle. The eagle reflects European fascist influence; it was not part of Afrikaner iconography. The Afrikaans motto reads: "My God, My Land, My People."
From the OB Collection, Cullen Library

Ossewabrandwag members drill at a wartime rally. No weapons are visible, since Prime Minister Smuts had officially disarmed the rural militia at the war's outset, but, privately, many OB members had access to firearms and explosives.
From the OB Collection, Cullen Library

is against the Government. We pray and hope that in the near future the Nationalists will still come to control our country. And that we will have the power to drive out of South Africa the rascally and filthy Jews. Like you did. I wish you all health and blessing for the future, for you and your volk. Heil Hitler.[56]

Subversion and the Politicians

In the heady atmosphere of 1939–1941, some unlikely individuals began to toy with the idea of a rightist revolution. These could include people previously considered moderates. The most striking case was General Hertzog himself, the leader of Reunited Afrikanerdom.

Hertzog's defense of English-speakers' rights had early on alienated militants in the Reunited National Party, including both conservative hard-liners like Strijdom and younger radicals like Verwoerd and C. R. Swart, the Orange Free State advocate, who was for a while deputy chairman of the Ossewabrandwag Great Council.[57] In late 1940 the embittered ex–prime minister left the Orange Free State congress of the party in disgust when it refused to support him on the question of equal rights for both language groups. He resigned as party leader and temporarily retired into the political wings. But within months Hertzog was to perform a stunning political turnaround that seemed to contradict everything he stood for. Angered at being outmaneuvered by the machinations of politicians, he turned to a model he had long quietly admired: Hitler's Germany. In October 1941 he issued a statement to the press in which he excoriated "liberal capitalism" and the multiparty system, praising, in contrast, National Socialism as reflecting the traditions of the Afrikaner, a system that, he argued, could only be adapted to South African needs by a dictator.[58] "National socialism," he continued, "as concerns its essence [*wese*], is not exclusively the creation or curious outgrowth [*eienaardige groeisel*] of any particular land or people. It is a plant which owes its origin to certain circumstances and certain requirements and needs in state life; and where all the necessary circumstances, requirements, and needs exist, it will be valid [*laat geld*]—whether it is in Germany or in South Africa, does not matter."

He went on:

Today in South Africa the discussions about national socialism . . . are generally paired with [*pleeg gepaard to gaan met*] another question which is closely related. . . . I mean the question of granting special powers to the governing person, or persons, by whom the appropriate form [*geskikte vorm*] of national socialism will have to be introduced, or applied and administered as a governing measure [*regeringsmaatreel*]; namely, the so-called dictatorship.

It is not necessary for me to go into the merits of this issue with you. It is sufficient to point out that the circumstances of the war and still more the circumstances under which peace will eventually be concluded, will necessarily and frankly unavoidably bring about the granting of dictatorial powers for a shorter or longer period to the person to whom the leadership of the state is entrusted. Therefore to quibble now about the question of whether at the conclusion of peace, democracy or dictatorship will be victorious, seems to me to be a waste of time which could be used more valuably.[59]

In the wake of Hertzog's shift, Van Rensburg and Weichardt, among others, immediately scrambled to reunite the various anti-war factions, by now hopelessly divided by personality and tactical differences. The Ossewabrandwag sent out a circular enclosing a letter from Hertzog expressing support for Van Rensburg's political direction: ". . . I have with the fullest agreement learned of his viewpoint in regard to our decadent democratic party system and the absolute necessity of the installation of a new state order through which the interests of the volk will be made more and those of the party and party leaders less of a special object of state concern and striving, than what is today the case in our democratic paradise."[60]

Weichardt, the best-known South African anti-Jewish activist of the thirties, resurfaced now in the hope of using Hertzog's name to political advantage. In November 1940 he had announced the reorganization of his Greyshirt movement as the South African National Socialist Union, supporting Oswald Pirow, the most outspokenly pro-Nazi figure in the National Party at that time. Weichardt had promised his followers' support for the party at election time.[61] Weichardt responded with political agility to Herzog's announcement several months later, and to the suggestion of his deputy, Isak le Grange, that he obtain Hertzog's support for a "National Socialist Volk Front" under the leadership of a triumvirate (presumably Weichardt, Hertzog, and Pirow, whose radical supporters had fallen into disfavor with

Malan). Hertzog would be the patron of this movement and the proposed future head of state.[62]

Hertzog responded with noncommittal interest to their overtures. Weichardt offered himself as an "honest broker" between the various nationalist factions, and early in 1942 he decided to appeal to Malan, Pirow, Van Rensburg, and E. A. Conroy (leader of the moderate Hertzogites who had left the National Party in sympathy with the general to form the Afrikaner Party).[63]

According to Weichardt's own papers, in an undated draft letter written around March 1942 he planned to ask for joint cooperation by these politicians in the face of the growing "totalitarianism" of Smuts's government:

In these circumstances I feel called, as a leader of a volk movement which has already been busy preparing the Afrikaner volk for eight years for the choice of National Socialism, on the one hand to energetically continue my work in my own circles [in eie kring] and on the other hand in the general interest to cooperate with all my opponents in the ranks of nationalist Afrikanerdom for the preservation [behoud] of our volk in every area where cooperation would not be in conflict with the principles of the South African National Socialist Union (Greyshirts).[64]

The politicians and would-be politicians failed yet again to reach agreement. But the underlying weaknesses of the right did not bring confidence to Smuts, who once again was despairing as Germany, joined now by Japan, won victory after victory. He had become convinced by late 1941 that his internal situation remained equally grave, and that all that remained to divide his enemies were personality differences.[65] There was still real government concern about the gravity of the situation. As late as August 1942 United Party secretary Louis Esselen still believed that Malan's old rival and recent convert to National Socialism, General Hertzog, was just waiting to be proclaimed savior of the volk once the war was lost.[66]

The possibility of an Axis victory was less certain in 1942 after Axis defeats at Stalingrad, El Alamein, and Midway, and, partly because of Hertzog's declining health, Smuts's position at home improved. The old general, the one man who might have been able to unite the right, died in November 1942. Without Hertzog, the Afrikaner nationalists fell once again into internecine feuding. Malan's Nationalists and the Ossewabrandwag, who could never agree on a program, accused each other of trespassing on their agreed-upon areas of jurisdiction, politics for the Nationalists and the ill-defined domain of "culture" for the OB.[67] Personality differences came to the fore again as Strijdom and Kemp, the party leaders in the Transvaal, charged the Ossewabrandwag with deliberately excluding top Nationalists in the OB from its senior positions.[68]

Weichardt could persuade no one to accept him as future Führer even under Hertzog's patronage, and without Hertzog to play Hindenburg to Weichardt's Hitler, the Greyshirt leader was out in the cold until, in late 1944, Smuts ran out of patience with Weichardt's propagation of National Socialism and had him interned.[69]

Malan, in turn, was unwilling to be replaced as the leader of Afrikanerdom, least of all by somebody lacking Hertzog's stature. Unlike many of his rivals, he was no newcomer to political life but one of the most experienced politicians in the country. He had long ago learned to tailor his political message to the times, readily moving from one end of the political spectrum to the other. As Harry Lawrence noted wryly in Parliament, Malan had as long ago as the time of the Bolshevik Revolution sharply contradicted his well-known anti-Communist reputation. Since in those days the Nationalists were seriously courting radicalized Afrikaner workers, Malan had felt compelled to state that "Communism in Russia stands for the same things as Nationalism in South Africa."[70] In the same way, by 1942, with the changing fortunes of the Axis, an alliance with the Radical Right was no longer the most strategically sensible path for the National Party.

With all the recurring squabbling on the right, the German Nazis could not agree on whether to support all the antiwar Afrikaner groups or just the currently most promising, the Ossewabrandwag. Yet even the pessimists in Berlin, like Harold Bielfeld at the Foreign Office, who believed it impossible to overthrow Smuts violently, hoped to tie down as many South African troops as possible at home so Smuts could not send them overseas.[71] The attractiveness of the Ossewabrandwag was, however, weakened by the fact that it had begun to threaten Malan's position just as much as Leibbrandt had threatened that of Van

Rensburg. The seasoned tacticians of the National Party were not going to allow this, and they had the background and experience to do something about it.

Furthermore, despite his dallying with authoritarianism, Malan apparently felt repulsed by the personal dictatorship he saw central to Nazism. This is clear from a speech to the Union-wide congress of the National Party on 3 June 1941 in which he stated that national socialism was contrary to the entire direction of Afrikaner history, with its origins in flight from Catholic, and later British, oppression.[72] Nonetheless, Malan made it clear that he did not wish to condemn National Socialism as a symbol for Germany itself:

[The Federal Council of the National Party] accepts that it [National Socialism] has done wonders there especially in reuniting the German people who had fallen into a condition of disintegration and decay in order to uplift them from the depths of humiliation to which the Treaty of Versailles had doomed them. We are also not indicating that we cannot learn anything from National Socialism. On the contrary, we are of the opinion that the anti-capitalism of that system should not be at all strange for our Afrikanerdom, because in our own country we have always been the anti-money power [*anti-geldmag*] and the anti-exploiter party.[73]

Perhaps the most important consideration, however, was that the extremism of the Ossewabrandwag and other ultranationalist organizations threatened to force the hand of the government against the National Party, a prospect made even less appealing as the Nazi juggernaut slowly ground to a halt in the snows of Russia.

Such changing circumstances strengthened Malan's argument that the radicals, by trying to replace the party with other novel organizations, were committing *moedermoord* ("matricide"). The party, as Malan pointed out in the same speech, was the tried and trusted mother of the achievements of Afrikaner nationalism, such as the will to preserve "white civilization." Only by closing ranks around the traditional focus of the Afrikaner right could the volk be saved from utter disintegration.[74]

Malan, distanced from the other more radical Afrikaner political factions, was able gradually, and with some difficulty, eventually to regain control of the direction of the Afrikaner nationalist movement and to consolidate support around the party. The mechanics of this process will be discussed later, but the most important consequence was that he achieved a resounding success in the 1943 general election, assuming the pre-1934 role of Hertzog as the only serious contender for the leadership of nationalist Afrikanerdom. This does not mean that the nationalist movement was yet sufficiently strong to achieve a parliamentary majority.

Although Malan captured a substantial share of the vote, and greatly improved on his position in the 1938 election, Smuts was returned to power with a large majority, drawing support from the entire English-speaking section and from a substantial minority of Afrikaners who remained loyal to Smuts, just as a minority among Afrikaners had supported him in pre-Fusion days. He had also been able to capitalize on the new Allied successes, and Stormjaer violence may have helped to discredit the antiwar parties among the voters, especially among families of soldiers fighting in North Africa and Italy, among whom were thousands of Afrikaners. An election in 1940, 1941, or even 1942 might have produced far fewer Afrikaner votes for the government, but by 1943 the tide had clearly turned against the German military machine. Equally important, the long-term impact of wartime needs had boosted food prices for farmers and temporarily eased white unemployment, and hence disaffection. The infighting in the Afrikaner right also caused many simply to abstain from voting, while numerous new arrivals in the cities, whose economic status may have caused them to have little affection for the ruling party, did not bother to register.[75]

Malan had nevertheless managed to neutralize his right-wing rivals, not one of whom was returned to Parliament.[76] He strengthened his hitherto shaky control of the white opposition and assumed Hertzog's mantle. Indeed, Frederik van Heerden, the leading Nationalist scholar on Afrikaner politics and National Socialism, has described Malan's consolidation of power by 1943 as "the victory of democracy" against his more avowedly authoritarian rivals.[77]

Although Van Heerden's assessment does contain an important kernel of truth, considering Malan's alternatives, it begs the question. Malan's conservative streak had indeed won out over the radicalism of the extreme right. The changing course of the war meant that the power balance was to be decided at the polls in South Africa and not by a violent revolution, which gave Malan the advantage over his professedly antiparliamentary competitors. None of this, however, could be equated with a victory of democratic values.

The entire nationalist movement, despite its many different shades, had been caught up in a wave of extremist and revolutionary hysteria that left no component part unscathed. Almost everyone in the National Party, from outspoken younger radicals like Eric Louw and Hendrik Verwoerd to old-guard conservatives, relative moderates in Nationalist terms, like Karl Bremer and Malan himself, had been affected to some degree by this baptism in the fires of war. For Hitler had, at least for a time, made so much seem possible that had previously been inconceivable for at least another generation.

Chapter Seven

The War and the Internal Transformation of the National Party

Despite the reunification of the Hertzogites and Malanites in early 1940, inside the broad Afrikaner nationalist movement there continued to be important differences in political opinion throughout the war years, and especially in the turbulent period up to 1943. On the left were the moderate Hertzogites, always sensitive to charges of a narrow ethnic-based nationalism, who left the Reunited National Party in sympathy with Hertzog's stand for English-speakers' rights at the end of 1940 to form a small new Afrikaner Party; and on the right were several groups: the huge Ossewabrandwag occupying the middle ground between fascism and the conservative populist nationalism of the Reunited Party; remnants of Weichardt's Greyshirts; and, still within the National Party, Oswald Pirow's pro-fascist New Order group.

After the 1941 rift between the Nationalist establishment and the Radical Right, and despite the Nationalists' growing antipathy toward South African imitations of National Socialism, the impact of the Radical Right was to change mainstream Afrikaner nationalism in a fundamental way. Hertzog's stunning turnaround on National Socialism had been only one particularly dramatic example of just how far this transformation could go.

Unity in Ambiguity: The Reunited National Party and the Radical Right

Early in the war widespread concern arose in the party about the activities of Pirow's New Order, after it took on a separate identity as a distinctive national socialist organization within the party. M. D. C. de Wet Nel, the secretary of the party in the Transvaal, wrote in agitation to a Nationalist member of Parliament, P. J. Bosman, after a tour of the Transvaal, that everywhere their supporters were upset about the disagreement over whether to adopt National Socialism as the party philosophy, as the New Order was advocating. The question was being asked: "Why does Mr. Pirow not discuss the matter with our top Party men and councils? Why the suspicion-sowing against the Party? Why a separate office with separate personnel, separate membership forms and fees? It creates suspicion, it brings further division and undermines our Party."[1]

The nature of De Wet Nel's argument is of particular interest here. His concerns were to be expected from any devoted party officer, yet his reasoning does not suggest ideological problems with the New Order, but rather a concern with party unity. Similar problems had arisen with the Ossewabrandwag, which, although from the start an organization separate from the National Party (unlike the much smaller New Order), had a close understanding with the party in the early years of the war.

In October 1940 Malan managed to persuade the Ossewabrandwag to define the scope of the agreement. Its role was to work for a "Christian National Republic"; to develop the religious, moral and economic life of the volk on the lines of the old Voortrekker principles, while pledging not to tolerate violence or "underground violent revolutionary activities" and not to undermine or prejudice the work of friendly political parties or bodies.[2]

The very nature of this pledge suggested Malan's own early forebodings about the Ossewabrandwag threat to the party, either indirectly through forcing Smuts's hand in the face of potential revolution, or more directly through a younger, more dynamic alternative to the party. The Nationalists and the Ossewabrandwag were necessarily uneasy bedfellows. It was only a matter of time before the advantages of such a pact became outweighed by the disadvantages. An early indicator of trouble was the growing inclination of many Nationalists to refuse to register to vote, on the grounds that the days of electoral politics were over, a view propagated widely in the Ossewabrandwag.[3] The OB caused the loss by a thousand votes of a Northmead

City Council election in a strongly Nationalist Witwatersrand area, when at four-thirty in the afternoon of the election, a time returning workers would be most likely to vote, the Ossewa-brandwag suddenly announced an evening rally, thus keeping many loyal Nationalist OB members away from the polls.[4] The OB ban on its officers serving as party officials made matters worse. Frans Mentz, party organizing secretary in the Witwa-tersrand, complained to Strijdom that outstanding party members who were appointed to OB positions were then compelled to resign from party offices.[5]

This kind of interference and mutual jealousy was one of the most important factors in ruining Nationalist-Ossewabrandwag relations, just as organizational rivalries helped to drive Pirow's New Order out of the National Party by the end of 1941. An additional factor was the opposition of individual Nationalists to the Radical Right on strictly philosophical grounds. At the height of the campaign among conservative Nationalists to expel the New Order, one such person wrote as follows to Otto du Plessis, the relatively radical young editor of the Eastern Cape Nationalist organ, *Die Oosterlig* (The Eastern Light):

We can best carry out the struggle by explaining both our difference with Pirow and those who follow him, and our own political position. We have already done so by showing him that we will not be led by foreign principles, like Nazism with its anti-Christian elements. But it is still not enough. . . . We must make it clear that the Reunited Party is not planning to play the role of Quislings for Hitler and his German Imperialism, like Advocate Pirow and his OB supporters. We will never hand over South Africa to Germany, still less to British Imperialism.[6]

Probably many committed Nationalists, especially of the older generation, shared this individual's concerns about the radicals' direction.

The Case of Otto du Plessis: The Contradictory Voice of the New Generation

Among many younger, more radical Nationalists, attitudes to National Socialism and similar regimes were ambivalent, if not downright contradictory. Nationalists were increasingly resentful about what they perceived as German interference in South African affairs, yet were too deeply impressed by the achievements of fascism, and especially German National Socialism, to reject everything the Radical Right represented. Perhaps the best example of this phenomenon was Otto du Plessis, a journalist of considerable talent, who, as editor of *Die Oosterlig,* operated in an area of the Cape with a strong Ossewabrandwag presence, where the local OB "general" was none other than John Vorster, the future South African prime minister.[7]

Du Plessis's most notable contribution during the early war years to the debate on the South African future was a short treatise published in 1941 as a pamphlet by Malan's Nasionale Pers. Since this publisher allowed Du Plessis to note his editorial rank on the title page of the pamphlet, it presumably had the status of a semiofficial party position paper. Entitled *Die Nuwe Orde* (The New Order), it discussed Du Plessis's views on the need for a local version of the worldwide revolution for a new sociopolitical and economic system to supplant liberal democracy. Du Plessis cited as examples such disparate regimes as those of Portugal's Salazar, Stalin, Mussolini, and Hitler himself.[8]

It is striking that from the distant vantage point of South Africa, the many important differences between these regimes seemed of less consequence than their similarities, which were contrasted with what was perceived as the far more distinctive liberal democratic system. Du Plessis declared German-style National Socialism to be inappropriate for South Africa, explaining, "The new order in South Africa cannot take the shape of German National Socialism, Italian Fascism, Spanish Falangism or any other foreign [*buitelandse*] form. It must take on its own South African character [*'n eie Suid-Afrikaanse vorm*]."[9] He proposed an indigenous version based on the old Boer republics. He still thought an Axis victory a strong possibility, but believed that, in any case, history was moving toward the destruction of capitalism and liberal democracy and that South Africans should take advantage of this trend.[10] His criticism of both the Nazis and the liberal democrats was in many respects a reaffirmation and explication of the implications of the Malanite position: military and political neutrality.

Nevertheless, it was precisely this lack of extremism, this apparent concordance with mainstream Nationalist thinking, that had demonstrated most clearly the extent of the change in Nationalist philosophy since the early thirties. With the war and the subsequent collapse of one democracy after another, Du Plessis could note with satisfaction in his treatise who the groups hardest hit were: the big capitalists; the "un-national" press; "unsettled and unassimilable elements" like the Jews and other population groups that placed their own interests above those of the volk; and "international" organizations like the Freemasons.[11]

Malan himself, until then hardly an extremist in matters of this sort, had intimated during a speech in early 1941 that measures against similar groups were under consideration for South Africa, declaring: "When we have the Republic the say of the inimical and un-national elements in our national affairs will be obliterated."[12]

Du Plessis spelled out some of the characteristics of his proposed South African republic: systematic racial segregation; a powerful military establishment; elimination of "an anti- and un-national Press"; a "disciplined" radio service as "the mightiest propaganda weapon"; and assimilation of English-speaking whites into Afrikanerdom on the basis of Christian Nationalism.[13] One of the most striking things about this vision is how closely it reflects later conditions in South Africa, with the single exception of elimination of the liberal press, which survived for many years as a remarkably strident critic of the post-1948 Nationalist government, at least until the emergency regulations imposed in 1985 and 1986. More notable is how far Nationalist thinking had strayed since the early thirties into outright authoritarianism, now to be imposed not only on black South Africans.

Yet despite the clarity of Du Plessis's authoritarian vision for South Africa, he became increasingly critical not only of the Radical Right but also of attempts by many Nationalists to appease such extremist groups. The maze of apparent contradictions is obvious. In striking contrast with the message of *Die Nuwe Orde*, he, soon appointed "Enlightenment Secretary" of the National Party in recognition of his knowledge of propaganda, began to advocate a message of scrupulous neutrality.

In a November 1942 National Party memorandum on the use of propaganda by the party, Du Plessis, who had apparently abandoned his early advocacy of the Boer model, attacked exclusivist references to a Boer state and argued for conversion of English-speakers to the republican cause.[14] He noted that many party supporters were now showing indifference or even hostility to Hitler's cause, and commented caustically: "The Germans are in reality not the great friends of our volk; they are also not the proponents of a really free republic in South Africa. They are just prepared to use every possible Quisling in South Africa for their own purposes."[15]

Nonetheless, Du Plessis's intense nationalism was pragmatic not only in openness to a greater party inclusiveness, but also in his willingness to use the best political techniques, whatever their source. He wrote to Malan in mid-1942 about the effectiveness of Nazi propaganda methods and suggested learning from them. He argued that efforts to recruit English-speakers could gain from the Nazis' success in gearing their message to each group in its own language. Du Plessis cited as valuable the use of short, pithy slogans like Hitler's "Away with Versailles, away with the Communists, away with the Jews,"[16] rather than the typically Nationalist lengthy quotations from the past.

The recourse to such examples does not necessarily imply endorsement of their content. Yet it does suggest that Du Plessis, like so many Nationalists of his generation, was so fascinated and impressed by the Nazi regime that his mind turned quite naturally and with an apparently complete lack of unease to examples of Nazi success *regardless* of their content or implications. Thus, in almost the same breath as he attacked the Nazis and rightist extremists in the earlier party memorandum on propaganda, he could look to Nazi Germany for advice on how best to achieve results for the National Party through stressing "positive" propaganda that deliberately omitted any traces of fanaticism. He said that "Hitler for example did not say that he wanted a National Socialist Germany before he accepted power. He took the standpoint that he first of all wanted to gain control, and then build Weimar Germany into National Socialist Germany."[17]

The implications of official Nationalist ambivalence or even silence on the specifics of a future South African republic were particularly ominous. Du Plessis's advice is certainly consonant with Malan's own hesitations on the nature of a republic. In the same speech Malan could profess an attachment to the right of protest and the Boer tradition of a popular say in Government and at the same time threaten elimination of unacceptable elements in the future state.[18] He confirmed cynics' fears with his statement that it was too soon to be advocating the suppression of political parties, a matter that could be decided *after* a republic had been established.[19] The Federal Council of the National Party was more forthright in indicating the nature of the future state, announcing in a March 1941 declaration that a republican government would have to exercise supreme power for a considerable time.[20] There was very little to separate such a view from Pirow's aim of a one-party authoritarian state.[21]

Du Plessis's wariness about getting too close to the Axis and his desire for a more inclusive type of Afrikaner nationalism cannot therefore simply be read at face value. The sometimes apparently very democratic warnings from such Nationalists, particularly those of the younger generation, were complicated by a strand of increasingly authoritarian thinking from the very same quarters. Du Plessis's was the new voice of mainstream Afrikaner nationalism, often bewilderingly contradictory in its assertions, opposed to anything that might detract from an authentically Afrikaner political vision, but thoroughly affected all the same by years of dabbling in Radical Right ideology.

The Transformation of the Youth

Yet Du Plessis was comparatively moderate compared with a still younger generation of Nationalists. By 1942 he was severely critical of the extremism of the youth wing of the National Party, the Nasionale Jeugbond (National Youth Union), formed in 1940, which often took a more accommodationist line toward the Radical Right than its elders in the party. He was especially unhappy about the Jeugbond's advocacy in its constitution of an exclusivist "Christian National Boer Republic" and a similar reference in this document to placing the youth organization at the service of the Afrikaner volk.[22]

The Transvaal wing of the Jeugbond, in its statement of principles, opposed foreign control of *any* kind, German or British, suggestive of an older tradition of Afrikaner nationalism. But in more radical language the organization aimed at the economic and spiritual salvation of the "Boer nation" rather than of (white) South Africa, theoretically the target community of the National Party.[23]

New members could be no younger than twelve and no older than thirty. Initiates declared their support for the establishment of a Christian-National Boer Republic and the salvation of their people through the "effective solution" of the following:

(a) the Native and Colored Question;
(b) the Asiatic Question;
(c) the Jewish Question;
(d) the Poor White Question;
(e) and all other national questions.[24]

Unlike the Cape National Party, but like the NP in the Transvaal, the Transvaal Jeugbond specifically excluded Jews. The constitution stated: "Any white person settled [*gevestig*] in South Africa, between the ages of 12 and 30 years, except a Jew, may become a member of the Bond."[25]

Even children as early as elementary-school age were taught an extremely exclusivist notion of Afrikanerdom and a belief that other groups were "questions" to be "solved," though the Jeugbond did not go as far as the Boerejeug, the youth wing of the Ossewabrandwag, which enrolled children from birth until the age of six as *Boerebabas* (Boer babies), from six to twelve years as *Boerekleingoed* (Boer little ones), and from twelve to eighteen years as *Boereseuns* and *Boeredogters* (Boer sons and Boer daughters).[26] The Ossewabrandwag parallels with similar arrangements for the youth in Nazi Germany are evident.

The distinction between conservative nationalism and OB Radical Right thinking was thoroughly blurred among the National Party youth. Apart from the constitution of the Transvaal Jeugbond, the draft resolutions proposed by individual branches of that organization at its first congress in October 1940 were permeated with extreme racism, with *völkisch* doctrines reminiscent of the Afrikaanse Nasionale Studentebond in the thirties, and with a thoroughgoing authoritarianism.

The Brakpan branch of National Party youth wanted Afrikaans as the first official language, with English enjoying only a supplementary status, with equality "where it is in the interest of the State and its inhabitants and good administration." The branch proposed a legal ban on undermining the authority of the future republic in any form; it proposed compensation of Afrikaners for their "indescribable oppression" from the "British-Jewish" quarter and a ban on intermarriage between Afrikaners and "unassimilable" *white* groups.[27]

The Pretoria Central branch recommended that only *Afrikaner* banks be supported; the Hercules branch rejected any Jewish assistance that might (however unlikely) be extended to the National Party, and Benoni demanded that under a Nationalist regime the ministries of education and finance be given to desirable individuals of "Christian National" sympathies.[28]

A slightly older party leader like Du Plessis took a marginally yet recognizably more moderate albeit sometimes more confusing stance than the youth. He perhaps knew he would have to work with senior establishment figures. For instance, A. L. Geyer, editor of Du Plessis's sister paper, *Die Burger,* was deeply worried about the extremist proponents of a Boer republic in which English-speakers would have second-class status. His concern was a practical one, because as a constitutionalist he believed that such extremism was ruining the chances of a republican electoral victory. In addition, Geyer shared the widespread Nationalist fear that the increasingly elitist Ossewabrandwag would not only divide the volk, but would shut out party loyalists from running a future republic: "That spiritual development makes the chances of a ballot victory very small. What then? Those people, it seems to me, fix all their hopes not only on a German victory, but on the foundation of our 'free republic' by Germany! *That* [country] will have to prescribe how our governmental system should be and which man should act as Führer here."[29] Geyer understood the dangers of accommodation to the Nazis.

But among the youth the radicals were so heavily entrenched that the Afrikaanse Nasionale Studentebond, which by 1943 was completely dominated by the Ossewabrandwag, had created strongholds in the Afrikaans teachers' training colleges. At the

Heidelberg college 125 out of 189 students were ANS members, at Pretoria Normal College 175 out of 215, and at Potchefstroom Normal College 244 out of 380.[30] These were extraordinarily high figures for as late a date as 1943, by which time the Nationalists were officially completely estranged from the Radical Right. The Studentebond was considerably weaker at Pretoria and Stellenbosch universities, which suggests that it appealed by then to a less affluent class of students.[31]

In the thirties most students at both types of institution could have been counted upon to support the party regardless of whether they were members of the Studentebond. Membership in the student group had never been an obstacle to joining the party. In the intervening years the political sympathies of younger Afrikaners had changed quite radically and the Studentebond had become officially distanced from the party through the ANS's Ossewabrandwag connections. Yet, considering the great numbers of students who were Studentebond members, it is plausible that many continued at least to vote for the party, if not to support it actively. More important, there were significant implications for the *future* political direction of Afrikaner nationalism in the widespread ANS membership among this generation.

Anti-English sentiment among these students went hand in hand with strongly pro-German sympathies. Comments by students at training colleges reflected their feelings on the war issue: "Please do away with every damned English word on the envelope. If you do not like to write in Afrikaans you can write in German. It disgusts me when I see the English on your letters."[32] Another such ANS member described the typical student evening schedule as eating, followed by listening to the German news.[33]

Their sympathies were hardly surprising, considering the books on which these students were being reared in the elementary and high schools. Recommended textbooks included *Die Moderne Wêreld* (The Modern World) by Mrs. De Vos Malan, wife of the superintendent-general of education in the Cape Province before the war, still being used in the schools in 1943. Mrs. Malan praised the work of the dictators and the advantages of totalitarian systems. A grammar primer by H. Hofmeyr, who was later interned for pro-Nazi activities, included practice sentences such as one stating that nobody believed in the German atrocities during the Polish campaign. Most common of all were novels and poems in school anthologies featuring horror stories about the British camps during the Anglo-Boer War.[34]

In such a climate, Geyer's concern about extremists was difficult to maintain among ordinary Nationalists, and almost impossible to sell effectively to the younger generation.

Krugerism, Neo-Feudalism, and the Structure of Traditional Afrikaner Political Life

At the height of pro-German sympathy in National Party ranks in the early years of the war, when the Nazis seemed on the verge of victory in Europe, as noted above, Nationalists like Du Plessis turned above all to the political systems of the old Boer republics for inspiration.

The *volksdemokrasie* (people's democracy) of President Paul Kruger and his Transvaal "South African Republic" of the nineteenth century especially suggested a "new" model for the many Afrikaners who had lost faith in the liberal democracy of the Western Allies but did not want an outright dictatorship. A key policy statement by the National Party Federal Council in April 1941 said:

The Boer nation, which is the creator and protector of our South African nationhood, developed in the Boer republics a system of our own which differs utterly from the British parliamentary system and yet also rests on a democratic basis, and which was so sanctified through the fire of sacrifice and suffering that it survived in the heart of all Afrikanerdom and today has become just as powerful a force as forty years ago.[35]

A detailed examination of the political system of Kruger's republic shows, however, how limited in scope was the democracy of this system. The regular round of elections and Kruger's great emphasis on the *volkswil* (people's will) do suggest the forms of a genuinely participatory state, but the reality was closer to a kind of neo-feudalism.

The Boers of the two nineteenth-century republics, the Transvaal and the Orange Free State, like warlike medieval barons, were a fractious people who quarreled incessantly, and periodically came to the verge of civil war.[36] They shared both a deep

devotion to strong leaders and a tendency to enshrine the hereditary principle in electing new ones. Thus when Transvaal
Commandant-General A. H. Potgieter died in 1854, his son assumed that position. The Boers in the western Transvaal under
the leadership of Andries Pretorius, victor of the epic struggle at
Blood River against the Zulu, transferred their allegiance to his
son, M. W. Pretorius, upon the father's death. Pretorius, Jr., was
later elected president of the Transvaal.[37] When the hereditary
principle failed to suggest the line of succession, formal elections
and other legal requirements were still effectively sidestepped.
After M. W. Pretorius had resigned in 1872, neighboring President Jan Hendrik Brand of the Orange Free State was asked to
stand for the Transvaal presidency. Brand declined, but recommended a similarly well-educated Cape man, Thomas Francois
Burgers, who was duly elected, notwithstanding the legal ban on
non-Transvaler nominees or on candidates not belonging to the
established Nederduitsche Hervormde Kerk (Dutch Re-Formed
Church). Both constitutional obstacles were simply amended by
the Volksraad (Parliament).[38]

Boer presidents were repeatedly reelected to successive terms,
rather than risk a change of leadership. M. W. Pretorius was president of the Transvaal from 1857 to 1871, Kruger from 1883
until his departure for Europe in 1900. J. H. Brand was president
of the Orange Free State for no fewer than twenty-five years.[39]
The presidents of the Boer republics were thus less like typical
Western-style democratic leaders than like elected monarchs,
along the lines of the kings of medieval Poland or Hungary, who
were chosen by a landed aristocracy constituting a self-styled
"nation," but which never made up more than ten percent of the
total population.

The franchise of the republics was extremely limited, restricted
to adult white males who had resided for at least five years in the
case of the Transvaal, or for six months in that of the Orange Free
State.[40] When in 1890 it became clear to Kruger that the non-Boer
miners who flooded into the Transvaal after the discovery of gold
would soon overwhelm his Boer oligarchy, he created a dual
franchise—all white male foreigners naturalized for two years
would be permitted to vote for a "Second Volksraad" with limited powers over local matters like mining and roads, but state

policy remained the preserve of the original "First Volksraad." The electorate for the latter, and in presidential elections as well, was restricted to voters enfranchised before the new law, and, thereafter, to those born in the Transvaal. The *Uitlander* (foreigner) element could only vote in this more selective category after being eligible for ten years for election to the Second Volksraad. The qualifications for eligibility as a candidate in elections to the Second Volksraad were highly specific: a candidate had to be at least thirty years old, enfranchised for two years before election, and also a Protestant resident owner of fixed property in the Transvaal.[41] It was not surprising that such conditions led to endless friction with the growing *Uitlander* community.

In theory both republics, the Transvaal and the Orange Free State, placed great emphasis on constitutional formalities and the expression of the popular will in the lawmaking process. In practice, a strong president could wield great power. In the Orange Free State, a president was independent of the Volksraad and could only be impeached by a two-thirds majority, and thus was very much "his own man," strengthened, as in the Transvaal, by the lack of either a party system or a regular cabinet. The five-man Executive Council of the Orange Free State included two of the president's own subordinates, the magistrate of the capital, Bloemfontein, and the government secretary. The council was also the final court of appeal,[42] which hardly made for a separation of powers, a notion that seems to have had little practical content in either republic.

In the isolated Transvaal, a man of Kruger's ability was able to use such a system to even greater advantage. Voters were encouraged to submit a steady stream of signed memorials, as the wily Kruger, a man with negligible formal education but remarkable political sophistication, liked to play off the Volksraad against the "popular will." In addition, he burdened an entire Raad committee with reading these documents, effectively limiting the theoretical sovereignty of the legislature by regularly reminding it of the duty to minister to the people's will.[43]

Cloaking his actions in the rhetoric of populism, he had built a highly authoritarian state that operated within formal structures rooted in an exclusivist ethnic nationalism that could nevertheless be passed off as democratic. This was the romanticized

model to which Afrikaner nationalists looked in the age of the
dictators, a model neither truly "fascist" nor recognizably in the
mold of the Western liberal democracies.

For instance, Kruger, a man convinced of a divine underpin-
ning of his rule, skillfully manipulated the system to enforce not
the people's will, but his own, refusing to apply to himself the
rule that Volksraad members should not speak more than twice
on the same topic. Members complained that he spoke too much
in the chamber and that he influenced them by his gestures even
when silent. Refusing to let anyone prevent him from speaking,
he tried to overcome the truculence of the Raad by summoning
its committees to his house, where he could influence them more
easily, intimidating members with his terrible temper when ordinary persuasion proved ineffective. In addition, together with
the state secretary, Dr. Leyds, himself a presidential appointee,
Kruger appointed heads of government departments who were
responsible to the two of them, and also high court judges.[44]

In effect this was a limited representative system rather than
a democracy, headed by a strongman. As J. S. Marais, the noted
historian of Kruger's republic, has pointed out, those who went
along benefited from a spoils system in which relatives and political supporters were regularly rewarded with offices for which
they were often unqualified. There is also considerable evidence
of lax management of state finances, corruption, and wasteful
spending.[45]

It hardly mattered that there were regular, occasionally fiercely
fought elections within this system. The strong ruler, the rewards
system, the lack of a highly developed state apparatus, and the
seat of ultimate power among a very small but fractious rural
aristocracy were all suggestive of a neo-feudal state.

The entire system rested on a rough-and-ready *realpolitik*.
Like the Germanic aristocracy of early medieval France, the rural
Boer patriarchs lacked the means, and in this case the expertise,
experience, or capital, to make the most of the land, leaving the
tilling of the soil to its older inhabitants.[46] Thus the mounted
Boer barons created a neo-feudal system of land tenure and labor
that underpinned their unruly oligarchic "democracy." Industrial activity was limited to mining on the Witwatersrand, and
to the production of sometimes lethal liquors that anesthetized

the minds of the troublesome but effectively disfranchised *Uit-landers*.[47] Industry was almost entirely in the hands of wealthy foreigners outside the inner political system, much like the Jewish entrepreneurs of the Middle Ages.

The Nationalists of the thirties and forties looked to this same rickety but workable model for inspiration as, fired by the spread of the "New Order" in so many countries overseas, they too sought to displace the widely discredited liberal parliamentary system. Their alternative model was likely to limit, rather than extend, the scope of popular participation. The top-heavy, ram-shackle state apparatus of Kruger's republic was also an unlikely basis for the kind of large-scale state intervention and control that the fiercely anticapitalist Nationalists of that era hoped to introduce to salvage their poorest constituents. In a similar way, their contemporaries like Hitler, along with a host of prophets of the New Order, looked to their remote past to legitimate their attempts to rescue the unemployed and downtrodden of their own nations from the poverty of postwar collapse, from untram-meled capitalist exploitation, and from economic depression.

There was another side to the heritage of Krugerism: the lack of experience of an indigenous democracy led to a deep suspicion that the modern liberal state system was hostile to the historic interests of Afrikaner nationalism. Thus Otto du Plessis wrote that "liberal individualism, constitutionalism and parliamentar-ism" had overemphasized individual interests, undermined Chris-tianity, provided a cover for big capitalists and the press to ex-ploit the masses, and denationalized the volk. He saw the struggle against liberal democracy as a direct outgrowth of that between Kruger and the *Uitlanders*. Du Plessis could hail the work of the fascist dictators as the "revolution of the twentieth century," to be emulated in an appropriately Afrikaner way, while looking to a "free Republic" through "volk organization" and "volk dis-cipline."[48] Nor was Du Plessis alone.

A Problem of Loyalty: The Case of Dr. Malan and Mrs. Denk

Just how much the very nature of a Nationalist's duties as a citizen and view of the liberal state had become uncertain in the wartime climate is perhaps best demonstrated by the famous Denk case. This involved not a youthful Nationalist, but the leader of the party himself. According to captured German documents found after the war, a Mrs. Denk, the wife of Hans Denk, a Nazi agent in South Africa, interviewed Malan in his Cape Town home on or around 16 January 1940. His longtime friend Karl Bremer, the Cape chairman of the National Party, had acted as interpreter. Mrs. Denk had given Malan a message from the German government about Nazi policy toward South Africa in the event of a separate peace. Although in 1946 Malan was cleared by a bipartisan parliamentary select committee of unethical conduct in this case, largely because it accepted his own explanation of what had happened, some questions were never satisfactorily answered.

The story of what actually occurred between Malan and Mrs. Denk (and its implications) is a rare example of evidence of direct contact between Nazi Germany and a National Party leader during the war, and is certainly the only case of such contact that was investigated at length.

Malan did not report his conversation with Mrs. Denk to the Union authorities, stating later in his defense to the Select Committee that he feared it was a government trap because such conversations happened frequently with people posing as German envoys, and that he did not think it a particularly important conversation since it contained nothing new to him.[49] On the other hand, Hans Denk, in his report to General von Karlowa, director of the Africa section at the German Foreign Office, reported that Malan was "extremely grateful for the news he received" and asked Mrs. Denk to convey his thanks to Herr Denk: "He gave the assurance that he would build up and work entirely on the lines suggested by us. He said, moreover, that he would at once talk with General Hertzog and all the leading National[ist] Afrikaners, with a view to influencing at once their respective speeches to be delivered in Parliament."[50]

The Select Committee did not accept this German statement at face value and took Malan's explanation in good faith. It also does not appear to have made much of the differences between the message as it was reported by Malan and as it appears in Von Karlowa's records. Either Denk or Von Karlowa may, of course, have represented the course of the interview in such a way as to make it seem more successful than it had actually been. Nevertheless, it is strange that Malan did not inform the authorities of the Nazis' message. He did not have to go to the police; he had ample access to members of the government as a senior opposition leader and former cabinet minister. On the other hand, under cross-examination Mrs. Denk stated that she was "inwardly disappointed" by Malan's reception.[51] She may, in turn, however, have been attempting to downplay the significance of her mission in the hope of easing her own legal difficulties with the Union government as a publicly exposed envoy of the Nazi government.

Malan had, according to the committee's findings, been courteous but noncommittal toward Mrs. Denk, stating cautiously that his views were well known.[52] Malan said she had spoken about the goodwill Germany had always held toward the Afrikaner people; she had expressed regret that South Africa had declared war against Germany; and she had noted German appreciation of Afrikaner aspirations about their own destiny. As the transcript of the investigation relates, Malan described her words as follows:

. . . if Germany won the war, then Germany wanted the Union to become independent and that the Union should then consist, I think it was mentioned separately, of the Cape Province, the Free State, the Transvaal and Natal, and that the British protectorates would be added. . . . I think she also said, but I do not remember quite clearly, something about Rhodesia and that, if the Union wanted to incorporate Rhodesia, it would at least have the approval of Germany after she gained the victory. With regard to South-West Africa, she said that Germany claimed the return of her colonies.[53]

He also said that she had offered channels for further negotiation,[54] hardly an insignificant communication, as Malan characterized it, since she suggested, in effect, a "South African Empire" with German backing.

In his autobiography Malan describes a similar incident in which he behaved in a similar way. He was approached during the war (he gives no date) by an individual who claimed to be in the service of Germany. This person told Malan that Germany was planning to land arms supplies in South Africa, with a view to promoting a rebellion there, and wanted to know where the most suitable place would be to do this, since the sympathy of the local whites would be crucial. Malan refused to have anything to do with the plot, but he made no attempt to report the incident, despite its obvious significance if it were true.[55]

Malan was not the only important Nationalist to keep crucial information from the authorities. Geyer, Malan's faithful lieutenant, relates in his wartime diary that he was well aware of the spying activities of two German agents, Schroder and Rooseboom, but discussed this only with Malan and with, of all people, J. A. Smith, the number-two man in the Ossewabrandwag.[56] And Geyer notes in the same entry that Commandant-General Van Rensburg on one occasion actually told Eric Louw that he was in contact with the German government,[57] but Geyer does not indicate what was actually said, nor is there any evidence that Louw ever reported this information.

There is only one way, it seems to me, that can explain Malan's behavior or Geyer's or Louw's without impugning their honor, and that is that their conduct epitomizes the confused loyalties of the time. In a profound sense, the Nationalists had come to distrust not only the Smuts government itself, but the very form of the South African state. Malan disagreed with Smuts's war policy, and with the entire current constitutional framework of which Smuts was the champion. Smuts, to Malan, had become identified as the enemy of Afrikanerdom just as Hitler was identified as the enemy of Smuts-style South African nationalism. This was not merely an issue of differences over policy, because, then, Malan would have been able to distinguish clearly between self-interest and loyalty to his party and to the volk on one hand, and a larger loyalty to the South African nation on the other. In that event he would have regarded a threat to Union sovereignty as a threat to Afrikaner sovereignty. In theory he did believe this, which led to his feud with the Ossewabrandwag, but in practice the issues were too blurred to make obvious ethical choices based on such distinctions.

The best option apparently seemed to be to keep out of trouble and say nothing. While Malan could not have been endangered from Smuts's quarter if he had reported the attempts of self-professed Nazi agents to co-opt him, it could, however, have damaged his credibility with militants in his own organization and on the Radical Right, which in early 1940 was not yet alienated from the National Party. Malan acted as though short-term interests of party and volk overrode interests of the nation, even where the long-term interests of Afrikaner independence were equally threatened. A deeply religious man like Malan could only take such a route if he thought that the primacy of his loyalty to the current state was so utterly compromised by its many objectionable features that it should give way to loyalty to a future republican state that existed in embryo in the Afrikaner nationalist movement.

This interpretation, while, of course, highly speculative, can make sense of Malan's curious behavior without suggesting that he was lying and that he really did have a working relationship with the Nazis. This interpretation is also consonant with the delicate but dangerous political tightrope performance he was trying to maintain. To report on Nazi contacts could bring no immediate benefit to the Nationalist cause and could conceivably do much harm. If failure to report these contacts had grave implications for the Smuts government, he could have reasoned, that was *its* problem.

In the absence of further evidence, the government could not pursue a case of failure to report treason against Malan, a punishable crime amounting to high treason under Roman-Dutch law.[58] Government lawyers working on the Denk case could only see a clear *moral* obligation resting on Malan to make known Mrs. Denk's approaches. In response to his defense, they argued that he had no way of knowing that she was *not* a genuine Nazi agent, nor was he entitled to constitute himself the sole judge of whether the message was important enough to warrant reporting it; in addition, the agent could have planned other more dangerous missions, notwithstanding Malan's own uncooperative response in this case.[59] Instead, it seems to me, Malan had denied the state information he knew to be potentially devastating to its security. He was acting as though the Nationalists constituted a state-within-a-state, with the right to act as a neutral political entity, rather than as subjects who differed from the government on a matter of policy.

This judgment assumes a shared moral viewpoint, one that

could support the notion of a common state with a common sovereignty and security, and that was precisely what had broken down during the early years of the war. Afrikaner nationalists, including even those relatively moderate leaders who consciously rejected any form of national socialism for South Africa, were beginning to assess basic issues of loyalty by a set of moral standards different from those of their compatriots. A more fundamental transformation of nationalist values would have been hard to imagine.

Afrikaner nationalists could assist the Axis cause, sometimes deliberately, but more often unconsciously, without feeling morally compromised, because their values and priorities had shifted so completely over the previous decade, and especially since September 1939, that the interests of the volk had become synonymous with those of the nation. For most Afrikaner nationalists, however, non-nationalist Afrikaners were traitors who set themselves apart from their own people. For some the volk was the Ossewabrandwag, for others it was the National Party, but until late 1941 when the rift occurred, for most Afrikaner nationalists it was both of these.

Despite the protestations about abiding by the pluralism of Boer republican tradition, in a much deeper sense Afrikaner nationalism was already far down the road to equating the party with the nation. The passions aroused by the war made a shift toward totalitarianism possible, and thus the doctrines of the European Radical Right made one of their most far-reaching inroads into Afrikaner nationalist values. In a fundamental sense, the New Right had secured an unlikely but ultimately significant success in a remote corner of the world and had succeeded in souring still further the chances for a democratic future in an already deeply troubled society.

Chapter Eight

The Road to Authoritarianism

Toward a Spirit of Elitism

The early war years saw a growing tendency among Afrikaner nationalists to lean toward more authoritarian policies, particularly as the succession of initial Nazi victories appeared to herald the demise of liberal democracy and of British hegemony in southern Africa. So pronounced was the new sense of destiny in the National Party that, at the beginning of 1940, one of its more obscure back-benchers, S. P. le Roux, the member for Oudtshoorn, questioned the right of any but Nationalist members of Parliament to vote on the war issue. The ten Jewish members in the Assembly, largely United Party supporters, were incapable of objectivity on the war, he asserted; the Native Representatives had no right to vote on a white man's war; the English-speakers were not real South Africans; and pro-government Afrikaners had no right to judge on this question, because they were just opportunists.[1]

A few months later, the Transvaal Nationalist leader, J. G. Strijdom, took up the same exclusivist theme. He argued that the rural constituencies should be represented in Parliament even more favorably than was already the case, since this was "the stable and conservative section of the people and therefore has special claims to representation."[2]

The proposition that Afrikaners were somehow more reliable South Africans than others could be traced in very general terms back to the late nineteenth century, even among the most moderate Afrikaners in the Cape Colony,[3] who had long accommodated themselves to membership in the British Empire, yet it had never been expressed as aggressively or explicitly as now. The unspoken elitism underlying it had become diffused in the conciliatory politics of Botha, Smuts, and eventually even the Hertzog of the thirties, but in time of national crisis, that spirit returned, and with a virulence that bespoke new influences.

For the assumptions underlying the striking language of Le Roux and Strijdom presupposed a higher court of authority than the South African state, one that had the right to decide the fate of the entire nation, and that was the Afrikaner nationalist movement. Such an assumption coexisted with and was a subtle but particularly far-reaching consequence of fascist thinking in South Africa: the notion that a political party, an organization or a movement, was somehow above regular state authority, that indeed the movement could sit in judgment upon the actions of the state and ultimately assume its functions in the name of a higher good.

Brotherly Conflict and the Draft Republican Constitution

Despite their minority status in the South African Parliament, the Nationalists and their sometime Radical Right allies were so confident of a republican victory in the early war years that they actually produced a draft constitution for their proposed republic, a revealing document with a complex and highly checkered history that says much about the wartime Afrikaner nationalist movement.

Relations between the National Party and its more extreme rivals, despite occasional setbacks, were particularly good at that time. Pirow's New Order remained inside the party until the end of 1941, but Malan went out of his way to placate his troublesome lieutenant, telling some three thousand people at Stellenbosch in March of 1941 that democracy as it was known in the British parliamentary system was a caricature and that the days of capitalism were numbered. Referring to Pirow's widely distributed pamphlet, *Nuwe Orde,* Malan said that perhaps 80 or 85 percent of the "new order" was already in the National Party program. It would be carried out "in letter and in spirit" when the party came to power. In the same speech he denied that Germany would impose national socialism on South Africa; he explained to considerable applause:

What Germany wants to achieve is the severance of the British connection, and she further apparently desires governments all over the
world to be friendly towards her. As far as that is concerned, Germany
can have no doubt about our own attitude. We intimated it on the 4th
September. We want to have peace with Germany and if we got power
in our hands today, we would make friends [*vriende maak*] with her
tomorrow.[4]

Pirow himself was stating that the National Party was the only
political home for the Afrikaner volk and that all Afrikaners
should belong to the party, the Ossewabrandwag, and Nico Diederichs's economic organization, the Reddingsdaadbond.[5] Louis
Weichardt was busy proclaiming the support of his reorganized
Greyshirt movement for the National Party during elections, expressing himself as pro-Pirow, antiwar, and in favor of Afrikaans
as the primary language of South Africa.[6]

The equally warm atmosphere between the party and the Ossewabrandwag in early 1941 was underlined by Malan, who
threatened that if Smuts dissolved the OB, the party would share
the consequences of any decision to follow a passive disobedience
policy. Malan continued: "The Ossewabrandwag is a mighty
organization which wants to discipline our volk and make it easy
to reach our ideals. We need the Ossewabrandwag on one hand
and the political party on the other. The one supplements the
other."[7]

The Ossewabrandwag–National Party relationship was so
congenial at that time that P. J. Luttig, who was both OB Chief
General of the North-Western Cape and also a member of the
Cape National Party Executive, a not unusual combination in
those heady days, told Van Rensburg that if he stuck with Malan,
his chances of succeeding the latter would be excellent.[8]

Within months, however, personality conflicts, intergroup rivalries, and dissension over points of ideological interpretation
created the ultimately permanent rift between these organizations. Malan came to believe that the political monopoly of the
National Party was being threatened by the Ossewabrandwag
and, to a lesser degree, by the New Order. Here was the much-
feared *broedertwis* (brotherly conflict) that had so often threatened the Afrikaner nationalist cause in the past.[9]

Apart from genuine ideological differences, Malan's refusal to
back down in the growing quarrel with the Ossewabrandwag

Oswald Pirow and his wife in 1938. Pirow was the best-known admirer of
Hitler's Germany in Hertzog's prewar cabinet; during the war he led a pro-
fascist splinter-group, the New Order, in the Reunited Nationalist parliamentary caucus. He was chief government prosecutor in the 1956–1961
"treason trial" of antiapartheid activists.
From the Cape Times *Collection in the South African Library*

J. F. J. ("Hans") van Rensburg, c. 1940. Van Rensburg was a former secretary of justice and administrator of the Orange Free State under Hertzog and
titular head of the Afrikaner Nasionale Studentebond; he was best known as
wartime commandant-general of the Ossewabrandwag (Ox-Wagon Guard)
and as chief of its militantly pro-Axis wing, the Stormjaers (Stormtroopers).
From the Cape Times *Collection in the South African Library*

Die O.B.

Ons
soek
eenheid
van
die
hele
Afrikaner-
volk.

Ons
soek
eenheid
en
nie
eensaam-
heid
nie.

Amptelike Ossewabrandwag-Mededelings. Vlugskrif No. 3.

Wat is die Geskil?

In September 1940 versoek die leier van die Herenigde Nasionale Party die Dagbestuur van die Groot Raad om 'n samespreking te reël met die Krisis-komitee van die Partykoukus ten einde 'n skakel te vind in verband met gesamentlike optrede in die krisis. Dr. Malan word as skakel aangewys in die gesamentlike strewe na 'n Republiek. 'n Paar weke later hou hy samesprekings met die Dagbestuur van die Ossewabrandwag en die Cradockse Ooreenkoms word aangegaan. Weer word in die ooreenkoms bevestig dat beide Party en Ossewabrandwag strewe na 'n Republiek. Vier maande later verwelkom dr. Malan die nuwe Kommandant-Generaal en verklaar: „dat hy die Ossewabrandwag hartlik gelukwens met die keuse van 'n Kommandant-Generaal, dr. J. F. J. van Rensburg" en voeg daarby: „Hy kon geen beter leier gekies het nie." Voortgaande verklaar hy: „Ek is 'n vriend van die Ossewabrandwag...

„ DIE O.B."

AMPTELIKE ORGAAN VAN DIE OSSEWABRANDWAG VIR KAAPLAND, TRANSVAAL, O. VRYSTAAT EN NATAL.

Hierdie vlugskrifte dien as voorloper vir „Die O.B." wat eersdaags weekliks sal verskyn.

Lede wat begerig is om „Die O.B." te ontvang moet onmiddellik hulle name en volledige posadresse inhandig by hul Kommandante of hoër offisiere. Die name moet dan onmiddellik deur die betrokke offisiere aan Hoofkwartier gestuur word, sodat die lede direk hul eksemplare kan ontvang.

voorsitter moet wees teneinde die gedagte aan subordinasie uit te skakel en dat elke leier van verskillende organisasies dus 'n volksleier op sy terrein is.

Eerste Moeilikheid Opgelos

Kort daarna egter bars die storm los. Beswaar is gemaak teen 'n verklaring te Elsburg deur die Kommandant-Generaal dat „nasionaal-sosialiste" (wat nog lede van die Herenigde Nasionale Party is) ook lede van die Ossewabrandwag kan wees.

Die geskil ontwikkel totdat dr. Malan 'n altimatum rig tot die Ossewabrandwag met die vier bekende else. Die Ossewabrandwag beroep hom op die Eenheidskomitee wat die vier punte behandel. Die Groot Raad aanvaar en handel in ooreenstemming met die bevindinge van die Eenheidskomitee en die geskil word as opgelos beskou.

Verbreking van Ooreenkoms

Daar eindig dit nie. 'n Geweldige veldtog word plotseling deur Partyleiers en die Pers op tou gesit, vol bitterheid en ongegrond beskuldigings teen die Ossewabrandwag e...

"Wat is die Geskil?" (What is the dispute?), a broadsheet of 5 November 1941 seeking to explain the Ossewabrandwag position on the National Party and downplaying responsibility for intra-Afrikaner division. The newspaper *Die O.B.* (announced in center box) evolved from such broadsheets.
From the OB Collection, Cullen Library

might best be explained by fear, jealousy, and unwillingness to make room for another organization, particularly one with the OB's dynamic image. There was a long history of bitter Afrikaner disputes based on such primacy of jurisdiction,[10] and the Malanites' careful guarding of their political turf was no exception in this regard.

For ironically enough, in its own way, Malan's National Party was becoming just as authoritarian as Van Rensburg's Ossewabrandwag. But Malan was careful of Afrikaner sensibilities about personal tyranny, especially one that could be charged to foreign manipulation.

Malan described the party as no ordinary party-political organization, but one that occupied a central position in Afrikaner ethnic life,[11] an historic role that the parvenu Van Rensburg had difficulty challenging. Malan's earlier claim that all members of the Ossewabrandwag were also members of the National Party makes sense in this light. That claim was now thoroughly discredited by the NP-OB rift.

Yet these differences between the Ossewabrandwag and the National Party, especially of ideology, were often exaggerated. They were used by pro-Nationalist historians to strengthen the thesis that the party, because of the eventual parting of the ways between it and the OB, was fundamentally unaffected by the rise of fascism. The limitations of this apologetic approach are especially evident in the case of the "Draft Constitution," which appeared in the Nationalist press in January 1942, several months after the split with the Radical Right had become obvious.[12]

The Draft Constitution represents the high-water mark of Radical Right influence on mainstream Afrikaner nationalist political thinking, although it has since come to be regarded as at worst an unfortunate historical aberration. The Nationalists later did their best to distance themselves from this document. It was never approved by any National Party congress.

What remains clear is that the published Draft Constitution is strikingly similar to the 1940 "Freedom Manifesto" of Piet Meyer's and Diederichs's radical Afrikaner Nasionale Studentebond, which was a document that advocated a form of fascism for South Africa. The constitution was published in summarized form in an Ossewabrandwag circular of July 1941,[13] though it was not an OB document in its origins.

A number of Afrikaner Broederbond intellectuals, including Diederichs and Meyer of the ANS and Verwoerd, Strijdom's right-hand man in the Transvaal National Party, had worked on the Draft Constitution at an earlier stage.[14] The involvement of the Broederbond is clear from a statement of its Executive thanking its policy committee for the Constitution during the Bond's annual gathering of 6 October 1941.[15] Van Rensburg stated that its authors included Verwoerd, T. E. Dönges, and J. H. Conradie, all three leading members of both the National Party and the Broederbond Executive.[16] Top Nationalists would appear, therefore, to have had a direct role in the formulation of this document.

The Draft Constitution was clearly a sensitive subject in National Party circles. Malan gave as one of his main reasons for the 1941 rift between the party and the Ossewabrandwag the publication of the Draft Constitution as an OB circular, which he considered an infringement of the Ossewabrandwag's agreement to leave the political sphere to the party.[17] Yet, according to Van Rensburg, that circular was simply the approved constitutional basis for cooperation agreed upon by the various member organizations of the Afrikaner Unity Committee early in 1941. This committee, consisting of representatives of the party, OB, Reddingsdaadbond, and FAK (the umbrella Afrikaner cultural organization), was intended to prevent friction between the various branches of the *Volksbeweging,* the volk movement. Van Rensburg maintained that Malan had been kept informed throughout the process of compiling the Draft Constitution and that, according to agreements, it could only be published with the permission of Malan.[18]

The Nationalists, the Broederbond, and the Ossewabrandwag were, therefore, all deeply involved in the compilation; if Malan was later deeply embarrassed by its contents, that must be because, by 1942, when it was published, such expressions of political extremism were no longer advantageous to his party's cause. In addition, by that time the whole issue of the Draft Constitution had become thoroughly entangled with organizational and personal rivalries.

In fact, contrary to Malan's later attempts to dissociate himself from connections with the compilers, the Draft Constitution was appended to a July 1941 declaration by the Unity Committee that advocated a republican form of government. This declaration was approved by Malan himself as evidence of support by the volk organizations for party policy.[19] Malan was admittedly unhappy about the idea of a committee's taking over what he regarded as the political functions of the party.[20]

It is also true that the Malan circle, the old guard of the Cape National Party, was particularly nervous about the ambitions of the constitution-makers on the Unity Committee. One reason was undoubtedly that several of the key members were Studentebond figures who were notoriously sympathetic to full-fledged national socialism, however much adapted to local conditions. Diederichs, as leader of the Reddingsdaadbond, sat on the committee. Its powerful secretary was the ubiquitous Piet Meyer.[21] This perhaps explains why the tone of the Draft Constitution was so reminiscent of that of the Studentebond's Freedom Manifesto. A. L. Geyer perceived the attempt by the Unity Committee constitution-makers to deal with the growing tensions between the party and the Ossewabrandwag over the July 1941 OB circular, among other things, in a manner revealing of many older Cape Nationalists' suspicions. He commented angrily, and with some exaggeration, in his diary: "I do not doubt that the pressure to refer the matter to the Unity Committee arises from (1) the desire to win time and (2) the knowledge that two of the other members, namely Diederichs and Meyer, are Nazis through-and-through and will stand by Van Rensburg."[22]

There was, however, almost certainly a second concern among Malan's circle, that is, the role of several ambitious Transvaal Nationalist Broederbond members in the formulation of the Draft Constitution. Figures inside the party itself were trying to push the Draft Constitution into a more radical direction than the old guard in the Cape, men like Geyer, Karl Bremer, or Malan himself, might have judged prudent.

Moreover, the Unity Committee, despite the heavy presence of figures known for their sympathy to Radical Right thinking and therefore likely to favor the Ossewabrandwag against the party, urged the Radical Right to withdraw its contentious circular, thus reestablishing the preeminence of the party in political matters.[23] This committee was surprisingly evenhanded in dealing with the party, and Malan's stubbornness in responding to their arbitration attempts consequently suggests as much his jealousy in guarding the party monopoly over political affairs as his substantive ideological concerns.

The picture is made still more complex by evidence that, at the time of the formulation of the Draft Constitution, many leading Ossewabrandwag members, especially in the Transvaal, were working closely with the party. One such OB member, who like many Nationalists before the split was both a National Party and Ossewabrandwag member, wrote to his superior, Strijdom, about the improvement in the situation in that province since some earlier rumblings of friction in late 1940. This change was, he noted, in stark contrast with the bad feelings many Nationalists held toward the dissident New Order: "There now exists a very nice relationship between the Party and the OB. The undermining work of certain elements has been stopped. In some places the OB even does the recruiting work for the Party. The relationship with the Controlling Council of the OB is also now very healthy."[24]

Conservatives in the party could hardly quarrel with such cooperative behavior, especially when so many of their members also belonged to the OB. Malan's sensitivity about the OB, especially about its role in drawing up the Draft Constitution, is, therefore, doubly puzzling.

The Totius Proposal, Van Rensburg, and Berlin

Malan's increasingly vehement denunciations of the Ossewabrandwag in the second half of 1941 and his attempt to distance himself from the Draft Constitution appear even more problematic when one considers his rejection of the so-called "Totius proposal." The celebrated Afrikaans poet J. D. du Toit ("Totius") had suggested that Malan take over the leadership of the entire volk, rather than just of the National Party. This proposal, which seemed likely to obtain Ossewabrandwag approval, would have entailed Malan's resignation from the leadership of the party, while Van Rensburg would agree to serve under Malan. Malan's position would be strengthened by the power to dismiss the leader of any volk organization.[25]

Malan politely rejected the offer on the grounds that he did not want dictatorial powers and that the FAK and Reddingsdaadbond, as "nonpolitical" cultural and economic organizations, would have problems accepting the leadership of a "political" leader. He suggested, in typically Cape Nationalist mode, that such powers be exercised instead by another committee.[26]

None of his arguments is wholly convincing. A committee already existed to resolve causes of friction between nationalist organizations, but he was wary of accepting *its* status as an arbitrator. The FAK and RDB, in turn, despite their nonpolitical character, had become involved earlier in 1941 in the Unity Committee, of which only *one* political party, that of Malan, was a member. Their control by the Broederbond, with its longtime resentment of old-fashioned Hertzogite nationalism[27] and intrinsic opposition to Smuts, still further weakened the claim that they were above party politics. Malan was, indeed, probably uncomfortable with the idea of acting as a dictator, but it had not been too difficult to persuade him earlier that year to assume near dictatorial powers within the party. The title *Volksleier* (volk leader),[28] which he held, is roughly analogous to the German appellation *Führer*.

Malan's own explanation for his stubborn refusal to patch up his quarrel with the Ossewabrandwag by accepting the Totius proposal is therefore implausible, but his rejection of the Totius plan makes sense if it is conceded that he was increasingly convinced of the need to rid himself of the potential threat from the OB, *regardless* of any attempts, however well-meaning, to negotiate a settlement. Van Rensburg, in particular, was becoming just too dangerous. Geyer noted with concern that on 28 August 1941 the pro-Nazi Zeesen Radio had summarized an article in the official *Deutsche Rundschau* in which Van Rensburg was revealed as the new Berlin-designated leader of Afrikanerdom. Geyer commented wryly: "Is it coincidence? I do not believe so."[29]

The Germans had presumably tired of the failure of the National Party to show sufficient enthusiasm for the idea of a German-directed regime in South Africa. Malan's endless quibbling over minor tactical points, his qualms about "national socialism," his jealous guarding of party prerogatives, and his rejection of violence could have provided little joy for Berlin. The promise of the first days of the war had not produced the desired political results, Malan had not emerged as the South African Quisling, and, therefore, a more accommodating leader had to be found.

By the end of 1941 Van Rensburg, sounding more and more sympathetic to Pirow and other exponents of national socialism,

was trying to backpedal on the earlier Ossewabrandwag under-
taking not to use violence or underground subversive activities,
an attempt that the cautious Malan regarded as counterproduc-
tive.[30] Notwithstanding the usual Nazi preference for working
with conservative nationalists, as in Eastern Europe too, rather
than those more openly committed to Radical Right policies,
like the various fascist movements in those countries, Van Rensburg, with his large Ossewabrandwag organization and the increasingly pro-Nazi tone of his leadership, must have appeared
the best German candidate for *Volksleier.* Here was a man who
seemed to understand the need for action and who was not hide-
bound by the scruples of the aging party-politician Daniel Malan.

The Draft Constitution and the Ambiguous Voice of Malanite Authoritarianism

The fundamental National Party view that it was the sole
party-political home for nationalist-oriented Afrikaners,[31] and
that all other Afrikaners were by inference "un-national," not
true Afrikaners, was a dogmatic judgment that indicates the
strength of anti-democratic currents in the wartime party. The
pedigree required of true Afrikaners was now to become still
more narrow and exacting than in the past, excluding not only
Smuts supporters, but also those to the right of Malan. This
same aura of authoritarianism found its way into the Draft Constitution. The document published by the Ossewabrandwag and
the version in the Nationalist press differed only in that in the
press legislative power was vested in the Volksraad (Parliament)
rather than in the presidency.[32] The Ossewabrandwag version of
1941, based on a still earlier draft issued as far back as April
1940 by the Transvaal OB, probably mainly the extremist
Stormjaer wing,[33] was generally more directly authoritarian in
tone and less carefully nuanced than the much fuller Nationalist
version, but they shared the same outline and the same spirit.

The publication by the party of its fuller version followed an
exceptionally lengthy debate in Parliament on a motion by Malan
to establish a republic, inevitably defeated by the pro-war Smuts
majority in the Assembly. Unlike the Draft Constitution, which
had gone through many hands, this motion is pure Malanite

philosophy, but it is generally in keeping with the spirit of the Draft. Malan urged a republic free of any links to the British Crown or any other power:

... such a republic shall not be cast on any foreign model, but shall be built up in accordance with our own national character and traditions based upon the principles of national government as embodied in the two former South African republics, departing from anything false and dangerous to the nation contained in the British liberalistic democracy as existing in this country and with the necessary adaptation to modern conditions.[34]

The tendency of the wartime National Party to try to be all things to all persons was underlined by Malan's implied sniping here not only at Smuts, but also at the New Order's alleged subservience to a "foreign model." Similarly, the republic was to be "Christian-national," a notion foreign to English-speakers, but its religious "substance and character" were to be based on "the true observance of equal language and cultural rights of both sections of the European population."[35] There was a reference to safeguarding whites in a spirit of guardianship of the black population, but this was a sentiment that could have come as easily from the more conservative sections of the United Party as from a Nationalist. But Malan showed a quite different spirit from that of the UP in the final clause of his motion, which emphasized the radical populism and xenophobia of the old Purified Party. And there were newer authoritarian undertones: ". . . it [the republic] shall be protected effectively against the capitalistic and parasitical exploitation of its people as well as against the undermining influences of hostile and unnational elements."[36]

The vagueness and general openness of this motion both to inclusive and exclusive varieties of Afrikaner nationalism no doubt reflected Malan's need to balance the militants' viewpoint with his own vestigial liberal scruples. Yet its very ambiguity permitted a hard-line interpretation no less threatening to traditional liberal democratic values.

The increasingly narrow self-perception of the National Party already allowed almost everyone outside its ranks to be considered "unnational." Now other questions necessarily arose. Were these people to be considered "hostile" to the republic in terms of Malan's motion? What would define a parasite? Would all capitalists be considered enemies of the state, or only those defined as such by a new republican government? It said much about the direction being taken by the party when a conservative and relatively moderate Nationalist like Malan advocated such a scheme.

When Malan at last gave permission for the Draft Constitution to be published in the Nationalist press "for discussion" only (suggesting reservations), *Die Transvaler* said he had considered the time "appropriate." As editor, Verwoerd stated openly that a thorough comparison between this piece and the party's program of principles and action, as well as Malan's recent republican motion in the Assembly, would show clearly that the party and its *Hoofleier* (chief leader) had accepted the scheme in its main principles and in its broad outlines.[37]

Verwoerd was obviously taking certain liberties with Malan's position on this issue, because the latter seems to have arranged for his own party organ, *Die Burger* in Cape Town, to dissociate itself from certain aspects of the Draft at the time of publication.[38] The two areas of contention were arbitrary restrictions on the franchise and the provision for Afrikaans as the only official language.[39] Nevertheless, there was clearly a great deal of support for the document in influential Nationalist circles, especially in the north, otherwise it would never have received such extensive treatment, being published in full over three days.

If Malan and the Old Guard in the Cape continued to have serious reservations about the Draft Constitution, they do not appear to have been very successful with the hard-liners in having this increasingly embarrassing scheme dropped. Alternatively, they may have been in substantial agreement with enough of this constitution not to be willing to split the party over minor points of contention.

A few years later the assistant commandant-general of the Ossewabrandwag in the Transvaal, J. A. Smith, said that, with a few amendments, the Draft Constitution had been accepted by the National Party as part of its program eighteen months after publication in the press, with the exception of the points rejected by *Die Burger* concerning restrictions on the franchise and Afrikaans as the sole official language. Smith argued that the

Ossewabrandwag had never distanced itself from this draft document,[40] suggesting a closer alliance of minds than is implied by the formal rift between the two organizations.

The influence of both German National Socialism and Kuyperian neo-Calvinism, with its references to sovereignty in each sphere, are particularly evident in the Draft Constitution. "Christian Nationalism" would be its basis. The flag would be the *Vierkleur* (four-colored flag) of Kruger's republic, the battle flag of the Anglo-Boer War. The head of state would be a president "responsible to God and the volk alone," but totally independent of the legislature,[41] chosen by enfranchised citizens, who were defined as those whites who could be expected to act in a *volksopbouend* way (roughly translated, a way constructive for the volk). The state would have the power to ensure that citizens as well as the mass media would not undermine public order, good morals, or the independence and dignity of the republic.[42]

The family sphere was to be given special priority, in keeping with the spirit of Kuyperian neo-Calvinism. The reason for the contentiousness of the proposals on language was clear: English was to be only a supplementary official language, with a status secondary to that of Afrikaans. Consonant with more authoritarian philosophies, the president was to be given wide powers, including the right to dismiss any cabinet minister. The president could give the prime minister the right to rule by decree in times of national emergency. This same provision in the otherwise democratic Weimar Constitution helped Hitler to concentrate all power in his hands.[43] Under certain circumstances, the president of the republic could submit referenda to the voters, the plebiscitary feature used to great effect by populist authoritarian rulers such as the Bonapartes in France and Paul Kruger in the Transvaal.[44] A similar technique would be used by Verwoerd in 1960 to create the long-awaited republic, and by P. W. Botha in 1983 to introduce a presidential system of government.

Parliament would consist of an elected Volksraad (literally translated, a People's Assembly) and a Communal Council, which, in the tradition of Italian Fascism, would be elected on corporatist lines by selected organizations like churches and professional bodies, rather than by direct vote. The council would also include presidential appointees, among them specialists on subjects such as "Indian infiltration" (*Indiërindringing*) and "Jewish overpopulation" (*Joodse oorbevolking*).[45]

There were no objections among the Nationalist establishment to the composition of the Communal Council. Jewish immigration had virtually stopped; if curbs on immigration were not to be the means of dealing with "Jewish overpopulation," the question arose as to how the suggested experts on the Communal Council would deal with their assigned problem. The party had come a long way indeed since the early thirties to feel comfortable with such proposals.

Although by the closing years of the war the Draft Constitution had become an embarrassment to the party and ever less was heard about it, it remains a crucial document for historians because it reveals the plans many Nationalists had in mind for South Africa, particularly in a context when an Axis victory seemed possible, even likely. It is true that this constitution foresaw a South African government that would allow for more pluralism than many conservative nationalist European and Latin American regimes of the period. There was no explicit ban on the existence of political parties other than the ruling one, elections were to be held at certain intervals, and there was some provision for public accountability. Nevertheless, the Draft Constitution needs to be read in conjunction with other evidence. Stalin's Soviet Constitution is a model of democratic values when read apart from its historical context; so too, the anti-Semitism in the South African Draft Constitution is a reflection of the Transvaal National Party ban on Jewish members, and of *Die Burger*'s rationalization of Hitler's mass removals of western European Jews to form labor gangs in Poland. The party's official organ argued that Jews were relentless enemies of Germany and had created problems in the occupied countries.[46]

Malan was increasingly uncomfortable with the Radical Right. But there was no change in the party attitude to the Jews even after the scope of Hitler's policies was clear. By December 1942 reports had reached South Africa that as many as two million Jews had been killed by the Nazis. A massive Day of Mourning was announced by the leaders of the South African Jewish community.[47] The Draft Constitution, appearing a year earlier, did not contradict the party's position, but affirmed it.

The Ambiguities of Authoritarian Volksdemokrasie

The liberal Native Representative, Donald Molteno, argued that Pirow split from the National Party at the same time as Malan's republican motion in Parliament only because the motion was not *sufficiently* pro-Nazi.[48] This was admittedly an interpretation that does not do justice to the significant differences of opinion between the National Party and its rivals on the Radical Right, but these differences were obviously becoming blurred for a significant section of public opinion.

Such differences were nonetheless very real in the perception of many leading Nationalists. For instance, T. E. Dönges, one of those behind the Draft Constitution, was convinced that Van Rensburg's acceptance of that document was just a ploy to appease the volk, which clearly wanted a "Christian National Republic." But he thought the commandant-general might later persuade the Ossewabrandwag to adopt full-scale national socialism, not only the *volksdemokrasie* favored by so many Afrikaners.[49]

Yet if Dönges and other Nationalists feared Van Rensburg as a potential despot, they had far fewer scruples about a tyranny of the party. Malan had indicated in August 1941 that one of the conditions of his accepting the mediation of the Unity Committee in the dispute with the Ossewabrandwag was an unambiguous acknowledgment by the committee that the National Party was the only organization exercising party-political leadership to represent "National-oriented Afrikanerdom" and that it had the right to the undivided loyalty of its members "in its own area."[50]

The Executive of the Transvaal National Party had been equally forthright in an earlier declaration of December 1940:

In the political sphere the Party demands the undivided loyalty of all its members. No member of the Party can therefore be a member of any other political party or any other organization with a political objective, which is declared by the Congress or by the Executive acting on behalf of the Congress as in conflict with the Principles of the Party or with the interests of the Party as a free and independent political body.[51]

Privately, Malan argued that it was a mistaken notion that the National Party and the Afrikaans press should be independent of each other. His views offended even his close friend A. L. Geyer, who retained some vestiges of the old Cape stand on freedom of the press.[52]

Despite Malan's opposition to overt personal dictatorship, he was very much part of the ambivalent concept of authoritarian *volksdemokrasie* now emerging. His political style inside the party was that of a one-man show, which makes it easier to understand why he did not have problems with most of the Draft Constitution.

Malan's approach to party management strengthens the argument that his feud with the Ossewabrandwag was based more on personal jealousy than on substantive concerns. He had been persuaded of the need to push through the special 1941 Union Nationalist Congress a reorganization scheme developed by Paul Sauer and P. W. Botha (later prime minister and then state president) that would place the party closer to the highly disciplined Ossewabrandwag.[53] The scheme was intended to replace the unwieldy complex of local branches, committees, and chairmen with cells of eight members each, headed by elected group leaders, and clustered in wards, with wards grouped in districts, each level headed by a "leader." Delegates to congresses would be elected by the district leaders. The aim was to increase grassroots party efficiency and control and, thereby, produce a highly effective political machine.[54] The similarity to the Nazi system of a tight network of membership units each grouped hierarchically into a *Gau* (district) is inescapable. Unlike the Nazis, or the similarly organized Ossewabrandwag, however, Nationalists were to elect their leaders rather than have them imposed from above, in keeping with the tradition of volk democracy. The principal difference from National Socialism was the plan to hold congresses and to call committees, at least at the higher levels of the party. Malan had ingeniously adapted something like the *Führerprinzip*, the Nazi principle of investing the leader with near-absolute power, to the needs of his own organization.

Malan organized the 1941 Union Congress to ensure that this scheme passed. He personally composed all proposals and sought out suitable proposers and seconders, accepting election as *Volksleier* only on condition of full support for this policy. This move left his outmaneuvered principal rival inside the party, Pirow, in utter silence. With *volmag* (full power) from the congress, Malan gained the support of many authoritarian-minded Ossewabrandwag followers who had previously opposed him.[55]

The younger men like Botha, Erasmus, and Sauer (all of them Cape Nationalists) had seen to it that the older institutions involved in reorganization would provide fewer obstacles to party leadership than in the past. Malan had tapped directly into the Kruger tradition of working inside a panoply of semidemocratic structures, while resorting to techniques of persuading, cajoling, and if necessary intimidating. Yet his approach was more streamlined than that of Kruger, and adapted to modern conditions, learning from the lessons of contemporary conservative authoritarian regimes, which similarly borrowed liberally from the currently ascendant Radical Right.

The "emergency" full powers assumed by Malan did not bode well for the kinds of powers that, under the Draft Constitution, might be entrusted by the president of the proposed republic to his prime minister in time of crisis. In the face of the possibility of a dramatic political realignment engendered by the highly fluid war situation, the congress resolved, subject to the approval of the provincial National Party congresses, to revise the system of party organization and to grant the party leader extraordinary powers:

Our Chief Leader . . . is therefore hereby empowered for the duration of the crisis or until the congresses themselves decide otherwise, to exercise all functions and conduct all dealings which fall within the power of any congress or of any party management, and insofar as he may deem it necessary or desirable in the interests of the unity and effectiveness of the party. These extraordinary powers will, whenever exercised in a specific case, be deemed to replace the effective powers of the congress or of the respective party management and not be a supplement to that.[56]

Malan thanked the Union Congress for these powers with a convincing display of humility; he denied that he wanted to be a dictator and expressed pleasure that he would still be subject to the provincial congresses.[57] His enthusiastic followers stood and applauded at the introduction of the proposal to entrust him with these powers, singing as they did so the Dutch song *Dat's Heeren Zeegen op u Daal* (That the Lord's Blessing Be upon You).[58]

The distinction between Malan's public emphasis on democratic niceties and private support for authoritarian practices reinforces the impression of a Janus-headed party beset by contradictions. Thus even Geyer, one of those least affected by imported authoritarian ideas, and sometimes downright hostile to them even in private, indicating as he had earlier in his diary his opposition for this reason to Diederichs and Meyer,[59] wrote to Otto du Plessis in March 1941: "When we achieve a republic, we can advocate a break with democracy if we consider it desirable, because then all anti-republican elements will have been eliminated [*uitgeskakel*]. But at this stage, while the course of the war and how it will affect us are still uncertain, a premature plea for the rejection of democracy can lead to serious disaster for the Afrikaner volk."[60]

It is true that the war had not made national socialists of the Nationalists. It had, however, forced the party into tactical arrangements and personal alliances with exponents of Radical Right philosophies that helped to nudge the Nationalists ever farther right. Despite the conscious rejection by the party leadership of "foreign ideologies," mainstream Afrikaner nationalism was now more authoritarian, more intolerant, and more elitist than in the past. Thus, while upholding the right of protest, the Federal Council of the National Party could in the same breath argue that the volk should not have to decide on whether to adopt "National Socialism" (the fashionable term for all the varieties of authoritarian nationalism current at the time) *before* the creation of a republic since ". . . with the achievement of the republic, the republican government will anyway need to have full power for some time to do everything to put the republic on a firm basis and to solve its most urgent questions."[61]

Of all the Nationalists, General Hertzog had made the most dramatic turnaround by his open advocacy of national socialism to resolve South Africa's problems. Yet his kind of radical alteration of standpoint was ultimately least significant, because he had already become marginal to the mainstream of the party. Similarly, proponents of full-fledged fascism like Pirow, Weichardt, and even Van Rensburg were all rendered irrelevant once the Germans' military fortunes changed. They ceased to pose a threat to the primacy of the National Party in Afrikaner politics; Malan's determination to adhere to his decision to break with the Far Right was therefore vindicated.

The changes in establishment Afrikaner nationalism were more cautious and less spectacular than Hertzog's belated conversion or the radicals' pseudofascism, but much more far-reaching. They were far more rooted in the Afrikaner past and more in touch with Afrikaner sensibilities than the policies of Pirow, Weichardt, or Van Rensburg. The authoritarian transformation of the National Party begun in the thirties and brought to fruition by 1942 was ultimately more acceptable to Afrikaners, primarily because of the way in which it was orchestrated by Malan and his experienced associates in the party.

By the time of the 1943 general election, Malan had isolated his right-wing Afrikaner opponents as exponents of foreign ideologies, as extremists with no sense of gratitude for what the party had done for Afrikanerdom. The mantle of Hertzog became more thoroughly Malan's than ever before, and with the passing of the old general in late 1942, lesser would-be Führers proved no match for the party and its leader. But the Nationalists had conceded much to make their program palatable. The radical populism of the thirties had been wedded to the authoritarian nationalism of the forties.

Chapter Nine

Healing the Schism

The Significance of the 1943 Election

The 1943 general election left Malan with a paltry 43 seats in the House of Assembly against 110 seats occupied by pro-war candidates. Within the pro-war coalition, including the small Labour and pro-imperial Dominion parties, Smuts's United Party had increased its representation from 71 seats at the dissolution of Parliament to 89. Malan had obtained a net increase of only three seats.[1] Seen superficially, Smuts had won his greatest victory, using an expanding wartime economy and a patriotic call to arms to win votes just as the likelihood of German defeat began to loom on the horizon. However, the United Party was not alone in profiting from these election results. The Nationalists' careful organizing had produced significant dividends and Malan had been substantially strengthened by the outcome of the election. Not only had most of Pirow's sixteen New Order members of Parliament refused to stand for reelection to this "liberal" legislature on ideological grounds,[2] but the remaining representatives of alternative varieties of Afrikaner nationalism, including both the moderate Afrikaner Party, with eight seats before the elections, and independent pro-Ossewabrandwag candidates, had all been soundly trounced. None of the candidates of the smaller Afrikaner groups was successful. Some Ossewabrandwag supporters may have voted for the National Party where there was no alternative way to register opposition to Smuts; others may have supported the Afrikaner Party, but many must have abstained, since the percentage poll (75.3 percent) was lower than in 1938 or 1948.[3]

Although the National Party lost some potential seats to Smuts because of the splitting of the antiwar vote by these "third party" candidates, Malan was now the unchallenged leader of the Afrikaner nationalist movement inside Parliament. The Radical Right gradually realized that the declining fortunes of the Third Reich left no alternative for taking power other than the ballot box. By April 1944 Strijdom was warning his top lieutenant in the Transvaal National Party, Verwoerd, that there was a strong possibility that Pirow, Weichardt, and Van Rensburg would soon team up to form a new party or at least some type of parliamentary front.[4]

Although no such alliance occurred, Van Rensburg did abandon his earlier disdain for elections and by late 1945 could tell a meeting of his followers, "the OB till now has considered the Parliamentary Front as secondary, but Stormjaers [Van Rensburg's extremist "stormtrooper" elite corps within the Ossewabrandwag] who are good enough to be sent to jail and concentration camps [a reference to Smuts's internment camps] are good enough to go to Parliament. The OB does not believe that its opponents have a monopoly in the area."[5]

Malan's pro-parliamentary strategy, based on a perceptive assessment of the likely direction of the war, had enabled him so successfully to dominate the field of Afrikaner nationalist politics that his rivals were left with no option but to confront him on his chosen battleground. At the time of the 1943 elections, however, when these opponents were not yet thoroughly convinced of the value of the electoral arena, Malan had demonstrated the National Party's greatly superior ability to elicit right-wing votes. The experienced National Party organization, which had never abandoned its belief in sound electoral preparedness, was a campaign machine against which its other nationalist rivals could not compete.

During the 1943 election the United Party identified the Nationalists, rather than the more flamboyant Ossewabrandwag, as the real threat to the Smuts government. Eric Louw, Strijdom's closest ally in the Cape National Party, disgustedly informed his friend of a revealing telegram from A. Oosthuizen, United Party organizing secretary, which had somehow fallen into Louw's hands. This telegram showed how far the pro-war forces were willing to go to thwart the National Party's advance. Oosthuizen, after consultation with United Party leaders, announced here the

withdrawal of his party in Louw's Beaufort West constituency—
in favor of a pro-OB independent candidate "to fight against
political enemy no. 1!"[6]

Oosthuizen's assessment was remarkably insightful. On 8 January 1947 the *Rand Daily Mail* would state that, according to
its own information, the Ossewabrandwag (which had once
claimed more than 100,000 members) had been reduced to perhaps 800 members, having increasingly lost supporters after the
rift with the National Party.[7] The Nationalists, on the other hand,
showed a continuing pattern of accelerating growth throughout
even the early war years, when the Ossewabrandwag was at its
strongest, and by 1943 the party was proving highly successful
in appealing to a broad range of Afrikaner voters. Without compromising on the essentials of their radical and "anti-capitalist"
republican creed, the Nationalists distanced themselves from the
more extreme rhetoric of the Ossewabrandwag, with its increasing emphasis on the "socialist" component of national socialism.
The OB alienated the most wealthy Transvaal farmers, whom the
party needed to make advances in that province.[8] The figures for
the Cape Party were particularly telling:

    1918: 17,000 members
    1929: 20,000
    1939: 35,000
    1940: 37,000
    1943: 76,000.[9]

In the last four years alone the Cape Party had more than doubled
its membership, something which had previously taken twenty
years to achieve.

Dan O'Meara notes that the growth of the National Party in
the years leading up to the 1943 election had another often forgotten dimension: by the end of the election campaign, Malan
had rid himself of almost all of the equivocating Hertzogite members of Parliament who had joined him at the time of reunification in early 1940. The twenty-nine former Fusionists had in
many cases joined either the extremist New Order on the right
or the moderate Afrikaner Party on the left. Others had been
expelled from the National Party or had retired from parliamentary politics. This left the much enlarged (at least in terms of

grass-roots support) Reunified National Party firmly in the hands of the hard-line and uncompromisingly republican leadership of the old Purified National Party.[10] Malan's position as Nationalist leader, already reinforced by his reorganization of the party, was therefore greatly strengthened.

Hertzog's former voters had increasingly drifted over to supporting the Malanite bloc. The 1943 election had shown a strong shift of support among the once pro-Fusion rural voters of the Transvaal and the Orange Free State to the Malanite Nationalists, formerly dominated by the urban and small-town Afrikaner petite bourgeoisie. The party gained ten new seats in the Transvaal (added to Strijdom's lone seat won in the 1938 election) and eight new seats in the heavily rural Orange Free State, giving them control of all but a single seat in that province.[11]

In 1938 approximately 60 percent of the Afrikaans-speaking vote had gone to Malan, while delivering him only 27 out of the 150 seats up for election (Native Representatives were elected separately), and the United Party had gained just over 40 percent of the Afrikaner vote. In 1943 the United Party dropped to about 32 percent, with a Nationalist gain of fifteen seats.[12]

Malan was rapidly reaching the point where his party could receive the percentage critically necessary in a winner-take-all system to gain a dramatically larger number of seats. Although Smuts continued to enjoy the support of a substantial number of Afrikaner voters, it was a declining minority.

Given the markedly more rapid growth of the Afrikaner population as against the English-speaking whites,[13] the Nationalists could look forward in the long term to ever greater prospects of success at the polls for Malan's party. This depended on garnering the remaining "national-minded" voters outside the party, particularly the Afrikaner working class and the section of the farmers' vote that Smuts still retained. If Smuts could only gain 32 percent of the Afrikaner vote with all the advantages of typical wartime patriotic support for the governing party, there was considerable potential for drawing away still more of his support once the war was over. Having warded off the threat from the extreme right in the early war years, Malan was now ready to expand beyond his traditional Afrikaner nationalist constituency to recruit additional support from moderate and radical Afrikaners alike.

Die Transvaler could well gloat in an April 1943 editorial, entitled "Have Confidence in the Future," about the increasing preponderance of Afrikaans-speakers among younger white South Africans, citing already dated 1936 census figures that actually underestimated the accelerating change in the composition of the white electorate: for every 100 English-speakers over twenty-one years, there were 115 Afrikaners; for every 100 English-speakers between the ages of seven and twenty-one, there were 185 Afrikaners; for every 100 English-speakers under seven, there were no fewer than 212 Afrikaans-speakers.[14]

But growth alone was not likely to produce substantial electoral gains for the National Party for some time. The party would have to look elsewhere for additional voters if it were to place itself within striking distance of victory in 1948, when the next election was due. This would mean in the first place the mobilization of the entire Afrikaner nationalist bloc, especially the alienated Radical Right.

The National Party Versus the Radical Right: A Nationalist Reading

To some extent, gaining the Radical Right vote appeared ever less of an obstacle to the National Party after 1943. By late 1944 Verwoerd could privately argue that, despite the lack of a clear swing away from the Ossewabrandwag, many still in the OB were waiting to see which way to jump, or were otherwise apathetic. In the long term, Verwoerd saw a tendency for Afrikaners to go over to the National Party, even among the intelligentsia, who were inclined to be the most critical of the party and to dabble most often in Radical Right alternatives.[15]

There was much to cause such dissatisfaction with the Ossewabrandwag among right-wing yet fundamentally conservative Afrikaners. In mid-1944 Frans Mentz, organizing secretary of the National Party on the Witwatersrand, was severely beaten by assailants presumed to be members of the extremist OB organization, the Stormjaers.[16] This attack led to a decree by Malan that congress decisions making Ossewabrandwag and National Party membership mutually irreconcilable be strictly enforced at all levels.[17] Brawling with Smuts supporters was one thing, but now even well-known Nationalists seemed fair game.

The Ossewabrandwag leadership took an openly pro–national socialist stand in the second half of the war, abandoning the earlier public convolutions. The OB youth wing, the Boerejeug (Boer youth), held "officers' training camps" with a syllabus of topics such as "Healthy National Socialism" and "National Socialism versus Capitalism and Communism."[18]

The worst fears of the party about the potential ideological direction of the Ossewabrandwag were being realized just as Van Rensburg was considering moderating his political stand sufficiently to permit participation in elections. By 1944 the Ossewabrandwag's official journal was blandly stating that while Pirow's professedly pro-Nazi New Order stood for national socialism, the OB lived it.[19]

The Nationalists' increasingly strident denunciations of national socialism, and of the Radical Right, suggested that any previous doubts about ideological differences between the party and its extremist rivals had been put to rest. The Nationalists now appeared to have nailed their flag firmly to the mast of at least a variant of parliamentary democracy, however much flawed by racism.

There is considerable evidence to support such an interpretation. Malan found himself in such a quandary over the course of the war that he told the party caucus that he feared that a German victory could actually be dangerous to the Nationalists (to which the incorrigible Strijdom replied that England would also be a threat, since it possessed Rhodesia).[20] Strijdom took an even stronger stance on principle when pressure was exerted by well-meaning Afrikaners to reconcile the party with the Radical Right. While those hopeful of a rapprochement between the Ossewabrandwag and the party stressed their joint opposition to large-scale "Jewish-British" capitalism and to the Union's connection with the British Crown, Strijdom declared angrily and revealingly to the equivocating Professor S. du Toit of Potchefstroom that the opposition of groups like the Ossewabrandwag and the New Order to British imperialism and capitalism pro-

vided as little common ground between them as these issues did
between the Nationalists and the Communists (the historic arch-
foe of Afrikaner nationalism):

The gulf between them and us consists in that while we build on the
democratic basis of the volk past in the religious as well as political
spheres, the destruction of democracy and the establishment of a National Socialist dictatorship, which Pirow conveniently calls an "Authoritarian" State and Van Rensburg an "Authority State," are a *sine
qua non* for both of them.[21]

The tendency of the National Party to moderate its views after
1943 to a more dramatic extent than after the 1941 rift with
the Ossewabrandwag was demonstated not only in its strenuous
opposition to any official rapprochement with the OB or New
Order, but in greater openness among some senior members to
a less exclusive notion of Afrikanerdom. T. E. Dönges, the powerful representative of the moderate wing of the party on the
Broederbond Executive and deputy chairman of the Bond from
1945, urged that the test of a true Afrikaner should not be a
person's descent, but his or her relationship to South Africa. For
purely pragmatic reasons, Dönges told his fellow members of the
Executive that as long as "right-minded" Afrikaners formed a
minority, support would have to be sought from friendly English-
speakers, without in any way diluting the republican principles
of the party. Pushing this Hertzog-like vision of nationalism, he
suggested that the Broederbond itself be used to persuade ordinary Afrikaners of the value of such support.[22]

This greater pragmatism and openness, which by 1947 led to
Malan's extending the hand of friendship to the Jewish community, although not without considerable resistance from party
hard-liners,[23] may be construed as a fundamental change of direction after a few "superficial experiments with National Socialism," as Nationalist historian F. J. van Heerden puts it.[24]
From this viewpoint, the most that could be said against Nationalist wartime behavior is that the party cynically but understandably enough hoped to make the most of the chances of a
German victory to promote its own republican program. As soon
as such a victory seemed unlikely, the party leadership changed
tack and returned to the historically tried and tested course of
trusting to the ballot box. It was logical that English-speaking

or even Jewish votes, however few in number, might be needed to obtain power for the Nationalists by that route. Afrikaner votes would be essential, but they might not be enough, especially if Smuts retained much of his Afrikaans-speaking support.

If one continues the Van Heerden line of thought, mainstream Afrikaner nationalism, apart from a little anti-Semitism in the thirties induced by the difficulties of economic competition during the Depression, along with a few minor lapses in democratic good sense, was seemingly not fundamentally affected by the rise of national socialism in Europe. The argument concludes that, because Afrikaner public opinion did not continue shifting rightward after the first year or two of the war, the winds of fascism had at most a highly visible but essentially temporary impact only on a few radical Afrikaner organizations, from which the National Party, in this view, did its best to distance itself.

The National Party and the Radical Right: The Continuing Courtship

This "democratic" interpretation of National Party activity during the age of the dictators falters, however, not only because it fails to take seriously the profound changes in attitudes and values in the party or the sheer scope of subversive and pro-Axis activity among many Afrikaner nationalists during the first half of the war. It also fails to consider the complex ways in which the National Party and the Radical Right were linked not only before 1943, but in which they also continued to flirt with each other in the years leading up to the historic 1948 elections. Every move by the National Party in the opposite direction, that of greater moderation and inclusiveness, has to be read in this context.

The party attitude on the war issue is a key pointer to the relative strengths or weaknesses of the argument that whatever support the Nationalists gave to the German cause in the early war years was at most opportunistic and transient. On at least one occasion Malan took a position about a possible German victory that was indistinguishable from that of the Radical Right, despite his earlier statements to the contrary. In late April 1943, just before the election campaign, Malan told an audience at

Vredendal in the Western Cape that, if the National Party came to power, it would halt the Union's active role in the war and recall South African troops, but that making peace would depend on *both* sides allowing the new government to do so. This was nothing more than a restatement of the traditional neutrality policy, but Malan gave a new twist to the old and partly discredited argument that a German victory would permit the creation of a republic, about which Malan obviously had some doubts. He used the "Red Menace" to make substantially the same point by a less direct route: "It is 100 times better that England and America lose the war because if England and America win the war, since Russia is winning it for them, then the leader of Communism will force Communism on the world."[25] At so late a date, after the decisive German defeats at El Alamein and Stalingrad, and after widespread Nazi atrocities had begun to be exposed,[26] Malan still preferred an Axis to an Allied victory. It was only the reasoning behind such a conclusion that had changed. As the Nazi cause became discredited by military defeat, Nationalist rhetoric on this subject changed. Now an Allied victory would not be a good thing because it would allegedly enhance the Communist threat. No self-respecting Afrikaner nationalist could disagree that the Communists, with their known support for black liberation and their potentially divisive influence on poor whites, would be a serious threat.

The indigenous Radical Right was a much more complex problem. As Hitler's fortunes waned, the Nationalists would have to come to some kind of an arrangement with their radical rivals. The National Party could never hope to attract moderates if it did not distance itself from anything that sounded like "national socialism," especially as the Nazis became increasingly discredited both by the military defeats of 1944 and 1945 and by the growing revelations of the magnitude of Nazi atrocities after the German surrender in May 1945.[27] Yet a Nationalist electoral victory would require support from the "antidemocratic" Radical Right. Both directions had to be followed simultaneously if the Afrikaner nationalist movement was to come to power at any point in the foreseeable future.

Thus, despite Verwoerd's public militancy in opposing cooperating with the Radical Right, his private relationships were often more complicated. After losing a 1943 libel suit against a Johannesburg pro-war newspaper, *The Star,* which had charged him with promoting Nazi propaganda, messages of support came from men long identified with the Radical Right. Diederichs, for example, sent a letter of support to his "dear friend" expressing shock at the court judgment; he told Verwoerd that he would encourage those in the nationalist movement to help defray the costs of the case.[28] Diederichs asked that his letter not be published.

Another independent radical, Albert Hertzog, who was on first-name terms with Verwoerd, wanted to know if the party-controlled Voortrekker Pers, which published *Die Transvaler,* was paying his friend's costs. He said that Verwoerd was attempting to fight "the whole money-power and the spiritually corrupt judicial benches which reign supreme in our land."[29] Just as the Smuts forces, savoring victory for the first time since the outbreak of war, were successfully targeting individual Afrikaner nationalists such as Verwoerd as traitors to South Africa, so nationalists now had to join forces against the hated alliance of Smuts's "British imperialism" and large-scale capitalists.

Verwoerd and Hertzog, like Diederichs, were for most of this period members of the Executive of the Broederbond.[30] The first two were not only personal friends; they also collaborated closely on the key Broederbond project of promoting the cause of all-Afrikaner trade unions to replace the "Leftist" and often non-segregated unions in the textile industry to which belonged many Afrikaans-speaking women.[31] This friendship and collaboration may explain why, once Hertzog had taken his late father's place on the board of *Die Vaderland,* the Afrikaner Party organ, which had hitherto been sympathetic to all non–National Party Afrikaner causes, it grew more tolerant of Verwoerd's abrasively Nationalist *Transvaler.*[32]

Hertzog and Diederichs represented some of the most radical trends in Afrikaner nationalism, roughly analogous respectively to those of the socialist-minded Strasser brothers and Party philosopher Alfred Rosenberg in the German Nazi movement. Albert Geyer, the editor of Malan's *Die Burger,* had, as noted earlier, privately described Diederichs as a "Nazi through-and-through."[33] Like the Ossewabrandwag during the second half of the war, the "anticapitalist" Hertzog was dedicated to improving the lot of the Afrikaner worker, especially on the mines. He aimed at having this class on the side of the Broederbond in "the coming revolution" and saving them from "the grip of Communism."[34]

Yet Hertzog's and Diederichs's radical views did not prevent Verwoerd from relating to these men on an intimate basis. They were members not only of the Broederbond Executive, but also of its still more powerful Management Committee.[35] Beyond that, their friendship, notwithstanding differences of opinion on issues like the Ossewabrandwag–National Party relationship,[36] suggests that Verwoerd was not particularly offended by their extreme views. The reason for this was simple enough.

Although sympathetic to both the Ossewabrandwag and the party, neither Hertzog, Jr., nor Diederichs was part of the OB establishment, which probably mattered a great deal to Verwoerd. Verwoerd's notoriously bitter feud with the Ossewabrandwag was based far more on personal and organizational jealousies than on fundamental differences in ideology. Indeed, some insiders believed the real reason for Verwoerd's animosity was the Ossewabrandwag's rejection of his candidacy for the position of its assistant commandant-general in the Transvaal.[37]

Hard-line party leaders like Verwoerd could deal quite comfortably with outspoken representatives of radical or authoritarian nationalism, but they could not abide a challenge to National Party control of Afrikaner nationalist politics. After the Nationalist victory in 1948, two of the new party backbenchers in the House of Assembly were none other than Albert Hertzog and Nico Diederichs.[38]

The radical-moderate dichotomy in party ranks did not necessarily coincide with one's degree of opposition to the Far Right. Hard-liners like Strijdom, Verwoerd, and Eric Louw were more likely to oppose attempts at Afrikaner unity than the Old Guard in the Cape party. Louw, for instance, was upset by a Geyer editorial in *Die Burger* advocating reconciliation between nationalist organizations after the 1943 elections.[39] Malan's paper in the Cape was one of the first parts of the National Party machine to move toward a pragmatic joining of Afrikaner nationalist forces now that the party's primacy had been established at the polls.

Strijdom was furious about a 1947 decision of the Cape National Party congress to admit members of the Ossewabrandwag into the party without requiring that they resign from their organization. The sole proviso was that applicants renounce OB principles that were in conflict with party membership. Strijdom regarded the fuzzy language of the Cape party resolution as "crazy," because it would encourage uncommitted Ossewabrandwag members to join the Nationalists while the Nationalists' prospective election partners in 1948, the Afrikaner Party, gained hard-line OB members because of its more lax membership rules.[40]

The far more exclusivist, anti-Semitic, and authoritarian tone of the nationalism of Verwoerd, Strijdom, and Louw suggests that they had more in common with the Radical Right than the Cape moderates. Yet the pragmatism of the Cape establishment and their supporters, like Dönges in the Transvaal, which allowed them the seeking of allies among non-Afrikaners, also permitted the bending of principle in the interests of Afrikaner unity, assuming that inherent conflicts of interest could be put aside.

The most obvious conflict of interest was Van Rensburg's attachment to a nonparty state, which would necessitate the destruction of the Nationalist machine. The tensions over this difference almost led to schism in the National Party in the months leading up to the 1948 election. Malan's developing strategy did not prove easy to sell to Nationalist hard-liners. The enthusiastic but cynical turnarounds Malan could perform so well could only depress if not exasperate those colleagues with a less flexible attitude to principle.

Strijdom, for instance, was deeply embittered by Malan's willingness to overlook Afrikaner Party leader Havenga's easygoing attitude toward Ossewabrandwag members of his organization. Malan was so keen to forge an electoral alliance with Havenga's otherwise moderate party, the embodiment of the old Hertzogite nationalist tradition, that he failed to pin down Havenga on the question of whether Ossewabrandwag members could stand as

Afrikaner Party candidates. This failure, along with Malan's turnabout on the Jewish question, which infuriated party right-wingers like Strijdom and C. R. Swart, the Orange Free State party leader, led Strijdom in September 1947 to threaten resigning as leader in the Transvaal.[41] Strijdom told Malan he would withhold a decision until after the elections, depending on what happened on cooperation between the party and the "Afrikaner Party–OB–New Order combination."[42] Strijdom informed Louw that if Malan and what he mysteriously described as his "new advisors" (who he did not specify) did not change their positions on the Ossewabrandwag and also on the Jewish issue, he would leave active politics forever.[43] In a letter to Swart, Strijdom stressed that pushing the Jewish question would lead to a schism in the party.[44]

Despite Malan's willingness to deal with the Afrikaner Party and other groups on a more open-ended and pragmatic basis than the purist republicans centered in the northern provinces, however, even he was unwilling to make too many concessions to his new ally, Havenga. The ugliness of the 1941 rift made impossible any easy transition to a really broad-based volk alliance. When John Vorster was put up as an Afrikaner Party candidate, Havenga was forced to yield to the Nationalist position that Ossewabrandwag members could not stand as actual candidates for the nationalist alliance. Vorster then stood as an independent, without Nationalist support, in the Witwatersrand town of Brakpan, and lost by four votes to the government candidate.[45] In this sense, the hard-nosed and authoritarian strategy that had come to characterize the National Party leadership during the early war years had not been discarded by even its most pragmatic figures. Malan could be just as stubborn and ruthless in his pragmatic pursuit of power as his tough northern colleagues were in their unforgiving attachment to alleged National Party principle and policy.

Ordinary party members, however, had become increasingly weary of all these professed stands on principle. Privately, some Nationalist candidates assured Van Rensburg that they were tired of such bitterness and that they accepted Ossewabrandwag members as "full-fledged Afrikaners" in the anti-Smuts alliance.[46] The same practical considerations that led Malan and the

Daniel Malan and his wife, Maria (preceding him), leaving Parliament in Cape Town. Malan, a former Dutch Reformed preacher, was first editor of the Nationalist newspaper *Die Burger*. A cabinet minister under Hertzog (1924–1934), he led the Purified Nationalists (1934–1940), and became deputy leader of the Reunited National Party, then leader, after Hertzog's departure from the party in 1940. He was prime minister from 1948 to 1954.

From the Cape Times *Collection in the South African Library*

J. G. ("Hans") Strijdom, c. 1946, pro-republican wartime leader of the National Party in the Transvaal, later prime minister (1954–1958).

From the Cape Times *Collection in the South African Library*

MALANITE FEARS OF IMMIGRATION

MR. LOUW AGAIN ON THE ATTACK

A new demand for the stoppage of Jewish immigration was made by Mr. Eric Louw (H.P., Beaufort West) when the Interior Vote was reached in Committee of Supply in the Assembly this afternoon.

MR. LOUW said the Herenigde Party was not against immigration provided full attention was given to the needs of South Africans and provided immigration was limited to desirable immigrants. The Herenigde Party was concerned about the employment position after the war and believed that, as there was already a Jewish question in the Union, Jewish immigration should be stopped.

As a result of the war a serious state of affairs would exist in Europe. Many thousands would be homeless and the problem of reabsorbing returned soldiers in employment would be difficult. It was said that this question would be discussed at the forthcoming conference of Dominion Prime Ministers.

A disturbing factor was the recent statement by the Minister of Lands that the Government was prepared, under Section 11 of the Land Settlement Act, to make land available to British returned soldiers after the war. The House wanted a clear statement of the Government's policy on post-war immigration.

"JEWISH PROBLEM"

During 1943 1,825 Jews had entered South Africa under temporary permits. The Minister had said that that number included Jews domiciled in South Africa who were returning to the Union after a short absence, but he had not stated how many of those people there were. From January, 1939, to December, 1942, 1,557 Jews had entered South Africa under permanent permits.

There was clearly a Jewish problem and one of the ways it could be tackled was by putting an immediate stop to the immigration of Jews into South Africa.

"GROWING HOLD"

The Opposition had already shown the growing hold of the Jewish population on the trade, industry and professions of the country. Their hold on the medical profession was especially pronounced. In the Witwatersrand Medical-School at present 442 of 823 students were Jews.

The alarm in the country was understandable. That was why the Opposition argued that all Jewish immigration should be stopped. He felt that the question could not be settled by stopping immigration because the damage had already been done. The only solution was to apply a quota system to all trades, professions and industries.

There had been a decided improvement in the matter of the changing of names. As the result of repeated protests from the Opposition the department was exercising more care in allowing such changes.

MR. M. ALEXANDER (U.P., Cape Town Castle) said if there was a Jewish question in the Union that was because it had been created by Mr. Louw and the Opposition in order to snatch votes. He would have thought that after the Opposition's melancholy experience of the last election they would have dropped this matter like a hot potato.

Mr. Louw, quoting from documents which he openly admitted were stolen, had used the method of taking a line or a sentence and distorting it. What was the House coming to when a member could introduce documents which he knew and admitted were stolen and when the Supreme Court had placed an interdict on their use?

If Mr. Louw had read the documents fully instead of quoting extracts out of their context he would have had no case at all.

WHOLESALE IMMIGRATION

Mr. Alexander said he stood fully by the declaration he had made in 1937, in reply to an accusation by Dr. Malan that Jewry was preparing to organise wholesale immigration of Jewish refugees from Europe. He had made that reply to Dr. Malan not only in his own name, but on behalf of the Jewish Board of Deputies.

It was recognised that immigration in South Africa was a national question. No organisation had ever sent money from South Africa to bring in immigrants. The Jewish people realised that the Opposition would make unscrupulous use of an increase in the Jewish population by immigration.

What the Jewish people objected to was discrimination in immigration.

"New Jewish Problem," an article in *Cape Argus*, 10 April 1944. Nationalist member of Parliament Eric Louw was persisting in leading attacks against further Jewish immigration; Louw proposed introduction of quotas limiting the numbers of South African Jews in each trade or profession. Morris Alexander was a prominent United Party parliamentarian and a leading figure in the Jewish community.

Cape leadership to an understanding with the Afrikaner Party led rank-and-file Nationalists, even in the Transvaal, to seek individual arrangements with local OB members. For instance, the Ossewabrandwag helped to elect Nico Diederichs to Parliament, despite Malan's strong disapproval of accepting its public support.[47] Ordinary party members had difficulty understanding why their leaders were now making so much fuss about the differences between themselves and their more outspokenly radical compatriots. Strijdom expressed extreme frustration at their failure to understand that "the differences between us and the OB are radical and profound differences of principle."[48]

It was not hard to see why many grass-roots Nationalists were alarmed at the intransigence of their leaders. A man like Pirow, the New Order leader, who had been the crucial intermediary between Hertzog and Malan back in 1940 on the allocation of seats to prevent the shipwrecking of nationalist Afrikanerdom reunification,[49] had been consigned to political oblivion by an unyielding leadership.

Malan, on the other hand, had sometimes been quite forgiving during the war on the issue of political violence, despite his constant denunciation of such methods. When two young OB Stormjaers, Visser and Van Blerk, were sentenced to death for their role in a fatal bombing attack, Malan, correctly judging that a move for clemency could only strengthen his position among militant republicans, led the successful campaign for commutation of their sentences.[50]

From the perspective of rank-and-file Nationalists facing a crucial election, if Malan was willing to mount a campaign to save the lives of convicted killers, why were he, and even more so, his lieutenants in the Transvaal, so determined to isolate rivals whose only sin had been to espouse the doctrines of Nazi Germany, once upheld in party circles as a model state?[51]

Similar questions could be asked about Strijdom's negative response when Theo Wassenaar, a prominent party activist in Pretoria, asked him to share a platform with OB officer and major Afrikaner intellectual Dr. Geoffrey Cronjé at a meeting against Smuts's postwar moves to give Indians a limited franchise that would allow them to elect three white representatives to the Assembly. Amid popular outrage at Smuts's "liberaliz-

ing,"[52] Wassenaar begged Strijdom to appear, since Cronjé was
an "expert" on the Indian question and because it would be a
good idea to further such volk cooperation at so crucial a juncture. Wassenaar noted that he had found much goodwill on a
visit to Barberton in the Eastern Transvaal, where Ossewabrandwag members had worked hard for the party cause on the local
election committee.[53] Yet Strijdom rejected in the strongest terms
speaking on the same platform as Cronjé or any other OB leaders,[54] but like-minded Nationalists such as Verwoerd found it
increasingly difficult to stop the growing pressure to reach an
agreement with the Ossewabrandwag. Verwoerd went so far as
to suggest publishing as a pamphlet a report by OB assistant
Commandant-General J. A. Smith highlighting the internal difficulties of the Ossewabrandwag. In Verwoerd's words, such a
project might kill the "reconciliation-among-the-volk stories."[55]

Yet the purist republicans failed to stem the tide of goodwill
between the two nationalist camps. During the by-election campaign for the rural Transvaal seat of Wolmaranstad, hundreds of
non-Nationalist voters approached former member of Parliament
Lodewyk Wentzel to stand as a candidate for the Radical Right.
However, during a meeting on 15 February 1947, his election
committee decided that he should stand back for the National
Party candidate, who stood "for a white South Africa, anti-Asian
[sic], anti-Communism, separation and the solution of the native
question."[56] There was too little to divide the Radical Right from
the party to make a third candidate plausible in a race against
Smuts and his alleged liberalism. Delegations from the Ossewabrandwag and the New Order in the Wolmaranstad district
therefore proceeded to a meeting of the party, where the radicals
offered to stand back in favor of the Nationalists in order to
further the Afrikaner cause against Smuts. This generous move
was received with warmth by the local party organization.[57]
Practical considerations had triumphed over the leadership's intransigence.

A similar spirit reigned elsewhere in the Transvaal. In the
Tzaneen district, where the party organization had hitherto been
weak, one E. J. Smit had developed a flourishing series of
branches by April 1947, drawing on the cooperation of Ossewabrandwag members, including OB officers, with himself as

party chairman. The local New Order leader, Dr. Ernest, gave his followers' unqualified support to Smit, who permitted all and sundry to join the party, in the hope of proving, as he put it, the "fraternal love" with which the Afrikaner cause was promoted in the far north. No fewer than six new party branches were set up on this basis in the Transvaal Lowveld.[58]

The Radical Right itself was beginning to realize that, with the destruction of the Nazi regime, Afrikaner nationalists would have to put their weight behind the National Party if they were to savor victory. Smit confided to his provincial secretary that local Ossewabrandwag members had recognized the need to return to the time-hallowed path of the ballot box and were returning to the party:

> In a private conversation, prominent OBs in Tzaneen declared that there had been a time when they had felt that the age of making crosses was past—but the war is over, and in the time in which we are now living, the feeling is that the means which the Reunited National Party offers are the only ones with which we can fight our volk enemies.[59]

Strijdom denounced the collaboration at Tzaneen in a circular sent to Transvaal party branches and representatives, declaring it in clear contravention of congress decisions. He angrily charged the Ossewabrandwag with wanting to set up "a dictatorship like those of Hitler, Mussolini or Stalin," hoping that such examples would shock his readers.[60] Times had changed. More than scare tactics or decrees were needed to prevent grassroots Nationalist support for reconciliation with the Ossewabrandwag.

The Nationalist leadership would have to find a way to match at an interorganizational level what they had already begun to achieve inside the party in policy, organization, and philosophy. The path to victory required a true wedding of the Old and the New Right under a single banner that would be democratic, authoritarian, and nationalist at the same time. After the 1943 elections, there could be no doubt as to whose banner this would be.

Chapter Ten

Unity Is Strength

The Afrikaner nationalist movement was not just the National Party anymore, but a vast conglomerate of organizations, many of them more or less clandestine, that had too much at stake to let personal pride or organizational jealousy stand in their way. The party's public stand against a broad volk alliance was doomed to failure. Outside the ranks of the party leadership, the many "volk organizations" such as the Reddingsdaadbond, the huge Federation of Afrikaner Cultural Organizations, and above all, the secret Afrikaner Broederbond (AB) were supplementing the efforts of grass-roots party activists to bring together those who they felt belonged together.

The Role of the Broederbond

General J. C. G. Kemp, the elderly co-leader of the Transvaal National Party and one of the few Hertzogites left in high party office, was one Nationalist who understood only too well how his fellow leaders' efforts were being countered by this alternative organizational network. In an address to the Transvaal party management committee in April 1944, he said:

This ostensibly peaceful crusade [Broederbond activities] was the most powerful instrument . . . with which the subversive bodies intended to bring about the realisation of their ideal, viz. to create a S. African Republic. . . . These subversive groups were never more dangerous [to the government] than they are today, as they have, after many years of bickering, found (through the Broederbond) a possible solution of the problem of uniting the great majority of the Afrikaans elements.[1]

Kemp grasped clearly here the manner in which, beneath all the factional rivalry, the cause of the *Volksbeweging*, the movement of the whole "national-minded" volk, was impelling the National Party toward an alliance between the Old and the New Right.

The Broederbond itself was never mentioned in the Afrikaans-language opposition press.[2] This was not surprising, for it was in the Bond that the party and the Radical Right confronted each other year in and year out, and it was in the Bond that they were forced to learn to work with each other.

The Broederbond had developed a veritable empire of front organizations in every field from education to economics. As far back as the turn of the century, early Afrikaner nationalists in the Western Cape had succeeded in obtaining widespread support for the Afrikaner banking and insurance companies that provided the financial support for the rise of the prosperous Cape National Party.[3] Now once again political mobilization on ethnic lines was paralleled by a growing financial mobilization of the Afrikaner people, but this time intended to reach into the most remote districts.

Business undertakings under direct Broederbond control had assets totaling close to eight million pounds. These included banks like Volkskas (people's bank), financial houses like Federale Volksbeleggings (federal people's investments), manufacturing plants, and both wholesale and retail commercial concerns such as the Uniewinkel (union store) chain.[4] The Broederbond had an impressive stake in the success of the Afrikaner nationalist movement, but this was something that required also a revival of political unity.

If the proven effectiveness of the National Party as an electoral machine could be united with the militancy and idealism of the Ossewabrandwag, and more especially with the genius of the volk associations in organizing on the most mundane social and economic levels, victory could be theirs. Smuts and the big capitalists, with their attentions focused constantly on international affairs and the problems of macro-economics, would, it seems to me, face an unprecedentedly well organized opposition movement, which understood the importance of carefully mobilizing Afrikaners in every sphere. The Broederbond had in mind an ethnic machine that would have been the envy of any fascist regime, but with the enormous added advantage of being able to function highly effectively inside a pluralistic and parliamentary state.

Like many authoritarian nationalist and fascist movements abroad, which often developed far more into broad rightist coalitions than their dictatorial leaders were ready to admit, the *Volksbeweging* spoke in both the language of socialism, as did Albert Hertzog, and of capitalism, as did Nico Diederichs. This capitalism was, however, to be of a special kind, geared not to the aggrandizement of individuals nor even of specific organizations, but to strengthening the nationalist movement as a whole, to the salvation of the entire volk, including its less privileged members. As Diederichs and his associate J. G. van der Merwe argued, in a presentation to the 1944 annual assembly or Bondsraad of the Broederbond, in order to *fight* capital, capital was necessary.[5] Thus enemies of traditional large-scale capitalism justified the creation of a financial and commercial empire. As with fascist movements abroad, this had a special appeal to small businessmen, in particular, and to the petite bourgeoisie, in general, but it could sound reassuring to many workers and to larger-scale businessmen as well.[6]

Indeed, the great strength of the Afrikaner *Volksbeweging* was that, long before achieving control of the state, it was developing a partnership between a mass political movement and a growing network of emergent sympathetic, and in this case self-made, capitalists like Diederichs. Unlike most analogous political movements abroad, there was to be considerable tolerance of political and economic pluralism within the *Volksbeweging,* at least until it could be consolidated under the banner of one political organization. From the viewpoint of the Broederbond, it was crucial that the ancient Afrikaner fractiousness be submerged in the interest of the greater good. In this spirit, even Verwoerd himself made no distinctions between nationalist Afrikaners of different ideological persuasions when he told the 1943 Broederbond annual assembly that there was no excuse for a *Broeder* who deliberately bought goods at a "foreigner's" shop when he could obtain similar goods in any Afrikaner establishment.[7]

There were many examples of politicians' joint involvement in Broederbond-organized economic ventures. There was, for instance, the Voortrekker Motor Club, a Bond front organization bold enough to use as its emblem a triangle like the Bond symbol. Despite the club's apparently innocuous purpose, its controlling committee included such prominent *Broeders* as Karl Bremer, F. C. Erasmus, and J. G. Strijdom, top party men in both the Cape and the Transvaal, and the first two very close to Malan himself. Similarly, Verwoerd, Diederichs, and I. M. Lombard, the pro-Ossewabrandwag secretary of the Broederbond during the war, although at odds on many political issues, were among eight directors of the Park Lane Nursing Home in Johannesburg, which was, characteristically, purchased through a Broederbond dummy concern, Gesondheidsdiens Eiendoms Beperk (Health Services Properties Limited).[8]

The potential for extending still further the scope of such ties was evident even in as well-known an opponent of Ossewabrand-wag–National Party cooperation as Verwoerd. According to a rare intelligence report, as spokesman for the Broederbond Executive, Verwoerd urged Bond members at their 1943 meeting to work not only on major national issues, but also at the most minute level in the interests of an all-embracing Afrikaner nationalist primacy:

They must attend to the little things. . . . It was also not sufficient merely to support each other. It was the calculated policy of the AB to gain control of as many key points as they could. Members of the AB should help each other to become members of school committees, village committees, town and city councils. In short, the AB must gain control of everything it could lay its hands on, in every walk of life in South Africa, and must not refrain from pushing its members into any key point whatsoever.[9]

Among those present at this meeting were Albert Hertzog, Diederichs, Dönges, Swart (a future state president), and H. J. Klopper, later longtime Nationalist speaker of the House of Assembly.[10]

The chairman of the meeting, Professor J. C. van Rooy, a man known for his Ossewabrandwag sympathies and long a key figure in the Radical Rightist ANS-Potchefstroom alliance, deplored the division between the party and the Ossewabrandwag, which he noted had, unbeknownst to the public, been played out "in the very heart of the AB." Van Rooy urged the 2,528 members of the Bond to unite against the real enemy, "the British-Jewish capitalists."[11]

Both Verwoerd and Van Rooy, although at opposite ends of the party-Ossewabrandwag spectrum in the Broederbond, had to acknowledge that the advancement of the volk was one issue upon which otherwise inveterate opponents could agree.

Thus when Smuts's enthusiastic young liberal-minded lieutenants such as E. G. Malherbe, the director of military intelligence, began to push for a program of school education taught in both English and Afrikaans, usually bitter enemies joined ranks. When the educational front organization of the Broederbond, the National Institute for Education and Training (usually known by its Afrikaans acronym, NIOO), was thrown full gear into this campaign, the pro-Ossewabrandwag Van Rooy thought nothing of nominating a rising party man such as Eben Dönges to the management committee of the institute.[12]

Backed by the party, the OB, New Order, Broederbond, and FAK, Dr. van Rhyn, editor-in-chief of the Nationalist daily in the Free State, *Die Volksblad,* and a staunch party member, was appointed full-time "Information Officer" to lead the campaign against dual-medium education.[13] On the other hand, among the full-time organizers for the Broederbond-orchestrated campaign was the Reverend G. D. Worst, an Ossewabrandwag member, who was also chairman of the Reddingsdaadbond in Potchefstroom and of the Synodal Commission for Training and Education of the powerful Transvaal Nederduitse Gereformeerde Kerk (the largest of the three Afrikaans Reformed churches in that province).[14]

One does not have to subscribe to a conspiracy theory of history that suggests the subordination of the National Party to the hidden hand of the Broederbond in order to see that on occasion the Bond did take on the role of a supra-party organization in the interests of protecting the volk cause. In August 1944, for example, Nico Diederichs raised the issue of a series of contentious articles in the popular magazine *Die Huisgenoot.* The articles concerned matters dealing with the struggle of Afrikaner clothing workers, an issue being dealt with by the Broederbond.[15]

Diederichs's fellow Bond Executive members acted swiftly to

squelch this unwanted interference, even though *Die Huisgenoot* was produced by the publishing house of the Cape National Party. The Executive decided to inform H. J. Otto, a fellow Bond member and chief manager of Nasionale Pers, Malan's own publishing vehicle in Cape Town, that it objected to publication of these articles. Absent Broederbond Executive member J. H. Conradie, a leading Cape Nationalist, would also specifically be informed about the matter, and Otto would "be made aware of the facts."[16]

Similarly, when the Broederbond was attempting to mediate between the Ossewabrandwag and the party, it could call upon the good offices of Dönges, as vice chairman of the Bond Executive, to present to Malan an AB plan. Thus the Broederbond would act as the supreme arbiter of nationalist Afrikanerdom. Dönges was detailed to find out Dr. Malan's and other party leaders' attitude about welcoming members of the Ossewabrandwag and New Order if the Broederbond declared that there was only one political party, Malan's, and that the Bond would use all its influence to ensure compliance with this position.[17] Although there is no indication that Malan ever accepted such a proposal, the Broederbond position was quite clear: if the National Party in its pride was not going to assist the cause of unity, the Broederbond was determined to step into the breach.

The interconnecting web between the party, the Broederbond, and the Ossewabrandwag, just as in the early war years, remained a powerful tool in structuring a new kind of Afrikaner nationalist politics in the years leading up to the 1948 elections. A family model—a quarrelsome family—seems appropriate to describe the relationship. Sometimes the family was more than a simile. *Broeder* C. F. Visser, strategically placed at the head of the large but ostensibly apolitical Afrikaner boy scout organization, the Voortrekkers, was married to the widow of N. J. van der Merwe, the revered late leader of the Free State National Party and longtime head of the FAK, the huge Broederbond cultural front organization. Mrs. Visser, in turn, headed the girls' branch of the Voortrekkers.[18]

At every level the *Volksbeweging* could outbid the Smuts camp in organization, efficiency, and devotion to promoting group interests. Only the Nationalist–Radical Right feud prevented the extension of its growing unity of purpose to the party-political sphere.

The Cronjé and Eloff Cases: Mainstream Nationalists and Radical Right Race Theorists

The myriad connections between the nationalist camps pushed them together in party politics as well. The patronage network was one key element in this process. This patronage system was firmly in the tradition of Kruger's republic,[19] but it was far more sophisticated and complex than anything in the old Transvaal's ramshackle patriarchal state. The nature of this patronage demonstrates the key role of the Broederbond in promoting the interests of volk unity.

A good example is the use of an April 1946 Bond circular to recommend for purchase *Broeder* Geoffrey Cronjé's new work, *Afrika Sonder die Asiaat* (Africa Without the Asian).[20] Cronjé was the key Ossewabrandwag intellectual, introduced in the previous chapter, with whom Strijdom had refused to share a platform, yet the heavily Nationalist Broederbond was now helping sell his book.[21]

Cronjé, like Verwoerd, Diederichs, and Hertzog, Jr., was a German-trained Afrikaner academic, and a leading sociologist. According to the South African sociologist and noted author on Afrikaner nationalism, Dunbar Moodie, "The foremost proponent of [the] racist strain in separate development theory was Geoff Cronje, whose ideas derive directly from National Socialist ideology within the OB."[22] Like many National Party men, he had also been an opponent of Jewish immigration. Cronjé's views on race were in contrast to the cultural-anthropological approach of more liberal Nationalists like W. W. M. Eiselen, later Verwoerd's secretary of native affairs.[23] Eiselen was concerned to preserve the heritage of each African ethnic group; Cronjé's books, in contrast, were based heavily on the fear of miscegenation and the disappearance of the white race. Both were extremely influential in the shaping of apartheid ideology. Cronjé provided one of the most important avenues for the application of national-socialist–influenced thought not only to the Jewish issue, but also to the treatment of South African blacks.

Equally important, his ideas were integrated into the influential pro-Eiselen faction in the Broederbond.[24]

On matters of racial policy, at least, the old Afrikaner right could assimilate the New Right with comparative ease. Cronjé was invited to address the landmark Broederbond-organized 1944 volk congress on Afrikaner racial policies.[25] His books *'n Tuiste Vir die Nageslag* (A Home for Our Posterity), published in 1945, and *Regverdige Rasse-Apartheid* (Just Racial Apartheid), published in 1947, read like a preparatory study for the Nationalist platform in 1948.[26] The 1947 book, published by the Christian Student Union of South Africa, had the additional prestige of being co-authored by Afrikaner churchmen E. P. Groenewald, a leading biblical scholar, and Willem Nicol, moderator of the Transvaal Nederduitse Gereformeerde Kerk (NGK), a former Broederbond chairman, and later administrator of the Transvaal under Malan. Their clear, all-embracing, and definitive "final solution" of the color issue in South Africa was the banner under which the nationalist movement would fight the next election.[27] This is not to say that they favored a genocidal approach, but rather that they were perhaps influenced by the tendency to seek all-embracing, visionary solutions that was so characteristic of the fascist era. *Regverdige Rasse-Apartheid* was one of the most important books on the ideology of apartheid. Underlying Cronjé's advocacy of an unprecedentedly thoroughgoing form of segregation was his conviction that interracial mixing in any form led to friction and (however paradoxically) to miscegenation. As he stated in his contribution to this book:

. . . the core of South Africa's racial problems [*rassevraagstukke*] . . . lies in the fact that racial conflict was born out of the superior position of the whites (and the subordinate position [*ondergeskiktheidsposisie*] of the non-whites).

Miscegenation and racial conflict—they are the core [*kern*] of South Africa's racial problems and they will remain the core of these problems as long as contact and the relationship between whites and non-whites continue as they currently are.[28]

In language prophetic of the future vision of Verwoerd and later architects of "grand apartheid" or "separate development," in which blacks would be expected to exercise their political rights on a "separate but equal" basis, Cronjé summarized his own solution to South Africa's "native question": "When race-apartheid is carried out consistently there will by the very nature of affairs no longer be such a thing as the superior position of one race group and the subordination of others because no horizontal division will exist any longer between the respective communities, but rather a vertical division will come about."[29]

Cronjé's work, despite Moodie's argument given above that it showed some national socialist influence, clearly aimed at more than brute racial oppression. The principles embodied in *Regverdige Rasse-Apartheid* soon provided the basis for an influential report by the Commission for Current Affairs of the Nederduitse Gereformeerde Federal Council of Churches.[30] Cronjé was hailed by a comparatively liberal Afrikaans Reformed churchman, the veteran writer on race relations, G. B. A. Gerdener, for his ideas on a more systematic form of racial segregation than had characterized South African society until then.[31] The Afrikaner church historian R. T. J. Lombard demonstrates how wide was the impact of Cronjé's ideas in commenting in his history of the Afrikaans Reformed churches and apartheid that the key 1950 congress on the "native question" held by the Nederduitse Gereformeerde Federal Mission Board "reveals the influence of Professor G. Cronjé's works on race relations," particularly in its advocacy of "autonomous development" (*eiesoortige ontwikkeling*) through which each population group (*volksgroep*) could be led "to its own destiny in the purest [*suiwerste*] and speediest way."[32] Interestingly, Lombard argues that this congress was one of the most important ever held in South Africa on this issue and that its influence was "far-reaching." Equally significant, the chairman of the congress was Cronjé's admirer, Gerdener.[33]

The desire to systematize segregation was at the core of the apartheid program from 1948 on. Although Cronjé's emphasis on "vertical division" is suggestive of more liberal influences, a "totalist" vision like that which had characterized fascist regimes in Europe and especially that of the Nazis permeated his apartheid program. It was to be a truly comprehensive and permanent solution, without the many loopholes of old-fashioned South African segregation. It was to be applied to African, "colored," and Indian with equal vigor. Yet Cronjé's views were considered sufficiently within the Nationalist mainstream to be admired by those at the heart of the Afrikaner establishment, like Moderator Nicol, Gerdener, the organizers of the 1944 Volkskongres or the 1950 church congress.

Nevertheless, Cronjé's wartime views appear to have been influenced by G. Eloff, whose *Rasse en Rassevermenging* (Race and Miscegenation), published in 1942, shows much more overt traces of Nazi thought. Indeed, Cronjé cites Eloff's claim of biblical support for maintaining racial purity in the opening chapter of *'n Tuiste Vir die Nageslag* and, like Eloff, devotes considerable space in this preparatory study for the later *Regverdige Rasse-Apartheid* to the biological damage caused by miscegenation. For example, he cites Eloff's argument that even a limited percentage of absorption of "colored" blood could seriously damage the racial composition of whites because of recessive traits that might not immediately be evident.[34] Eloff's targeting of miscegenation was not surprising in the South African society, but his reasoning suggested influences from beyond South Africa. He argued that mixed races were genetically inferior to "pure" ones, tending, for instance, he said, to suffer from higher rates of mental retardation and tuberculosis. In the eugenic tradition of Nazi pseudoscience, Eloff claimed that the Afrikaners were especially fitted biologically to promote "white Christian civilization," combining the best of superior Alpine and Nordic races, and even improving on them by being both taller on average than either group, as well as darker in complexion, which was beneficial in so hot a climate.[35] As Eloff explained:

Armed with a strong constitution, a tanned [*bruinende*] skin which protects us against the sun-rays, adequate sweat glands for cooling off in the warm climate, an abundant progeny, and a persistent disposition with most of the characteristics of the Nordic race, an aversion to miscegenation, a people rooted in this land through adaptation and tradition who stretch over 10 generations—behold the conditions for self-preservation, see there the grounds for my belief in the Boer and his future in this country.[36]

Eloff's theories outdid Ossewabrandwag chief Van Rensburg's musings about a nonparty state in borrowing from fascist, and especially Nazi, thinking in Europe. His book was nonetheless published by the National Party's Nasionale Pers, which suggests some support in Nationalist quarters. When he was inexplicably

reduced to taking a job that was a lowly one for so highly qualified an academic, the Broederbond promptly stepped in to help
him. It was not one of the Ossewabrandwag members of the
Executive but Verwoerd who raised the matter. Just as the Broederbond had promoted Cronjé's work, so Verwoerd asked the
Bond Executive to consider assisting Eloff to obtain a more fit-
ting position as a scientist. It was not typical Broederbond procedure to bring up such a question at a meeting of the Executive,
as is attested by the minutes of this period; Verwoerd was, therefore, going out of his way to assist him. Verwoerd's fellow party
man on the Executive, J. H. Conradie, raised the possibility of
a lectureship in zoology at the University College of the Orange
Free State; the Executive agreed to provide a supplementary al-
lowance of twenty-three pounds per month until Eloff could find
a decent position.[37]

The crucial point seemed to be that individuals outside the
National Party should avoid references to a political system that
would challenge its hegemonic position. Nazi racial theories, on
the other hand, were treated with sympathetic interest. Not that
Nationalist leaders favored genocide, but eugenic and *Herren-
volk*-type theories were less offensive than one-party state mod-
els.

Cronjé's theories, for example, drawing on Eloff's own, were
centered around the belief that racial mixing was a crime against
the white race, typically committed by degenerates or low-class
immigrants. This was a point with which few "national-minded"
Afrikaners would wish to quarrel, given their determined campaign from at least the mid-thirties to pass a wide-ranging antimiscegenation law. Cronjé's authoritarianism was similarly un-
problematic, since he did not propagate a dictatorship but rather
argued that agitators against a future apartheid regime should
be silenced.[38]

It is significant that the work in which Cronjé espoused this
view was not only published under the auspices of the highly
authoritarian Ossewabrandwag,[39] but was analyzed and debated
nationwide in the hundreds of local cells, the grass-roots base
of the Broederbond.[40] In 1945 the National Party had already
declared the concept of apartheid to be official party policy.[41] In
1948 Malan's election manifesto would take up Cronjé's apart-

heid program virtually in its entirety, including a statement that steps would be taken against those who undermined this policy and who propagated ideas that were *volksvreemd* (alien to the volk).[42]

When faced by the major perceived threat to Afrikaner nationalist interests, that posed by the vast black majority, the National Party and the Radical Right could join ranks in the interests of a higher cause. In so doing, the party once again shifted decidedly to the right.

The Radicalization of the Nationalist Youth

Despite the demise of the Nazi regime, its shadow continued to loom over the Afrikaner nationalist movement. Many mainstream Nationalists had been profoundly influenced by the years of semifascist rhetoric and the constant jockeying with the radicals. The process helped to close the electorally dangerous gap between the party and the Radical Right.

It was not surprising, in consequence, that younger Nationalists posed a special problem for the party leadership, which was trying, in order to broaden its electoral base at both extremes, to clarify and improve its image as a forward-looking and relatively moderate force in white politics, at least on issues like the nature of a future republic.

Nationalist youth, however, continued to take an equivocal and often radical stance long after the 1943 election. One person who was disturbed by this was Professor E. F. Gey van Pittius of Potchefstroom, a loyal party man. He wrote to Strijdom in April 1945 of his concern regarding the extreme rightist political opinions of the Nationalist student group on his campus. Like Strijdom, he had hoped that attitudes would change with the end of the war, but confessed sadly: "I must honestly admit that I am not very optimistic: I fear that we will still have to fight hard against the foreign ideologies [Nationalist code language for both communism and fascism], because many of those ideas have already worked their way in deeply among some of our people."[43]

Gey van Pittius was referring to the Christian Republican Student Union, a Nationalist group based in Potchefstroom and

Bloemfontein that, like the more orthodox "Republican Student Union" at Pretoria University, was working to create an alternative organization to the pro-Ossewabrandwag ANS. The "Christian" Republican Student Union rejected dictatorship but it used in its projected constitution much of the language of the discredited 1942 Draft Constitution, particularly in the opening articles of both documents. The language of Article 2(a) of the Christian RSU's constitution supported a theocratic and highly authoritarian version of Kruger's republican model:

Aware of their volk vocation and familiar with the principles of a pure Christian Republic with a Volk Head who enjoys full authority and who with his Government makes and executes all laws, bound only in his conscience to the revelation of God and the Constitution of the State, defined by the Volksraad [People's Assembly] . . .[44]

The proponents of this scheme advocated a political system that was unmistakably authoritarian. They tried to sell their position as official party policy to the more orthodox Nationalist students in Pretoria. One of the Potchefstroom group, F. B. Scheepers, who was also divisional secretary of the party in that constituency, told his Pretoria colleagues that the party wanted a strong central government and that it favored a separation of legislative and executive powers only for the present. Dismissing the separation of powers as a product of the French Revolution and "false Empire democracy" ("*valse* Empire *demokrasie*"), Scheepers claimed that the party would not uphold this distinction much longer and suggested that the hard-line republican Strijdom, "the heir of Dr. Malan," supported the position taken in Article 2(a).[45]

Scheepers proved remarkably prophetic in this regard, for after 1948 Malan moved to have Parliament declared the highest court in the land in order to overcome the entrenched provisions for the Cape "colored" franchise in the Union constitution. His successor, Strijdom, would go still further in abrogating the separation of powers by packing the Senate with nearly forty Nationalist appointees, thus almost doubling the size of the upper house, and by almost doubling the size of the appeal bench of the Supreme Court through the addition of compliant judges, thereby enabling "colored" voters to be removed from the common roll. Similarly, the powerful presidency envisaged by Scheepers and his fellow students was in many respects realized in the national security state system of the 1983 Botha constitution, in which most power was concentrated in the hands of the state president and the National Security Council, rather than of Parliament, the voters, or even the Nationalist caucus.[46]

But in 1945 Strijdom was still expressing disappointment at the undemocratic position of the Potchefstroom students, especially of P. J. Van der Walt, organizing secretary of Nasionale Jeugbond, the youth wing of the National Party. In *Stryd* (Struggle), the journal of the Jeugbond, Van der Walt had advocated the "organic volk concept" and had attacked liberal democracy as "the liberalistic life- and world-view with its mechanistic ethnic concept of a mongrelized [*mengelmoes*] population, who are all citizens of the state with full citizens' rights."[47] Strijdom showed an unusually sympathetic grasp of why this position had been taken up by many of the party youth and acknowledged that deeply Radical Right thinking still permeated Nationalist ranks even at so late a date:

For me it seems as if many of our people, especially during these war years of confusion, although they have taken a position against the foreign ideologies which have been proclaimed here, still to a degree have been influenced by them even to make unhealthy concessions to the proponents of these alien things, from which comes the common talk, even in our ranks, about such ideas as an authoritarian state and an organic volk concept.[48]

Strijdom could not recognize that many of the party youth were not simply being misled, but were reacting to a mass of contradictory messages from the party establishment itself. It was the general impression among these younger Nationalists that the direction of the party had shifted in the direction of a more authoritarian and elitist nationalism, and that this had not been fundamentally altered by Malan's post-1943 strategy of pragmatism.

The National Party and the Greyshirts

Strijdom's brave opposition to "unhealthy concessions" to the Radical Right was to wither rapidly when he was in power and faced with the constraints of the rule of law even in a deeply flawed version of the Westminster system. In practice, the democratic scruples of an older and more conservative nationalism gave way when confronted by the exigencies of power. In order to remain in control after 1948, the Nationalists would sometimes resort to highly authoritarian methods, and also would make their peace with some of the most outspoken elements of the wartime Radical Right. For among those appointed to Strijdom's "enlarged Senate" was Louis Weichardt, the former Greyshirt leader, whose presence in that chamber was considered so scandalous by Jewish parliamentarians such as Senator Leslie Rubin that Rubin refused to greet the man who he recalled had described the Jewish people as "vermin."[49]

Weichardt and his Greyshirts epitomize the difficulty of making immutable distinctions between conservative mainstream Afrikaner nationalism and the Radical Right. One of the first representatives of national socialism in South Africa, Weichardt had never been embarrassed about proclaiming his unqualified support for this ideology; he had adopted the swastika as the symbol of his organization.[50]

On the other hand, Weichardt had never confused ideological principle with political interest. He had repeatedly thrown his weight behind the National Party during elections, both in 1938 and again in the early war years.[51] The many points of coincidence between the policies of both organizations, such as ardent nationalism, full-scale segregation, anti-Semitism, and the denunciation of large-scale capitalism and liberal democracy, made such cooperation much easier. By 1944, with Hitler's forces facing imminent defeat, Weichardt was once again willing to cooperate with the Nationalists in the interests of the need to *saamtrek* (pull together) against yet another Smuts term in office. His support was widely acknowledged. Greyshirt meetings were advertised in the Nationalist press, although no publicity for the Ossewabrandwag was permitted in party organs.[52] Jan van Niekerk, Nationalist member of Parliament, along with other party leaders, publicly thanked the Greyshirts for their official support during the NP's successful 1944 Wakkerstroom by-election campaign. It seemed to many Nationalists an omen of the future, much as a similar result in that constituency had heralded Hertzog's 1924 general election victory. The same Nationalist leaders expressed their gratitude for the *unofficial* support extended to the party by the Ossewabrandwag during this by-election campaign. The OB had, by refusing to give a definite order on how to vote, opened the way for members to support the republican National Party candidate without losing face.[53]

If there were few major ideological differences between the Greyshirts and the Ossewabrandwag, there were almost none between the Greyshirts and the New Order, the third major representative of the Afrikaner Radical Right. Despite the closeness of the Greyshirts to the National Party,[54] in a characteristically mercurial move, Weichardt, only months after Wakkerstroom, formed an alliance with the New Order's Pirow.[55] The Nationalists, who would not have dealings with Pirow, did not hold this step against Weichardt. Later in 1944, when Weichardt was detained for failure to observe Smuts's wartime ban on propagating Nazism, Nationalist member of Parliament P. J. van Nierop intervened with the authorities on Weichardt's behalf and promised to press his case with the government.[56]

This difference in attitude can partly be explained by the relative insignificance of the Greyshirts as a serious threat to the National Party. Weichardt had long since passed the peak of his popularity. Jewish immigration had been almost wholly stopped by the end of the thirties, and Weichardt's overt attachment to full-blown "national socialism" could have little appeal to Afrikaners, especially now that the Nazis faced defeat. Anti-Semites could find support in the National Party program without having to become South African Nazis. On the other hand, from the party viewpoint, defending Weichardt after Smuts's heavy-handed treatment of him so late in the war was a good selling point with the many Afrikaners who saw the general as an insensitive tyrant.

Yet there is more to the difference between the Nationalist treatment of Weichardt and of the New Order and the Ossewabrandwag. Pirow was an exponent of full-blown fascism, although more on the lines of Mussolini's Italy, and the New Order had been dealt a mortal blow when it lost its parliamentary representatives in 1943. The New Order, unlike the Ossewabrandwag, was no more of a threat to the party than were the Greyshirts. Yet Pirow had been associated with the Ossewabrandwag since the 1941 rift and had committed the fatal error of challenging the Nationalist leadership from inside the party. His followers had campaigned against the National Party from late 1941 to 1943. The New Order could not be forgiven for such behavior, short of totally abandoning its radical program and returning to the party as chastened and loyal individual members. The Greyshirts did not fall under this rubric and therefore, despite adherence to "national socialism" and their outward paraphernalia of a Nazi-style movement, they could be accepted unconditionally into the volk alliance.

From Volk Front to Victory

As the war drew to a close, although the creation of an independent republic remained an important priority for Afrikaner nationalists, dealing with the rapidly urbanizing black population became an even more urgent matter. On this issue, even Malan's rhetoric left little to distinguish between the National Party and the Radical Right. In April 1943 Malan was telling his supporters that the holding of dance parties by whites and blacks was indicative of the link between the threat of communism and the "black danger," a "black sin-flood." White and black soldiers were playing football together; still more shocking, at the medical college in Durban, black students stood by when the professors performed operations on whites, and wore the same coats as their white counterparts.[57]

Similar racial concerns led Ossewabrandwag boss Hans van Rensburg to despair at the intransigence of the Nationalist leadership in failing to respond to gestures of reconciliation from his organization. In a September 1947 speech in the Pretoria Koffiehuis, he declared: "We are all Afrikaners, whites on a non-white continent, and we are all threatened by the same dangers. It is becoming high time that the emphasis be laid on the common points which are innumerable, rather than the points of difference, which are few."[58]

Although some organizations, such as the businessmen's Afrikaner Handelsinstituut (Afrikaner Commercial Institute or AHI), were unwilling to go far beyond United Party prescriptions lest they be deprived of cheap black labor, the much more radical approach Cronjé advocated was gaining wide support in Nationalist ranks. Especially in the Afrikaans press and in the Afrikaans Reformed churches there was a growing demand for comprehensive apartheid, an all-embracing segregation to be applied in every sphere, even in the economy, regardless of the cost. This vision was most fully articulated by the Broederbond's front research organization, set up specifically for the purpose, the South African Bureau for Racial Affairs (SABRA).[59] Notwithstanding considerable differences on the exact tactics to be used in achieving this vision, the priorities of Afrikanerdom were once again clear.

This perhaps explains why after the war Malan was willing to change his stance on the Jewish issue and to form an alliance with Havenga's Afrikaner Party, despite the presence of many Ossewabrandwag members in its ranks. All whites would need to stand together behind the Afrikaner nationalist banner if the volk were to survive. Only for the sake of appearance did Malan insist on a ban on Ossewabrandwag members standing as Afrikaner Party candidates.

Not everybody in the party agreed with Malan's pragmatism. On the Jewish issue in particular, Strijdom, Swart, Louw, and other committed anti-Semites refused to budge for several years. Not until the 1951 National Party merger with Havenga's followers did Strijdom permit the removal of the ban on Jewish membership of the Transvaal party. For the moment, however, they preferred to swallow their pride rather than risk a schism.[60] In October 1947 Strijdom complained to Louw how upset he was that Malan, who as late as 29 December 1946 had given notice in the Government Gazette of his intent to introduce a private members' bill to stop a new wave of Jewish immigration, had now performed a complete turnaround on the subject, under the influence of his "new advisors."[61]

Verwoerd confessed privately that he, along with many younger Nationalists, was not pleased with Malan's new stress on equal rights for English-speakers. English-speakers who became assimilated as Afrikaners were not a problem, in Verwoerd's view, but he hoped to see the English "Afrikanderised" and to have Afrikaans established as the predominant and, ultimately, the only language in South Africa. Verwoerd thought that Malan sounded too accommodating to the English,[62] a charge that had once pronounced a death knell for another Nationalist leader, General Hertzog.

Malan, however, was an experienced professional who had long ago learned to balance ideological principle with a hard-nosed awareness of political reality. Unlike Hertzog, he was not about to make too strong a stand on an issue that would alienate him from his core Afrikaans-speaking constituency. Yet, although it is doubtful whether he gained anything more than the most negligible Jewish or English-speaking support in the 1948 elections, his generally more moderate message must have reassured key Afrikaner Party supporters and disaffected Afrikaans-speaking United Party and Labour Party followers.

The old reliable combination of the majority of white agriculture and of white labor would thus be solidly in the right column on election day, as had not been the case since Fusion.[63] As long as the key supporters of the Far Right were among these voters, Malan would have what he needed to reach the threshold necessary to carry his alliance to victory.

By putting the Radical Right behind him (quite literally) through the arrangement with Havenga, Malan was assured of most Ossewabrandwag votes as well as those of whatever remained of Pirow's followers, without suffering from a "national socialist" image among Afrikaners. Malan received wholehearted support from Weichardt, whose Greyshirts, resurrected as the "White Workers' Party," provided crucial support in some constituencies for the "White Front."[64]

Malan emerged from the 1948 elections with seventy seats (twenty-two more than at dissolution) and Havenga with nine, to provide a narrow Afrikaner nationalist majority of five.[65] The surprise result was as much the product of an intensive mobilization of the Radical Right vote as of support from Havenga's more moderate followers.[66] Malan's *Volksfront* strategy had worked, without requiring the kind of concessions to the radicals that would have alienated more moderate Afrikaner voters. By seeking allies outside the party, Malan had also checked the overweening ambitions of Strijdom and Verwoerd in the north.

Malan's triumph has been the subject of endless debate. He was certainly assisted by the incompetence of several Smuts ministers, the poor organization and divisions between liberals and conservatives in the United Party, economic difficulties with postwar reconstruction, and the always serviceable battle cry about the "black danger," rendered more immediate by the competition in the cities between white and black workers. As economist Merle Lipton shows in *Capitalism and Apartheid,* white labor felt understandably threatened; during the war, the absence of so many of their number had opened up numerous opportunities to blacks, especially in the semiskilled sector. The veterans returned to unemployment, concluding that there had been a general erosion of segregation at their expense. The urgency of the race issue was brought home by large-scale black political radicalization: the rise of the uncompromising Non-European Unity Movement in the Cape "colored" community, the emergence of the African National Congress Youth League, the massive 1946 black mineworkers' strike, and the resulting collapse of the principal means for channeling black African protest along traditional lines, the Natives' Representative Council.[67]

Not since 1929 had the overwhelming majority of Afrikaners supported the cause of militant nationalism.[68] The *Volksbeweging* and its political spearhead, the National Party, had succeeded in achieving not just the unity of nationalist Afrikanerdom, but also control of the South African state itself, far more speedily than anybody could have imagined. The extraordinary organizing abilities of that movement could now be directed at the shaping of a political system more in keeping with its own authoritarian yet populist nationalism.

Assisted by the *Volksbeweging,* Malan's work of consolidating National Party control of Afrikaner nationalist politics had at last been brought to fruition, obtaining the radicals' votes without conceding anything substantial. That he did not have to make any concessions is attributable precisely to the National Party's having long before taken the path of gradual, almost imperceptible, but nevertheless fundamental accommodation to its rivals on the right.

This is why when Hitler and the war issue passed from the world stage, the radicals could comfortably return to the Nationalist fold. All that would be required was an acknowledgment of party supremacy. For the National Party to which the radicals returned after 1948 was of a very different kind from that which had split in 1934 over Fusion; 1948 was no repeat of 1929. The nationalism Malan's National Party preached was essentially more authoritarian, more elitist, and more exclusive than the simple, often racist, but nevertheless relatively inclusive populist nationalism of Hertzog's old party, which had at times appealed to English, Jewish, and even "colored" voters.

The apartheid state would not, however, be a pale imitation of an imported fascist model, but would draw on the lifeblood of a much older, indigenous tradition, that of Krugerism. The new state would be both republican and autocratic, both populist and despotic, both radically modern—indeed revolutionary in its massive social engineering—yet incorrigibly, even passionately, reactionary in its determination to re-create the simpler world of the old Boer republics.

Epilogue: The Years in Power

The Impact of the Nationalist Victory

Smuts realized only too well the enormity of the Nationalist triumph in May 1948. His opinion of the new government was summed up neatly in some words of warning to Sam Kahn, the first Communist Party member to be elected to the Union Parliament. On Kahn's arrival in the Assembly in January 1949, the old general took the novice Native Representative aside in the House lobby, saying, "I hope you are being cautious. These people will put you in gaol, you know."[1]

Smuts, who, despite his reputation among Afrikaner nationalists as a tyrant, had patiently refrained from overreaching his hand in combating the Radical Right, was as good a judge of his inveterate opponents as anybody. They too understood clearly the difference between their methods and his. As Pirow, that longtime admirer of Mussolini, later admitted, Smuts had probably saved his life in the war; another leader might have panicked and put him and several others up against a wall for their activities.[2]

A flight of foreign capital from the Union, with a considerable effect on the economy over the next decade, especially in the manufacturing sector, underlined Smuts's alarm at the Nationalist victory.[3] Privileged whites recognized the significance of the election results. So did blacks, on other grounds. One black observer commented bitterly to Hofmeyr: "We Africans had cause to grieve against your government, but we never believed for a moment that the European electorate would decide as was shown 26th [sic]."[4] The black majority could be certain of one thing about the new government, that Malan would not tolerate any "liberalizing" on race relations. All of his supporters were committed to a more thoroughgoing form of white supremacy,

The cabinet that introduced apartheid, with Prime Minister Daniel Malan and Governor-General G. Brand van Zyl, 1948. Front (left to right): C. R. Swart, E. G. Jansen, Malan, Van Zyl, N. C. Havenga, J. G. Strijdom, P. O. Sauer; back: B. J. Schoeman (second), F. C. Erasmus, T. E. (Eben) Dönges, A. J. Stals, Eric Louw, S. P. le Roux.

Jansen was the first Nationalist governor-general (1951–1960). Swart, Nationalist leader in the Orange Free State, was governor-general (1960–1961) and then state president (1961–1967).

Dönges was a member of the Broederbond executive. Sauer (with P. W. Botha) was architect of the wartime restructuring of the party. Erasmus, as secretary of Malan's Cape NP, directed the purge of non-Nationalists from the security forces. Havenga, leader of the more moderate Afrikaner Party, briefly restrained the Nationalists' more radical policies; his group merged with the NP in 1951.

Courtesy The Argus

whether they were farmers or businessmen finding increasing difficulty in obtaining cheap black labor, workers or petit bourgeois elements threatened by black competition for their jobs, or clergymen and other intellectuals ideologically committed to the political salvation and domination of the Afrikaner volk. Such a commitment to more overt forms of segregation and white control was in stark contrast to Smuts's complaint to his old British friends, the Gilletts, that he had "no time for these tiresome racial conundrums" and that he wished that colors and languages did not exist.[5]

The commitment to dramatic change was soon expressed in concrete legislative terms. As liberal member of Parliament Margaret Ballinger later noted, whatever the faults of the new Nationalist government, it could not be accused of inertia. As soon as the Nationalists recovered from the shock of gaining power, they demonstrated their vigor and will to remold South African society.[6]

Not everything in their election program could be implemented: there was, for instance, no nationalization of the mines, which would have been disastrous for foreign relations and prohibitively costly if compensation had been provided.[7] Similarly, a truly "Christian National Republic," such as had been touted during the war years, did not prove feasible in the real world of parliamentary politics, since Malan had to make so many compromises with his ally Havenga and even with the business interests backing the white opposition, in order to effect the principal part of his program, apartheid.[8] Within the National Party itself there was also an ongoing debate between the pragmatists, often businessmen, who did not want to move too quickly in the direction of economic apartheid and an end to cheap black labor, and the ideologues, who were determined to enact the full vision of "total apartheid" as quickly as possible.[9] Malan could be no Mussolini, let alone an Adolf Hitler; there would be no formalized dictatorship here.

Nevertheless, the new regime was not just a case of old wine in new flasks. For the first time since Union, the ruling cabinet was uniformly made up of Afrikaners. Despite tactical differences, the new leadership was united in its determination to find a way out of the quagmire of increasing racial integration, especially in the economic sphere, with its associated threat of growing demands for an extension of black political rights. Apartheid was intended to be such a way out. Its proponents were uniformly distinguished from earlier campaigners for segregation by the conviction that apartheid was not just a practical solution but the Afrikaners' divine mission in southern Africa, acting on behalf of the white race.[10] This belief was analogous in some ways to the Nazis' belief in the German mission to save the Aryan race, and was in large part influenced by rightist Afrikaner Broederbond ideologues like Cronjé who were now key opinion-makers behind the scenes, as many of the associated Bureau of Racial Affairs elements in the Broederbond were appointed to important positions in the new government.[11] Apartheid meant government by blueprint, in which state planning would ensure that measures regulating economic development, interracial contact, and Afrikaner political control would be mutually complementary, part of a single vision, rather than the intermittent ad hoc measures of the past.

The groundwork had been well established by the Broederbond. Although its relationship with the Nationalist government was by no means secure until Verwoerd's accession to the prime ministership in 1958,[12] the 1948 victory nevertheless positioned reliable Broederbond leaders at the very heart of the ruling establishment. Not only were most members of the National and Afrikaner Party caucuses ordinary Bond members,[13] but Eben Dönges was in the cabinet, and Albert Hertzog, Henning Klopper, a founder of the Bond, and Nico Diederichs were all sitting as freshmen members of Parliament on the Nationalist back benches, the last two elected with open Ossewabrandwag support. Verwoerd, yet another longtime Broederbond Executive member, failed to win a seat precisely because of his rejection of Ossewabrandwag support. Malan consequently had to find him a place in the Senate, to which representatives were elected by the caucuses of the major parties in the Assembly and provincial councils.[14]

In 1945 the Broederbond Executive had decided that "for historical and practical reasons the Reunited National Party is the only political organization within which Afrikanerdom can realize its political ideals in a united deployment of strength."[15]

This policy of consolidating forces had now paid its dividends, and the Broederbond Executive extended its congratulations personally to new members of the legislature.[16] The elitism of the European New Right was introduced by the Broederbond into the very heart of the South African government through the Bond's already established interlocking arrangement with more traditional nationalist forces.

The Return of the Radical Right

Malan did not forget those he had once admired: he expressed pleasure at the increasingly favorable treatment of Germany in the face of growing international fears of the communist threat.[17] Even those who had not always been so friendly to the cause of *volksdemokrasie,* such as the would-be assassin, Leibbrandt, and the man behind Zeesen Radio, Eric Holm, could now be forgiven; both were released within a month of the Nationalist victory, eliciting outrage from the opposition. Hofmeyr considered this move an extraordinary blunder at so early a stage, given the Nationalists' election campaign attempt to project a more moderate image, and commented, "Perhaps people will now begin to realize that the leopard hasn't changed his spots."[18]

To some degree, there was considerable evidence to confirm the suspicions of Hofmeyr and others who were increasingly convinced, however unfairly, that fellow travelers of the wartime fascists had come to power in South Africa in the guise of the Nationalists. Apart from the more or less clandestine Broederbond presence in the government, the new cabinet included such far more visible hard-liners as Strijdom and Swart, as well as Louw, leader of the anti-Semites in the party.[19] Malan appointed Willem Nicol, co-author with Cronjé of *Regverdige Rasse-Apartheid,* to be administrator of the Transvaal.[20] Otto du Plessis, that former admirer of the world revolution that would usher in a new order, became state director of information, and later served as administrator of the Cape Province.[21]

After all of Malan's moderate pre-election rhetoric, he now seemed to go out of his way to project a radical and even revolutionary image. Contrary to precedent, he kept Governor-General Brand van Zyl waiting for several days before answering the call to form a new government and, contrary to established government practice, ignored him for long spells.[22] He released Leibbrandt and Holm even *before* requesting Van Zyl's legally required assent for such a pardon.[23]

Malan's longtime factotum, Cape NP Secretary F. C. Erasmus, as the new minister of defense promptly dismissed the director of military intelligence, Colonel Charles Powell, and in the words of Powell's predecessor, E. G. Malherbe, proceeded to remove two truckloads of "secret files dealing with information which the military authorities had obtained during the war concerning the subversive activities of certain people: members of the Ossewabrandwag and the Broederbond."[24] In what might be interpreted as a complementary move, one of the first acts by the new government was the lifting of Smuts's ban on OB and AB members joining the civil service.[25]

Johannes Strauss von Moltke, the former Greyshirt and leader of the South African Fascists, emerged as leader of the National Party in South-West Africa, which in 1950 received six seats in the House of Assembly.[26] With a high proportion of German-speakers in this all-white electorate, these constituencies were comparatively safe Nationalist seats after the anti-Nazi crackdowns by the United Party government during the Smuts years. Van Rensburg returned to the National Party, and his Ossewabrandwag gradually faded into political oblivion, lacking any obvious political base now that the war was over and the Malanites had appropriated the support not only of many Afrikaner farmers in the Transvaal but also of most blue-collar Afrikaner workers.[27] Pirow had long since ceased to be a significant force in Afrikaner politics, though one of the main thoroughfares in Cape Town is named after him, and he did enjoy some visibility as chief government prosecutor in the 1956–1961 "treason trial" of antiapartheid activists, a role cut short by his death in 1959.

In keeping with the long-standing cool but polite relationship between the Nationalists and the Greyshirts, Louis Weichardt was able to negotiate a particularly smooth merger, without any loss of face to his organization. He had not changed his stance on his old primary political concern, stating in 1949 at the final conference of his White Workers' Party (the latest formal name for the Greyshirt movement) that he was still hostile to the Jews;

he advised them to exercise the option to go to Israel.[28] The communist threat and the black "problem" necessitated a new strategy of unity. Weichardt told the conference: "Let us dissolve the White Workers' Party to realize the further road to unity. Let us try to tie together the family bond, because the Reunited National Party, Afrikaner Party, OB and New Order are our family, we cannot seek unity outside the family."[29] The conference agreed that the Greyshirts would be retained as a "movement" but not as a political party. Weichardt learned in a long discussion with Malan, who, he said, had shown great sympathy with their difficulties, that the National Party was trying to find positions for the most senior office-bearers of the White Workers' Party.[30]

Weichardt toured the country as a popular speaker for the Nationalist cause, standing unsuccessfully for the party in the 1953 elections.[31] He was elected honorary president of the Nasionale Jeugbond, the party youth wing, in the Cape Town suburb of Observatory, as well as chairman of the National Party branch in that area.[32] As his reward, he ended his political career as a member of Strijdom's "packed" Senate and thus helped to erase the constitutionally entrenched rights of the Cape "colored" voters.[33]

Other well-known pro-Nazi figures took longer to gain positions in the Nationalist establishment. Not until 1953 was the former Ossewabrandwag general and member of the militant Stormjaer organization, B. J. Vorster,[34] elected to Parliament on a Nationalist ticket.[35] By then, the feud with the Ossewabrandwag was something from the past, although his statement during the war continued to provide ammunition for the enemies of the National Party: "We stand for Christian Nationalism which is an ally of National Socialism. . . . You can call such an anti-democratic system a dictatorship if you like. In Italy it is called Fascism, in Germany National Socialism and in South Africa Christian Nationalism."[36]

After Verwoerd became prime minister in 1958, the Nationalists moved more sharply to the right. Diederichs, Albert Hertzog, and Vorster were included in Verwoerd's cabinet.[37] In 1959 Vorster's close associate, Piet Meyer, was appointed head of the state-controlled South African Broadcasting Corporation, which

Hendrik Verwoerd, who in 1937 became first editor of the Nationalist newspaper *Die Transvaler*. Verwoerd was elected to the Broederbond executive in 1939 and became a senator after the 1948 Nationalist victory. As minister of "native" (later "bantu") affairs from 1950 and prime minister (1958–1966) he was chief architect of the homelands "grand apartheid" scheme.

Courtesy The Argus

B. J. (John) Vorster, a wartime general in the Ossewa-brandwag, who was interned on suspicion of subversion. He became a Nationalist member of Parliament in 1953, Verwoerd's minister of justice from 1962 to 1966, prime minister from 1966 to 1978, and, finally, state president from 1978 to 1979.

Courtesy The Argus

he soon transformed into even more of a Nationalist fief.[38] He also emerged at the head of the Broederbond, of which he was chairman from 1960 to 1972. Another Vorster intimate, former Ossewabrandwag officer and fellow internee Hendrik van den Bergh, became head of the feared Bureau of State Security, which Vorster established in 1968.[39]

In the sixties, in the ranks of the church, Vorster's brother Koot, convicted during the war of subverting a naval officer,[40] became the regional ecclesiastical strongman as the Moderator of the Cape Nederduitse Gereformeerde Kerk. Unlike many of his former associates on the Far Right, Koot Vorster remained unrepentant. As late as 1964 he told an interviewer in an unsolicited reply that he preferred Nazism to communism, although he denied that he had been pro-German.[41]

To the casual observer of the first two decades of Nationalist rule, the Afrikaner establishment seemed to have become overrun by "Nazis" and fellow travelers. Those who thought so could not detect the subtle nuances that distinguished the variety of ideological schools within the National Party. For instance, Vorster was unquestionably authoritarian, but as a former disciple of Pirow and Van Rensburg was no doctrinaire exclusivist nationalist; he accepted all whites who supported his belief in the need for a strong state and a disciplined nation. Like the authoritarian and even pro–national socialist General Hertzog of 1941–1942, Vorster had no difficulty associating with accommodating English-speakers, an approach in stark contrast with that of hard-line ethnic nationalists like Strijdom and especially Verwoerd, with his emphasis on a purely Afrikaner Christian Nationalism, and yet who firmly defended the need for at least the trappings of a parliamentary system.[42]

The Nationalist Departure from the Past

Yet despite the many differences of opinion inside the National Party, there was a broad consensus on what needed to be done to save South Africa for the white man, especially the Afrikaner. A tide of legislation overwhelmed the country after 1948. Havenga's quibbling about upholding the "Hertzog tradition" delayed but did not halt the chosen direction of the party.

In criticizing Havenga, Strijdom pointed out that Hertzog had differed from the Malanite party on most of the issues at the heart of the apartheid program:

separate representation of "colored" voters;
removal of Hertzog's separate white representatives of Africans from the Assembly;
industrial segregation of whites and "coloreds," and not just Africans;
banning interracial marriages;
legally enforced white/"colored" residential segregation.[43]

The new-style Afrikaner nationalism differed even more fundamentally from the Smuts regime than from that of Hertzog. In his old age, Smuts had shown signs of an openness, however reluctant, to a more flexible racial policy, if only in recognition of the social and economic realities of postwar South Africa. The war had enhanced the importance and scope of the manufacturing and commercial sectors, as well as of black workers, all of whom desired reforms that would strengthen opportunities for an established black urban working class.[44] Wartime needs had temporarily forced the relaxation of the color bar in jobs and training, and had encouraged a more open, competitive labor market that would have replaced whites with cheaper black workers, as had already happened in agriculture.[45]

Smuts's own Fagan Commission recommended on the eve of the 1948 election that the permanence of African urbanization be accepted and the conditions of Africans in the towns be substantially improved.[46] His proposals for Indian parliamentary representation, however limited, were another sign of how far this once ruthless practitioner of white supremacy was willing to go in the direction of a more open political and economic system. None of this affected his conviction, which even J. H. Hofmeyr shared, about the need for white leadership in South Africa for the foreseeable future.[47] Nevertheless, Smuts's designation just before the 1948 election of Hofmeyr, the one outspoken liberal in his cabinet, as his deputy prime minister[48] could be seen as suggesting that Smuts would countenance still more "liberalization."

The Nationalists tried to profit politically from Hofmeyr's

public indiscretions. Their own constituency could see no advantage in integration. It offended their social sensibilities; it seemed contrary to their received history; and it threatened their socioeconomic status. Most Afrikaners still perceived themselves as in too marginal an economic position to compete in an open market with blacks, while the wealthy minority of farmers or emergent capitalists felt threatened by policies that might dry up their source of labor and drive up black wages. Above all, political integration posed a challenge to the Afrikaner's one opportunity to gain exclusive control of the South African state. Hofmeyr symbolized all these threats.

In a propaganda pamphlet compiled by future president P. W. Botha, who thirty-six years later would, somewhat ironically, end the days of all-white parliamentary politics, Hofmeyr was attacked for his statement on 15 January 1947 that Africans and Indians would "eventually" have to be represented in Parliament by their own people: "Minister Jan Hofmeyr wants Kaffirs and Indians and Coloreds on the same voting rolls as whites. He wants Kaffirs, Indians and Coloreds to take up seats in Parliament. He advocates political equality between white and non-white."[49]

Hofmeyr's premature death in late 1948 robbed South Africa of one of its most outstanding leaders, but one for whom the white electorate was not ready. In an atmosphere of intense racial suspicion, the new government set about turning the clock back in what they hoped would be an irreversible way. Yet like so many New Right regimes of the interwar years, the climate of reaction was deeply enmeshed with a radical, even revolutionary spirit, the vision of a systematically, totally segregated universe, of government by blueprint, without the many loopholes that Smuts and even Hertzog had tolerated.

The Nationalist New Order

Among the mass of legislation introduced in the decade that led from crude "negative" apartheid to Verwoerd's "positive" "separate development," complete with a constellation of independent African homelands (as the small and fragmented rural reserves, residual territories in which Africans could own property, came to be called), three major groups may be distinguished. These were the racial purity laws, general measures affecting human rights, and the main body of apartheid legislation. Each in its own way reflected, however opaquely, the years of involvement with Radical Right philosophy.

The Eloffs and the Cronjé's had their way almost immediately. The first major piece of apartheid legislation banned interracial marriage, followed a year later in 1950 by three closely related measures. The much more limited 1927 prohibition on extramarital sexual relations between whites and Africans was expanded to include "coloreds" and Indians as well in terms of an "Immorality Amendment Act," which was revised again in 1957 so as to allow convictions for even a kiss across the color line. The penalty for infraction of the 1957 measure was draconian: up to seven years in prison, with the added option of lashes for the male partner.[50] (The miscegenation laws were repealed decades later in 1985 as part of limited reforms initiated by President P. W. Botha.)

Together with the ban on interracial marriage (which had occurred principally between whites and "coloreds"), this legislation could easily be compared with similar provisions in Hitler's Law for the Protection of German Blood and Honor.[51] The main difference was that whites, not "Aryans," were the protected class, and blacks, not Jews, the targeted group.

White racial purity was to be further protected by the Group Areas Act of 1950, which legally enforced the often customary, but widely ignored, residential segregation of whites and "coloreds." In order to make the whole system work with maximum efficiency, the 1950 Population Registration Act compelled every resident of the Union to be classified as a member of a statutorily defined racial group, with a bewildering variety of subcategories. There were no fewer than seven for the "colored" group, including "Cape colored," "Cape Malay," and "other colored." Identity documents were to carry the required information.[52] Those whose status was in question could appeal to a race classification board.

No expense was to be spared in this extraordinarily costly exercise, nor did enthusiasts of total segregation stop at bars between whites and others. Although in practice the main racial divide remained that between whites and others, by the 1950s the spirit of racial purification had become so pervasive among government officials that it was possible for P. J. Oosthuizen, superintendent of the African township at Stellenbosch, to send a circular to employers asking them to stop contacts between "coloreds" and "natives," because this was thought to lead to racial intermixture and the deterioration of both communities.[53]

Security legislation and laws relating to individual freedom were another important area of change. Since 1927 there had existed "riotous assemblies" legislation, intended mainly to hinder political organizing by blacks.[54] In addition, Hertzog had at least considered in 1939 a stringent bill to control the press.[55] Yet in the past the government had lacked either the will or the desire to ignore any public outrage at the wholesale curbing of such basic freedoms. In this sense, the liberal state still existed in the Union before 1948. Radical groups like the Communist Party could still freely organize, provided that they did not break any laws, due process was for the most part still maintained, and the press was restricted principally by common law provisions barring libel or slander.

This began to change dramatically after 1948. Under the 1951 Suppression of Communism Act, not only was the small Communist Party banned and its representatives in the Assembly (elected by African voters) ejected from Parliament, but individuals could be "named" by ministerial decree as falling within the definition of "Communism." A "banning" procedure permitted the minister of justice to deprive a named person of the right to engage in politics for either a fixed or an indefinite period. Additional curbs on personal freedom could include a prohibition against the affected individual's teaching or publishing, or leaving his or her magisterial district without special permission, or leaving home after dark, or even being with more than one person in the same room.

The definition of communism under this law was sufficiently broad to encompass, at least theoretically, almost any kind of opposition activity.[56] Again, there are obvious parallels with similar ostensibly anti-Communist legislation in Hitler's Germany, especially the 1933 Enabling Act. The act, intended to outlaw

Communist activity, was also soon used against a much broader spectrum of political opposition.

Other measures of the new Nationalist government included the 1948 Citizenship Act, under which citizenship rights other than those established by birth were made subject to the whim of the minister of the interior alone.[57] The aim was to limit any increase in the number of non-Afrikaner voters, made urgent by the narrow Nationalist majority in Parliament. British-born citizens were naturally concerned by this development, a fear confirmed by the Nationalist purge of many English-speakers from senior positions in the military and the civil service, replacing them with reliable party supporters (usually Broederbond members). Junior Afrikaner lawyers were consistently appointed as new judges; the government moved its accounts to Bond-controlled financial institutions such as Volkskas; and appointments to the boards of the many state corporations were almost exclusively given to Afrikaners.[58]

The Nationalists made no attempt to create a fascist-style corporate state, with parliamentary representation along professional and occupational lines, as in Mussolini's Italy, and with overarching umbrella organizations for both employers and employees, replacing trade unions and employer associations, as in both Germany and Italy. But they did attempt to crush African trade unionism, barring Africans from membership in state-recognized unions in 1953, removing their right to strike, and offering an alternative system of "plant-level committees" and state-appointed labor officers. When some employers continued to recognize African trade unions, the government prohibited the deduction of dues. Although "coloreds" and Indians could still belong to mixed state-recognized unions, no new mixed unions received government recognition, and trade union leaders were often "named" under the Suppression of Communism Act and banned or detained.[59]

Just as Hitler and Mussolini forged an alliance of state and capital to promote "national" economic interests, so the Nationalist government used the massive expansion of state involvement in the economy to further the interests of an indigenous Afrikaner entrepreneurial class, and to reduce the threat of a

widening gap between rich and poor Afrikaners. State corporations multiplied in number, including not only the long-estab-
lished ISCOR (Iron and Steel Corporation) and ESCOM (Elec-
tricity Supply Commission) as well as South African Railways,
but also SASOL, the state oil company, the Atomic Energy Board,
and ARMSCOR, the state armaments and munitions monopoly.
Furthermore, the state-run Industrial Development Corporation,
the instrument which the Nationalists hoped to use to encourage
expansion in manufacturing, developed a close relationship with
private Afrikaner companies like Federale Kunsmis (Federal Fer-
tilizer), and by 1960 the Development Corporation had invested
171 million pounds in industrial projects, partly through loans,
but primarily in the form of holdings in new enterprises. Such
developments strengthened the role of the Afrikaner-controlled
state in the economy and helped to create and train Afrikaner
capitalists who would otherwise have been unable to compete
with established English-speaking and often British-owned economic interests.[60]

At the same time, white workers, predominantly Afrikaners,
were protected by statutory measures that allowed the minister
of labor, in terms of the 1956 Industrial Conciliation Act, to
reserve jobs for particular racial groups "in any industry, trade
or occupation." Three years later this law was amended to permit the minister to reserve jobs even where the autonomous
white-controlled industrial council of a particular industry opposed such steps.[61]

A planned economy could not accommodate resistance from
whites who failed to see the advantages of such a system; such
a degree of state regulation of labor went far beyond long-standing reservation of better-paying mining jobs for whites, and Hertzog's encouragement in the twenties of a "civilized labor" policy
that favored the employment of whites or, to a lesser extent, of
"coloreds" rather than Africans in both the public and the private sector. The post-1948 Nationalists wanted a more exclusivist, comprehensive, and statutorily enforced policy more in
keeping with government by blueprint.

Under Strijdom, Hertzog's concessions to the English-speaking community, permitting the use of the Union Jack and "God
Save the King" alongside the Union Flag and "Die Stem," were

also abolished: in terms of measures introduced in 1957 there was to be one flag and one anthem. Once Verwoerd was in power, the royal connection was finally severed not by the broad will of the (white) people, as the Nationalists had long promised, but by a simple majority in a 1960 referendum. The republic would not, however, be along the lines of the controversial 1942 Draft Constitution, but rather a modestly modified version of the Union constitution as amended by that time, with a purely ceremonial state president (C. R. Swart) replacing the governor-general. Yet many English-speakers could justifiably feel that nothing would stop the government from getting anything more that it wanted, perhaps eventually moving to declare Afrikaans the sole official language.

The image of an unstoppable government which no longer abided by the rules and which was willing to use patronage, overt manipulation, and even force to maintain and extend its power was what gave the strongest impression of a quasi-fascist state. There was plentiful evidence that Mussolini and Hitler had similarly successfully purged the state apparatus of most undesirable incumbents and replaced them with their own appointees or, where that was not possible, had created parallel party-based agencies such as the SS or the Nazi Auslandsorganisation.

Following in the footsteps of the Suppression of Communism Act, the 1953 Public Safety Act further eroded the rule of law, giving the minister of justice the power to declare a state of emergency and to suspend the separation of powers (which had never been constitutionally entrenched) by effectively granting him martial law authority. The Population Registration Act and the Group Areas Act were similarly enforced at the whim of individual ministers, or of officials appointed by them, who could administratively reclassify an individual from one race to another with the stroke of a pen, or who could declare a whole community unfit to live in a particular residential area.[62] All of these measures had their roots in past laws; under the 1927 Native Administration Act, for instance, the governor-general had enjoyed enormous powers over Africans, removing most of the protection of the courts.[63] Now the same principles were to be applied to everybody.

The rapidly increasing use of detention without trial and the increasing curbs on the press which followed in the sixties and seventies were an extension of this process. For a while at least, the opposition forces were demoralized, beaten into submission, or driven underground or into exile.

Despite the development of a close relationship with Israel, anti-Semitism survived among some senior Nationalists just beneath the surface. This was demonstrated by numerous outbursts over the years in Parliament.[64] Veteran Jewish human rights campaigner Helen Suzman was met with anti-Semitic abuse when she attempted in 1959 to raise in Parliament the terrible conditions in which many African workers lived on white-owned farms. Suzman's biographer, Joanna Strangwayes-Booth, explains that Nationalist backbenchers produced reports of cases of Jewish farmers ill-treating their black workers. One of these members, J. F. Schoonbee, stated, "I just want to say that if I were today of Jewish descent, I would be the last person to raise the matter in the House." When Suzman refused to back down, Schoonbee shouted, "Go preach in the synagogue!" An anonymous Nationalist added, "We don't like your screeching Jewish voice."[65] As late as 1973 Justice Minister Jimmy Kruger made threatening remarks toward Suzman, the main thrust of which was that Jews could not criticize South African legislation because of their allegedly dubious loyalties.[66]

Well-known pro-Nazis visited South Africa during the 1960s. Oswald Mosley, the notorious leader of the Union of British Fascists, crossed the ocean and met the prime minister and various cabinet ministers a number of times. Similarly, Adolf von Thadden, leader of the German neo-Nazis, was in contact with leading members of the National Party.[67]

Yet there was nothing to match the sheer daring of Verwoerd's "grand apartheid," the gradually crystallizing master plan to make South Africa a land with a white majority by means of limited partition rather than Smuts's expedient of massive European immigration, which would surely have swamped the Afrikaner people. For Nationalist rule meant much more than "petty apartheid" measures. It meant more than just the immense expense of multiple signs for segregated facilities under the 1953 Separate Amenities Act. Nor was it just the cost of building a host of ethnic universities under the 1959 Extension of University Education Act or of implementing the application of the hated pass laws to African women, long exempt from these measures.[68]

For the Verwoerdian vision of grand apartheid meant the massive restructuring of an entire society. The impoverished rural African reserves were, at least theoretically, to be developed into something that could pass for viable countries, three and a half million people would be shunted across South Africa in the largest peacetime forced removals of the century in order to tidy up the racial map, and massive state subsidies were to underpin the business operations that would provide the illusion of geographic separation and economic independence. White taxpayers would have to pay millions of dollars in such subsidies to support "border industries" near homelands and the ubiquitous bus services to bring commuters from closer homelands to work, but not live, in the white cities.[69] In addition, white manpower would be increasingly needed in the ranks of the military to defend this authoritarian system.

By the seventies the promise of grand apartheid had already begun to show some visible cracks, as the tide of black migrants to the cities failed to be reversed. Meanwhile, the homelands deteriorated into dumping grounds for the unwanted, run by individuals who increasingly represented only themselves and the coterie of clients who benefited in some way from the largesse Pretoria provided to its black allies. When black rage in the cities exploded in the mid-seventies and again in the eighties, white capitalists of both language groups lost faith in the old schemes, and even the Nationalists had to explore new ways to preserve party rule. In the face of necessity, apartheid could always be reformed; as in the Malan years, the party could show extreme flexibility on tactics. As before, ultimate Nationalist control, however, could still not be open to debate. That was the unalterable effect of adopting an authoritarian nationalist model. Power, once achieved, would not readily be surrendered.

The Limitations of the New Order

The increasing state control of most aspects of life through the fifties, sixties, and seventies, from jobs, universities, and the-

aters to the ambulance to the inevitably segregated hospital, suggested to many that the National Socialist–influenced personnel
who were rising to the top in the new administration were in a
position to effect their ideas on a massive scale. Yet South Africa
remained in many ways a world apart from the "classic" fascist
model. The Union retained a parliamentary system of sorts, regular elections were held (although gradually bereft of even the
last vestiges of black participation), and for a long time a surprisingly vigorous opposition press survived. Through the fifties
at least, the African National Congress and other protest organizations were able to organize remarkably effective campaigns
that would have been impossible in Nazi Germany, Fascist Italy,
or even Franco's Spain or Salazar's Portugal.

It is true, of course, that the rise of the nonracial Congress
Movement, an alliance of the ANC and like-minded white, Indian, and "colored" groups, was cut short by the five-year "Treason trial" of 1955 to 1961, a show-trial in which more than a
hundred activists were effectively removed from the political
mainstream.[70] Nevertheless, South Africa was not Hitler's Germany or Stalin's Russia. All the treason defendants were ultimately acquitted. Although Nationalist rule came to be widely
equated with a police state, and although South Africa built up
a fearsome reputation as the most prolific executioner in the
Western world, there were nothing like death camps or a Gulag
Archipelago. Mass disappearances were not even suspected until
the mid-eighties during the Botha states of emergency.

Even amid the slow erosion of the rule of law and of the power
of the courts to challenge government excess (Supreme Court
testing rights were largely emasculated during the struggle over
the "colored" franchise), the Nationalists retained a notable concern to uphold the appearance of legality. Every new ministerial
power was carefully shepherded through Parliament in the regular manner, signed, and gazetted. Policemen dutifully quoted
the chapter and verse of the laws that enabled them to bring the
much-feared four-o'clock morning knock to citizens' front doors.

Very few leading Nationalists were willing to speak of white
supremacy as the brutally honest Strijdom did with his constant
talk of the need to preserve *baasskap* (boss-ship). Only occasionally did his successor, Verwoerd, let the veil fall with com-

ments such as his well-known reference to "Bantu education"'s being necessary to train Africans for the menial work they were meant to do, rather than for white-collar jobs in "white" South Africa.[71] From the seventies, such gaffes would be increasingly rare, at least at the highest levels, as apartheid underwent modification and modernization to meet changing economic and political realities. The authoritarian heart of the system became heavily camouflaged by an overlay of reformist rhetoric and successive waves of repealing the most obviously repressive apartheid measures. Only recurring mass police action, the growing militarization of society, and the gradual concentration of real power in the hands of a small core-group around the new state president, no longer merely a ceremonial figure as before 1984, intimated that the reintroduction of the liberal state and fundamental democratization were not on the immediate agenda.

Ironically, the racial and ethnic pluralism so encouraged by the National Party meant that a totalitarian regime, which was never fully achieved even in Hitler's Germany, could not have been realized. The constant multiplication of bureaucratic agencies, especially after the advent of the homelands and aggravated in more recent years by the tricameral Parliament of the Botha constitution, provided for an endless overlapping of authority and sometimes conflicting sources of patronage, and blunted the administrative edge of authoritarian legislation.

In addition, sheer black numbers contributed to the Nationalists' inability to destroy completely mass black opposition as the Nazis or the Italian Fascists had succeeded in crushing internal resistance. Moreover, although the power of white opposition political parties to influence the making of law gradually withered after 1948 and Afrikaners gradually challenged the old English monopoly over industrial and commercial life, a wealthy English-speaking "liberal" establishment survived outside the main structures of power, although under Piet Meyer the Broederbond worked mightily to weaken this bloc through state-controlled education and broadcast media propaganda.[72]

In a much more fundamental sense, the corporate rather than person-based nature of Nationalist authoritarianism tended to limit dictatorial ambitions on the part of the leadership. The endless maze of associations, committees, and departments responsible for the effective functioning of the *volksdemokrasie* ensured a healthy dose of interorganizational rivalry, while the eternal round of National Party and other congresses, Afrikaans Reformed synods, and more specific topical conferences allowed for a degree of grass-roots participation that would have been hard to achieve in a truly fascist state. The importance of this tradition for Afrikaners is demonstrated both by the attacks of the Far Right breakaway Conservative party on P. W. Botha's so-called imperial presidency and by the 1989 revolt of the National Party caucus against Botha's attempts to concentrate all power in presidential hands. *Volksdemokrasie* never meant one-man rule.

The Success of an Indigenous Model of Authoritarianism

Indeed, it was the very broad-based character of the Nationalist regime, rooted in every town and village with a labyrinthine organization which touched every member of the volk, that made the new government so strong. The Nationalists could assume the trust of their people and make any necessary changes in tactics without risking a palace revolution. The importance of keeping friction, no matter how fierce, beneath the facade of monolithic unity had been learned in the war years. Decapitation of the top leadership could not threaten the system, which was a well-greased machine that could produce a host of like-minded individuals.

But the effect of all this on the possibility of developing a viable alternative liberal Afrikaner tradition was devastating. In the confining structures of the *Volksbeweging*, which underpinned Nationalist rule, dissidents had always existed, but they faced ostracism and the threat of expulsion from the volk. Only the breakdown of unity inside the *Volksbeweging*, such as began in 1982 with a major split by conservative Afrikaners on the Far Right, opened up opportunities on the left for breathing some life into this long-stunted alternative political tradition through the Independent Party, the New Democratic Movement, the Democratic Party, and similar smaller but vocal splinter groups with significant Afrikaner support, especially among the intelligentsia. Lesser splits, even on the right, such as Albert Hertzog's

Herstigte Nasionale Party (Reconstituted National Party) in 1969, were dealt with summarily by the Broederbond network, which expelled all HNP members.

Until the early 1980s, when the first really serious cracks in the system began to develop, the post-1948 regime had built up a uniquely successful and long-lasting model of authoritarian nationalism, one which in many ways outdid "classical" German National Socialism and Italian Fascism in its sophistication, in its flexibility in changing circumstances, and in its adaptation to local conditions. Malan and his successors had successfully appropriated much of the spirit and even the content of the European Radical Right, yet had fed this into the indigenous Afrikaner context. Authoritarian nationalism was presented not as something borrowed or foreign, but as in keeping with the best traditions of Afrikaner history.

Malan and the National Party proposed, at least in principle, to extend to other groups in South Africa their Christian National *volksdemokrasie*. In the vision more fully articulated by Verwoerd and the Bureau of Racial Affairs, each volk would have its own democracy, disciplined, orderly, and motivated by the highest Christian ideals. The premier volk in the land would, of course, in no way concede any control over the region it claimed as its own. As David Chidester explains, the option taken by the post-1948 Nationalists was one of hegemony, "only a slightly less violent disposition toward otherness" than that of fascism, in which "all difference is systematically violated, yet this violation is accomplished in a somewhat less violent manner."[73] Those outside the dominant group were theoretically permitted, even encouraged, to exist as distinct entities, yet in practice were denied substantive autonomy.

The Malan government and its successors used language, ideas, and institutions in an increasingly Orwellian fashion to give the aura of legitimacy and democracy to their methods. Such an assessment does not mean that the party leadership was *insincere* in describing apartheid as "separate development" or its increasingly authoritarian oligarchy as genuinely democratic. For such a form of ideological hegemony is a two-edged sword that can be ultimately even more compelling in the attractiveness of its argument to its creators than it is to its targets.

This approach was not something invented in the face of post-1948 realities; the Nationalists had developed precisely this dualistic hegemonic strategy during the war years. Caught between the inclusive nationalism of Smuts and the "national socialism" of the Radical Right, the National Party had been forced to develop its own workable philosophy, one both plausibly rooted in its own conservative yet populist past, but at the same time radical in its authoritarianism and social vision. It is true that all the talk of ending unfair capitalism and the structures of British parliamentarianism came to nothing when the Nationalists came to power; these were not feasible objectives, nor were they necessary for a party in control of the machinery of state. Now capitalism and parliamentarianism could be made to work for the National Party cause.

Nevertheless, subtle yet important changes had to be effected. The state apparatus had to be purged of non-Nationalists, and the Broederbond economic war had to be maintained and expanded to bring reliable Afrikaners into the halls of commerce and industry. The parliamentary system also had to be altered to produce reliably desirable results. The additional seats for South-West Africa, the struggle over the "colored" franchise, and the granting of the vote to the predominantly Afrikaans-speaking eighteen-year-olds were all steps along this road.

Malanite nationalism was democratic only in the sense that Kruger's republic had been. During the long years in the hardest school of all, out in the political wilderness, the Nationalists had learned to combine the trappings of democracy with the spirit of Krugerism: authoritarian, stubborn, and intolerant of dissent, yet extraordinarily patient, willing to bide their time and organize behind the scenes, all the time insisting, and even believing, that their policies were based on the highest principles of popular participation.

The Nationalists had never become in any real sense "Nazi" nor even "fascist," although they had been beguiled by the unquestionable material advances made by Germany and Italy under these regimes. The National Party included many who would not only have welcomed a German victory, but who would very likely have assisted German war aims, provided that, like the Bulgarian and Rumanian kings or Admiral Horthy in Hungary, they were permitted to retain their own state forms and autonomy.

By the end of the war a subtle yet profound change had occurred within the main body of Afrikaner nationalism, a change brought about by years of flirtation with the Radical Right. For every protestation of democratic values, for every rejection of dictatorship, for every declaration of Christian allegiance, there was a National Party move in the opposite direction, toward accommodating radical sentiment, in the interest of capturing the broadest possible Afrikaner nationalist support while at the same time distancing themselves from the real conservatives in South Africa, the United Party. For in contrast with the Nationalists, the United Party stood for the preservation of white dominance without a dramatic break with the liberal state or with laissez-faire economics, and for the retention of a unitary South African state without partition.

Thus, when the Nazi cause lost, the Radical Right could, without feeling unduly compromised, find a home in a National Party that professed pluralism and democratic values. But there was a much more fundamental conviction among Nationalists that the only true South Africans were those who professed allegiance to the volk as defined by the party, and, in turn, that the only true members of the volk were those who supported the party, who adhered to official party philosophy and accepted an apartheid future.

To depart in any real sense from this limited vision of nationhood came to amount to the rejection of the most deeply held principles of postwar nationalism. To question such principles, much less to pose any real challenge to the Nationalist hold on power, was to challenge the assumption that only the National Party had the experience and the ability to take charge of South Africa's future. This is why, despite the tactical ingenuity and flexibility of the Nationalist rulers, when the original vision of apartheid ceased to have any credibility, real reform came so slowly, hesitantly, and, all too often, too late to make a substantial impact on black or world opinion. This is also why the belated power-sharing schemes of the eighties did not and could not mean surrender of any fundamental control at the center, and why even the most limited reforms entailed such a sense of betrayal inside the Afrikaner community and such angry resistance from the distrustful and embittered intended beneficiaries of such change.

By 1989 the Afrikaner leaders of the wartime generation were all dead, with the lone exception of P. W. Botha, in the war years a relatively junior figure in the National Party. With the passing in 1978 of State President Nico Diederichs, followed by the deaths of John Vorster in 1983 and of Piet Meyer in 1984, the last of the wartime leadership was gone. A new, more pragmatic generation was in power, dependent almost as much on English-speaking votes as on traditional Afrikaner support, and espousing, however reluctantly, the rhetoric of change and of justice for all. Yet the Nationalists faced formidable difficulties in leading their people out of the morass of apartheid to a genuinely non-racial society. Caught between fearful whites and suspicious blacks, they had become the captives of their own history, trapped by their past actions, their philosophy, style, and structures, and even by their own followers, many of whom increasingly looked for an alternative to the Conservative Party as the repository of the old-time Verwoerdian faith in segregation and partition. The old entanglement with the Radical Right had, despite the many changes of recent years, left a legacy which the National Party could escape not by incremental limited reforms but only by a dramatic and definitive break with its past.

Notes

Preface

1. Cf. William Henry Vatcher, *White Laager: The Rise of Afrikaner Nationalism* (New York and London: Frederick Praeger, 1965), pp. 58–75.
2. Brian Bunting, *The Rise of the South African Reich* (Harmondsworth, Middlesex: Penguin, 1969).
3. See Hans Strydom and Ivor Wilkins, *The Super-Afrikaners: Inside the Afrikaner Broederbond* (Johannesburg: Jonathan Ball, 1978), and J. H. P. Serfontein, *Brotherhood of Power: An Exposé of the Secret Afrikaner Broederbond* (Bloomington and London: University of Indiana Press, 1978).
4. For instance, Dan O'Meara, the best-known Marxist scholar in this field, has dismissed Strydom and Wilkins's work as reflecting "a widespread belief in a monolithic party controlled by the 'super Afrikaners' of the secret Afrikaner Broederbond . . . , able to unite the *volk* behind its implacable position." Cf. *Volkskapitalisme: Class, Capital and Ideology in the Development of Afrikaner Nationalism 1934–1948* (Johannesburg: Ravan, 1983), p. 2.
5. D. W. Krüger, *The Making of a Nation: A History of the Union of South Africa 1910–1961* (Johannesburg and London: Macmillan, 1969), p. 213.
6. B. J. Liebenberg, "From the Statute of Westminster to the Republic of South Africa, 1931–1961," in C. F. J. Muller, ed., *Five Hundred Years: A History of South Africa* (Pretoria and Cape Town: Academica, 1969), p. 422.
7. J. C. Moll, *Fascisme: Die Problematiek van Verklaringsvariante; Fascisme en Suid-Afrika* (Bloemfontein: Publication Series C no. 9, University of the Orange Free State, 1985), p. 164.
8. Frederik Jacobus van Heerden, "Nasionaal-Sosialisme as Faktor in die Suid-Afrikaanse Politiek, 1933–1948" (Bloemfontein: Unpub. D.Phil. dissertation, University of the Orange Free State, 1972), p. 357.
9. Ibid., pp. 357 and 385.
10. George Cloete Visser, *OB: Traitors or Patriots?* (Johannesburg: Macmillan, 1976), p. 209.
11. Ibid., p. 207.
12. Heribert Adam, "Perspectives in the Literature: A Critical Evaluation," in H. Adam and Hermann Giliomee, eds., *The Rise and Crisis of Afrikaner Power* (Cape Town: David Philip, 1979), p. 25.
13. O'Meara, *Volkskapitalisme*, pp. 9–11.

14. Cf. Sipho Mzimela, *Apartheid: South African Nazism* (New York et al: Vantage Press, 1983); Alexandre Kum'a N'dumbe III, "La Politique Africaine de l'Allemagne Hitlerienne 1933–1943" (2 vols.) (Lyons: Unpub. doctoral thesis, Lyons University II, 1974); see also his "Afrikapolitik des dritten Reichs," *Afrika Heute* 21/22 (November 1972), pp. 456–459; "Hitler, L'Afrique du Sud et la Menace Imperialiste: Les Relations Secretes entre Hitler et l'Afrique du Sud," *Les Temps Modernes* 29 (October 1973), published as a separate pamphlet; and *Relations between Nazi Germany and South Africa: Their Influence on the Development of the Ideology of Apartheid* (United Nations Centre Against Apartheid: Notes and Documents no. 12, May 1976).

15. See Mzimela, *Apartheid,* pp. 179–180, and Kum'a N'dumbe, "Hitler," pp. 13–14.

16. Cf. Howard Simson, *The Social Origins of Afrikaner Fascism and Its Apartheid Policy* (Uppsala: Uppsala Studies in Economic History 21, 1980); also "The Afrikaner Nationalist Movement/Regime in Comparative Perspective" (Unpub. paper for Joint Committee on African Studies conference on "South Africa in the Comparative Study of Class, Race and Nationalism," New York, 8–12 September 1982).

17. Simson, *Afrikaner Fascism,* pp. 14–15.

18. Ibid., pp. 160ff.

19. Ibid., p. 200.

Introduction: Between Crown and Swastika

1. Throughout this study, distinction will be made between the National Party and its individual members, the Nationalists, on the one hand, and Afrikaner nationalism and nationalists, in the sense of the much broader political movement, on the other.

2. For instance, when Archbishop Desmond Tutu appeared in debate with Foreign Minister Pik Botha on the American television program "Nightline" in 1986, Botha expressed outrage at his opponent's claim that the South African government was the most vicious regime since that of the Nazis. Botha pointed out that South Africa had fought on the side of the Allies in the Second World War. He omitted any mention of his own party's stance during that conflict.

3. See, for instance, William Henry Vatcher, *White Laager: The Rise of Afrikaner Nationalism* (New York and London: Frederick Praeger, 1965), pp. 58–75, and Brian Bunting, *The Rise of the South African Reich* (Harmondsworth, Middlesex: Penguin, 1969).

4. The most notable relevant work in this tradition is Dan O'Meara's *Volkskapitalisme: Class, Capital and Ideology in the Development of Afrikaner Nationalism* (Johannesburg: Ravan, 1983).

5. See, for instance, Heribert Adam's comments in "Perspectives in the Literature: A Critical Evaluation" in H. Adam and Hermann Giliomee,

eds., *The Rise and Crisis of Afrikaner Power* (Cape Town: David Philip, 1979), p. 25.

6. During the seventies and early eighties the *Sunday Times,* a weekly with the biggest circulation in South Africa, often featured accounts of "fifth column" activities of the war years.

7. In late 1940 a German spy named Trompke informed Berlin that the OB at that time had some 170,000 members, but it is likely that the OB, which had by no means peaked at that date, grew still larger in the following year, when Nazi successes continued almost daily. (See Washington, U.S. National Archives, Microfilm Series T-120, Captured German Foreign Office Records, Reel 318/24184, Telegram, Trompke to Berlin, 6 November 1940).

8. See George Cloete Visser, *OB: Traitors or Patriots?* (Johannesburg: Macmillan, 1976), and Hans Strydom, *For Volk and Führer: Robey Leibbrandt and Operation Weissdorn* (Johannesburg: Jonathan Ball, 1982).

9. See, for instance, Frederik Jakobus van Heerden, "Nasionaal-Sosialisme as Faktor in die Suid-Afrikaanse Politiek, 1933–1948" (Bloemfontein: Unpub. D.Phil. dissertation, University of the Orange Free State, 1972), and J. C. Moll, *Fascisme: Die Problematiek van Verklaringsvariante: Fascisme en Suid-Afrika* (Bloemfontein: Publication Series C No. 9, University of the Orange Free State, 1985).

10. For good overviews of Italian Fascism and German Nazism, cf. Walter Laqueur, ed., *Fascism: A Reader's Guide* (Berkeley and Los Angeles: University of California Press, 1976), Part II, pp. 125ff.; Stanley G. Payne, *Fascism: Comparison and Definition* (Madison: University of Wisconsin Press, 1980), pp. 42–67; and F. L. Carsten, *The Rise of Fascism* (Berkeley and Los Angeles: University of California Press, 2nd ed. 1980), pp. 45ff.

11. For some problems of definition, see the impressive essay by Juan J. Linz, "Some Notes Toward a Comparative Study of Fascism in Sociological Historical Perspective" in Laqueur, ed., *Fascism,* pp. 3–121. See also the survey by J. C. Moll, *Fascisme,* and Eugen Weber, "The Right: An Introduction" in Hans Rogger and Eugen Weber, eds., *The European Right: A Historical Profile* (Berkeley and Los Angeles: University of California Press, 1966), pp. 1–28.

12. On clerico-fascism and other varieties of Radical Right movements, cf. Rogger and Weber, eds., *The European Right*; Stanley G. Payne, "Fascism in Western Europe" in Laqueur, ed., *Fascism,* pp. 295–311; Payne, *Fascism,* pp. 105–160; and Carsten, *Rise of Fascism,* pp. 194–229.

13. Mary Benson, *The African Patriots: The Story of the African National Congress of South Africa* (London: Faber and Faber, 1963), p. 94. Benson notes that the lack of enthusiasm for the Allied cause on the part of many Afrikaners greatly increased the importance of the black contribution to the South African war effort. This role was, however, never recognized in any tangible way by the authorities, except, somewhat

ironically, by Prime Minister Smuts's threat to arm black South Africans after the Japanese attack on Pearl Harbor, which threatened to introduce the possibility of an invasion along the east coast.

14. The Marxian works of O'Meara and Howard Simson (see *The Social Origins of Afrikaner Fascism and Its Apartheid Policy* [Uppsala: Uppsala Studies in Economic History 21, 1980]) cannot be considered to have redressed the balance, since they are almost devoid of unpublished archival data. Structuralist theory, however compelling, is not a substitute for detailed archival research.

15. One of the most obvious examples of such factionalism is the split between the Cape Province in the south, traditionally (but not always) more moderate in its nationalism, and the Transvaal in the north, which has produced a long succession of hard-liners. In contrast with Cape pragmatists like Malan and P. W. Botha are such northern-based prime ministers as J. G. Strijdom and the Dutch-born Hendrik Verwoerd. Similarly, Andries Treurnicht's Far Right Conservative Party, which broke away from the Nationalists in 1982, draws most of its electoral support from former Nationalists in the Transvaal.

Chapter 1: The Coming of the Shirt Movements

1. Johannesburg, University of the Witwatersrand, Cullen Library, Manuscripts Department, J. H. Hofmeyr Papers, D: South-West Africa, Confidential "Memorandum on German Activities in South-West Africa" by Professor Eric Emmett of the University of Cape Town, based on official documents, including German ones, supplied by the Political Investigation Section of the Administration of South-West Africa, ca. 1937.

2. University of Cape Town, Jagger Library, Archives and Manuscripts Department, H. G. Lawrence Papers, E5.45, "Nazi Activities in the Union of South Africa Before and During the War," December 1945, p. 1.

3. Lawrence Papers, E3.262, Otto von Strahl, Confidential report, "Protect Your Home Country," 18 July 1941, p. 6. See also Jeremy Lawrence, *Harry Lawrence* (Cape Town and London: David Philip, 1978), p. 114. Bohle's evidence seems fairly reliable on most matters. For instance, his comments in this report on detailed plans by the Colonial Section of the Nazi Party in Berlin for renewed German control of the former colonies (p. 18) are supported by the discussion of these elaborate schemes in the work of Wolfe Schmokel, one of the few scholars to have produced a detailed published study of Nazi interest in Africa. Schmokel unfortunately provides very little specific discussion of German activities in South Africa or South-West Africa. See *Dream of Empire: German Colonialism 1919–1945* (New Haven and London: Yale University Press, 1964), pp. 137–184.

4. "It DID Happen Here! Nazi Propaganda in S. Africa," pamphlet reprinted by G. Saron from *Common Sense*, January, February, and March numbers, 1940, for prospective use by the anti-Nazi Union Unity Truth

Service, p. 2. *Common Sense* was a respected journal published jointly by South African Jewish and Christian leaders to fight anti-Semitic activity in that country. On Ernst Bohle's English birthplace, see Karl Dietrich Bracher, *Die Deutsche Diktatur* (Frankfurt et al: Ullstein Materialien, 1969), p. 351.

5. Lawrence Papers, "Nazi Activities," p. 9.

6. Lawrence Papers, von Strahl, "Protect Your Home Country," pp. 6 and 10.

7. Ibid., pp. 7–8.

8. Lawrence Papers, "Nazi Activities," p. 9.

9. Lawrence Papers, E5.44.4, White Book on Nazi Activities in the Union of South Africa, 1933–1939, vol. 5, pp. 480–481. As in the case of many figures featured in this chapter, particularly those in secondary roles, Krause's first name is not mentioned in the source. German and South African practice in documentation of the period was often to mention only the last name, sometimes adding an initial or two for further identification.

10. See, for instance, the hundreds of pages of descriptive reports contained in U.S. National Archives Microfilm Series, T-120, Captured German Foreign Office Records, Reel 3017/E490824ff., Akten Pol.X, Betreffend: Innere Politik, Parlaments- und Parteiwesen in Südafrika, 1936–1937.

11. Bloemfontein, Instituut vir Eietydse Geskiedenis, Greyshirts (L. T. Weichardt) Records, File 115, Address by Weichardt to White Workers' Party Conference, 10 June 1949, p. 1.

12. Private communication from Robert Shell.

13. University of Cape Town, Archives and Manuscripts Department, Morris Alexander Papers, Jewish Materials List IV: File 24, "A Memorandum on the Anti-Jewish Movements in South Africa," 1935, p. 2.

14. *The Anti-Jewish Movements in South Africa: The Need for Action* (Johannesburg: Executive Council of the South African Jewish Board of Deputies, 1936), p. 4.

15. "It DID Happen Here!" pp. 4–5.

16. *Anti-Jewish Movements in South Africa,* pp. 4–5. On De Waal, see also Alexander Papers, "Memorandum on Anti-Jewish Movements," pp. 5–6.

17. Ibid. For the date of the appearance of the Blackshirts, see the memorandum on anti-Jewish movements cited above, p. 7.

18. Greyshirt Records, File 2, Weichardt to editor, *Die Burger,* 5 September 1935, and File 4, Weichardt to Smuts, 21 February 1940, enclosing a similar earlier missive to Hertzog.

19. Greyshirt Records, File 4, Circular from Weichardt to party members, 27 February 1940.

20. Greyshirt Records, File 2, Weichardt to editor, *Die Burger,* 5 September 1935.

21. Greyshirt Records, File 2, O. von Derfelden to secretary, *Die Waarheid,* 23 April 1935.

22. Greyshirt Records, File 3, Walter Stark to SANP, 8 January 1937.
23. Donald M. McKale, *The Swastika Outside Germany* (Kent, Ohio: Kent State University Press, 1977), p. 95.
24. Lawrence Papers, E3.266, Otto von Strahl, "Strictly Confidential: List of Dangerous Nazis," 1942.
25. Lawrence Papers, E3.9, "Very Confidential Memorandum Relating to Nazi Activities in the Union of South Africa," 28 October 1939, p. 5.
26. The minutes of Greyshirt conferences and congresses clearly demonstrate Weichardt's concept of "responsible leadership." Although a chairman supposedly controlled these meetings, and all delegates were theoretically permitted to air their views, jeers by Weichardt's supporters could remove an item from the agenda and he dominated all proceedings. He continually interrupted speakers with lengthy admonitions and clarifications, and never failed to get his own way.
27. Alexander Papers, Jewish Materials List IV: File 24, "Who is Weichardt? Who are the Greyshirts?" ca. 1935, and "Afrikaners, Greyshirts and Nazis: What the South West African Commission Has Revealed," ca. 1935.
28. Alexander Papers, Jewish Materials List IV: File 24, "The Greyshirts are South African Nazis: What the South West African Commission Has Revealed," ca. 1935, pp. 2–3. The correspondence of Weigel is also presented in the South African Jewish Board of Deputies' 1936 pamphlet *The Anti-Jewish Movements in South Africa*, pp. 21–22.
29. Alexander Papers, ibid., p. 1. I have not located the German original documents. The translator of this correspondence is unidentified in the source, which may explain the awkward syntax.
30. Ibid., p. 2.
31. Greyshirt Records, File 1, L. Kunze to Weichardt, 25 May 1934, and Weichardt to Kunze, 29 May 1934.
32. Alexander Papers, "Memorandum on Anti-Jewish Movements," pp. 7–8.
33. *Anti-Jewish Movements in South Africa,* pp. 8–9.
34. Greyshirt Records, File 4, "The Song of the Gentile," anonymous music manuscript, ca. 1938, verse 3.
35. Otto von Strahl discusses the "German reading circles" set up by the Nazis all over the Union to lend books to interested individuals. See Lawrence Papers, E5.44.4, Confidential White Book on Nazi Activities in the Union of South Africa 1933–1939, Volume 5, pp. 477 and 599–601.
36. Greyshirt Records, File 121, First SANP Congress: Minutes, 19 December 1934, p. 12.
37. Lawrence Salomon, "The Economic Background to the Revival of Afrikaner Nationalism" in Jeffrey Butler, ed., *Boston University Papers in African History,* Vol. 1 (Boston: Boston University Press, 1964), p. 222.
38. For comparative discussions of these developments, see Stanley G. Payne, *Fascism: Comparison and Definition* (Madison: University of Wisconsin

Press, 1980); F. L. Carsten, *The Rise of Fascism* (Berkeley and Los Angeles: University of California Press, 1980); and Hans Rogger and Eugen Weber, eds., *The European Right: A Historical Profile* (Berkeley and Los Angeles: University of California Press, 1966).

39. Hertzog Papers, Vol. 51(v), in the Central Archives Depot, Pretoria, contain a long series of threatening letters sent to the general during 1932, in which the authors protested that his policies were proving ruinous to many whites. See also Salomon, "Economic Background," p. 232.

40. Salomon, "Economic Background," pp. 231–232.

41. The scholarship on the process of coalition and the ensuing fusion of the two major parties is both dense and voluminous. The most detailed account may be found in the massive study by J. H. le Roux and P. W. Coetzer, *Die Nasionale Party: Deel 3* (Bloemfontein: Instituut vir Eietydse Geskiedenis, 1982). See also S. L. Barnard and A. H. Marais, *Die Verenigde Party: Die Groot Eksperiment* (Durban: Butterworth, 1982), pp. 1–27. The most useful accounts in English may be found in D. W. Krüger, *The Making of a Nation: A History of the Union of South Africa* (Johannesburg and London: Macmillan, 1969), chapter 10, and T. Dunbar Moodie, *The Rise of Afrikanerdom: Power, Apartheid and the Afrikaner Civil Religion* (Berkeley and Los Angeles: University of California Press, 1975), chapter 7. An alternative Marxian interpretation is available in Dan O'Meara, *Volkskapitalisme: Class, Capital and Ideology in the Development of Afrikaner Nationalism 1934–1948* (Johannesburg: Ravan, 1983), chapter 2.

42. Hertzog Papers, Vol. 97, "Verklaring deur Generaal Hertzog en Generaal Smuts aangaande Samewerking," 1933. See also T. R. H. Davenport, *South Africa: A Modern History* (Johannesburg and London: Macmillan, 2nd ed. 1978), pp. 213–216.

43. See Payne, *Fascism,* pp. 107–118. In 1928 the Communist International instructed the South African Communist Party to promote a "black republic," resulting in severe disaffection on the part of its until then mainly white supporters.

44. Davenport, *South Africa,* p. 215.

45. See Hermann Giliomee, "Constructing Afrikaner Nationalism," *Journal of Asian and African Studies* 18:1–2 (January/April 1983), pp. 91–92. For a discussion of the historic roots of the development of the Western Cape as the most bourgeois section of the Afrikaner nationalist movement, see Giliomee's "Western Cape Farmers and the Beginnings of Afrikaner Nationalism," *Journal of Southern African Studies* 14:1 (October 1987), pp. 38–65.

46. On A. J. Werth's various political roles, see Le Roux and Coetzer, *Nasionale Party: Deel 3,* p. 730, and J. H. le Roux and P. W. Coetzer, eds., *Die Nasionale Party: Deel 4* (Bloemfontein: Instituut vir Eietydse Geskiedenis, 1986), pp. 14 and 97.

47. Cape Town, Cape Archives, A. L. Geyer Papers, Vol. 1, Werth to Geyer, 14 March 1934.

48. Geyer Papers, Vol. 1, Werth to Geyer, 9 July 1934.
49. Greyshirt Records, File 14, J. H. H. de Waal, Jr., to his father, 22 February 1934. Also File 115, SANP Conference: Minutes, 19 August 1938, p. 3. On De Waal's role in the pre-Fusion NP, see Giliomee, "Western Cape Farmers," p. 62.
50. Greyshirt Records, File 14, De Waal, Jr., to father, 22 February 1934.
51. Greyshirt Records, File 115, SANP Conference, Minutes, 19 August 1938, p. 3.
52. Greyshirt Records, File 3, D. M. Hoffman, A. Dreyer, and T. Leonhardt to Weichardt, 4 October 1937.
53. Johannesburg, University of the Witwatersrand, Cullen Library, Manuscripts Department, South African Institute of Race Relations (SAIRR) Records, Part I, B 88.6.1, Morris Alexander to J. D. Rheinallt-Jones, 28 November 1933.
54. SAIRR Records, Part I, B 88.6.1, flyer advertising S.A. National Democratic Movement (Blackshirts) meetings in eight rural Transvaal centers, May 1934. Also Greyshirt Records, File 1, L. Kunze to Weichardt, 25 May 1934.
55. SAIRR Records, Part I, B 88.6.1, J. Conradie to J. D. Rheinallt-Jones, 25 June 1934.
56. Ibid.
57. Greyshirt Records, File 14, De Waal, Jr., to father, 22 February 1934.
58. Cape Town, Cape Archives, Senator D. H. van Zyl Papers, Vol. 6, "Junior Nationaliste: Oranjehemp-Drag," a four-page set of guidelines with illustrations for male and female uniforms. With the exception of one minor passing reference, I have been unable to find any other reference to the Orangeshirts.
59. C. M. van den Heever, *General J. B. M. Hertzog* (Johannesburg: APB Bookstore, 1946), pp. 248ff. See also *Bylae* A "Program van Beginsels van die Verenigde Suid-Afrikaanse Nasionale Party, 1934" in Le Roux and Coetzer, *Nasionale Party: Deel 3*, pp. 630–635.
60. See David Yudelman, *The Emergence of Modern South Africa: State, Capital, and the Incorporation of Organized Labour on the South African Gold Fields, 1902–1939* (Cape Town and Johannesburg: David Philip, 1984), pp. 251ff.
61. Gideon Shimoni, *Jews and Zionism: The South African Experience (1910–1967)* (Cape Town: Oxford University Press, 1980), p. 115.
62. Instituut vir Eietydse Geskiedenis, W. Bruckner de Villiers Papers, File 2, Notes for an undated speech "Waarom Koalisie wat bedoel was op Samesmelting uiteenloop aangegaan."
63. Geyer Papers, Vol. 1, Notes for editorial "Die Hoofvyand in die Nasionale Stryd," 15 November 1934.
64. Hofmeyr Papers, Aa 485, O. D. Schreiner to Hofmeyr, 11 October 1934. Also Hofmeyr Papers, Ga 18, S. G. Millin to Hofmeyr, 8 October 1934.
65. SAIRR Records, Conradie to Rheinallt-Jones, 25 June 1934.
66. Greyshirt Records, File 3, M. Kotze to W. Laubscher, 20 October 1937.

67. J. L. Basson, *J. G. Strijdom: Sy Politieke Loopbaan van 1929 tot 1948* (Pretoria: Wonderboom-Uitgewers, 1980), pp. 162, 164–165, and 170.

68. Greyshirt Records, File 3, Hoffman, Dreyer, and Leonhardt to Weichardt, 4 October 1937.

69. Greyshirt Records, File 7, M. van Zyl to Manager, *Die Waarheid,* 28 September 1937, and reply, 1 October 1937.

70. See relevant correspondence in Greyshirt Records, File 3, 1937. Also Bloemfontein, Instituut vir Eietydse Geskiedenis, Senator M. P. A. Malan Papers, File 8, "Uit die Amptelike Notule van die Hoofbestuur van die Nasionale Party, Kaapland," Minutes of Dagbestuur (management committee), Cape National Party, 30 July 1937, p. 6.

71. Ibid.

72. Greyshirt Records, File 121, SANP Congress, ca. late 1937, Minutes, p. 28.

73. M. P. A. Malan Papers, File 8, Minutes of Dagbestuur, Cape National Party, 30 July 1937, pp. 6–7.

74. Greyshirt Records, File 3, F. C. Erasmus to W. R. Laubscher, 28 September and 25 October 1937.

75. Greyshirt Records, File 3, Laubscher to Erasmus, 22 September 1937.

76. Greyshirt Records, File 3, Erasmus to Laubscher, 28 September 1937.

77. Greyshirt Records, File 3, Erasmus to Laubscher, 1 September 1937.

78. Le Roux and Coetzer, *Nasionale Party: Deel 4,* p. 131.

79. Greyshirt Records, File 3, Hoffman, Dreyer, and Leonhardt to Weichardt, 4 October 1937.

80. Greyshirt Records, File 3, Erasmus to Laubscher, 28 September 1937. The Afrikaans reads: "'n Party wat oënskynlik in so 'n noue verband staan met en geinspireer word deur die politieke bedrywighede van 'n ander land, hoe bevriend ons daarmee ook al mag wees."

81. Bloemfontein, Instituut vir Eietydse Geskiedenis, Eric Louw Papers, File 2, Malan to Louw, 9 December 1936.

82. Greyshirt Records, File 3, Erasmus to Laubscher, 25 October 1937.

83. Ibid.

84. See Greyshirt Records, File 14, F. von Hasselt to J. von Moltke, 20 January 1935.

85. Greyshirt Records, File 3, "Van" to Weichardt, 9 December 1936.

86. See "It DID Happen Here," reprint from *Common Sense,* January, February, and March Numbers, 1940, p. 11. A photographic copy of the relevant pages of that issue of *Die Rapport* exists in the South African Institute of Race Relations Records at the University of the Witwatersrand. See SAIRR Records, Part 1, B 88.6.1, enclosure with letter from I. M. Goodman, Secretary of the S.A. Jewish Board of Deputies, to J. D. Rheinallt-Jones, 27 April 1934. On Olivier's role in this case, see *Die Burger,* 23 August 1934.

87. *Die Rapport,* 13 April 1934, p. 2. Report given in English.

88. *Die Burger,* 23 August 1934. The judgment was reprinted as a pamphlet entitled *Die Waarheid van die Gryshemde* (see Alexander Papers, List IV,

File 24). The original Afrikaans, referring also to two further anti-Semitic documents which the defendants had claimed originated in the Jewish Emmanuel Hall, states: "Die hof is daarvan oortuig dat die dokumente onmiskenbare tekens verraai dat dit opgestel is deur 'n lid of lede van die Gryshemp-beweging en dat dit maklik deur Inch of Von Moltke of een van die twee opgestel kon gewees het." (tr. "The court is convinced that the documents display unmistakable signs that it [sic] was composed by a member or members of the Greyshirt Movement and that it [sic] could easily have been composed by Inch or Von Moltke or one of the two.")

89. Ibid.; see also the Board of Deputies pamphlet *The Anti-Jewish Movements in South Africa*, p. 7.

90. See Greyshirts Records, File 2, Weichardt to Minister of Justice, 4 April 1935, and Director of Prisons to Weichardt, 27 July 1935.

91. Gus Saron, "Four Eventful Decades," in South African Jewish Board of Deputies, *The Story of Fifty years 1903–1953* (reprint from *Jewish Affairs*, SAJBD monthly, June 1953), p. 35, in University of Cape Town, Archives and Manuscripts Department/Kaplan Center for Jewish Studies, A. M. Jackson Miscellany.

92. Alexander Papers, Board of Deputies File 7, Legal opinion for board by attorneys P. Millin and I. Isaacs, "In Re S.A. Jewish Board of Deputies," 30 March 1937, p. 1.

93. Ibid.

94. Ibid.

95. Greyshirt Records, File 3, W. R. Laubscher to Weichardt, 13 October 1937.

96. University of Cape Town, Archives and Manuscripts Department/Kaplan Center for Jewish Studies, I. M. Goodman Papers, one-page typed transcript of judgment by Mr. Justice Centlivres "In the matter between Isaac Meyer Goodman, Petitioner, and Johannes von [sic] Strauss von Moltke, Respondent," Cape Town, 22 February 1938.

97. Goodman Papers, typed transcript of affidavit "In Re Petition of Isaac Goodman Petitioner versus Johannes von Strauss von Moltke Respondent for an Interdict," 31 January 1938, pp. 5 and 7.

98. Ibid., p. 5.

99. *Die Suiderstem*, 27 June 1938, cited in Alexander Papers, Board of Deputies File 59, G. Saron to Alexander, 6 July 1938.

100. Basson, *J. G. Strijdom*, p. 165.

101. This is supported by the abundant documentation collected by the 1935 South West Africa Commission and the 1946 commission (U.G. 16-1947) set up to investigate the deportation of German aliens from that territory. The latter listed individuals known for their pro-Nazi activities or sympathies.

Chapter 2: Jewish Immigration and the Tide of Nationalist Anti-Semitism

1. Cf., for instance, Milton Shain, *Jewry and Cape Society: The Origins and Activities of the Jewish Board of Deputies for the Cape Colony* (Cape Town: Historical Publication Society, 1983), pp. 3ff.

2. Gideon Shimoni, *Jews and Zionism: The South African Experience (1910–1967)* (Cape Town: Oxford University Press, 1980), p. 45.

3. Ibid., p. 65.

4. Shain, *Jewry and Cape Society*, pp. 45ff.

5. Ibid. I have not located any copy of this journal. Shain notes (p. 116) that Hoggenheimer originated as "Hoggenheimer of Park Lane" in a musical comedy, *The Girl from Kay's*, first produced in London in November 1902.

6. Ibid., pp. 57ff.

7. Gus Saron, "The Struggles and Achievements of Four Eventful Decades," in *The South African Jewish Board of Deputies: The Story of Fifty Years 1903–1953* (Reprinted from *Jewish Affairs*, June 1953), pp. 29–30. See also Muriel Horrell, comp., *Laws Affecting Race Relations in South Africa (To the End of 1976)* (Johannesburg: South African Institute of Race Relations, 1978), p. 5.

8. Saron, "Struggles and Achievements," pp. 31–32.

9. Shimoni, *Jews and Zionism*, pp. 41–47 and 90–93. See also Richard Stevens, "Smuts and Weizmann" in Richard Stevens and Abdelwahab Elmessiri, eds., *Israel and South Africa: The Progression of a Relationship* (New Brunswick, N.J.: North American, revised ed. 1977), pp. 34–56.

10. Shimoni, *Jews and Zionism*, pp. 92–94.

11. Ibid.

12. University of Cape Town, Jagger Library, Archives and Manuscripts Department, Morris Alexander Papers, Jewish Materials List IV: File 24, Malan to Alexander, 10 July 1924.

13. *Die Burger*, 22 March 1929.

14. I wish to thank Sharon Friedman of the Kaplan Center for Jewish Studies at the University of Cape Town for giving me access to hitherto "lost" immigration records of the South African Jewish Board of Deputies. An immigration register of the board for the late twenties shows Jewish immigrants to have come almost exclusively from towns in Lithuania, along with neighboring areas of Poland and the Soviet Union. This document had not yet been filed in the archival catalog at the time of consultation.

15. Alexander Papers, Board of Deputies File 3, Transcript from *Cape Times*, "A Bill Against Jews?" 3 February 1930.

16. Shimoni, *Jews and Zionism*, pp. 100–101.

17. Alexander Papers, Board of Deputies File 3, "Antwoord op brief in *Die Burger* van 23.11.36," pp. 2–3.

18. Ibid., pp. 3–4.
19. Alexander Papers, Board of Deputies File 3, Telegram from Johannesburg Board of Deputies Office to Alexander, 7 February 1930. See also telegram from same office to Alexander, 31 January 1930.
20. Bloemfontein, Instituut vir Eietydse Geskiedenis, E. H. Louw Papers, File 2, Malan to Louw, 10 June 1930.
21. Shimoni, *Jews and Zionism*, p. 91.
22. Ibid., p. 18. Reformed Judaism was a movement founded in nineteenth-century Central Europe, and which embraced an openness to integration into the broader Gentile community. Its ideal was assimilation, not an exodus to Palestine. Hasidism was a form of ultraorthodoxy, often found among sections of Polish Jewry, and which rejected the concept of the Zionist state on the grounds that the Messiah had not yet come to found it.
23. Sharon Friedman, "Jews, Germans and Afrikaners: Nationalist Press Reaction to the Final Solution" (Cape Town: Unpub. B.A. [Hons.] thesis, University of Cape Town, 1982), p. 2.
24. *Der Afrikaner* (Yiddish-language newspaper), 24 May 1929, election statement, cited in Shimoni, *Jews and Zionism*, p. 51.
25. André du Toit, "Puritans in Africa? Afrikaner 'Calvinism' and Kuyperian Neo-Calvinism in Late Nineteenth-Century South Africa," *Comparative Studies in Society and History* 27:2 (April 1985), pp. 225, 230–231.
26. Malan's rhetoric in the thirties was sometimes ambivalent in this regard, but usually he left his audiences in no doubt that he considered Afrikaans-speakers the most reliable and "truest" South Africans. His references to the volk almost always implied only Afrikaans-speakers. See, for instance, Pretoria, State Archives (Transvaal Archives Depot), Mrs. S. Kieser Collection, 1936 Transvaal National Party Congress, Minutes, p. 46.
27. Cape Archives, Senator D. H. van Zyl Papers, Vol. 40, 1934 Cape National Party Congress, Minutes, Appendix D, Opening Speech of Dr. D. F. Malan, p. 29. My translation. The original Afrikaans reads: "Daar is gesê dat die koalisie gevorm moet word om 'n end te maak aan rassehaat. Die ondervinding het egter geleer dat sodra gepraat word van die s.g. rassehaat, daar iets anders agter sit. As daardie masker weggetrek word, sal 'n mens altyd daar sien die stale, berekenende, gulsige gelaat van Hoggenheimer."
28. See the many cartoon illustrations in P. W. Coetzer and J. H. le Roux, eds., *Die Nasionale Party: Deel 4* (Bloemfontein: Instituut vir Eietydse Geskiedenis, 1986).
29. See, for instance, Dan O'Meara, *Volkskapitalisme: Class, Capital and Ideology in the Development of Afrikaner Nationalism 1934–1948* (Johannesburg: Ravan, 1983). Classic examples of this approach can also be found in Martin Legassick, "Legislation, Ideology and Economy in Post-1948 South Africa" in *Journal of Southern African Studies* 1:1 (October 1974): 5–35, and Harold Wolpe, "Capitalism and Cheap Labour-Power in South Africa: From Segregation to Apartheid" in *Economy and*

Society 1:4 (November 1972): 425–456; also Belinda Bozzoli, "Capital and the State in South Africa" in *Review of African Political Economy* no. 11 (January–April 1978): 40–50.

30. Van Zyl Papers, Vol. 40, 1934 Cape National Party Congress, Minutes, Appendix D, p. 28.

31. Ibid., p. 29.

32. 1934 Cape National Party Congress, Minutes, Annual Report of Executive, p. 15.

33. See chapter 1.

34. *Cape Argus,* 24 February 1934.

35. *Die Burger,* 4 December 1933.

36. University of Cape Town, Kaplan Center for Jewish Studies/Archives and Manuscripts Department, South African Jewish Board of Deputies Archive, Bound Minutes 1934–1937, Minutes of Cape Committee, 5 June 1935, p. 4.

37. See, for instance, Berlin, Nazi Party Main Archive (Microfilmed by Hoover Institution, Stanford, 1960), Reel 34, Folder 656, Education Director, *Ortsgruppe* Zehlendorf to NSDAP Party Archive, 25 August 1934. This is accompanied by a complete issue of the Greyshirt journal *Die Waarheid/The Truth* of 18 May 1934, detailing the transformation of Louis Weichardt's South African Gentile National-Socialist Movement and the South African Greyshirts into the South African National Party (SANP), usually known simply as the Greyshirts.

38. Board of Deputies Archive, Minutes 1934–1937, Report of Board Conference, 27 March 1935, p. 4. Also Minutes of Cape Committee, 8 September 1935, p. 4, and 8 December 1935, p. 3.

39. *The Immigration of Jews into the Union, 1926–1935 (With Appendices for the Year 1936): An Analysis of Official Statistics* (N.p.: South African Jewish Board of Deputies, 1937), pp. 8 and 13.

40. Ibid., p. 13.

41. Ibid., pp. 8, 10 and 15.

42. Kieser Collection, 1936 Transvaal National Party Congress, Minutes, p. 18.

43. Ibid., p. 22.

44. Ibid., p. 20.

45. Ibid., pp. 21–23.

46. Ibid., pp. 27–28.

47. Ibid., pp. 31–32.

48. G. C. Cuthbertson, "Jewish Immigration as an Issue in South African Politics, 1937–1939" in *Historia* 26:2 (May 1981), p. 120.

49. See University of the Witwatersrand, Cullen Library, Manuscripts Department, J. H. Hofmeyr Papers, Dh 1, Anti-Semitism and Immigration, File 1, "Memorandum on European Immigration to South Africa for Submission to the Hon. the Prime Minister," 30 March 1936, p. 9.

50. See the complex and lengthy correspondence on this issue in Hofmeyr Papers, Dh 1, File 1, 1936.

51. Kieser Collection, 1936 Transvaal National Party Congress, Minutes, pp. 40 and 47.
52. Ibid., p. 50.
53. Ibid. "Dat hierdie Kongres, met die oog op die aangenome mosie insake Joodse immigrante, die Federale Raad dringend versoek om in sy Beginsel-Program die toelating van Jode as lede van die Nasionale Party te verbied, oor die Unie."
54. Ibid., p. 47. It is interesting to note that, like so many white South African politicians of his day, Malan simply ignored black South Africans in his calculation of such percentages.
55. Cuthbertson, "Jewish Immigration as an Issue," p. 121.
56. University of Cape Town, Kaplan Center for Jewish Studies/Archives and Manuscripts Department, Jewish Immigration Collection, A. "Draft Recollections of the Jewish Immigrants from Germany 1933–1936," by L. Raphaely, pp. 2–3.
57. Die Transvaler, 1 October 1937.
58. Hertzog's papers contain frequent requests from the Jewish community for action against the anti-Semites. Usually these were met with brusque responses merely "noting" their contents.
59. S.A. Jewish Board of Deputies Archive, Bodenstein to S.A. Jewish Board of Deputies, 28 August 1934.
60. Pretoria, State Archives, J. C. Smuts Papers, Vol. 123, Copy of Letter, H. D. Bodenstein for Prime Minister to President of Board of Deputies, 19 August 1936.
61. Ibid.
62. Cuthbertson, "Jewish Immigration as an Issue," pp. 121–124.
63. Ibid., p. 125.
64. Bloemfontein, Instituut vir Eietydse Geskiedenis, Senator M. P. A. Malan Papers, File 8, "Notules en Uittreksels uit Notules," Minutes of Cape NP Executive, 2 June 1939.
65. Ibid.
66. Cape Argus, 16 April 1937.
67. Cape Argus, 12 April 1937.
68. Alexander Papers, Board of Deputies File 7, Malan to G. Saron, 1 February 1938.
69. Alexander Papers, Board of Deputies File 59, Alexander to Lyons, 17 February 1938.
70. Kieser Collection, "Die Nasionale Party se Verkiesingsmanifes: Algemene Verkiesing 1938," Art. 4.
71. Alexander Hepple, Verwoerd (Harmondsworth, Middlesex: Penguin, 1967), pp. 223–225.
72. Ibid.
73. Alexander Papers, Board of Deputies File 7, A. J. van Zyl, Manager of Voortrekker Press, to Secretary, Board of Deputies, Johannesburg, 12 October 1937. This document is apparently an English translation of the original.

74. Ibid.
75. Alexander Papers, File 7, G. Saron to A. J. van Zyl, 19 October 1937.
76. Alexander Papers, Board of Deputies File 7, Van Zyl to Saron, 28 October 1937.
77. Hofmeyr Papers, Dh File 2, Press Report no. 122.
78. Hofmeyr Papers, Dh File 2, "Louw's Aliens' (Amendment) and Immigration Act, 1939: An Analysis." This memorandum analyzes the bill section by section.
79. Ibid., p. 2.
80. Alexander Papers, C. File 31, Malan cited in Cape Committee Report to Meeting of Deputies, 12 November 1939, p. 2.
81. Hofmeyr Papers, Dh File 2, "Eric Louw's Bill," p. 1.
82. Ibid., pp. 1–2.
83. Interview with Africopa News Service in *Daily News,* cited in United Party *Newsletter,* 92 (August 1947), pp. 3–4.

Chapter 3: The Berlin Connection

1. See editorial "Der Union von Südafrika zum 31. Mai 1935" in *Afrika-Rundschau* 1:2 (June 1935), p. 31, in which South Africa was described as enjoying the greatest German interest among the British dominions.
2. Ibid., p. 32. See also Werner Schmidt-Pretoria, *Der Kulturanteil des Deutschtums am Aufbau des Burenvolkes* (Hannover: Hahnsche Verlagsbuchhandlung, 1938), a highly propagandistic work, which deals in detail with the contribution of Germany to Afrikaner culture.
3. The best recent work on the racially mixed ancestry of the Afrikaner is H. F. Heese's *Groep Sonder Grense: Die Rol en Status van die Gemengde Bevolking aan die Kaap, 1652–1795* (Belville: Western Cape Institute for Historical Research, 1984).
4. See M. F. Katzen, "White Settlers and the Origin of the New Society, 1652–1778" in Monica Wilson and Leonard Thompson, eds., *A History of South Africa to 1870* (Cape Town: David Philip, 1982), pp. 174, 194, and 229; also E. H. Raidt, *Afrikaans en Sy Europese Verlede: Van Tacitus tot Van Wyk Louw* (Cape Town: Nasou, 2nd ed. 1982), pp. 83–85.
5. See, for instance, University of Cape Town, Jagger Library, Archives and Manuscripts Department, H. G. Lawrence Papers, E3.262, Otto von Strahl, "Protect Your Home Country," detailing prewar Nazi activities in South Africa.
6. F. A. van Jaarsveld, *The Awakening of Afrikaner Nationalism 1868–1881* (Cape Town: Human and Rousseau, 1961), pp. 70, 145–146, and 192.
7. J. S. du Plessis, "The South African Republic" in C. F. J. Muller, ed., *Five Hundred Years: A History of South Africa* (Cape Town and Pretoria: Academica Press, 2nd ed. 1975), pp. 266 and 275–276.
8. Ibid., p. 287.
9. Ibid., p. 289.

10. J. S. Marais, *The Fall of Kruger's Republic* (Oxford: Clarendon Press, 1961), p. 99.

11. Ibid., p. 291.

12. M. C. van Zyl, "States and Colonies in South Africa, 1854–1902" in Muller, ed., *Five Hundred Years*, pp. 309 and 312.

13. Ibid., p. 337.

14. Marais, *Fall of Kruger's Republic*, p. 47.

15. Leslie Rubin, "Afrikaner Nationalism and Nazi Germany: The Roots of Apartheid" (Unpub. paper, 1985), p. 2.

16. Donald M. McKale, *The Swastika Outside Germany* (Kent, Ohio: Kent State University Press, 1977), pp. 31 and 45ff.

17. Ibid., pp. 47–48.

18. Lawrence Papers, E3.9, "Very Confidential Memorandum Relating to Nazi Activities in the Union of South Africa," 28 October 1939, p. 6.

19. Lawrence Papers, E3.262, Otto von Strahl, Confidential Folder "Protect Your Home Country," 18 July 1941, p. 10.

20. See also the extensive discussion of the role of the *Deutsch-Afrikaner* in Lawrence Papers, E5.44, White Book on Nazi Activities in the Union of South Africa 1933–1939, Vol. 5, pp. 477–481, 544–548, and 567–578.

21. Ibid., pp. 546–547.

22. Ibid., pp. 554–555.

23. Ibid., p. 556.

24. Ibid., p. 570.

25. Ibid., p. 573.

26. Ibid., pp. 599–601. A detailed report on Nazi activity in one of the most famous German schools, that at Hermannsburg in Natal, can be found in H. G. Lawrence Papers, E3.221, "Nazi Activities and Propaganda in Schools in Natal," 22 February 1940.

27. Ibid., pp. 1 and 11, and annexures A, B, and E.

28. Ibid., Annexure H.

29. See Lawrence Papers, E3.212–E3.215, Correspondence regarding Deutsche Berufsgruppen, 30 August 1939ff.

30. Lawrence Papers, E3.262, Von Strahl, "Protect Your Home Country," pp. 6 and 10.

31. Lawrence Papers, E3.213, Translated transcript of captured correspondence, "AA of the German Berufsgruppen," Hamburg, to all office bearers, 11 June 1935.

32. Lawrence Papers, E3.214, "Translation of Extracts from: Instructions for the Establishing of New *Stützpunkte* and *Zellen* Abroad," a mimeographed four-page report, part of correspondence seized at the outbreak of war, enclosed with a secret letter from the Secretary for South-West Africa in Windhoek to the Chief Control Officer, Department of Justice, Pretoria, 30 August 1940.

33. University of Cape Town, Archives and Manuscripts Department, Morris Alexander Papers, C. File 29, "German Nazis Organise in South Africa," reprinted from *Forward,* 1938.

34. Lawrence Papers, White Book on Nazi Activities in the Union of South Africa, 1933–1939, Vol. 2, p. 185.

35. Ibid., p. 232.

36. Lawrence Papers, White Book on Nazi Activities in the Union of South Africa, 1933–1939, Vol. 3, p. 293.

37. U.S. National Archives Microfilm Series, T-120, Captured German Foreign Office Records (hereafter USNAMS, T-120), Reel 3017/E491148, Dieckhoff to Smuts, 20 August 1936.

38. T. Dunbar Moodie, *The Rise of Afrikanerdom: Power, Apartheid and the Afrikaner Civil Religion* (Berkeley and Los Angeles: University of California Press, 1975), p. 155.

39. USNAMS, T-120, Reel 317/241170, Leitner to Foreign Office, 15 June 1939, p. 2.

40. USNAMS, T-120, Reel 3017/E491215, Stiller to Foreign Office, 28 April 1937.

41. P. J. Meyer, *Nog Nie Ver Genoeg Nie: 'n Persoonlike Rekenskap van Vyftig Jaar Georganiseerde Afrikanerskap* (Johannesburg and Cape Town: Perskor, 1984), pp. 10–11.

42. Rubin, "Afrikaner Nationalism and Nazi Germany," p. 5.

43. Ibid.

44. Interview with Leslie Rubin, 7 June 1985.

45. Fichte, the German nationalist philosopher, particularly admired the kingdom of Prussia as a model state. He would no doubt have been horrified to see some of the uses to which his ideas, like those of Nietzsche, Herder, and Schleiermacher, were put to use by pro-Nazi academics. The use of the term "neo-Fichteanism," following Moodie (*Rise of Afrikanerdom*, pp. 154ff.) and Rodney Davenport, *South Africa: A Modern History* (Toronto and Buffalo: University of Toronto Press, 1987), p. 318, does not imply that the ideas of Fichte, or indeed those of other nineteenth-century German philosophers, are in any way analogous to those of Hitler or other Nazi ideologues.

46. Meyer, *Nog Nie Ver Genoeg Nie,* pp. 11–12.

47. Lawrence Papers, White Book, Vol. 3, p. 314.

48. Ibid., pp. 303–304.

49. Ibid., p. 294.

50. Ibid., pp. 311–313.

51. USNAMS, T-120, Reel 317/241191–241192, "Unterredung mit Professor Diederichs, Suedafrika, am. 19. Mai 1939," pp. 1–2. The original German of this passage reads: "Sehr viele ihrer heute führenden Leute seien doch noch zu weitgehend befangen in demokratischen Ideen. Infolgedessen werde für eine völlige nationale Erhebung ein weitgehender Führerwechsel Voraussetzung sein. Die Hoffnung liege da bei der Jugend und man sei sich im nationalen Lager einig darüber, dass jeder neugeborene Bure einmal Nationalist sein würde. Der Endsieg sei infolgedessen niemanden fraglich."

52. Ibid., pp. 2–3. This extract reads: ". . . habe die hauptsächlichste Sorge

der Heranbildung von Fachleuten zu gelten, die hernach nicht nur gesinnungsmässig, sondern auch fachlich in der Lage seien, die Regierung zu übernehmen. Dieser Aufgabe werde sich in Zukunft mit kleinsten Anfängen beginnend, der "Broederbond" widmen. Mit der Bitte, dies als streng vertraulich zu betrachten, sagte mir Prof. Diederichs dann, dass er vor kurzem die Leitung des "Broederbonds" übernommen habe. Der "Broederbond" sei eine Geheimorganisation, in die eine Aufnahme erst nach eingehender Prüfung möglich sei. Ziel der Organisation sei, das ganze Land, vor allem auch die führenden Stellen, zu durchdringen und das gesamte Staatswesen auf diese Weise von innen her zu erobern."

53. Ibid., p. 4. ". . . er glaube nicht, dass die innere Stärke der Nationalen Partei dann schon genügen würde, eine Regierung zu bilden nach dem Muster der autoritären Staaten. Diese allein aber könne auf die Dauer seine Stellung südlich des Äquators sichern."

54. USNAMS, T-120, Reel 317/241190, "Bemerkungen von H. Bohle," 30 May 1939.

55. "It DID Happen Here! How the Nazis Conducted Propaganda in South Africa" in *Common Sense*, January 1940, pp. 9–10.

56. Ibid., p. 10.

57. USNAMS, T-120, Reel 317, "Bemerkungen von H. Bohle."

58. USNAMS, T-120, Reel 318/241238, Undated memorandum "Aufzeichnung für den Empfang des Wirtschafts- und Verteidigungsministers der Union von Südafrika Pirow," p. 1.

59. See copy of Pirow's letter of thanks to German Foreign Minister Ribbentrop in Stanford, 26 November 1938, Hoover Institution, German Foreign Office Collection, File 540/147841. On Pirow's visit to Germany and Italy, see also USNAMS, T-120, Reel 318/241235–241242, documents regarding Pirow's visit, 1938, including a discussion of Mussolini's impressions of Pirow, which were extremely uncomplimentary. See Telegram, Mackensen to Berlin, 28 November 1938.

60. Pretoria, State Archives, J. C. Smuts Papers, Vol. 56, S. G. Millin to Smuts, 12 November 1938.

61. Johannesburg, University of the Witwatersrand, Cullen Library, Manuscripts Department, S. G. Millin Papers, C1, Hofmeyr to Millin, 16 December 1938.

62. Ibid.

63. Ibid.

64. Ibid.

65. Millin Papers, C1, Hofmeyr to Millin, 19 June 1938.

66. USNAMS, T-120, Reel 3017/E491047, "Abschrift: Die Neuwahlen zum Unionsparlament im Juni kommenden Jahres, Kapstadt, ende Oktober 1937," p. 3.

67. Ibid. The text reads: ". . . sind sie natürlichen Voraussetzungen für ein Zusammengehen der Malan Partei und der Grauhemden durchaus vorhanden. Beide stehen sie in ehrlicher und offener Opposition zur Regierung, beide halten sie die Judenfrage und den Bolschewismus für einen

wesentlichen Kernpunkt ihrer Programme, beide wollen die Unabhängigkeit des südakfrikanischen Geldmarktes vom internationalen Judentum durch Errichtung einer rein südafrikanischen National Bank sicherstellen."

68. Ibid.
69. Alan Bullock, *Hitler: A Study in Tyranny* (New York: Harper and Row, 1964), p. 188.
70. A good account of the rise and fall of the German National People's Party can be found in John A. Leopold, *Alfred Hugenberg: The Radical Nationalist Campaign Against the Weimar Republic* (New Haven and London: Yale University Press, 1977).
71. Bloemfontein, Instituut vir Eietydse Geskiedenis, Greyshirts (L. T. Weichardt) Records, File 3, F. C. Erasmus to W. R. Laubscher, 25 October 1937. See also Erasmus to Laubscher, 28 September 1937.
72. Bullock, *Hitler,* pp. 147–150.
73. See Peter Stachura, "The Nazis, the Bourgeoisie and the Workers during the *Kampfzeit,*" in P. D. Stachura, ed., *The Nazi Machtergreifung* (London: George Allen and Unwin, 1983), pp. 15–32, and Dan O'Meara, *Volkskapitalisme: Class, Capital and Ideology in the Development of Afrikaner Nationalism, 1934–1948* (Johannesburg: Ravan, 1983), pp. 49ff. O'Meara points out that the large-scale Cape sheep farmers were particularly steadfast supporters of Malan, bound as they were by strong trade ties both to Germany and to Great Britain.
74. Ibid., p. 50.
75. Moodie, *Rise of Afrikanerdom,* p. 154.
76. E. W. F. Tomlin, *The Western Philosophers* (London et al: Hutchinson, 1968), p. 215.
77. Robert Waite, *The Psychopathic God: Adolf Hitler* (New York: Basic Books, 1977), pp. 98–102.
78. Ibid., p. 144.
79. Robert Pois, ed., *Alfred Rosenberg: Selected Writings* (London: Jonathan Cape, 1970), Introduction, pp. 17–18.
80. Ibid., p. 19.
81. Moodie, *Rise of Afrikanerdom,* p. 162.
82. USNAMS, T-120, Reel 217/241195, "Unterredung mit Professor Diederichs," p. 5. The text reads: ". . . die Vereinigte Partei ihre Sitze im Wesentlichen lediglich den Stimmen der Juden zu verdanken habe."
83. Nicolas Diederichs, *Vom Leiden und Dulden* (Bonn: Ferdinand Dümmlers Verlag, 1930).
84. N. Diederichs, *Nasionalisme as Lewensbeskouing en Sy Verhouding tot Internasionalisme* (Bloemfontein et al: Nasionale Pers, 1936), p. 3.
85. Ibid., pp. 17–18 and 63.
86. *Die Volksblad,* 25 April 1935, cited in Moodie's translation in *Rise of Afrikanerdom,* p. 160.
87. Moodie, *Rise of Afrikanerdom,* pp. 54–55.
88. Ibid., p. 155.

89. Ibid.
90. O'Meara, *Volkskapitalisme,* p. 51. Although by 1931 the Broederbond had begun to grow in the southern provinces, O'Meara's view that its base was the Transvaal is nowhere contradicted by the Broederbond materials I have used. Furthermore, for the first eleven years of the Bond's existence, branches were restricted to the Transvaal. Bond annual meetings were held in Johannesburg or Pretoria until 1938, when they were moved to the more centrally located Bloemfontein. See the Bond's official history by A. N. Pelzer, *Die Afrikaner-Broederbond: Eerste 50 Jaar* (Cape Town: Tafelberg, 1979), pp. 36–37 and 43. Furthermore, Transvalers held the chairmanship of the Bond until 1952 (Pelzer, p. 46). Of sixty candidates for the Bond Executive Council in 1941, at least thirty-six were Transvalers even at this relatively late date, when the Bond included branches in all provinces. See J. H. P. Serfontein, *Brotherhood of Power* (Bloomington: Indiana University Press, 1978), pp. 79–80.
91. O'Meara, *Volkskapitalisme,* p. 62.
92. C. J. H. de Wet led an agitation for a radical "Christian Nationalist" program during 1936–1937. This was only one of many crises reflected in the party minutes of those years. See Pretoria, State Archives, J. G. Strijdom Papers, Vol. 36, C. J. H. de Wet to Secretary, Transvaal NP, 16 April 1937. As late as January 1939 the NP on the Witwatersrand had only been able to reduce its debt from 550 to 320 pounds, and the payment of constituency dues was being described as "a matter of seriousness." See Strijdom Papers, Vol. 36, Transvaal NP Executive, Minutes, 21 January 1939, p. 3.
93. O'Meara, *Volkskapitalisme,* p. 60.
94. N. Diederichs, *Die Kommunisme: Sy Teorie en Taktiek* (Bloemfontein et al: Nasionale Pers, 1938), pp. 162–163.
95. Foreword to ibid.
96. A. J. H. van der Walt, N. Diederichs, J. F. J. van Rensburg, and others, *Hedendaagse Politieke Strominge* (Johannesburg: Voortrekkerpers, n.d.).
97. Moodie, *Rise of Afrikanerdom,* pp. 169–170.
98. Ibid., p. 230.
99. *Die Afrikaner* (Bloemfontein: Nasionale Pers, 1941), pp. 55–56, cited by Moodie in his own translation in *Rise of Afrikanerdom,* p. 163.
100. P. J. Meyer, *Die Toekomstige Ordening van die Volksbeweging in Suid-Afrika* (Stellenbosch, ANSB, 1942), p. 12, cited in Moodie, *Rise of Afrikanerdom,* p. 230.
101. USNAMS, T-120, "Unterredung mit Professor Diederichs," p. 4.
102. *Die Transvaler,* 4 October 1937.
103. Ibid.
104. *Die Waarheid,* 23 February 1934.

Chapter 4: The Initial Transformation of the National Party

1. Dan O'Meara, *Volkskapitalisme: Class, Capital and Ideology in the Development of Afrikaner Nationalism* (Johannesburg: Ravan, 1983), pp. 51–52. Hermann Giliomee argues, contrary to O'Meara, that too much should not be made of the British connection, which affected primarily the wool trade. Giliomee points out that the wine and wheat industries, the other two staples of Cape agriculture, were geared minimally toward export to Britain. See Giliomee, "Constructing Afrikaner Nationalism," *Journal of Asian and African Studies* 18:1–2 (January/April 1983), pp. 91–92.

2. See chapter 1.

3. Pretoria, State Archives, J. G. Strijdom Papers, Vol. 35, Strijdom to T. Wassenaar, 18 June 1936.

4. Strijdom Papers, Vol. 36, Strijdom to J. J. Erasmus, 29 January 1939.

5. Leslie Rubin, reminiscing on his own days in the South African Senate (1955–1960), recalled how different Strijdom was from the intellectual Verwoerd. Strijdom, despite his tough reputation, was always polite and greeted even his enemies, albeit always in Afrikaans. Verwoerd came across as cold and arrogant even toward his own lieutenants, and especially toward those of a different political persuasion. Interview, 7 June 1985.

6. Bloemfontein, Instituut vir Eietydse Geskiedenis, Senator M. P. A. Malan Papers, File 8, "Notules en Uittreksels uit Notules," Cape National Party Management Committee, Minutes, "Punte wat as Fundamenteel Beskou Word by die Opstel van die Program van Beginsels en Program van Aksie vir die Nuwe Party," p. 11.

7. Ibid., p. 13.

8. "Program van Beginsels van die Vereenigde party, 5 Desember 1934," in F. A. van Jaarsveld, ed., *Honderd Basiese Dokumente by die Studie van die Suid-Afrikaanse Geskiedenis 1648–1961* (Cape Town: Nasou, 1980), pp. 232–233.

9. M. P. A. Malan Papers, File 9, "Jaarverslae van die Federale Raad van die NP 1916–1951," Annual Report of Cape NP Executive, 25 July 1934, p. 6.

10. M. P. A. Malan Papers, File 9, Annual Report of NP Federal Council, 25 September 1939, p. 1.

11. M. P. A. Malan Papers, File 7, "Notules en Uittreksels uit Notules 1908–1961," 1925 Cape NP Congress, Minutes, p. 23.

12. J. L. Basson, *J. G. Strijdom: Sy Politieke Loopbaan van 1929 tot 1948* (Pretoria: Wonderboom-Uitgewers, 1980), pp. 168–169.

13. Newell M. Stultz, *Afrikaner Politics in South Africa, 1934–1948* (Berkeley and Los Angeles: University of California Press, 1974), pp. 57–58.

14. Ibid., p. 57.

15. Cape Town, Cape Archives, Senator D. H. van Zyl Papers, Vol. 9, "Hierdie vergadering van vroue van De Aar . . ."

16. Stultz, *Afrikaner Politics,* p. 57.
17. Van Zyl Papers, Vol. 40, 1937 Cape NP Congress, Minutes, p. 27.
18. Ibid.
19. Ibid., pp. 5 and 16.
20. Compare the single paragraph on "Non-white races" in the 1936 Program of Principles of the Orange Free State NP, usually centrist in Nationalist terms on the race issue, with the references to segregation in the 1938 Nationalist Federal Program of Action. The latter deals with segregation not only in the section on "The Native Question," but also in those on labor policy and social welfare. (See Van Jaarsveld, ed., *100 Basiese Dokumente,* p. 236, and Van Zyl Papers, Vol. 40).
21. Pretoria, State Archives (Transvaal Archives Depot), Mrs. S. Kieser Collection, 1936 Transvaal NP Congress, Minutes, 5 October 1937, p. 2.
22. Strijdom Papers, Vol. 36, Transvaal NP Executive, Minutes, 5 October 1937, p. 2.
23. Strijdom Papers, Vol. 36, 1937 Transvaal NP Congress Minutes, p. 5.
24. Corporatism, theoretically drawing on the government of medieval towns by trade guilds, held that the most appropriate way of overcoming regional and class divisions within the state was for citizens to be represented in legislatures according to trade or profession. Under this theory, both employers and employees would belong to the same occupational organizations, which would send delegates to law-making bodies; this arrangement would obviate the need for trade unions, which were seen as fomenters of class war. Corporatism received its greatest support from Mussolini's Fascists and from the clerico-fascist regimes of Franco in Spain and Salazar in Portugal.
25. Strijdom Papers, Vol. 36, 1937 Transvaal NP Congress, Minutes, p. 2.
26. Strijdom Papers, Vol. 35, Transvaal NP Executive, Minutes, 25 May 1937, p. 2.
27. A. N. Pelzer, *Die Afrikaner Broederbond* (Cape Town: Tafelberg, 1979), pp. 37 and 43.
28. Only male Afrikaners over twenty-five could become members of the AB. Dan O'Meara discusses the effective exclusion of workers from the AB in favor of petit bourgeois elements. See *Volkskapitalisme,* p. 63. A 1939 Broederbond circular explicitly insisted that prospective middle-aged members, as opposed to younger recruits, should "at least be influential people who occupy key positions." See Cape Archives, T. E. Dönges Papers, Vol. 86, Broederbond Circular 1/38/39, 2 August 1939.
29. Strijdom Papers, Vol. 36, 1937 Transvaal NP Congress, Minutes, p. 4.
30. Ibid., p. 5.
31. O'Meara, *Volkskapitalisme,* pp. 51–52 and 98.
32. Pelzer, *Afrikaner Broederbond,* pp. 9–10. This source is unique in that it was commissioned by the AB Executive Council as the semiofficial history of the Bond. Despite an inherent bias, Pelzer cites records that are obviously beyond the reach of the independent researcher.
33. Serfontein, *Brotherhood of Power,* p. 40.

34. Ibid.
35. Henry Kenney, *Architect of Apartheid: Verwoerd—An Appraisal* (Johannesburg: Jonathan Ball, 1980), p. 46. Dönges was invited to act as a legal advisor for the AB as early as 1936, and in the same year introduced a resolution at the AB annual conference or Bondsraad. (See Pelzer, *Afrikaner Broederbond*, pp. 72–73).
36. Serfontein, *Brotherhood of Power*, p. 50.
37. Ibid.
38. Bloemfontein, Instituut vir Eietydse Geskiedenis, Dr. J. H. O. ("Otto") Du Plessis Papers, File 1, Albert Hertzog to Du Plessis, 9 February 1939.
39. B. M. Schoeman, *Die Broederbond in die Afrikaner-Politiek* (Pretoria: Aktuele Publikasies, 1982), p. 18. This is an invaluable source on AB activities, because its author had been expelled from the Bond in the late sixties for his extreme right-wing sympathies. He appears to have had access to particularly sensitive records.
40. Pelzer, *Afrikaner Broederbond*, p. 46.
41. Ibid. Also Dönges Papers, Vol. 72, 1937 FAK Congress, Minutes, p. 8.
42. Ibid., p. 8.
43. Ibid., p. 10.
44. Harry Lawrence, for instance, although no great liberal on the race question at that time, was attacked by the Nationalists for permitting "colored" United Party members to be involved in his Salt River constituency organization. Cf. University of Cape Town, Jagger Library, Archives and Manuscripts Department, H. G. Lawrence Papers, B13.1, Louis Esselen to Lawrence, 4 November 1935. See also *Die Burger*, 8 August 1935.
45. Dönges Papers, Vol. 73, "Verslag van die Hoofwerksaamhede van die FAK voorgelê op die Derde Vergadering van die Afrikaanse Nasionale Kultuurraad," 2–3 July 1940, pp. 3–4.
46. Ibid., p. 5.
47. Schoeman, *Broederbond in die Afrikaner-Politiek*, p. 13.
48. Dönges Papers, Vol. 73, "Verslag van die Hoofwerksaamhede van die FAK," p. 7.
49. J. H. O. du Plessis Papers, File 1, letterhead on correspondence, A. Hertzog to Du Plessis, 4 March 1939.
50. Serfontein, *Brotherhood of Power*, p. 80.
51. Dönges Papers, Vol. 73, Afrikaanse Nasionale Kultuurraad circular from Meyer, 22 March 1939, p. 2.
52. Dönges Papers, Vol. 73, Afrikaanse Nasionale Kultuurraad circular from Meyer, "Die Reddingsdaadfonds en Ekonomiese Volkskongres," p. 4.
53. Serfontein, *Brotherhood of Power*, p. 50.
54. Dönges Papers, Vol. 72, 1937 FAK Congress, Minutes, p. 4.
55. Ibid., p. 12.
56. See A. P. J. van Rensburg, "Die Simboliese Ossewatrek van 1938," *Historia* 17:1 (March 1972), pp. 12–46. For details of the wedding and baptism ceremonies accompanying the centenary, see Pretoria, State Archives, Records of the Voortrekker Centenary Committee, Heidelberg

(Transvaal). I wish to thank Robert Shell for information about the baptism of children during the Centenary.

57. Bloemfontein, Instituut vir Eietydse Geskiedenis, J. D. Jerling Papers, File 6, leaflet "Sentrale Voortrekker-Eeufees 1838–1938," p. 3.
58. Ibid., p. 5.
59. Cape Town, Cape Archives, A. L. Geyer Papers, Vol. 1, handwritten notes on Fusion, ca. 1933, p. 1.
60. Alan Paton, *Hofmeyr* (Cape Town: Oxford University Press, abridged ed., 1971), pp. 239–240.
61. Hofmeyr Papers, Aa 1353, L. R. Macleod to Hofmeyr, 8 May 1939.
62. University of Cape Town, Archives and Manuscripts Department, Sir Patrick Duncan Papers, F. C. Sturrock to Duncan, 28 August 1936.
63. Paton, *Hofmeyr*, p. 196.
64. William Russell Kienzle, "German Policy Towards the Union of South Africa, 1933–1939" (unpub. Ph.D. dissertation, Pennsylvania State University, 1974), p. 62.
65. Bloemfontein, Instituut vir Eietydse Geskiedenis, E. H. Louw Papers, File 71, *Ierland Toon die Weg Aan: Konstitusionele Ontwikkeling Sedert 1921* (Cape Town: Nasionale Pers, 1939).
66. *Die Vaderland*, 15 August 1939.
67. Ibid.
68. Du Plessis Papers, File 1, N. Coertze to Du Plessis, 16 May 1939.
69. Pretoria, State Archives, General J. C. Smuts Papers, Vol. 60, Smuts to John Martin, 3 August 1939.
70. See Lawrence Papers, E3.264, Appendix to "Interim Report on the Afrikaner *Broederbond*," 11 November 1941.
71. Paton, *Hofmeyr*, p. 236.
72. Ibid., pp. 219–220.

Chapter 5: A Pro-War Majority in a Climate of Subversion

1. University of Cape Town, Jagger Library, Archives and Manuscripts Department, Duncan Papers, A27.2, Memorandum by Sir Patrick Duncan on the war crisis, 4 September 1939, p. 1. The Status Act defined the nature of Union sovereignty in terms of negotiations and ensuing British legislation over the preceding decade that had established the character of self-governing dominions within the British Commonwealth. The question of the "indivisibility of the Crown," was, however, the one constitutional issue on which Hertzog and Smuts could not reconcile their interpretations, even after Fusion. A key aspect of this issue involved whether a dominion could stay out of a war involving Britain.
2. Cited in W. K. Hancock, *Smuts: The Fields of Force 1919–1950* (Cambridge: Cambridge University Press, 1968), p. 285.
3. Ibid., p. 286.
4. Malan promised Hertzog support on this issue during a long discussion on 1 September, their first since the split of 1934. See University of Cape

Town, Archives and Manuscripts Department, H. G. Lawrence Papers, K4.34, Questionnaire from Joomas Kirsi to Lawrence, October 1972, item "General Hertzog and Dr. Malan Confer, 1 September 1939."

5. Duncan Papers, Memorandum on the war crisis, p. 2.
6. Duncan Papers, A27.8, High Commissioner (L. H. Clark) to Duncan, 13 September 1939.
7. South Africa, House of Assembly Debates, Vol. 36, 4 September 1939, col. 20.
8. Ibid.
9. Jeremy Lawrence, *Harry Lawrence* (Cape Town: David Philip, 1978), p. 112.
10. Ibid., p. 107.
11. Duncan Papers, A27.3, Duncan to Hertzog, 5 September 1939.
12. Lawrence Papers, Kirsi Questionnaire, "General Hertzog and Dr. Malan Confer."
13. Assembly Debates, 4 September 1939, col. 21.
14. Ibid.
15. Ibid., col. 21.
16. Ibid., cols. 22–23.
17. Ibid., cols. 24–25.
18. Ibid., col. 28.
19. Ibid., col. 49.
20. Ibid., cols. 49–50.
21. Ibid., col. 49.
22. Ibid., col. 51.
23. Ibid., cols. 51–52.
24. Duncan Papers, Memorandum on the war crisis, p. 3.
25. Newell M. Stultz, *Afrikaner Politics in South Africa 1934–1948* (Berkeley and Los Angeles: University of California Press, 1974), pp. 61 and 64.
26. Ibid., p. 64.
27. Duncan Papers, Duncan to Hertzog, 5 September 1939.
28. Ibid.
29. University of Cape Town, Archives and Manuscripts Department, Donald Molteno Papers, C7.8, Molteno to Sir Howard d'Egville, 3 November 1939. Also Pretoria, State Archives, General J. C. Smuts Papers, Vol. 60, Smuts to John Martin, 30 November 1939.
30. Michael Roberts and A. E. G. Trollip, *The South African Opposition 1939–1945: An Essay in Contemporary History* (London et al: Longman, Green and Co., 1947), pp. 17–19.
31. Ibid., pp. 21–37.
32. Pretoria, State Archives, General J. C. G. Kemp Papers, Vol. 6, "Ooreenkoms Tussen Generaal Hertzog en Dr. Malan," p. 1.
33. Ibid.
34. Ibid.
35. Stanford, Hoover Institution Archives, German Foreign Office Collection,

File 540, contains a long series of these telegrams, covering developments inside the Union in great detail.

36. German Foreign Office Collection, File 540, 240565–240567 and 240568–240569, Telegrams, Werz to Berlin, 9 November 1939 and 14 November 1939.

37. T. R. H. Davenport, *South Africa: A Modern History* (Johannesburg: Macmillan, 2nd ed. 1978), p. 233.

38. C. M. van den Heever, *General J. B. M. Hertzog* (Johannesburg: APB Bookstore, 1946), p. 283.

39. Ibid., pp. 286–287.

40. University of Cape Town, Archives and Manuscripts Department, Margaret Ballinger Papers, B2.1, Transcript of article "Nazi Principle in Blatant Form" for *Forum*, 20 April 1940, p. 10.

41. University of Cape Town, Archives and Manuscripts Department, Waterson Collection, A3.9.8, Cypher telegram, Smuts to Waterson, 27 November 1940.

42. Smuts Papers, Vol. 150, Cypher telegram, Close to Smuts, and reply, 13 and 14 February 1942.

43. Smuts Papers, Vol. 63, Smuts to Gilletts, 10 July 1940.

44. Pretoria, State Archives, J. G. Strijdom Papers, Vol. 46, "Verslag van Hoofbestuur," 1940 National Party Congress.

45. German Foreign Office Collection, File 540, 240588, Telegram, Trompke to Berlin, 20 February 1940.

46. *Ons Leiers Wys op Gevare van Genl. Smuts se Studeerkamer-Oorlog* (Pretoria: Transvaal National Party, 1940), pp. 1–2.

47. German Foreign Office Collection, File 540, 240595, Telegram, Trompke to Berlin, 6 June 1940.

48. Johannesburg, University of the Witwatersrand, Manuscripts Department, J. H. Hofmeyr Papers, Hofmeyr to Kenneth Underhill, 23 April 1939.

49. Smuts Papers, Vol. 60, Smuts to Martin, 3 August 1939.

50. Johannesburg, University of the Witwatersrand, Cullen Library, Manuscripts Department, South African Institute of Race Relations (SAIRR) Records, Part I, 42.12.2, J. D. Rheinallt-Jones to Piet van der Byl, 8 December 1939.

51. SAIRR Records, Part I, 42.12.2, Van der Byl to Rheinallt-Jones, 25 November 1939.

52. Smuts Papers, Vol. 61, Brookes to Smuts, 21 June 1940.

53. University of the Witwatersrand, Manuscripts Department, Union Unity Truth Service (UUTS) Records, File 175, "Thane: Broederbond I," ca. 1940. According to this memorandum, Holm's name was found on a list of AB members.

54. Lawrence Papers, E3.90, Confidential Memorandum, Wilson to Lawrence, 10 November 1939.

55. University of Cape Town, Archives and Manuscripts Department, Morris

Alexander Papers, South African Jewish Board of Deputies File 4, Secretary, Johannesburg Committee to Secretary, Cape Committee, 26 April 1940.

56. Lawrence Papers, E3.101, "Usual Broadcast from Zeesen, Monday Oct. 30, 1939," pp. 7–8.

57. Ibid., p. 8.

58. Lawrence Papers, Zeesen Reports, E3.103, 2 November 1939, p. 11, E3.108, 30 December 1939, p. 10, and E3.114, 31 December 1939, p. 2.

59. Lawrence Papers, E3.103, Zeesen Report, 2 November 1939, p. 11.

60. Hans Strydom, *For Volk and Führer: Robey Leibbrandt and Operation Weissdorn* (Johannesburg: Jonathan Ball, 1982), p. 275.

61. Lawrence Papers, E3.108, Zeesen Report, 7 November 1939, p. 10.

62. *Die Burger,* 3 December 1940.

63. Ibid., 17 December 1940.

64. Ibid., 6 December 1940.

65. Ibid., 4 December 1940.

66. M. Ballinger Papers, B5.19, "Parliamentary Review," early 1940.

Chapter 6: The Rise of the Ossewabrandwag and the Specter of Revolution

1. Stanford, Hoover Institution Archives, German Foreign Office Collection, File 540, 24056, Telegram, Luitpold Werz to Berlin, 9 November 1939. Also University of Cape Town, Jagger Library, Archives and Manuscripts Department, H. G. Lawrence Papers, E3.9, "Very Confidential Memorandum Relating to Nazi Activities in the Union of South Africa," 28 October 1939, p. 1.

2. Johannesburg, University of the Witwatersrand, Cullen Library, Manuscripts Department, Ossewabrandwag Collection, Series A, Circular from Controlling Council, 10 February 1941, and undated memorandum "Volksdiens-Organisasie van die O.B."

3. J. H. P. Serfontein, *Brotherhood of Power: An Exposé of the Secret Afrikaner Broederbond* (Bloomington and London: Indiana University Press, 1978), pp. 59ff.

4. *Ons Party en die OB: Samewerking Misluk* (collected party statements) (Cape Town: Cape National Party, ca. 1941), pp. 4 and 6. See also *Die Transvaler,* 25 March 1941.

5. OB Collection, "Notule van die Eerste Laer van Ossewabrandwag Offisiere," 13 and 14 October 1941, p. 6.

6. See the OB pamphlet *Leier van die Gedissiplineerde Afrikanerdom: Dr. J. F. J. van Rensburg—Lewensbeskrywing en Drie Toesprake* (Johannesburg: Voortrekkerpers, n.d.), p. 16.

7. Ibid., p. 3.

8. M. S. B. Kritzinger, *Handige Woordeboek* (Pretoria, J. L. van Schaik, 1976), p. 73.

9. F. L. Carsten, *The Rise of Fascism* (Berkeley and Los Angeles: University of California Press, 1980), pp. 207–208.

10. See chapters 3 and 4.

11. OB Collection, "Notule van die Eerste Laer," pp. 4–5.

12. Lawrence Papers, E5.47, "Strictly Confidential Report on the Affidavit of Dr. Luitpold Werz," by Lt. George Visser, 25 November 1946, p. 2. Werz's 36-page affidavit treats the activities of this network of agents in detail.

13. Washington, U.S. National Archives, Microfilm Series T-120, Captured German Foreign Office Records (hereafter USNAMS, T-120), Reel 318/241284, Telegram, Trompke to Berlin, 6 November 1940.

14. USNAMS, T-120, Reel 318/241282–241283, Telegram, Trompke to Berlin, 2 February 1943.

15. Lawrence Papers, Affidavit by Luitpold Werz, 14 September 1946, p. 30.

16. Ibid.

17. Ibid.

18. See George Cloete Visser, *OB: Traitors or Patriots?* (Johannesburg: Macmillan, 1976), pp. 26ff. for a detailed discussion of the Stormjaers.

19. Ibid., pp. 100–105.

20. Ibid., p. 135.

21. Ibid., p. 138.

22. University of Cape Town, Archives and Manuscripts Department, Leonard Marquard Papers, E4.3, Notes by Marquard on a conversation with Van Rensburg, 29 June 1942.

23. Visser, *OB: Traitors or Patriots?*, p. 17.

24. University of the Witwatersrand, Manuscripts Department, J. H. Hofmeyr Papers, Ga 30, Hofmeyr to Underhill, 26 July 1942.

25. Lawrence Papers, E3.60, Undated affidavit by Lawrence and E3.61, Notes "Rex vs. Wilkens and Others," August 1941.

26. By way of example of how widespread this sort of thing had become, my grandmother remembers a woman in a house down the street in Port Elizabeth being taken away by the police for sending radio signals to German vessels offshore.

27. Ernest Malherbe, director of military intelligence during the war, notes that political internees like Vorster, held on suspicion of planning or participating in subversive activities, were treated comparatively well under the circumstances, especially in contrast with the conditions under which Axis political prisoners were held. Convicts cleaned their houses, an officer was given the full-time task of listening to their complaints, gifts could be received, and daily tea, cake, and beer were provided in addition to the usual meals. Despite this, some internees, including Vorster, behaved in a defiant manner and were consequently sentenced to solitary confinement. See E. G. Malherbe, *Never a Dull Moment* (Cape Town: Howard Timmins, 1981), p. 213.

28. House of Assembly Debates, Vol. 42, 19 March 1941, col. 4897.
29. Ibid.
30. A journalistic but useful account of this venture is Hans Strydom's *For Volk and Führer: Robey Leibbrandt and Operation Weissdorn* (Johannesburg: Jonathan Ball, 1982).
31. Ibid., p. 104.
32. See Serfontein, *Brotherhood of Power,* pp. 57–63, for details of the endless squabbles over the nature and leadership of the nationalist struggle.
33. H. G. Lawrence, "The Leibbrandt Trap" in *Sunday Times Color Magazine,* 1 April 1973, pp. 14–15.
34. Strydom, *For Volk and Führer,* p. 146.
35. Lawrence, "Leibbrandt Trap," pp. 14–15. See also Strydom, *For Volk and Führer,* p. 148.
36. Ibid., pp. 186ff. See also Lawrence Papers, E3.267, Major Jan Taillard, Memorandum "The Leibbrandt Case," 5 September 1942, pp. 1–16.
37. Strydom, *For Volk and Führer,* p. 262.
38. University of Cape Town, Archives and Manuscripts Department, G. Brand van Zyl Papers, Unpublished "Reminiscences," Vol. 5, p. 86.
39. Pretoria, State Archives, General J. C. Smuts Papers, Vol. 60, G. W. Wessels to Smuts, 16 May 1939.
40. Smuts Papers, Vol. 61, J. Coetzee to Smuts, 17 March 1940.
41. Lawrence Papers, E3.234, OB Secretary, Bloemfontein, to P. K. Zondagh, no date.
42. Visser, *OB: Traitors or Patriots?* pp. 94–95.
43. Smuts Papers, Vol. 61, Colonel B. C. Judd to Louis Esselen, 10 February 1940.
44. Smuts Papers, Vol. 61, Vere Stent to Smuts, 17 June 1940.
45. Smuts Papers, Vol. 132, "Secret" Memorandum from Commandant-in-Chief, Burger Commandoes, 17 November 1939. The commandoes and district rifle associations provided a rural militia that was called out in emergencies. The crucial importance of retaining their loyalty in so explosive a political atmosphere is obvious, especially given the radical nationalist sentiments of many farmers in the outlying areas.
46. Smuts Papers, Vol. 132, Memorandum "Most Secret: Security of Our Own Forces," no date.
47. See, for instance, Lawrence Papers, E3.80, Censorship Summary, "Subversive Activities in Schools of the Union," 30 January 1941.
48. Lawrence Papers, "East Rand School Position" and "Statement by Mr. L. D. Turner" in Censorship Summary, 30 January 1941.
49. *Sunday Times,* 25 February 1940.
50. Ibid.
51. Dan O'Meara, *Volkskapitalisme: Class, Capital and Ideology in the Development of Afrikaner Nationalism 1934–1948* (Johannesburg: Ravan, 1983), p. 60.
52. *Rand Daily Mail,* 30 January 1940.
53. Ibid.

54. *Rand Daily Mail,* 14 March 1940.

55. Lawrence Papers, E3.80, Intelligence Report, 13 December 1940, in Censorship Summary, 30 January 1941.

56. USNAMS, T-120, Reel 318/241231–241232, letter to Adolf Hitler, received 7 November 1938.

57. Bloemfontein, Instituut vir Eietydse Geskiedenis, J. D. Jerling Papers, File 11, G. Yssel to Jerling, 13 July 1940, and File 13, OB Great Council, Minutes, 9 July 1940, p. 1. See also Michael Roberts and A. E. G. Trollip, *The South African Opposition: An Essay in Contemporary History* (London et al: Longman, Green and Co., 1947), pp. 35–36.

58. Pretoria, State Archives, J. B. M. Hertzog Papers, Vol. 34, "Persverklaring," 22 October 1941.

59. Ibid.

60. Jerling Papers, File 30, "Genl. Hertzog Spreek tot die Jeug," 1942.

61. Instituut vir Eietydse Geskiedenis, Greyshirts (L. T. Weichardt) Records, File 4, transcript of letter to *Die Burger,* 5 November 1940.

62. Greyshirt Records, File 4, "Memo I/s Konsep Brief Genl. Hertzog," Isak le Grange to Weichardt, ca. 1941, judging by internal evidence.

63. The Afrikaner Party and Hertzog parted company, however, on the latter's views on National Socialism.

64. Greyshirt Records, File 5, Draft letter by Weichardt, ca. March 1942.

65. University of Cape Town, Archives and Manuscripts Department, Sir Patrick Duncan Papers, D1.35.60, Smuts to Duncan, 30 October 1941.

66. University of Cape Town, Archives and Manuscripts Department, Waterson Collection, A3.9.57, Louis Esselen to Sidney Waterson, 20 August 1942.

67. See, for instance, Jerling Papers, File 21, Circular from OB Controlling Council, 29 May 1941, accusing the National Party of duplication of OB structures through the recent reorganization of the party along cell lines.

68. *Die Transvaler,* 1 September 1941.

69. Greyshirt Records, File 6, T. Stoffberg to Colin Steyn, 27 November 1944.

70. University of Cape Town, Archives and Manuscripts Department, Donald Molteno Papers, D2.54, "The Week in Parliament," ca. March 1943, p. 2.

71. Lawrence Papers, "Strictly Confidential Report on the Affidavit of Dr. Luitpold Werz," p. 3.

72. Speech at Union Congress of National Party, 3 June 1941, in S. W. Pienaar and J. J. Scholtz, eds., *Glo in U Volk: D. F. Malan as Redenaar* (collected speeches) (Cape Town: Tafelberg, 1964), pp. 41–42.

73. Ibid., p. 41.

74. Ibid., p. 38.

75. Merle Lipton, *Capitalism and Apartheid: South Africa, 1910–1986* (Aldershot, UK: Wildwood House, 1986), p. 273.

76. For an interesting discussion of the 1943 elections, see Newell M. Stultz,

Afrikaner Politics in South Africa 1934–1948 (Berkeley and Los Angeles: University of California Press, 1974), pp. 67ff. Stultz sees the election results as crucial to understanding why Malan needed only a marginal swing away from the government five years later in order to topple Smuts from power. In 1943 the winner-take-all single-member constituency system led to election results that belied the actual proportion of votes going to Afrikaner nationalists, whose impact was greatly reduced by a split vote on the right.

77. Frederik Jacobus van Heerden, "Nasionaal-Sosialisme as Faktor in die Suid-Afrikaanse Politiek, 1933–1948" (Unpub. D.Phil. dissertation, University of the Orange Free State, 1972), p. 357.

Chapter 7: The War and the Internal Transformation of the National Party

1. Pretoria, State Archives, J. G. Strijdom Papers, Vol. 36, M. D. C. de Wet Nel to P. J. Bosman, 28 April 1941.
2. Pretoria, State Archives, General J. C. G. Kemp Papers, Vol. 6, "Onderhoud tussen Dr. Malan en die Grootraad van die Ossewa-Brandwag, 29 Oktober, 1940."
3. Strijdom Papers, Vol. 40, Frans Mentz to Strijdom, 17 April 1941.
4. Bloemfontein, Instituut vir Eietydse Geskiedenis, Dr. H. F. Verwoerd Papers, File 3/1/1, F. Mentz to Verwoerd, 7 June 1941.
5. Ibid.
6. Bloemfontein, Instituut vir Eietydse Geskiedenis, Dr. J. H. O. ("Otto") du Plessis Papers, File 3, letter to Du Plessis, 23 August 1941.
7. Du Plessis Papers, File 3, Report from Graaff-Reinet of OB meeting held by Vorster, Eastern Province General, 3 November 1941.
8. Otto du Plessis, *Die Nuwe Orde: Die Revolusie van die Twintigste Eeu* (Port Elizabeth: Nasionale Pers, 1941), pp. 7, 10.
9. Ibid., p. 20.
10. Ibid., p. 7.
11. Ibid., p. 12.
12. *Die Transvaler,* 25 March 1941.
13. Du Plessis, *Die Nuwe Orde,* pp. 26–27.
14. Du Plessis Papers, File 3, "Memorandum: Insake die Propaganda van die Herenigde Nasionale Party," ca. November 1942, pp. 4–6.
15. Ibid., p. 12.
16. Du Plessis Papers, File 3, Draft letter, Du Plessis to Malan, ca. July 1942.
17. Du Plessis Papers, "Insake die Propaganda van die Herenigde Nasionale Party," p. 2.
18. *Die Transvaler,* 25 March 1941.
19. *South African "Nationalism": Its Black Record in the War, 1939–1945* (Pretoria: United Party, ca. 1945), p. 18.
20. Ibid.

21. For the policies of the New Order, see Oswald Pirow, *Nuwe Orde vir Suid-Afrika* (Pretoria: Christelike Republikeinse Suid-Afrikaanse Nasionaal-Sosialistiese Studiekring, 1941).

22. Du Plessis Papers, "Insake die Propaganda van die Herenigde Nasionale Party," p. 18.

23. Strijdom Papers, Vol. 58, "Konstitusie van die Nasionale Jeugbond Soos Aanvaar op die Eerste Provinsiale Kongres," Johannesburg, 19 October 1940, p. 1.

24. Ibid.

25. Ibid.

26. University of Cape Town, Jagger Library, Archives and Manuscripts Department, H. G. Lawrence Papers, E3.75, Report by Controller of Censorship, "Most Secret: Report on Subversive Influences in Training Colleges and Schools," 1 August 1943, p. 5.

27. Strijdom Papers, Vol. 58, Nasionale Jeugbond Congress, Minutes, 19 October 1940, pp. 7–8.

28. Ibid.

29. Cape Town, Cape Archives, A. L. Geyer Papers, Vol. 1, Diary, 27 December 1940.

30. Lawrence Papers, "Subversive Influences in Training Colleges and Schools," p. 6.

31. Ibid., p. 8.

32. Ibid.

33. Ibid., pp. 11–13.

34. Ibid.

35. *Die Burger,* 10 April 1941.

36. J. S. du Plessis, "The South African Republic," in C. F. J. Muller, ed., *Five Hundred Years* (Pretoria and Cape Town: Academica, 1969), pp. 255–256.

37. Ibid., p. 253.

38. Ibid., p. 258.

39. Ibid., pp. 241, 255, and 258.

40. Ibid., p. 282. See also Trafford B. Barlow, *President Brand and His Times* (Cape Town and Johannesburg: Juta, 1972), p. 26.

41. Du Plessis, "South African Republic," pp. 282–283.

42. Barlow, *President Brand,* p. 27.

43. J. S. Marais, *The Fall of Kruger's Republic* (Oxford: Clarendon Press, 1961), pp. 11–12.

44. Ibid., pp. 11–14.

45. Ibid., pp. 19–21. Richard Mendelssohn's research on the role of Jewish entrepreneur Samuel Marks in the Transvaal Republic has revealed a curiously enigmatic and labyrinthine state record-keeping system, quite arbitrary in its arrangement, that must have facilitated the efforts of unscrupulous officials. (Private communication)

46. Donald Denoon and Balam Nyeko, *Southern Africa since 1800* (London and New York: Longman, 2nd ed. 1984), pp. 126–127 and 143.

47. Ibid., p. 104.
48. Otto du Plessis, *Die Nuwe Suid-Afrika*, pp. 1, 8–9, and 28.
49. Union of South Africa, S.C. 5-'46, *Report of the Select Committee on German Foreign Office Documents*, 1946, pp. xiii–xiv. For the debate in Parliament during which Harry Lawrence raised the issue of the captured documents, see South Africa, House of Assembly Debates, Weekly Edition, 7 May 1946, cols. 6948ff.
50. "Excerpt from the Report by Herr Hans Denk on his journey in South Africa," appendix in *Report of Select Committee*, p. iii. See also "Notes for the Reich Foreign Minister" from Chief Advisor Karlowa, 29 March 1940, in *Akten zur Deutschen Auswärtigen Politik 1918–1945: Aus dem Archiv des Deutschen Auswärtiges Amts*, Series D, Vol. 9 (Frankfurt: P. Keppler Verlag, 1962), pp. 36–37.
51. *Report of Select Committee*, pp. x–xv.
52. Ibid., p. xiii.
53. Ibid., p. 30.
54. Ibid., p. 31.
55. Daniel Malan, *Afrikaner-Volkseenheid en My Ervarings op die Pad Daarheen* (Cape Town et al: Nasionale Boekhandel, 1959), pp. 220–221.
56. Geyer Papers, Diary, 6 June 1941.
57. Ibid.
58. University of the Witwatersrand, Cullen Library, Manuscripts Department, J. H. Hofmeyr Papers, Df, "Ex Parte Minister of Justice: Opinion" by H. M. Bloch and L. de V. van Winsen, 17 June 1946, p. 1.
59. Ibid., p. 6.

Chapter 8: The Road to Authoritarianism

1. *The Star*, 31 January 1940.
2. Margaret Ballinger, "Nazi Principle in Blatant Form: Exclusive Conception of Afrikaner Culture, Sentiment and Tradition" in *Forum*, 20 April 1940, p. 10.
3. Hermann Giliomee, "Constructing Afrikaner Nationalism," *Journal of Asian and African Studies* 18:1–2 (January/April 1983), p. 85.
4. *Die Burger*, 25 March 1941.
5. *Die Transvaler*, 4 March 1941.
6. Bloemfontein, Instituut vir Eietydse Geskiedenis, Greyshirt Records, File 4, Copy of letter by Weichardt in *Die Burger*, 5 November 1940. See also Instituut vir Eietydse Geskiedenis, Dr. J. H. O. ("Otto") Du Plessis Papers, File 2, Letter and accompanying circular from Weichardt to Du Plessis, 31 October 1940, promising electoral support to the National Party. Weichardt's turnabout on the language issue, compared with his strict bilingualism in the thirties, demonstrated throughout the Greyshirt minutes of the period, is just another example of his extraordinary political agility.
7. *Die Transvaler*, 25 March 1941.

8. Instituut vir Eietydse Geskiedenis, Senator P. J. H. Luttig Papers, File 2, unpub. manuscript "My Lewensbeskouing en Politieke Loopband," p. 43.

9. Among the more obvious examples are the bitter Hertzog-Malan feud over Fusion, the original Hertzog breakaway from Botha's South African Party in 1913, and the continual factionalism of the old Transvaal Republic, which had repeatedly exposed the Boers to attack by the British or by surrounding black states.

10. See André du Toit, "Puritans in Africa? Afrikaner 'Calvinism' and Kuyperian Neo-Calvinism in Late Nineteenth-Century South Africa," *Comparative Studies in Society and History* 27:2 (April 1985), p. 215.

11. T. Dunbar Moodie, *The Rise of Afrikanerdom: Power, Apartheid and the Afrikaner Civil Religion* (Berkeley and Los Angeles: University of California Press, 1975), p. 217.

12. See *Die Transvaler*, 22–24 January 1942, in which the draft was published in three parts.

13. Compare *Vryheidsmanifes van die A.N.S. (1 Julie 1940)* (Bloemfontein: Nasionale Pers, 1940) and University of the Witwatersrand, Cullen Library, Manuscripts Department, Ossewabrandwag Collection, C1, OB *Uniale Omsendbrief* no. 1/41, 3 July 1941, with the Draft Constitution as published in *Die Transvaler*, 22–24 January 1942.

14. Moodie, *Rise of Afrikanerdom*, p. 215.

15. J. H. P. Serfontein, *Brotherhood of Power: An Exposé of the Secret Afrikaner Broederbond* (Bloomington and London: University of Indiana Press, 1978), pp. 50–51.

16. OB Collection, "Notule van die Eerste Laer van Ossewa-Brandwag Offisiere van die Unie en Daarbuite," Bloemfontein, 13–14 October 1941, pp. 6–7.

17. Cape Town, Cape Archives, A. L. Geyer Papers, Diary, 30 August 1941.

18. OB Collection, "Notule van die Eerste Laer," p. 7.

19. Moodie, *Rise of Afrikanerdom*, p. 220.

20. Ibid.

21. Alexander Hepple, *Verwoerd* (Harmondsworth, Middlesex: Penguin, 1967), p. 92.

22. Geyer Papers, Diary, 29 August 1941.

23. Ibid., 3 September 1941.

24. Pretoria, State Archives, J. G. Strijdom Papers, Vol. 40, letter to Strijdom, 28 March 1941.

25. Bloemfontein, Instituut vir Eietydse Geskiedenis, Dr. H. F. Verwoerd Papers, File 1/1/3, "Afskrif van Voorgestelde Verklaring deur Dr. J. D. du Toit ('Totius')," ca. late 1941, p. 2.

26. Ibid., p. 3.

27. This dated back to his denunciation of the AB in 1935. See chapter 4.

28. *Die Burger*, 4 June 1941.

29. Geyer Papers, Diary, 30 August 1941.

30. Bloemfontein, Instituut vir Eietydse Geskiedenis, J. D. Jerling Papers, File 11, Malan to Van Rensburg, 8 December 1941.

31. *Ons Party en die O.B.: Samewerking Misluk* (collected party statements) (Cape Town: Cape National Party, ca. 1941), pp. 4 and 6.

32. Moodie, *Rise of Afrikanerdom*, p. 220.

33. Ibid., p. 215.

34. House of Assembly Debates, Vol. 43, 13 January 1942, col. 33.

35. Ibid., col. 34.

36. Ibid.

37. *Die Transvaler*, 22 January 1942.

38. Moodie, *Rise of Afrikanerdom*, pp. 220–221.

39. Ibid.

40. *Die O.B.*, 17 January 1945.

41. Stanford, Hoover Institution Archives, W. H. Vatcher Collection, *Konsep-Grondwet van die Republiek* (reprinted from *Die Transvaler*, 22–24 January 1942), pp. 1ff.

42. Ibid.

43. This is not to say that the emergency powers were in themselves sufficient for his purposes, since the later Enabling Act, passed by an attenuated Reichstag, was at least as important, as was the Night of the Long Knives in the following year.

44. See chapter 7.

45. *Konsep-Grondwet van die Republiek*, p. 6.

46. *Die Burger*, 12 December 1942.

47. See *Jewish Affairs*, December 1942. The entire issue was devoted to revelations about these atrocities.

48. University of Cape Town, Jagger Library, Archives and Manuscripts Department, Donald Molteno Papers, D2.35, "The Week in Parliament," ca. January 1942.

49. Cape Town, Cape Archives, T. E. Dönges Papers, Vol. 90, Notes by Dönges on the NP-OB rift, ca. late 1941.

50. Geyer Papers, Vol. 1, Reply of Dr. Malan to Piet Meyer, Secretary of Unity Committee, 30 August 1941.

51. Strijdom Papers, Vol. 36, Transvaal National Party Executive, Minutes, 3 December 1940, p. 1.

52. Geyer Papers, Diary, 14 March 1942.

53. Ibid., 25 May and 6 June 1941.

54. Ibid. See also F. C. Erasmus and Eric Louw, *Handleiding van die Herenigde Nasionale Party* (Cape Town: Nasionale Pers, n.d.), pp. 14–16.

55. Geyer Papers, Diary, 6 June 1941.

56. *Die Burger*, 4 June 1941.

57. Ibid.

58. Ibid.

59. Geyer Papers, Diary, 29 August 1941.

60. Du Plessis Papers, File 2, Geyer to Du Plessis, 1 March 1941.

61. *Die Burger*, 5 June 1941.

Chapter 9: Healing the Schism

1. Newell Stultz, *Afrikaner Politics in South Africa, 1934–1948* (Berkeley and Los Angeles: University of California Press, 1974), pp. 85 and 89.
2. Pirow's followers believed that the days of elections were numbered and that liberal democratic procedures were both outdated and farcical. They had been elected to Parliament in the 1938 elections under the banner of Hertzog and, in one case, that of Malan.
3. Stultz, *Afrikaner Politics,* pp. 85ff.
4. Bloemfontein, Instituut vir Eietydse Geskiedenis, Dr. H. F. Verwoerd Papers, File 1/56/1, Strijdom to Verwoerd, 29 April 1944.
5. Pretoria, State Archives, J. G. Strijdom Papers, Vol. 56, Transvaal National Party Circular No. 5, 10 September 1945, p. 1.
6. Bloemfontein, Instituut vir Eietydse Geskiedenis, Eric Louw Papers, File 3, Louw to J. G. Strijdom, 12 July 1943.
7. *Rand Daily Mail,* 8 January 1947, cited in Stultz, *Afrikaner Politics,* p. 101.
8. Dan O'Meara, *Volkskapitalisme: Class, Capital and Ideology in the Development of Afrikaner Nationalism, 1934–1948* (Johannesburg: Ravan Press, 1983), pp. 132–133.
9. Verwoerd Papers, File 1/65/1, Telegraphed press report of Malan's speech, Vredendal, 30 April 1943, p. 4.
10. O'Meara, *Volkskapitalisme,* pp. 132–133.
11. Ibid., p. 133.
12. Stultz, *Afrikaner Politics,* pp. 58 and 88.
13. Ibid., p. 93.
14. *Die Transvaler,* 26 April 1943. These figures are discussed in Stultz, *Afrikaner Politics,* p. 93.
15. Verwoerd Papers, File 1/56/1, Verwoerd to Strijdom, 28 August 1944.
16. Strijdom Papers, Vol. 56, OB District Circular No. C3/44 from "General" C. L. de Jager, 26 July 1944. De Jager defended the assault on Mentz on the grounds that the latter had libeled the OB emergency fund for internees, an act that could not be punished through the courts and therefore had been dealt with through alternative channels.
17. Strijdom Papers, Vol. 56, Circular from Malan to all Cape National Party leaders, 10 November 1944. See also O'Meara, *Volkskapitalisme,* p. 132.
18. Johannesburg, University of the Witwatersrand, Cullen Library, Manuscripts Department, J. H. Hofmeyr Papers, Da, "Supplementary Report on Subversive Influences in Training Colleges and Schools," 12 January 1944, p. 4.
19. Strijdom Papers, Vol. 56, Strijdom to Editor, *Die Vaderland,* 27 October 1944.
20. Bloemfontein, Instituut vir Eietydse Geskiedenis, Senator P. J. H. Luttig Papers, "Teleurstellende Gebeurtenisse op die Politieke Pad van die Nasionale party," n.d., p. 2.

21. Strijdom Papers, Vol. 56, Strijdom to Professor S. du Toit, 15 September 1944.

22. Cape Town, Cape Archives, Dr. T. E. Dönges Papers, Vol. 85, Broederbond Executive, Minutes, 1–2 February 1944, p. 8.

23. Gideon Shimoni, *Jews and Zionism: The South African Experience (1910–1967)* (Cape Town: Oxford University Press, 1980), pp. 163–168.

24. Frederik Jakobus van Heerden, "Nasionaal-Sosialisme as Faktor in die Suid-Afrikaanse Politiek, 1933–1948" (Bloemfontein: Unpub. D.Phil. dissertation, University of the Orange Free State, 1972).

25. Verwoerd Papers, File 1/65/1, Telegraphed press report of Malan's speech, Vredendal, 30 April 1943, pp. 9–11.

26. See, for instance, the special issue of the South African periodical *Jewish Affairs,* December 1942, giving details about the Holocaust.

27. For the manner in which the party struggled to accept the truth of the Holocaust, see Sharon Friedman's useful study, "Jews, Germans and Afrikaners: Nationalist Press Reaction to the Final Solution" (University of Cape Town: Unpub. B.A. (Hons.) thesis, 1982).

28. Verwoerd Papers, File 1/65/1, Diederichs to Verwoerd, 20 July 1943.

29. Verwoerd Papers, File 1/65/1, "Albert" to Verwoerd, 20 July 1943. The letterhead is that of Hertzog.

30. Cf. Dönges Papers, Vol. 85, containing minutes of the AB Executive for 1940–1947.

31. Dönges Papers, Vol. 85, AB Executive, Minutes, 5–6 May 1944, p. 7. Women of all races could still legally engage in collective bargaining, from which pass-bearers—that is, African men—were excluded. The pass laws were extended to cover African women only after the Nationalists came to power in 1948.

32. University of the Witwatersrand, Manuscripts Department, Union Unity Truth Service (hereafter UUTS) Records, Confidential Report "The Spreading Ramifications of the 'Afrikaner *Broederbond,'*" 25 April 1944, p. 6.

33. Cape Town, Cape Archives, A. L. Geyer Papers, Vol. 1, Diary, 29 August 1941. See chapter 8.

34. Dönges Papers, Vol. 86, AB Bondsraad, Minutes, 2–3 October 1944, p. 8.

35. Dönges Papers, Vol. 86, AB Executive: Management Committee, Minutes, 29 August 1947, p. 1.

36. Cf. J. H. P. Serfontein, *Brotherhood of Power: An Exposé of the Secret Afrikaner Broederbond* (Bloomington and London: University of Indiana Press, 1978), pp. 60–63. In 1941–1942 Verwoerd sometimes clashed angrily with both Hertzog and Diederichs because of their willingness to overlook differences of principle between the party and the OB in the interests of Afrikaner nationalist unity.

37. Verwoerd repeatedly blocked attempts by the AB Executive to heal the

rift between the OB and the party during the years leading up to the 1948 elections. See, for instance, Dönges Papers, Vol. 85, AB Executive, Minutes, 11 August 1945, p. 5, and 25 September 1945, p. 3. For the charge that Verwoerd's opposition to the OB was inspired by the latter's rejection of him for a top position, see Geyer Papers, Vol. 1, "Baby" to "Anna," 30 November 1941.

38. Hofmeyr Papers, Da, Report by United Party Head Office, "Who Governs South Africa? The People Versus the *Broederbond*," November 1948, p. 2.

39. Louw Papers, File 3, Louw to Strijdom, 12 July 1943.

40. Verwoerd Papers, File 1/56/1, Strijdom to Verwoerd, 29 April 1947.

41. Verwoerd Papers, File 1/56/1, Strijdom to Malan, 24 September 1947.

42. Ibid.

43. Strijdom Papers, Vol. 47, Strijdom to Louw, 29 October 1947.

44. Strijdom Papers, Vol. 47, Strijdom to Swart, 19 November 1947.

45. Verwoerd Papers, File 1/1/3, Press release on Van Rensburg speech at OB meeting, Klerksdorp, 17 April 1948, p. 2. See also O'Meara, *Volkskapitalisme*, p. 265.

46. Ibid., pp. 4–5.

47. T. Dunbar Moodie, *The Rise of Afrikanerdom: Power, Apartheid and the Afrikaner Civil Religion* (Berkeley and Los Angeles: University of California Press, 1975), p. 157.

48. Verwoerd Papers, File 1/56/1, Strijdom to Verwoerd, 5 March 1947.

49. Geyer Papers, Vol. 1, Diary, 28 January 1940.

50. J. F. J. van Rensburg, *Their Paths Crossed Mine: Memoirs of the Commandant-General of the Ossewabrandwag* (Johannesburg: Central News Agency, 1956), p. 232.

51. As far back as 1937, at the very inception of *Die Transvaler*, Verwoerd had set the tone for many Nationalist leaders' views when he declared that Fascism and Nazism, although imperfect, had done much good for Italy and Germany. This suggested, Verwoerd noted, the need to study such experiments, but not simply imitate them, although he saw nothing wrong with a politician wanting to apply to his own country some of the lessons from Germany and Italy. Cf. *Die Transvaler*, 4 October 1937.

52. He actually wanted only to give the Indians of Natal similar rights to those of qualified Cape African voters, who since 1936 had elected three white representatives to the House of Assembly. In return for this small concession, Smuts was planning to limit Indian property rights in Natal, in order to appease the conservative English-speaking electorate there.

53. Strijdom Papers, Vol. 56, Wassenaar to Strijdom and General J. C. G. Kemp, 3 May 1946.

54. Strijdom Papers, Vol. 56, Strijdom to Wassenaar, 6 May 1946.

55. Verwoerd Papers, File 1/56/1, Verwoerd to Strydom, 28 November 1946.

56. Verwoerd Papers, File 1/56/1, Declaration handed by National Party Office, Wolmaranstad, to *Die Transvaler*, 15 February 1947.

57. Verwoerd Papers, File 1/56/1, Report of meeting at Wolmaranstad, 15 February 1947, pp. 1–3.

58. Strijdom Papers, Vol. 57, E. J. Smit to Secretary, National Party, Pretoria, 19 April 1947.

59. Strijdom Papers, Vol. 57, E. J. Smit to Secretary, Transvaal National Party, 3 May 1947.

60. Strijdom Papers, Vol. 57, Circular from Strijdom to all National Party divisions, branches, and representatives, 1947.

Chapter 10: Unity Is Strength

1. Johannesburg, University of the Witwatersrand, Cullen Library, Manuscripts Department, Union Unity Truth Service (hereafter UUTS) Records, File 175, Report "The Spreading Ramifications of the 'Afrikaner Broederbond,'" p. 1.

2. Ibid.

3. Hermann Giliomee, "Western Cape Farmers and the Beginnings of Afrikaner Nationalism," *Journal of Southern African Studies* 14:1 (October 1987), p. 49.

4. UUTS Records, File 175, Memorandum on AB Economic Activities, ca. 1944, p. 1. See also University of Cape Town, Jagger Library, Archives and Manuscripts Department, Leo Marquard Papers, E4.8, E. G. Malherbe, Memorandum "The Afrikaner Economic Movement." This dimension of Afrikaner nationalism is dealt with in much greater detail in Dan O'Meara's *Volkskapitalisme* (Johannesburg: Ravan, 1983), which is largely devoted to this topic.

5. Cape Town, Cape Archives, Dr. T. E. Dönges Papers, Vol. 86, AB Bondsraad, Minutes, 2–3 October 1944, p. 9.

6. For analogies with the cross-class appeal of the Nazis, to cite just one case, see Thomas Childers, *The Nazi Voter: The Social Foundations of Fascism in Germany, 1919–1933* (Chapel Hill and London: University of North Carolina Press, 1983), especially pp. 262ff.

7. UUTS Records, File 175, Memorandum on AB Economic Activities, p. 8.

8. UUTS Records, File 175, Memorandum on AB Economic Activities, pp. 6–7.

9. UUTS Records, File 176, "Special Observation: Twenty-fifth Anniversary Meeting of the A.B.," 13 December 1943, p. 12. This is a report by an observer from the pro-war camp who managed to attend the celebration incognito. It is one of the very few such reports by an outsider on an AB annual assembly.

10. Ernest G. Malherbe, *Education in South Africa Vol. II: 1923–1975* (Cape Town and Johannesburg: Juta, 1977), pp. 672–674. As wartime military intelligence chief, Malherbe had access to reports on such meetings.

11. UUTS Records, File 176, "Twenty-fifth Anniversary Meeting," p. 18.

12. Johannesburg, University of the Witwatersrand, Manuscripts Department, J. H. Hofmeyr Papers, Da, Copy of letter, L. J. Odendaal, General Secretary of NIOO, to Professor J. G. Meiring, Stellenbosch, 29 February 1944.

13. Hofmeyr Papers, Da, Department of Military Intelligence Memorandum "Secret and Confidential: re NIOO," 9 March 1944, p. 1.

14. Hofmeyr Papers, Da, Hastings Beck, "Most Secret: Report on Nasionale Instituut vir Opvoeding en Onderwys," 29 November 1944, p. 9.

15. Dönges Papers, Vol. 85, AB Executive, Minutes, 18–19 August 1944, p. 4.

16. Ibid. On the remarkably successful resistance of the garment workers to these AB-organized efforts, see Jon Lewis, "Solly Sachs and the Garment Workers' Union," and John Mawbey, "Afrikaner Women of the Garment Union During the Thirties and Forties," in Eddie Webster, ed., *Essays in Southern African Labour History* (Johannesburg: Ravan, 1978), pp. 181–206.

17. Dönges Papers, Vol. 86, Note in Dönges's handwriting on back of "Ontleding van Veldm. Smuts se Toespraak (Volgens Verslag *Rand Daily Mail*)," ca. 1944.

18. Hofmeyr Papers, Da, "Highlights from the Opposition Press No. 138: The Spreading Ramifications of the 'Afrikaner Broederbond,'" 25 May 1944, p. 4.

19. See chapter 7.

20. Dönges Papers, Vol. 86, AB Circular 7/45/46, 2 May 1946, p. 2.

21. By the time of the Nationalist victory in 1948, the AB included among its members at least 60 of the 79 National and Afrikaner Party parliamentarians elected in that year (cf. Hofmeyr Papers, Da, "Who Governs South Africa?" p. 2).

22. T. Dunbar Moodie, *The Rise of Afrikanerdom* (Berkeley and Los Angeles: University of California Press, 1975), pp. 154 and 274.

23. Ibid., pp. 272–274.

24. Ibid., pp. 274–275.

25. Ibid., p. 275.

26. Cf. Geoffrey Cronjé, *'n Tuiste Vir die Nageslag: Die Blywende Oplossing van Suid-Afrika se Rassevraagstukke* (Johannesburg: Publicité Handelsreklamasies, 1945), and G. Cronjé, Willem Nicol, and E. P. Groenewald, *Regverdige Raase-Apartheid* (Stellenbosch: Christen-Studenteverenigings-maatskappy van Suid-Afrika, 1947).

27. Interestingly, the subtitle of Cronjé's *'n Tuiste Vir die Nageslag* translates as "The Permanent Solution of South Africa's Race Questions."

28. Cronjé et al., *Regverdige Rasse-Apartheid,* p. 70.

29. Ibid., p. 103.

30. The report was not, however, unanimously accepted in church circles. See, for instance, the letter from Ben Marais, published in *Die Kerkbode,* 14 July 1948. This letter was just the beginning of a long and fierce correspondence in the official organ of the Nederduitse Gereformeerde Kerk over whether apartheid was prescribed by the Bible. According to

Marais, the principles in this church report had previously been incorporated into a highly popular book on race relations. His evidence suggests that this was *Regverdige Rasse-Apartheid,* a conclusion confirmed by S. du Toit's "Press Comment" in the Gereformeerde Kerk (a smaller Afrikaans Reformed church) paper, *Die Kerkblad,* 20 January 1950. The commission report was adopted in 1948 by the Transvaal synod of the NGK, which found that "its policy of apartheid is born not only out of circumstance, but has its basis in Holy Scripture." Cf. *Die Kerkbode,* 3 August 1949.

31. G. B. A. Gerdener, review in *Die Kerkbode,* 10 November 1948.
32. R. T. J. Lombard, *Die Nederduitse Gereformeerde Kerke en Rassepolitiek: Met Spesiale Verwysing na die Jare 1948–1961* (Pretoria: NG Kerkboekhandel Transvaal, 1981), p. 259.
33. Ibid., p. 94.
34. Cronjé, *'n Tuiste Vir die Nageslag,* pp. 8 and 44.
35. G. Eloff, *Rasse en Rassevermenging: Die Boerevolk Gesien van die Standpunt van die Rasseleer* (Bloemfontein: Nasionale Pers, 1942), pp. 50–61 and 74ff.
36. Ibid., p. 61.
37. Dönges Papers, Vol. 85, AB Executive, Minutes, 14 February 1946, p. 2.
38. Cf. Cronjé, *'n Tuiste Vir die Nageslag,* pp. 39–63 and 80–88. For the campaign for antimiscegenation legislation, see Patrick Furlong, *The Mixed Marriages Act: An Historical and Theological Study* (University of Cape Town: Center for African Studies, 1983).
39. Moodie, *Rise of Afrikanerdom,* pp. 274–275.
40. W. A. de Klerk, *The Puritans in Africa: A Story of Afrikanerdom* (London: Rex Collings, 1975), pp. 219–220.
41. Ibid., p. 220.
42. *Die Burger,* 29 March 1948.
43. Pretoria, State Archives, J. G. Strijdom Papers, Vol. 58, E. F. Gey van Pittius to Strijdom, 26 April 1945.
44. Strijdom Papers, Vol. 58, "Konsep Grondwet: van Christelik [*sic*] Republikeinse Studentebond," ca. 1945, p. 1.
45. Strijdom Papers, Vol. 58, Scheepers to F. Smit, 14 April 1945.
46. For details of this constitution, see Patrick Furlong, "Apartheid and Neo-Apartheid: Impressions of an Insider," *Thresholds* 1 (January 1985): 80–93. For a pro-government exposition of the constitution, see the pamphlet by the National Party chief information officer, Jan Grobler, *Constitution '83 in a Nutshell,* sent to all white households during the referendum campaign preceding the adoption of this new system.
47. Strijdom Papers, Vol. 58, Gey van Pittius to Strijdom, 12 April 1945.
48. Strijdom Papers, Vol. 58, Strijdom to Gey van Pittius, 19 April 1945.
49. Interview with Leslie Rubin, 7 June 1985.
50. See chapter 3.
51. See chapters 1 and 6.
52. Strijdom Papers, Vol. 56, L. J. du Plessis to Strijdom, 6 September 1944.

53. Ibid. See also Strijdom Papers, Vol. 56, Strijdom to Editor, *Koers,* 28 August 1944.

54. See, for instance, Bloemfontein, Instituut vir Eietydse Geskiedenis, Greyshirt Records, File 6, General J. C. G. Kemp to Weichardt, 12 April 1944, expressing appreciation of the promise of Greyshirt support, and a warm letter of thanks from Weichardt to Kemp, 13 April 1944.

55. Greyshirt Records, File 6, F. C. Coetzee, New Order, to P. J. Joubert, S.A. Nasionaal-Sosialistiese Bond, 4 October 1944.

56. Greyshirt Records, File 6, Unknown Greyshirt author (probably the current secretary of the movement) to Dr. T. Stoffberg, 10 December 1945.

57. Bloemfontein, Instituut vir Eietydse Geskiedenis, Dr. H. F. Verwoerd Papers, File 1/65/1, Telegraphed press report of Malan speech, Vredendal, 30 April 1943, pp. 12ff.

58. Verwoerd Papers, File 1/1/3, Transcript of Van Rensburg speech, 24 September 1947, p. 1.

59. Deborah Posel, "The Meaning of Apartheid Before 1948," *Journal of Southern African Studies* 14:1 (October 1987), pp. 128–129 and 135–136.

60. See the fascinating correspondence between Malan's factotum, F. C. Erasmus, and J. G. Strijdom on this topic in Instituut vir Eietydse Geskiedenis, F. C. Erasmus Papers, correspondence on Jewish issue, 10 November to 15 December 1947. See also Gideon Shimoni, *Jews and Zionism: The South African Experience (1910–1967)* (Cape Town: Oxford University Press, 1980), pp. 211–212.

61. Strijdom Papers, Vol. 47, Strijdom to Louw, 29 October 1947. The "new advisors" were probably Havenga and rising lights in the National Party like propaganda secretary P. W. Botha, a loyal Cape Malanite who was elected to Parliament for the first time in 1948.

62. UUTS Records, File 175, "Copy: Johannesburg Report 1745. 1.9.44 Special," 1 September 1944, pp. 1–2.

63. See Merle Lipton, *Capitalism and Apartheid: South Africa, 1910–1986* (Aldershot, UK: Wildwood House, 1986), pp. 261ff.

64. Cf., for instance, Greyshirts Records, File 9, Chief Secretary, White Workers' Party and Greyshirts, to Private Secretary, Prime Minister, 7 June 1948, enclosing telegram of congratulations from Weichardt to Malan, 28 May 1948. Cf. also File 9, Fanie Labuschagne, Afrikaner Party MP for Klip River, to Chief Secretary, White Workers' Party, 12 June 1948, in which Greyshirt support is described as having been vital in Labuschagne's victory.

65. Cf. Newell Stultz, *Afrikaner Politics in South Africa, 1934–1948* (Berkeley and Los Angeles: University of California Press, 1974), pp. 135 and 143 for figures on the election results.

66. Hofmeyr Papers, Ab 1, Diary, 7 June 1948. Malan himself admitted his surprise to A. Oosthuizen, the UP organizing secretary.

67. Stultz, for instance, argues that the apartheid slogan had nothing to do with Malan's victory, which simply amounted to the remobilization of

the Afrikaner nationalist vote after the final collapse of the Fusion experiment (*Afrikaner Politics,* pp. 147ff.). O'Meara, while equally deprecating the apartheid argument, strenuously attacks both Stultz and the view that Malan succeeded due to his garnering of the "floating vote." Instead, O'Meara sees the election result as the product of a successful new alliance of class forces, based on the traditional Nationalist core of the urban and small-town petite bourgeoisie, and strengthened by new inroads among Transvaal farmers and white workers (*Volkskapitalisme,* pp. 225–226). More recently, Merle Lipton has argued for a combination of the class alliance and floating vote arguments, maintaining that unfavorable economic conditions led the floating vote to return to the NP, as it had in 1929 (*Capitalism and Apartheid,* pp. 274–278). It was widely believed at the time, however, that Smuts's deputy, Hofmeyr, was primarily responsible for the shift in votes, because of his well-known relative liberalism in racial matters. After the election a major effort was made to oust Hofmeyr from his position in the UP. Cf. Hofmeyr Papers, Ab 1, Diary, 4 November 1948.

68. Lipton, *Capitalism and Apartheid,* pp. 277–278.

Epilogue: The Years in Power

1. University of Cape Town, Jagger Library, Archives and Manuscripts Department, Margaret Ballinger Papers, A2.19, Handwritten notes, 28 January 1949, detailing a discussion with Smuts. Native Representatives were elected at fixed intervals which did not coincide with elections by white and colored voters.

2. Johannesburg, University of the Witwatersrand, Cullen Library, Manuscripts Department, J. H. Hofmeyr Papers, Aa 1905, J. A. Gray, London, to Hofmeyr. Pirow informed Gray of his feelings on this subject.

3. Merle Lipton, *Capitalism and Apartheid: South Africa, 1910–1986* (Aldershot, UK: Wildwood House, 1986), p. 286.

4. Hofmeyr Papers, Aa 1908, C. M. D. Ndawe to Hofmeyr, 6 June 1948.

5. Pretoria, State Archives, General J. C. Smuts papers, Vol. 77, Smuts to Gilletts, 9 November 1945.

6. Margaret Ballinger Papers, B1.2, "South Africa's Last Five Years," draft of article for *African World,* March 1953, p. 1.

7. Lipton, *Capitalism and Apartheid,* pp. 285–286.

8. T. Dunbar Moodie, *The Rise of Afrikanerdom: Power, Apartheid and the Afrikaner Civil Religion* (Berkeley and Los Angeles: University of California Press, 1975), p. 281. Malan filled the ranks of his cabinet mainly with Cape Nationalists whom the moderate Havenga could trust.

9. On the intra–National Party debate, see Deborah Posel, "The Meaning of Apartheid before 1948: Conflicting Interests and Forces Within the Afrikaner Nationalist Alliance," *Journal of Southern African Studies* 14:1 (October 1987), pp. 123ff.

10. Ibid., p. 125.

11. Ibid., p. 124.
12. Moodie, *Rise of Afrikanerdom*, p. 256.
13. Hofmeyr Papers, Da, Report by United Party Head Office, "Who Governs South Africa? The People versus the Broederbond," November 1948, p. 2.
14. Moodie, *Rise of Afrikanerdom*, p. 257.
15. Cape Town, Cape Archives, Dr. T. E. Dönges Papers, AB Executive, Minutes, 11 August 1945, p. 5.
16. See, for instance, the telegram from the Executive to Senator D. H. van Zyl on his election to the Senate. Cf. Cape Archives, D. H. van Zyl Papers, Vol. 5, Telegram, J. P. van der Spuy to Van Zyl, 10 September 1948.
17. Ballinger Papers, G16, "Foreign Policy of the Union of South Africa" (Statements by Malan, 1948–1949), p. 12.
18. Hofmeyr Papers, Ab1, Diary, 12 June 1948.
19. T. R. H. Davenport, *South Africa: A Modern History* (Johannesburg: Macmillan, 2nd ed. 1977), plate 7, portrait of Malan cabinet.
20. Ernst G. Malherbe, *Never a Dull Moment* (Cape Town: Howard Timmins, 1981), p. 242.
21. Leslie Rubin, "Afrikaner Nationalism and Nazi Germany: The Roots of Apartheid," unpub. paper, 1985, p. 1.
22. See Hofmeyr Papers, Aa 1928, Helen McIntosh to Hofmeyr, 29 May 1948, and University of Cape Town, Archives and Manuscripts Department, G. Brand van Zyl Papers, Unpublished "Reminiscences," Vol. 5, p. 86.
23. Ibid.
24. E. G. Malherbe, *Education in South Africa Vol. II: 1923–1975* (Cape Town and Johannesburg: Juta, 1977), p. 683. See also Malherbe, *Never a Dull Moment*, p. 248.
25. Alan Paton, *Hofmeyr* (Cape Town: Oxford University Press, abridged ed. 1971), p. 393.
26. Davenport, *South Africa*, p. 260.
27. Hans van Rensburg, *Their Paths Crossed Mine: Memoirs of the Commandant-General of the Ossewabrandwag* (Johannesburg: Central News Agency, 1956), pp. 207–208. During the 1948 election the Labour Party did not even bother to field candidates in many of the mining constituencies that had traditionally been the heartland of its support, so overwhelmingly had the Nationalists succeeded in capturing this much-coveted voting bloc. Cf. Dan O'Meara, *Volkskapitalisme: Class, Capital and Ideology in the Development of Afrikaner Nationalism* (Johannesburg: Ravan, 1983), p. 240.
28. Bloemfontein, Instituut vir Eietydse Geskiedenis, Greyshirt Records, File 115, SA White Workers' Party Conference, 10 June 1949, Minutes, p. 3.
29. Ibid. Dönges sent a personal letter of thanks to Weichardt for dissolving his party in the interests of the Nationalist cause. This letter arrived many months after this decision, which suggests that Weichardt's complaints

about Nationalist ingratitude may have had something to do with this attempt to placate him. Cf. Greyshirt Records, File 115, Dönges to Weichardt, 30 May 1950.

30. Greyshirt Records, File 115, SA White Workers' Party Conference, 10 June 1949, Minutes, pp. 1–3.
31. Greyshirt Records, File 115, Weichardt to J. H. Viljoen, 22 July 1955, and Mrs. J. van Rooyen to Weichardt, 25 October 1950. See also File 115, Mrs. S. Human to Weichardt, 5 June 1950, for an invitation from the party to share a platform with Minister Dönges at a "National Struggle Day" at Rustenburg in the Transvaal.
32. Greyshirt Records, File 115, Weichardt to P. J. Luttig, 28 February 1950, and Weichardt to J. H. Viljoen, 22 July 1955. The Luttig letter is part of an extensive correspondence regarding the collection of a gift of money by Nationalist parliamentary representatives in belated recognition of Weichardt's efforts on behalf of the Nationalist cause. At that point, Weichardt felt that his colleagues in the Greyshirts had received little gratitude for all their sacrifices.
33. Alexander Hepple, *Verwoerd* (Harmondsworth: Penguin, 1967), p. 87.
34. For Vorster's Stormjaer links, see Moodie, *Rise of Afrikanerdom*, p. 257.
35. O. Geyser, ed., *Geredigeerde Toesprake van die Sewende Eerste Minister van Suid-Afrika* (Bloemfontein: Instituut vir Eietydse Geskiedenis, 1976), p. 27.
36. Malherbe, *Never a Dull Moment*, p. 245.
37. Henry Kenney, *Architect of Apartheid: H. F. Verwoerd—An Appraisal* (Johannesburg: Jonathan Ball, 1980), pp. 163 and 208.
38. For Meyer's own account of his activities in this position, see his autobiography, *Nog Nie Ver Genoeg Nie: 'n Persoonlike Rekenskap van Vyftig Jaar Georganiseerde Afrikanerskap* (Johannesburg and Cape Town: Perskor, 1984), pp. 103–159.
39. Leonard Thompson and Andrew Prior, *South African Politics* (New Haven and London: Yale University Press, 1982), p. 176.
40. David Harrison, *The White Tribe of Africa: South Africa in Perspective* (Berkeley and Los Angeles: University of California Press, 1981), pp. 133–134.
41. University of Cape Town, Archives and Manuscripts Department, Leo Marquard Papers, E4.31, Transcript of interview, Gert Pretorius with Koot Vorster for *Cape Argus Weekend Magazine*, 27 June 1964.
42. Moodie, *Rise of Afrikanerdom*, pp. 292–293.
43. Bloemfontein, Instituut vir Eietydse Geskiedenis, Dr. H. F. Verwoerd Papers, File 1/56/1, Strijdom to Malan, 24 September 1947.
44. See Lipton, *Capitalism and Apartheid*, p. 273.
45. Ibid., p. 196.
46. Davenport, *South Africa*, p. 245.
47. Paton, *Hofmeyr*, p. 368.
48. Davenport, *South Africa*, p. 282.
49. Verwoerd Papers, File 1/1/3, P. W. Botha, *Aanvalle op Dr. Malan oor sy*

Kleurbeleid: Wanvoorstellings en die Feite (Johannesburg: Voortrekker-pers, 1947), p. 4.

50. For details of this legislation, see P. J. Furlong, "The Mixed Marriages Act, 1949: A Theological Critique Based on the Investigation of Legislative Action and Church Responses to this Legislation" (Unpub. M.A. dissertation, University of Cape Town, 1985), pp. 115–116.

51. Cf. Alan Bullock, *Hitler: A Study in Tyranny* (New York: Harper and Row, 1964), p. 339.

52. Davenport, *South Africa*, p. 258.

53. Marquard Papers, E4.14, Circular from P. J. Oosthuizen, 3 August 1955.

54. Donald Denoon and Balam Nyeko, *Southern Africa Since 1800* (London and New York: Longman, 1984), p. 169.

55. Hofmeyr Papers, Aa 1353, Lewis Rose Macleod to Hofmeyr, 8 May 1939.

56. Ballinger Papers, "South Africa's Last Five Years," p. 2. Old-style African National Congress leaders who had never espoused Marxism of any sort were among the early targets of this legislation.

57. Ibid., p. 6.

58. Lipton, *Capitalism and Apartheid*, pp. 283–284.

59. Ibid., pp. 27–28.

60. Ibid., pp. 283–285.

61. Ibid., p. 24.

62. Marquard Papers, E4.13, Gerald Gordon, "Is South Africa Losing Its Democratic Freedom? Nationalism's Final Steps Towards Creating a Corporative State," Reprint from *Cape Times*, 28 January 1954.

63. Marquard Papers, E4.17, "Democracy or Dictatorship: Which Do We Want?" Reprint from *Cape Times*, 14 February 1956.

64. Rubin, "Afrikaner Nationalism," p. 21.

65. Joanna Strangwayes-Booth, *A Cricket in the Thorn Tree: Helen Suzman and the Progressive Party* (Johannesburg: Hutchinson, 1976), p. 144.

66. *Die Burger*, 15 May 1973.

67. Rubin, "Afrikaner Nationalism," p. 21.

68. Davenport, *South Africa*, pp. 269–270.

69. Cf. Joseph Lelyveld, *Move Your Shadow: South Africa, Black and White* (New York: Penguin, 1985), pp. 119ff.

70. Davenport, *South Africa*, pp. 280–281.

71. Kenney, *Architect of Apartheid*, p. 118.

72. Cf. Piet Meyer's speech to the AB annual assembly on the subject of integrating English-speakers into the Afrikaner nationalist worldview, 3 October 1966, Annexure J in J. H. P. Serfontein, *Brotherhood of Power: An Exposé of the Secret Afrikaner Broederbond* (Bloomington and London: University of Indiana Press, 1978), pp. 230–242.

73. David Chidester, "Religious Studies as Political Practice," *Journal of Theology for Southern Africa* 58 (March 1987), p. 13.

Essay on Sources

The secondary literature, its value, and its limitations have been discussed at some length in the Preface, and hence this essay focuses more exclusively on the primary sources. These consist of two principal groups: published material, including biographies, governmental records, and newspapers; and unpublished archival collections. Most primary sources are South African in origin, although some are located among the German documents captured by the Allies at the end of the Second World War and housed in the German Foreign Office in Bonn, the Federal Archive in Koblenz, and the Documentation Center in West Berlin.

The biographical literature is surprisingly thin for this period, and what exists tends to be rather silent on many of the issues that most interest a researcher dealing with the impact of Nazism and Italian Fascism on Afrikaner nationalist politics. On the wartime government side are works including individual useful gems of information, but they tend to be more concerned with broader questions of administration and international affairs. In this group are Hancock's magisterial study of Smuts (which delivered nothing of value for this study), Hancock and Van der Poel's multivolume edition of selections from Smuts's writings, and Alan Paton's marvelous biography of Hofmeyr, by common consensus probably the greatest biographical study to come out of South Africa. Jeremy Lawrence's book on his father, Harry, the wartime minister of the interior, is of limited use to the scholar because of the lack of footnotes; the historian is better advised to go to the main source for this biography, the Lawrence Papers in the library of the University of Cape Town.

Biographical studies of the major National Party figures are still more problematic. Van den Heever's life of Hertzog is substantial and reasonably reliable but is dated, although better than Pirow's study of the general. H. B. Thom's life of Malan, while an improvement on Malan's own autobiography, *Afrikaner Volkseenheid en My Ervarings op die Pad Daarheen*, is similarly episodic and hagiographic in nature, and tends to skim over long periods of Malan's life (most notably the early war years). Malan's collected speeches are more useful, although they necessarily give a one-dimensional portrait.

There are no studies of Pirow or Weichardt, while Van Rensburg's autobiography, *Their Paths Crossed Mine,* says surprisingly little about the Ossewabrandwag's relationship with the National Party that could not be gleaned from the general secondary literature. Nor are there any really good studies of Verwoerd, although Hepple's little book (long banned in South Africa) is remarkably insightful, despite its demonological assumptions. Vorster and Diederichs still await published studies, as do the lesser figures such as F. C. Erasmus or Eric Louw, although there are a recent autobiography of Piet Meyer (more useful for the postwar period) and an adoring work on P. W. Botha that says very little about his early years in politics.

As regards more general reference works, there are very few recent archive-based contributions in English on the major white parties or organizations. What exists is the product of Afrikaner nationalist scholars, dutifully thorough in its ransacking of the main archival collections, if often plodding in style, but reluctant to provide any truly critical analysis. G. D. Scholtz's multivolume study of Afrikaner thought is perhaps the most notable example of the older scholarship in this tradition: it reflects far more of post-1948 Nationalist thinking than of what actually happened in earlier times. The vast and as yet incomplete history of the National Party edited by J. H. Le Roux and P. W. Coetzer is a good reference series, but, like so much of the genre, it tends to be uncritical at all the points where a serious critique is most needed and is bogged down by excessive minor details. On the thirties, it is of limited use for an analysis of National Party–Radical Right relationships; the volume covering the period 1940–1948 was still in preparation at the time of writing.

Newspapers and government records such as the published Debates of Parliament (Hansard) have uniformly greater interest for the historian, but are in some respects of lesser value for this type of study than might otherwise be the case. Although valuable for official policy statements and speeches, by their very nature they do not record what the major parties did not want the rest of the world to see. This is accentuated by the heavily partisan nature of the South African press: the Nationalist newspapers of the period are striking for their editorial comments, even in major stories, and for their unapologetically biased stand on issues affecting party interests. Malan is always presented as a hugely popular, larger-than-life figure, while Smuts is usually depicted in semidiabolical terms. The pro-Smuts newspapers are hardly better; one librarian informed me that it is difficult to find good coverage of the Afrikaner opposition in these papers, because during the war their journalists were discouraged from giving exposure to movements critical of the war effort.

For all that, newspapers are often useful precisely because of their highly partisan character, especially for obtaining a general sense of the ongoing struggle inside the National Party between the major factions. The editors of the provincial party newspapers tended to be very close to the leaders of their respective wings of the party. For instance, *Die Burger* is a very reliable source for the mind-set of Malan's inner circle in the Cape, while Verwoerd's *Die Transvaler* strongly expresses the more militant position of the Strijdom bloc in the north. The Ossewabrandwag had its newspaper, *Die O.B.*, as did the Greyshirts, *Die Waarheid/The Truth*, an organ devoted mainly to anti-Semitism. None of these are easily available in the United States, although limited runs can be obtained through the Cooperative Africana Microfilm Project, and a long microfilmed run of the *Transvaler* is kept at the Hoover Institution at Stanford.

German sources were often more useful, although the materials from the huge sets of microfilmed Captured Nazi Party and German Foreign Office

Records available through the Hoover Institution and the Center for Research Libraries in Chicago provided less valuable material than might have been expected. Many of these records relate to the German minority in South Africa or consist of very general position papers on the changing political situation in the country. Most valuable here was the secret telegraphic correspondence between the German agents in Lourenço Marques and Foreign Office headquarters in Berlin. Much of this material can be located via George O. Kent's massive four-volume *A Catalog of Files and Microfilms of the German Foreign Ministry Archives 1920–1945* (Stanford: Hoover Institution, 1964). Curiously, one of the most important runs of South Africa–related material is not indexed in this study, but can be found in the German Foreign Office Collection in the archives of the Hoover Institution. The published records of the German Foreign Office cover very little material on South Africa compared with these microfilmed materials and are best bypassed by the student of Afrikaner politics.

Inevitably, the relevant South African archival collections are much more valuable than any of these sources. Right of access to these varies from easy (most collections held by the Libraries of the Universities of Cape Town and the Witwatersrand) to impossible (most official records in the Central State Archives Depot, Pretoria). The records of the Governor-General's Office, Prime Minister's Office, Foreign Ministry, Ministry of the Interior, Defense Force, and Police for the thirties and forties are still closed. They are all subject to a hundred-year rule. The records of the National Party and of most Afrikaner nationalist organizations, kept in various locations, are almost as difficult to consult, because of the strict conditions for use, which would be problematic for most academic historians.

Fortunately, such conditions do not apply to all the relevant archival collections, and many individuals, to whose papers access is typically much easier to obtain, often kept copies of materials otherwise only available in such closed collections. Most notable in this category are the papers of Smuts, Strijdom, Hofmeyr, and especially Harry Lawrence, who as minister in charge of internal security during the war kept a veritable treasure trove of documents on subversive activities. Special permission (not difficult to obtain) was required to consult General Hertzog's papers (somewhat surprisingly, far less useful than the above collections) and those of Albert Geyer, whose wartime diary was probably the most valuable single item consulted in researching this study.

The papers of leading liberals of the period sometimes also delivered interesting individual bits of information, as was the case with the papers of Senator William and Mrs. Margaret Ballinger, a collection split between the libraries of the Universities of Cape Town and the Witwatersrand. None of the Ballinger documents in the latter location proved relevant for this study.

The major depository for the private papers of leading Nationalists is the Instituut vir Eietydse Geskiedenis (Institute for Contemporary History) at the University of the Orange Free State in Bloemfontein. Such collections may be consulted only under certain conditions, but this material is really too valuable to be overlooked, especially since access to official papers in the State Archives is virtually impossible. Occasionally there are important gaps in these collections, most notably in the papers of Eric Louw, whose absorbing private correspondence stops in 1937 and is not resumed until 1943. What survives nevertheless makes an investigation all the more worthwhile.

Some of the less likely locations are often the most valuable. For instance, the papers of Eben Dönges in the Cape Archives are of special interest to the historian, are readily available for the forties, and include one of the few substantial sets of Broederbond materials in an open collection. Similarly, there is a small but fascinating collection of Ossewabrandwag pamphlets and other memorabilia at the University of the Witwatersrand, which also holds the invaluable records of the Union Unity Truth Service, which specialized in investigating and exposing antiwar activities. Scholarly prudence does, however, suggest that, given the nature of the Truth Service, its materials should be used with some caution. On the other hand, nothing found here or in similar collections, such as that of Harry Lawrence, obviously contradicted anything found in the papers of Afrikaner nationalists themselves.

On anti-Semitism, the papers of Morris Alexander are a major source, but researchers are warned that, at the time of my consultation, individual documents were difficult to find in this large collection which has been through several attempts at reorganization, often resulting in conflicting file and document labels. The South African Jewish Board of Deputies Archive, recently acquired by the Kaplan Center for Jewish Studies of the University of Cape Town, had not yet been properly organized at the time of consultation; it is potentially a very useful resource. The minute books of the Board of Deputies were an especially good indicator of the growing tide of anti-Semitic activity in the middle to late thirties.

Finally, pamphlets, often held in smaller collections or as a section of a larger one, are useful to consult. During the war, the Ossewabrandwag and the National Party regularly published major policy pronouncements in pamphlet form, and the shirt movements and their opponents, lacking the funds for larger publications, often relied on this format. Sometimes even a souvenir pamphlet, such as those issued during the 1938 Ox-Wagon Trek Centenary celebrations, will include key information on organizers and speakers that gives hints as to which other organizations may have been involved in such events.

Even the most unlikely materials need to be considered in such a study, particularly when access to many of the most obvious collections is so difficult. Yet the amazing thing about researching this book is that, despite all the problems attending the writing of a work on so sensitive a subject, there was never a poverty of suitable sources. On the contrary, given the exigencies of time and money, the greatest obstacle facing the author was always the question of sorting out which materials should be included and which should be left to another project. Despite all the difficulties surrounding the study of modern South African history, even in the most traditional fields such as white party politics and political culture, it remains a very young and fertile area for future research. There is still much virgin soil to till.

Finally, I should add a comment on a few technical points. All translations are my own unless otherwise noted. Most quotations from German documents are given in the original language in the notes. For Afrikaans sources, where I have considered a word or term ambiguous, I have given the original in parentheses in the text. The full names of many lesser figures discussed in German or Afrikaans sources are unknown. The common practice in correspondence of the time was to sign or address letters or memoranda with an initial and the last name. Sometimes only the last name is given, making identification still more difficult. I have in all cases given as much information as I have been able to glean from the documents themselves and from related sources.

Selected Bibliography

This bibliography is classified as follows:

A. Archival and Other Documentary Collections

1. State Archives (Central Depot), Pretoria
2. Transvaal Archives Depot, Pretoria
3. Instituut vir Eietydse Geskiedenis, University of the Orange Free State, Bloemfontein
4. Manuscripts Department, Cullen Library, University of the Witwatersrand, Johannesburg
5. Cape Archives Depot, Cape Town
6. Archives and Manuscripts Department, Jagger Library, University of Cape Town
7. Kaplan Center for Jewish Studies/Archives and Manuscripts Department, University of Cape Town
8. Archives of the Hoover Institution for War, Revolution and Peace, Stanford
9. Microfilmed Collections of Captured German Documents
10. Documents in Private Possession

B. Official Publications and Papers

1. German Government Records
2. South African Government Records

C. Newspapers and Journals
D. Articles
E. Books and Pamphlets
F. Unpublished Papers and Theses
G. Miscellaneous

A. Archival and Other Documentary Collections

1. State Archives (Central Depot), Pretoria

Abraham Papers, J. H. Vols. 2–4.
Duits-Afrikaanse Hulp-Aksie, Records of the.

Hertzog Papers, General James Barry Munnik. Vols. 33, 34, 50, 51, 52, 62, and 97.
Kemp Papers, General J. C. G. ("Jan"). Vols. 4–6.
Smuts Papers, General Jan Christiaan. Vols. 53–64, 77, 123–125, 129, 132, 142–146, 150, 160, 162, 164–169, and 388/1.
Strijdom Papers, J. G. ("Hans"). Vols. 35, 36, 40, 46, 47, and 56–58.
Van der Westhuizen Collection, Mrs. J. S.
Van Heerden Papers, Dr. G. D. S.
Van Rensburg Collection, Dr. J. F. J. ("Hans").
Voortrekker Centenary Committee of Heidelberg (Transvaal) Records.
Voortrekker Movement Records. Vol. 1.

2. Transvaal Archives Depot, Pretoria

Kieser Collection, Mrs. S.

3. Instituut vir Eietydse Geskiedenis, University of the Orange Free State, Bloemfontein

Afrikaner Party Records. Files 1, 2, 4, 5, and 21.
De Villiers Papers, W. B. ("Bruckner"). Files 1, 2, 6, and 8.
Du Plessis Papers, Dr. J. H. O. ("Otto"). Files 1–4, 6, 7, 21, and 24.
Erasmus Papers, F. C.
Greyshirts (L. T. Weichardt) Records. Files 1–11, 14, 115, and 121.
Jerling Papers, J. D. Files 6, 8, 11, 13, 15, 21, 24, 27, 29, 30, and 36.
Louw Papers, Eric. Files 2, 3, 33, 71, 89, and 90.
Luttig Papers, Senator P. J. H. File 2.
Malan Papers, Senator M. P. A. Files 2, 4, and 7–10.
Pirow Papers, Oswald. Files 1, 2, and 5.
Verwoerd Papers, Dr. Hendrik. Files 1/1/3, 1/1/4, 1/24/1, 1/30/1, 1/39/2/1, 1/56/1, 1/65/1, and 3/1/1.
Von Moltke Papers, Johannes Strauss. Files 2, 4, and 5.

4. Manuscripts Department, Cullen Library, University of the Witwatersrand, Johannesburg

Hofmeyr Papers, J. H. File Series Aa, Ab, Da, Df, Dh, and G.
Millin Papers, Sarah Gertrude. File C1.
Ossewabrandwag Collection.
South African Institute of Race Relations Records, Part I. B1–43, B57–88.
Stubbs Papers, Brigadier-General Ernest. File B2.
Union Unity Truth Service Records. Files 141, 146, and 173–176.

5. Cape Archives Depot, Cape Town

Dönges Papers, Dr. T. E. ("Eben"). Vols. 72–75, 85, 86, 90, and 100.
Geyer Papers, A. L. Vol. 1.
Louw Papers, C. R. Vol. 8.
Van Zyl Papers, Senator D. H. Vols. 5, 6, 9, and 40.

*6. Archives and Manuscripts Department, Jagger Library,
University of Cape Town*

Alexander Papers, Morris. Letter and Case Books; Jewish Materials C, Files
26–27, 29–32, 34, and 43–45; Jewish Pamphlets Collection; Jewish Mate-
rials List IV: Files 18 and 24; Board of Deputies Files 3–7, 49, and 59.
Ballinger Papers, Margaret. File Series A2, A3, B, D4, D16, E, and G.
Ballinger Papers, Senator William.
Buyskes Papers, Hilda.
Duncan Papers, Sir Patrick.
Friedlander Papers, Zelda.
Gutsche Collection, Thelma.
Lawrence Papers, H. G. ("Harry"). File Series B–E, G, and K.
Marquard Papers, Leonard. File Series C, D, and E.
Molteno Papers, Donald.
Norton Papers, Victor.
Sibbett Papers, Cecil.
Theron Papers, Major-General Frank.
Van Zyl Papers, G. Brand.
Waterson Collection.

*7. Kaplan Center for Jewish Studies/Archives and Manuscripts
Department, University of Cape Town*

Goodman Collection, I. M.
Jackson Miscellany A. M.
Jewish Immigration Collection.
South African Jewish Board of Deputies Archive. Minute books, 1934–1942;
Files on Anti-Semitism and Discrimination, Publications Act and Parliamen-
tary Matters.

*8. Archives of the Hoover Institution for War, Revolution and
Peace, Stanford*

Communist Party of South Africa Collection.
German Foreign Office Collection. File 540.
Vatcher Collection, William Henry.

9. Microfilmed Collections of Captured German Documents

German Foreign Office Records, Captured. U.S. National Archives Microfilm
Series, T-120. Material relating to South Africa. Reels 317, 318, 3016, 3017,
3404, 4357, and 5023.
Nazi Party Main Archive, Berlin Document Center. Microfilmed by Hoover
Institution, Stanford, 1960. Material relating to South Africa and South-
West Africa. Reel 34, Folders 656 and 657.

10. Documents in Private Possession

Rubin Collection, Senator Leslie.

B. Official Publications and Papers

1. German Government Records

Akten zur Deutscher Auswärtigen Politik 1918–1945: Aus dem Archiv des Deutschen Auswärtiges Amts. Series D, Vol. 9. Frankfurt: P. Keppler Verlag, 1962. Vols. 1, 4, 8–11, and 13.

2. South African Government Records

Debates of the House of Assembly (Hansard).
Debates of the Senate.
Emergency Regulations Proclamation—Annexure to 1941 War Measures Act: War Measure no. 14, 1941.
S.C. 5-'46. Union of South Africa. Report of the Select Committee on German Foreign Office Documents, 1946.
U.G. 16-1947 Report of the Commission to Recommend for Deportation.

C. Newspapers and Journals

Die Burger	*Rand Daily Mail*
Cape Argus	*The Star*
Cape Times	*Sunday Times*
Common Sense	*Die Transvaler*
Forum	*United Party Newsletter*
Jewish Affairs	*Die Vaderland*
Die Kerkblad	*Die Waarheid*
Die Kerkbode	*Die Wa-Ketting*
Die O.B.	

D. Articles

Bozzoli, Belinda. "Capital and the State in South Africa." *Review of African Political Economy* no. 11 (January–April 1978), pp. 40–50.

Chidester, David. "Religious Studies as Political Practice." *Journal of Theology for Southern Africa* 58 (March 1987), pp. 4–17.

Cuthbertson, G. C. "Jewish Immigration as an Issue in South African Politics, 1937–1939." *Historia* 26:2 (May 1981), pp. 119–133.

Du Toit, André. "No Chosen People: The Myth of the Calvinist Origins of Afrikaner Nationalism and Racial Ideology." *American Historical Review.* 88:4 (October 1983), pp. 20–52.

———. "Puritans in Africa? Afrikaner 'Calvinism' and Kuyperian Neo-Calvinism in Late Nineteenth Century South Africa." *Comparative Studies in Society and History.* 27:2 (April 1985), pp. 209–240.

Furlong, Patrick. "Apartheid and Neo-Apartheid: Impressions of an Insider." *Thresholds* (Journal of the Graduate Student Association, University of California at Santa Barbara) 1 (January 1985), pp. 80–93.

Giliomee, Hermann. "Constructing Afrikaner Nationalism." *Journal of Asian and African Studies.* 18:1–2 (January/April 1983), pp. 83–98.

———. "Western Cape Farmers and the Beginnings of Afrikaner Nationalism, 1870–1915." *Journal of Southern African Studies* 14:1 (October 1987), pp. 38–63.

Kum'a N'dumbe III, Alexandre. "Afrikapolitik des dritten Reichs." *Afrika Heute* 21/22 (November 1972), pp. 456–459.

Legassick, Martin. "Legislation, Ideology and Economy in Post-1948 South Africa." *Journal of Southern African Studies* 1:1 (October 1974), pp. 5–35.

Nasson, Bill, and John, J. M. "Die Lewe en Dood van Abraham Esau." *Die Suid-Afrikaan* (June 1986), pp. 23–25.

O'Meara, Dan. "The Afrikaner Broederbond 1927–1948: Class Vanguard of Afrikaner Nationalism." *Journal of Southern African Studies.* 3:1 (October 1976), pp. 156–185.

Posel, Deborah. "The Meaning of Apartheid Before 1948: Conflicting Interests and Forces Within the Afrikaner Nationalist Alliance." *Journal of Southern African Studies* 14:1 (October 1987), pp. 123–139.

Salomon, Laurence. "The Economic Background to the Revival of Afrikaner Nationalism." In *Boston University Papers in African History.* Volume 1. Edited by Jeffrey Butler. Boston: Boston University Press, 1964, pp. 217–242.

"Der Union von Südafrika zum 31. Mai 1935." *Afrika-Rundschau* 1:2 (June 1935), pp. 1–2.

Van Rensburg, A. P. J. "Die Simboliese Ossewatrek van 1938." *Historia* 17:1 (March 1972), pp. 12–46.

Villa-Vicencio, Charles. "South Africa's Theologized Nationalism." *Ecumenical Review.* 29:4 (October 1977), pp. 373–382.

Wolpe, Harold. "Capitalism and Cheap Labour-Power in South Africa: From Segregation to Apartheid." *Economy and Society* 1:4 (November 1972), pp. 425–456.

E. Books and Pamphlets

Adam, Heribert, and Giliomee, Hermann, eds. *The Rise and Crisis of Afrikaner Power.* Cape Town: David Philip, 1979.

Andrews, W. H. *The Nazi Danger in South Africa.* London: Labour Monthly, ca. 1942.

The Anti-Jewish Movements in South Africa: The Need for Action. N.p.: South African Jewish Board of Deputies, 1936.

Barlow, Trafford B. *President Brand and His Times.* Cape Town and Johannesburg: Juta, 1972.

Barnard, S. L., and Marais, A. H. *Die Verenigde Party: Die Groot Eksperiment.* Durban: Butterworth, 1982.

Basson, J. L. *J. G. Strijdom: Sy Politieke Loopbaan van 1929 tot 1948.* Pretoria: Wonderboom-Uitgewers, 1980.

Benson, Mary. *The African Patriots: The Story of the African National Congress of South Africa.* London: Faber and Faber, 1963.

Blackshirts! Greyshirts! Hunger! Slavery! Oppression and War! Johannesburg: League Against Fascism and War, late 1930s.

Bracher, Karl Dietrich. *Die Deutsche Diktatur.* Frankfurt et al.: Ullstein Materialien, 1969.

Bullock, Allan. *Hitler: A Study in Tyranny.* New York et al.: Harper and Row, revised ed. 1964.

Bunting, Brian. *The Rise of the South African Reich.* Harmondsworth, Middlesex: Penguin, 1969.

Campaign for Right and Justice. *For Right and Justice: Against Fascism.* Johannesburg: Palladium Publishers, 1944.

Carsten, F. L. *The Rise of Fascism.* Berkeley and Los Angeles: University of California Press, 2nd ed. 1980.

Childers, Thomas. *The Nazi Voter: The Social Foundations of Fascism in Germany, 1919–1933.* Chapel Hill and London: University of North Carolina Press, 1983.

Cilliers, A. C. *Die Stryd om Volkseenheid.* Stellenbosch: Pro Ecclesia-Drukkery, 1941.

Cronjé, Geoffrey. *'n Tuiste Vir die Nageslag: Die Blywende Oplossing van Suid-Afrika se Rassevraagstukke.* Johannesburg: Publicité Handelsreklamasies, 1945.

Cronjé, Geoffrey, Nicol, Willem, and Groenewald, E. P. *Regverdige Rasse-Apartheid.* Stellenbosch: Christen-Studenteverenigingsmaatskappy van Suid-Afrika, 1947.

Davenport, T. R. H. *South Africa: A Modern History.* Johannesburg: Macmillan, 1978.

De Gruchy, John W., and Villa-Vicencio, Charles, eds. *Apartheid Is a Heresy.* Cape Town: David Philip, 1983.

De Jonge, Alex. *The Weimar Chronicle: Prelude to Hitler.* New York: New American Library, 1979.

De Klerk, W. A. *The Puritans in Africa: A Story of Afrikanerdom.* London: Rex Collings, 1975.

Denoon, Donald. *A Grand Illusion: The Failure of Imperial Policy in the Transvaal Colony During the Period of Reconstruction 1900–1905.* London: Longman, 1973.

Denoon, Donald, and Nyeko, Balam. *Southern Africa since 1800.* London and New York: Longman, 2nd ed. 1984.

Diederichs, Nicolaas. *Die Kommunisme: Sy Teorie en Taktiek.* Bloemfontein et al.: Nasionale Pers, 1938.

———. *Nasionalisme as Lewensbeskouing en Sy Verhouding tot Internasionalisme.* Bloemfontein et al.: Nasionale Pers, 1936.

———. *Von Leiden und Dulden.* Bonn: Ferdinand Dümmlers Verlag, 1930.

Die Duerckheim Rapport: Offisiële Dokumente oor Nazi Komplot in die Unie—Beoogde Anneksasie. Johannesburg: Unity Truth Service, 1939.

Du Plessis, Otto. *Die Nuwe Suid-Afrika: Die Revolusie van die Twintigste Eeu.* Port Elizabeth: Nasionale Pers, 1941.

Eloff, G. *Rasse en Rassevermenging: Die Boerevolk Gesien van die Standpunt van die Rasseleer.* Bloemfontein: Nasionale Pers, 1942.

Erasmus, F. C., and Louw, Eric. *Handleiding van die Herenigde Nasionale Party.* Cape Town: Nasionale Pers, n.d.

Fascism Means War: What the Blackshirts Stand For. Johannesburg: South African Anti-Fascist Movement, ca. 1935.

Fest, Joachim C. *Hitler.* Translated by Richard and Clara Winston. New York: Vintage Books, 1975.

Furlong, Patrick. *The Mixed Marriages Act: An Historical and Theological Study.* Communications No. 8. Cape Town: Center for African Studies, University of Cape Town, 1983.

Geyser, O., ed. *Dr. H. F. Verwoerd die Republikein: Hoofartikels uit Die Transvaler 1937–1948.* Cape Town and Johannesburg: Tafelberg, 1972.

———, ed. *Geredigeerde Toesprake van die Sewende Eerste Minister van Suid-Afrika.* Bloemfontein: Instituut vir Eietydse Geskiedenis, 1976.

Geyser, O., and Marais, A. H., eds. *Die Nasionale Party: Deel 1.* Bloemfontein: Instituut vir Eietydse Geskiedenis, 1983.

Giliomee, Hermann, and Elphick, Richard, eds. *The Shaping of South African Society 1652–1820.* London and Cape Town: Longman, 1979.

Grobler, Jan. *Constitution '83 in a Nutshell.* Cape Town: National Party, 1983.

Hancock, W. K. *Smuts.* 2 vols. Cambridge: Cambridge University Press, 1962 and 1968.

Harrison, David. *The White Tribe of Africa: South Africa in Perspective.* Berkeley and Los Angeles: University of California Press, 1981.

Heese, H. F. *Groep Sonder Grense: Die Rol en Status van die Gemengde Bevolking aan die Kaap, 1652–1795.* Belville: Western Cape Institute for Historical Research, 1984.

Hepple, Alexander. *Verwoerd.* Harmondsworth, Middlesex: Penguin, 1967.

Hexham, Irving. *The Irony of Apartheid: The Struggle for National Independence of Afrikaner Calvinism against British Imperialism.* New York and Toronto: Edwin Mellen Press, 1981.

Hildebrand, Klaus. *Vom Reich zum Weltreich: Hitler, NSDAP und Koloniale Frage 1919–1945.* Munich: Wilhelm Fink Verlag, 1969.

Hitler, Adolf. *Mein Kampf.* Translated by Ralph Manheim. Boston: Houghton Mifflin, 1943.

The Immigration of Jews into the Union, 1926–1935 (With Appendices for the Year 1936): An Analysis of Official Statistics. N.p.: South African Jewish Board of Deputies, 1937.

Joubert, Dion. *Oorlogsverklaring 1939: Drama in die Volksraad.* Cape Town and Johannesburg: Tafelberg, 1972.

Kater, Michael H. *The Nazi Party: A Social Profile of Members and Leaders, 1919–1945.* Cambridge, Mass.: Harvard University Press, 1983.

Kenney, Henry. *Architect of Apartheid: Verwoerd—An Appraisal.* Johannesburg: Jonathan Ball, 1980.

Krüger, D. W. *The Making of a Nation: A History of the Union of South Africa 1910–1961.* Johannesburg and London: Macmillan, 1969.

Kruger, Jannie. *President C. R. Swart*. Cape Town et al.: Nasionale Boekhandel, 1961.

Kum'a N'dumbe III, Alexandre. *Hitler, L'Afrique du Sud et la Menace Imperialiste: Les Relations Secretes entre Hitler et l'Afrique du Sud*. Pamphlet Reprint from *Les Temps Modernes* 29 (October 1973).

———. *Relations between Nazi Germany and South Africa: Their Influence on the Development of the Ideology of Apartheid*. United Nations Centre Against Apartheid: Notes and Documents no. 12 (May 1976).

Laqueur, Walter, ed. *Fascism: A Reader's Guide*. Berkeley and Los Angeles: University of California Press, 1976.

Lawrence, Jeremy. *Harry Lawrence*. Cape Town: David Philip, 1978.

Leier van die Gedissiplineerde Afrikanerdom: Dr. J. F. J. van Rensburg—Lewensbeskrywing en Drie Toesprake. Johannesburg: Voortrekkerpers, n.d.

Lelyveld, Joseph. *Move Your Shadow: South Africa, Black and White*. New York: Penguin, 1985.

Leopold, John A. *Alfred Hugenberg: The Radical Nationalist Campaign Against the Weimar Republic*. New Haven and London: Yale University Press, 1977.

Le Roux, J. H., and Coetzer, P. W. *Die Nasionale Party: Deel 2*. Bloemfontein: Instituut vir Eietydse Geskiedenis, 1980.

———. *Die Nasionale Party: Deel 3*. Bloemfontein: Instituut vir Eietydse Geskiedenis, 1982.

———, eds., *Die Nasionale Party: Deel 4*. Bloemfontein: Instituut vir Eietydse Geskiedenis, 1986.

Lipton, Merle. *Capitalism and Apartheid: South Africa, 1910–1986*. Aldershot, UK: Wildwood House, 1986.

Lombard, R. T. J. *Die Nederduitse Gereformeerde Kerke en Rassepolitiek: Met Spesiale Verwysing na die Jare 1948–1961*. Pretoria: NG Kerkboekhandel Transvaal, 1981.

Long, B. K. *In Smuts's Camp*. London et al.: Oxford University Press, 1945.

Mack Smith, Denis. *Mussolini: A Biography*. New York: Vintage Books, 1983.

Malan, Daniel F. *Afrikaner-Volkseenheid en My Ervarings op die Pad Daarheen*. Cape Town et al.: Nasionale Boekhandel, 1959.

Malherbe, Ernst G. *Education in South Africa Vol. II: 1923–1975*. Cape Town and Johannesburg: Juta, 1977.

———. *Never a Dull Moment*. Cape Town: Howard Timmins, 1981.

Mann, Golo. *The History of Germany Since 1789*. Translated by Marian Jackson. New York: Praeger, 1968.

Marais, A. H., ed. *Politieke Briewe 1909–1910: Deel 1*. Bloemfontein: Instituut vir Eietydse Geskiedenis, 1971.

Marais, J. S. *The Fall of Kruger's Republic*. Oxford: Clarendon Press, 1961.

Maylam, Paul. *A History of the African People of Southern Africa: From the Iron Age to the 1970s*. Cape Town and Johannesburg: David Philip, 1986.

McKale, Donald M. *The Swastika Outside Germany*. Oxford, Ohio: Kent State University Press, 1977.

Meyer, P. J. *Die Afrikaner*. Bloemfontein: Nasionale Pers, 1940.

————. *Nog Nie Ver Genoeg Nie: 'n Persoonlike Rekenskap van Vyftig Jaar Georganiseerde Afrikanerskap.* Johannesburg and Cape Town: Perskor, 1984.

Michalka, Wolfgang. *Nationsozialistische Aussenpolitik.* Darmstadt: Wissenschaftliche Buchgesellschaft, 1978.

Moll, J. C. *Fascisme: Die Problematiek van Verklaringsvariante; Fascisme en Suid-Afrika.* Bloemfontein: Publication Series C no. 9, University of the Orange Free State, 1985.

Moodie, T. Dunbar. *The Rise of Afrikanerdom: Power, Apartheid and the Afrikaner Civil Religion.* Berkeley and Los Angeles: University of California Press, 1975.

Muller, C. F. J., ed. *Five Hundred Years: A History of South Africa.* Pretoria and Cape Town: Academica, 1969.

Mzimela, Sipho. *Apartheid: South African Nazism.* New York et al.: Vantage Press, 1983.

Nazi Activities in South-West Africa (As Stated in the Report of South West Africa Commission, March, 1936). London: Friends of Europe, 1936.

Odendaal, André. *Vukani Bantu: The Beginnings of Black Protest Politics in South Africa to 1912.* Cape Town and Johannesburg: David Philip, 1984.

O'Meara, Dan. *Volkskapitalisme: Class, Capital and Ideology in the Development of Afrikaner Nationalism 1934–1948.* Johannesburg: Ravan, 1983.

Ons Leiers Wys op Gevare van Genl. Smuts se Studeerkamer-Oorlog. Pretoria: Transvaal National Party, 1940.

Ons Party en die OB: Samewerking Misluk. Cape Town: Cape National Party, ca. 1941.

Paton, Alan. *Hofmeyr.* Cape Town: Oxford University Press, abridged ed. 1971.

Payne, Adam. *Nazi Plot in South Africa.* London: Todd Magazines, ca. 1941.

Payne, Stanley G. *Fascism: Comparison and Definition.* Madison: University of Wisconsin Press, 1980.

Pelzer, A. N. *Die Afrikaner Broederbond: Eerste 50 Jaar.* Cape Town: Tafelberg, 1979.

Pienaar, S. W., ed. *Glo in U Volk: Dr. D. F. Malan as Redenaar.* Cape Town: Tafelberg, 1964.

Pirow, Oswald. *Nuwe Orde vir Suid-Afrika.* Pretoria: Christelike Republikeinse Suid-Afrikaanse Nasionaal-Sosialistiese Studiekring, 1941.

Pois, Robert, ed. *Alfred Rosenberg: Selected Writings.* London: Jonathan Cape, 1970.

Raidt, E. H. *Afrikaans en Sy Europese Verlede: Van Tacitus tot Van Wyk Louw.* Cape Town: Nasou, 2nd ed. 1982.

Remak, Joachim, ed. *The Nazi Years: A Documentary History.* New York: Simon and Schuster, 1969.

Roberts, Michael, and Trollip, A. E. G. *The South African Opposition 1939–1945: An Essay in Contemporary History.* London et al.: Longman, Green and Co., 1947.

Rogger, Hans, and Weber, Eugen, eds. *The European Right: A Historical Profile.* Berkeley and Los Angeles: University of California Press, 1966.

Schmidt-Pretoria, Werner. *Der Kulturanteil des Deutschtums am Aufbau des Burenvolkes*. Hannover: Hahnsche Verlagsbuchhandlung, 1938.

Schmokel, Wolfe W. *Dream of Empire: German Colonialism 1919–1945*. New Haven and London: Yale University Press, 1964.

Schoeman, B. M. *Die Broederbond in die Afrikaner-Politiek*. Pretoria: Aktuele Publikasies, 1982.

Scholtz, G. D. *Die Ontwikkeling van die Politieke Denke van die Afrikaner: Deel VIII 1939–1948*. Johannesburg: Perskor, 1984.

Serfontein, J. H. P. *Brotherhood of Power: An Exposé of the Secret Afrikaner Broederbond*. Bloomington and London: University of Indiana Press, 1978.

Shain, Milton. *Jewry and Cape Society: The Origins and Activities of the Jewish Board of Deputies for the Cape Colony*. Cape Town: Historical Publication Society, 1983.

Shimoni, Gideon. *Jews and Zionism: The South African Experience (1910–1967)*. Cape Town: Oxford University Press, 1980.

Simson, Howard. *The Social Origins of Afrikaner Fascism and Its Apartheid Policy*. Uppsala: Uppsala Studies in Economic History 21, 1980.

The South African Jewish Board of Deputies: The Story of Fifty Years 1903–1953. Reprinted from *Jewish Affairs*, June 1953.

South African Jews in World War Two. Johannesburg: South African Jewish Board of Deputies, 1950.

South African "Nationalism": Its Black Record in the War, 1939–1945. Pretoria: United Party, ca. 1945.

Sowden, Lewis. *The Land of Afternoon: The Story of a White South African*. New York: McGraw-Hill, 1968.

Stachura, Peter, ed. *The Nazi Machtergreifung*. London: George Allen and Unwin, 1983.

Stevens, Richard, and Elmessiri, Abdelwahab, eds. *Israel and South Africa: The Progression of a Relationship*. New Brunswick, N.J.: North American, Rev. ed. 1977.

Stoecker, Helmuth, ed. *German Imperialism in Africa: From the Beginnings Until the Second World War*. Translated by Bernd Zöllner. London/Atlantic Highlands, N.J.: C. Hurst/Humanities Press International, 1986.

Strangwayes-Booth, Joanna. *A Cricket in the Thorn Tree: Helen Suzman and the Progressive Party*. Johannesburg: Hutchinson, 1976.

Strydom, Hans. *For Volk and Führer: Robey Leibbrandt and Operation Weissdorn*. Johannesburg: Jonathan Ball, 1982.

Strydom, Hans, and Wilkins, Ivor. *The Super-Afrikaners: Inside the Afrikaner Broederbond*. Johannesburg: Jonathan Ball, 1978.

Stultz, Newell M. *Afrikaner Politics in South Africa 1934–1948*. Berkeley and Los Angeles: University of California Press, 1974.

———. *The Nationalists in Opposition 1939–1948*. Cape Town and Pretoria: Human and Rousseau, 1975.

Templin, J. Alton. *The Theological Foundation of Afrikaner Nationalism*. London and Westport, Conn.: Greenwood Press, 1984.

Thom, H. B. *D. F. Malan*. Cape Town: Tafelberg, 1980.

Thompson, Leonard. *The Political Mythology of Apartheid*. New Haven and London: Yale University Press, 1985.

Thompson, Leonard, and Prior, Andrew. *South African Politics*. New Haven and London: Yale University Press, 1982.

Thompson, Leonard, and Wilson, Monica, eds. *A History of South Africa to 1870*. Cape Town: David Philip, 1982.

Toland, John. *Adolf Hitler*. New York: Ballantine, 1984.

Vail, Leroy, ed. *The Creation of Tribalism in Southern Africa*. London/Berkeley and Los Angeles: James Currey/University of California Press, 1989.

Van den Heever, C. M. *General J. B. M. Hertzog*. Johannesburg: APB Bookstore, 1946.

Van der Poel, Jean. *Selections from the Smuts Papers*. Vol. 5–7. Cambridge: Cambridge University Press, 1973.

Van der Walt, A. J. H., Diederichs, N., Van Rensburg, J. F. J. et al. *Hedendaagse Politieke Strominge*. Johannesburg: Voortrekkerpers, n.d.

Van Jaarsveld, F. A. *The Awakening of Afrikaner Nationalism 1868–1881*. Cape Town: Human and Rousseau, 1961.

———, ed. *100 Basiese Dokumente by die Studie van die Suid-Afrikaanse Geskiedenis, 1648–1961*. Cape Town: Nasou, 1980.

Van Rensburg, J. F. J. *Their Paths Crossed Mine: Memoirs of the Commandant-General of the Ossewabrandwag*. Johannesburg: Central News Agency, 1956.

Vatcher, William Henry. *White Laager: The Rise of Afrikaner Nationalism*. New York and London: Frederick Praeger, 1965.

Villa-Vicencio, Charles, and De Gruchy, John W., eds. *Resistance and Hope: South African Essays in Honour of Beyers Naudé*. Cape Town and Grand Rapids, Mich.: David Philip and William B. Eerdmans, 1985.

Visser, George Cloete. *OB: Traitors or Patriots?* Johannesburg: Macmillan, 1976.

Waite, Robert L. *The Psychopathic God: Adolf Hitler*. New York: Basic Books, 1977.

Webster, Eddie, ed. *Essays in Southern African Labour History*. Johannesburg: Ravan, 1978.

Yudelman, David. *The Emergence of Modern South Africa: State, Capital, and the Incorporation of Organized Labour on the South African Gold Fields, 1902–1939*. Cape Town and Johannesburg: David Philip, 1984.

F. Unpublished Papers and Theses

Friedman, Sharon. "Jews, Germans and Afrikaners: Nationalist Press Reaction to the Final Solution." Cape Town: Unpub. B.A. (Hons.) thesis, University of Cape Town, 1982.

Furlong, Patrick J. "The Mixed Marriages Act, 1949: A Theological Critique Based on the Investigation of Legislative Action and Church Responses to this Legislation." Cape Town: Unpub. M.A. Dissertation, University of Cape Town, 1985.

―――. "National Socialism and the National Party of South Africa, 1934–1948." Paper presented to the African Studies Association annual conference. New Orleans, November 1985.

Kienzle, William Russell. "German Policy Towards the Union of South Africa, 1933–1939." Unpub. Ph.D. dissertation, Pennsylvania State University, 1974.

Kum'a N'dumbe III, Alexandre. "La Politique Africaine de l'Allemagne Hitlerienne 1933–1943." 2 vols. Lyons: Unpub. doctoral thesis, Lyons University II, 1974.

Rubin, Leslie. "Afrikaner Nationalism and Nazi Germany: The Roots of Apartheid." Unpub. paper, 1985.

Simon, Howard. "The Afrikaner Nationalist Movement/Regime in Comparative Perspective." Unpub. paper for Joint Committee on African Studies conference on "South Africa in the Comparative Study of Class, Race and Nationalism." New York, 8–12 September 1982.

Van Heerden, Frederik Jakobus. "Nasionaal-Sosialisme as Faktor in die Suid-Afrikaanse Politiek, 1933–1948." Bloemfontein: Unpub. D.Phil. dissertation, University of the Orange Free State, 1972.

G. Miscellaneous

Interview with Leslie Rubin, 7 June 1985.

Index

About the Author

Patrick Furlong grew up in South Africa and studied at the University of Cape Town. He received his Ph.D. in 1987 from the University of California at Santa Barbara and returned to South Africa to research this book. He has taught at Presbyterian College in Clinton, South Carolina, and is now assistant professor of history at Bethany College in Lindsborg, Kansas.

About the Book

Between Crown and Swastika was composed on a Mergenthaler Linotron 202 in Sabon. Sabon was designed by the late Swiss typographer, teacher, scholar, book designer, and type designer Jan Tschichold.

The book was composed by Brevis Press in Bethany, Connecticut, and designed by Kachergis Book Design in Pittsboro, North Carolina.

University Press of New England

publishes books under its own imprint and is the publisher for Brandeis University Press, Brown University Press, Clark University Press, University of Connecticut, Dartmouth College, Middlebury College Press, University of New Hampshire, University of Rhode Island, Tufts University, University of Vermont, and Wesleyan University Press.

Library of Congress Cataloging-in-Publication Data

Furlong, Patrick Jonathan, 1959–
   Between crown and swastika : the impact of the radical right on the Afrikaner nationalist movement in the fascist era / Patrick Furlong.
     p. cm.
   Includes bibliographical references.
   ISBN 0-8195-5229-1 (alk. paper)
   1. South Africa—Politics and government—20th century. 2. Fascism—South Africa—History. 3. South Africa—Race relations. 4. National Party (South Africa)—History. I. Title.
DT1924F87 1991
320.5′3′0968—dc20

90-11944